119589

P9-EDF-093

D0123494

Joh. P. Meyer

As in this centennial year we thank God for His many blessings to Wisconsin Lutheran Seminary, we think especially also of the constant encouragement to search the Scriptures and to live in them which Professor Joh. P. Meyer, through his own example and guidance, has given to his students, colleagues, and brethren in the ministry during his forty-three years of service on the faculty. That we might gratefully share with others the blessing of such encouragement, we offer his study of II Corinthians.

The Centennial Committee

Carl Lawrenz, President
Wisconsin Lutheran Seminary

MINISTERS OF CHRIST

MINISTERS
of CHRIST

A COMMENTARY ON THE
SECOND EPISTLE OF PAUL TO THE CORINTHIANS

By Prof. Joh. P. Meyer

NORTHWESTERN PUBLISHING HOUSE

Milwaukee 8, Wisconsin

PREFACE

There is a twofold significance to the appearance of this commentary on Second Corinthians as part of the centennial observance of Wisconsin Lutheran Seminary.

That it should be Second Corinthians that is presented in this work, is itself a factor related to the genius which is peculiar to the Seminary and to the type of theological study which has prevailed in it. When the Apostle undertakes to dictate this letter to *the church of God which is at Corinth, with all the saints which are in all Achaia* (1:1), it is not a moment for dealing in the first place with matters of Christian doctrine as these are dealt with in the Epistles to the Romans and the Ephesians; nor is it a time for disposing of great practical problems in Christian life in the light of Christianity's leading doctrines, as these concerns are handled in the Epistles to the Galatians and to the congregation at Thessalonica. Paul's Second Letter to the Corinthians is rather a pouring-out of the man Paul himself. It is surely not overstating the case to say that we learn more from this letter about the great Apostle's personality and temperament than we do from all his other writings put together.

Behind the words of the Apostle in this letter, expressing great personal concern as they do, we still see him working with the clarity of insight that marks the theologian; we see him in his care for the whole Church of Christ which marks the Apostle commissioned for that task; the peculiar needs and problems of a church founded on the pagan soil of first-century Corinth here fill the heart of the man whom the Lord Himself has designated as His *chosen vessel* to bear His name *before the Gentiles* (Acts 9:15); the welfare of each blood-bought soul here again lies close to the heart of Paul the *Seelsorger* (2:7).

In this epistle, then, we have the picture of the divinely commissioned and inspired Apostle expressing himself on a great variety of concerns, telling his Corinthians and us precisely how and why he thinks and feels as he does in the situation in which he and the recipients of his letter at the moment find themselves. In the commentary on the letter we have not only an exposition of the great thoughts and words of the divinely inspired writer, but particularly a study of the emotional overtones attending these words, and in great detail a delineation of the concrete situations out of which this writing grew and toward which it was directed. What thoughts Paul intended his words to convey and why he framed them as he did; how his words were received at Corinth and what sort of effect they wrought— these are the matters that receive primary consideration in the book before us.

To set forth the thoughts which the original writer intended to convey to his original readers is the broad task that the author of this *Commentary* has set himself. In studying a book of Scripture in this way, the author is consciously following the approach to all study of Scripture that has been characteristic of Wisconsin Lutheran Seminary both in its days in Wauwatosa and now in its time at Mequon. In molding this kind of theological attitude, the author of this commentary has himself, so far as the present generation is concerned, played a major part.

If it can be said of any man living that he is the embodiment of Wisconsin Synod theology, such a statement can be made of Professor Joh. P. Meyer. Therefore it is a cause for special rejoicing and thanksgiving that the committee chose as a Seminary centennial publication just this *Commentary* by Professor Meyer, since it is the mature fruit of a devoted lifetime of study, observation, and participation in the Synod's work.

Now in his ninety-first year of life and the forty-fourth of his work at the Seminary, Professor Meyer is a very vivid link with our Synod's past. Himself a student of Dr. Adolf Hoenecke and a onetime colleague of Professors August Pieper and J. P. Koehler, it has been under his personal guidance that the characteristic approach to Scripture that was dubbed "The Wauwatosa Theology" has remained the self-evident approach also in the Seminary's new home at Mequon. All of his colleagues on the faculty except one studied under him at the Seminary, and even that one had Professor Meyer as his instructor earlier, in his preministerial training.

To one hurriedly paging through the annual catalogs of Wisconsin Lutheran Seminary for the past several decades, it would certainly appear that Professor Meyer is the "dogmatician," the teacher of systematic theology, at the Seminary. Yet, when his Synod asked him some years ago to publish his materials on dogmatics in book form in connection with the observance of the centennial of the Synod, Professor Meyer demurred. The reason he gave at the time was that he feared that such publication would give too much encouragement to a trend that he could observe in modern theology, namely, that of paying careful attention to the pronouncements of some teacher while paying only lip service to the Sacred Text.

Though Professor Meyer may have taught dogmatics, his was in only a very secondary manner a course in "systematic theology." Instead, the words of the Old and New Testaments were constantly held before his classes, these words to be understood and applied as the original writers had intended they should be.

Those of us who have been closely associated with the author of this *Commentary* have good reason to surmise, however, that his great joy in teaching at the Seminary was the course in the New Testament that he has given year after year to the men of the incoming class. Though entitled "Isagogics," the course was not one in Introduction in the ordinary sense of the word. Matters of Introduction the men had studied in their college years. But now, on the basis of the Greek text, they were led through the thought of the Book of Acts and the epistles of the New Testament by a master. Without hesitation he could give, in Greek, the Pauline expression for any given concept and who could account, so far as this can be done at all, for the particular sphere of activity in which any New Testament figure was engaged during any season of a given year. In this course Professor Meyer *lived* the New Testament, and his students, to a degree, lived it with him. His *Commentary on Second Corinthians* has been an outgrowth of a part of that course.

We are certain that the author of this work has no greater hope than that the use of his book will induce the reader of it to apply a little more consciously to himself the now time-worn injunction that needs emphatic repetition in our day:

> *Te totum applica ad textum;*
> *Rem totam applica ad te.*

FREDERIC E. BLUME

CONTENTS

INTRODUCTION

The Chronology

It may help our understanding of Second Corinthians if we assemble a few dates in connection with it. We shall gather the material from the Book of Acts and the two extant letters of Paul to the Corinthian congregation.

In the year 60 A.D. the Roman governor Porcius Festus arrived in Caesarea, where Paul had been kept in custody for two years (Acts 24:27). This fixes the time of Paul's arrest in Jerusalem as the year 58, shortly after Pentecost (Acts 20:16; 24:11). He had observed the Passover festival of that year in Philippi (Acts 20:6) Three months of the winter 57-58 he had spent in Corinth (Acts 20:3). This places the date of Second Corinthians somewhere in the second half of 57.

In 56 Paul had visited Corinth to present his plan of a collection for the needy Christians in Jerusalem (II Cor. 8:10; 9:2). His plan was enthusiastically received and endorsed by the congregation. Paul left Corinth with the promise to return before long, then to visit Macedonia from Corinth, and after his return from Macedonia to Corinth to go to Jerusalem to deliver the collection (II Cor. 1:15, 16).

Not very long after this visit the incest case happened in Corinth. This, together with the misread letter of Paul to the Corinthians (not extant), stirred up considerable trouble (I Cor. 5:9). The Corinthians sent a delegation with a letter to Paul (I Cor. 7:1; 16:17), who received additional information from members of Chloe's house. About the same time the false apostles must have arrived, stirring up more trouble.

About Easter time in 57 Paul answered the Corinthians in what we now call the First Epistle to the Corinthians. In order to give the Corinthians time to deal with this heinous case themselves, Paul had already at this time changed his travel plans (I Cor. 16:5; II Cor. 1:23ff.). In Corinth many doubted whether he would come at all (I Cor. 4:18-21). Was Timothy the carrier of the letter (I Cor. 4:17; 16:10)? About the end of May or the beginning of June Paul left Ephesus for Corinth via Macedonia (I Cor. 16:8; Acts 20:1 — the festival of Diana being held about that time of the year). He had sent Titus to Corinth to assist the congregation in overcoming the disturbances. In Macedonia Paul met his assistant, who had returned from Corinth with a favorable report.

Then Paul penned Second Corinthians.

Outline

The Epistle easily falls into three major parts of unequal length: chapters 1–7; 8–9; 10–13. In the first part the general topic is the ministry of Paul. The second deals with the collection for the needy Christians in Jerusalem. The third takes up the matter of the false apostles who had invaded the Corinthian congregation.

The first part is not easy to subdivide. All thoughts are closely joined together like the links of a chain. So closely are they meshed that it sometimes is almost impossible to say just where the one stops and the next begins. We may roughly group them into four general parts.

In speaking about his ministry Paul first stresses his sole concern for the welfare of the Corinthians (1:3–2:11). In the second group he paints a picture of the wonderfully great "treasure in earthen vessels" (2:12–5:10). He next points out how careful he is to avoid giving any offense (5:11–6:10). Lastly he pleads with the Corinthians for an understanding of his spirit and purpose (6:11–7:16).

SECOND CORINTHIANS

I. PAUL'S MINISTRY

Chapters 1-7

THE SALUTATION

Chapter 1:1, 2

The salutation follows the usual pattern: the writer identifies himself, he names the addressees, and adds his greetings.

The writer in this case is Paul, who is *an apostle of Jesus Christ by the will of God.* This is the same form which he used in First Corinthians. Only there he had mentioned that he was *called* to be an apostle, κλητός. In writing the second letter, he has Timothy as an associate. He calls him the *brother.* When Paul wrote First Corinthians, Timothy was not with him; he was on his way to Corinth via Macedonia (Acts 19:22). In First Corinthians, Paul mentions the brother Sosthenes as his associate.

We take up the salutation itself. It is the same in both epistles: *"Grace to you and peace from God our Father, and the Lord Jesus Christ."*

The name of the addressees is also the same in both letters, τῇ ἐκκλησίᾳ τοῦ θεοῦ τῇ οὔσῃ ἐν Κορίνθῳ, *to the Church of God which is in Corinth.* In Second Corinthians, others are joined to this church as belonging to the addressees of the letter: σὺν τοῖς ἁγίοις πᾶσιν τοῖς οὖσιν ἐν ὅλῃ Ἀχαίᾳ, *together with* (the Corinthians the letter is addressed to) *all the saints who are in all Achaia.* Attica was joined to the province of Achaia by the Romans. There was a group of Christians in Athens. There was also a congregation in the harbor town of Corinth, Cenchrea (Rom. 16:1). These and other Christians scattered through-

out the province are included in the addressees. The letter is addressed
to the Corinthians in the first place, but throughout, and particularly
when Paul adds a πάντες, the other Christians in Achaia must be included. The matters discussed in the letter, including the case of church
discipline, concern them all.

The first letter was addressed strictly to the congregation in Corinth.
The members there were reminded of their peculiar standing in the
world: ἡγιασμένοις ἐν Χριστῷ Ἰησοῦ, κλητοῖς ἁγίοις, *sanctified in Christ
Jesus, called (as) saints.* Then they were further reminded that they
are such σὺν πᾶσιν τοῖς ἐπικαλουμένοις τὸ ὄνομα τοῦ κυρίου ἡμῶν Ἰησοῦ
Χριστοῦ, *jointly with all those that call upon the name of our Lord
Jesus Christ.* They were not to consider themselves as an isolated body,
nor to act without consideration for the other Christians in the
world. Paul underscored this latter thought by adding ἐν παντὶ τόπῳ,
αὐτῶν καὶ ἡμῶν, *in every place, theirs and ours.* Yes, the place where
they are located is theirs, their home, but it is also ours.

Thus Paul in the salutation of his first letter impressed upon the
Corinthians the fact which they never must lose sight of: that the
confessing Christians (ἐπικαλουμένοις) have common interests and
mutual obligations. This is then most tersely stressed in I Corinthians
14:36: "What, came the word of God out from you? or came it unto
you only?" In the second letter Paul stresses that congregations living
in the vicinity of each other often have common problems, which
they will have to work out jointly.

A. PAUL'S SOLE CONCERN THE WELFARE OF THE
CORINTHIANS

Chapter 1:3 to Chapter 2:11

1. 1:3-7

In reading this brief section, our attention is arrested by the repetition of παρακαλεῖν, either as a verb or in noun formation. It occurs
10 times. This root can represent various shades of meaning according to the context in which it is used. Its general meaning is to
urge. This may take the form of admonition, of exhortation, of encouragement, of comfort, etc. Since our present section introduces God

as "the Father of mercies," and speaks about παράκλησις as a remedy for θλῖψις, the meaning of comfort and consolation is clearly indicated.

(3) The Apostle begins by voicing his praise to the God and Father of our Lord Jesus Christ. Εὐλογητὸς ὁ θεὸς καὶ πατὴρ τοῦ κυρίου ἡμῶν Ἰησοῦ Χριστοῦ, *Blessed be the God and Father of our Lord Jesus Christ.* The whole work of our redemption is couched in these words in an appealing, heart-warming way, gushing forth from a heart deeply concerned about the readers and overfilled with joy at the blessing which this Savior-God has showered on both writer and readers.

At once Paul, by the use of an apposition, designates this author of our salvation as *the Father of mercies and God of every comfort,* ὁ πατὴρ οἰκτιρμῶν καὶ θεὸς πάσης παρακλήσεως. There is but one article joining πατήρ and θεός into a single concept: the One who is both Father and God. Οἰκτιρμός, usually found in the plural, means pity or mercy. It is the love of God as it manifests itself over against misery. It occurs only six times in the New Testament, twice coupled with σπλάγχνα, the intestines, the heart. (Once in the genitive, σπλάγχνα οἰκτιρμῶν, Col. 3:12; and once as united by καί: σπλάγχνα καὶ οἰκτιρμοί, Phil. 2:1.) The genitive in our text is best read as qualifying: the Father who is characterized by mercies, merciful in His heart, and practicing mercy, delighting in doing so. The genitive παρακλήσεως is also qualifying: God is a God who is rich in dispensing comfort. Paul adds πάσης. His comfort is not limited. He has comfort for every occasion.

(4) God has manifested Himself as such, and is continuing to do so. He is acting as Comforter: ὁ παρακαλῶν ἡμᾶς ἐπὶ πάσῃ τῇ θλίψει ἡμῶν, *our Comforter in our entire tribulation.* The Greek present participle has the force of an English noun ending in -er or -or which names the person performing an action; ὁ παρακαλῶν equals: the Comforter. Ἐπί with the dative indicates the occasion, which in this case was πᾶσα ἡ θλίψις of Paul and his associates. Πᾶς in the predicative position with the definite article makes of the θλῖψις, of all its various forms and manifestations, one coherent thing, a unit. Paul is now not thinking of all the many tribulations which befell him in his career as an Apostle as so many isolated events; he sees in them simply links in a long unbroken chain. And throughout God proved Himself to be the Comforter.

Paul next mentions one of the results of this characteristic of God, εἰς τὸ δύνασθαι ἡμᾶς παρακαλεῖν τοὺς ἐν πάσῃ θλίψει, *so that we are able to comfort those in every trouble.* Εἰς may express purpose, but if Paul had meant to stress the idea of purpose, he probably would have chosen πρός in preference to εἰς. Paul is here interested in the actual result of his tribulations and God's comfort which he experienced in them. It was this that through God's comfort he acquired a certain ability, the ability to pass on to others the comfort by which he himself had been sustained in his afflictions. Speaking about the others, he again uses πᾶς, but without an article, *in every tribulation,* whatever form it may assume in any given case.

Although the cases may vary, and though the comfort may have to take on different forms in the individual cases, yet virtually, in its essence, it is always one and the same comfort, διὰ τῆς παρακλήσεως ἧς παρακαλούμεθα αὐτοὶ ὑπὸ τοῦ θεοῦ, *by means of the comfort with which we ourselves are being comforted by God.* We take note that παρακαλούμεθα is the present tense. The comfort which Paul can pass on to others is not something which he has received at some time in the past; no, just as his tribulation is one unbroken chain, so also the comfort which God supplies reaches him in continuous succession.

(5) The tribulations which Paul suffers may surpass those of others in severity because of his office as an Apostle, but in kind they are those which are common to Christians. This is a thought for which Paul is quietly preparing his readers, although he does not state it directly until a little later. He calls his afflictions the παθήματα τοῦ Χριστοῦ, *the sufferings of Christ.* The genitive τοῦ Χριστοῦ does not here mean the sufferings which Christ Himself endured in His own person. It might mean that they are sufferings which Christ imposes, but it seems most likely that it points to such sufferings which everybody must expect who is united with Christ in faith, just because of his connection with Christ. Christ Himself said that everyone who would follow Him as His disciple must take his cross upon himself. Paul warned the Galatians that there is no other way into the kingdom of heaven than through tribulation (Acts 14:22). These are the sufferings of Christ.

Of these Paul says that they abound, περισσεύει, in his case, but that they are always matched by the abounding comfort. Ὅτι καθὼς περισσεύει τὰ παθήματα τοῦ Χριστοῦ εἰς ἡμᾶς, οὕτως διὰ Χριστοῦ περισσεύει καὶ ἡ παράκλησις ἡμῶν, *for just as the sufferings of Christ abound in us, so also through Christ does our comfort abound.*

(6) In verse 4 Paul had spoken in a general way about people who were in trouble, τοὺς ἐν θλίψει. He now turns directly and specifically to the Corinthians, saying twice ὑπὲρ τῆς ὑμῶν παρακλήσεως, *for, or in behalf of, your comfort.* Note that he has ὑμῶν in the attributive position, thereby giving it some prominence. The comforting of the Corinthians is the aim to be achieved. To this he adds the first time καὶ σωτηρίας, *and (in behalf of) your salvation.* Nothing less than their salvation is at stake. Their salvation will be advanced by the comfort which Paul dispenses, and contrariwise, their salvation will suffer if Paul would withhold his comfort, or if they would refuse to accept it, or would in some way or other squander it.

For the purpose of emphasis Paul divides between his own sufferings, on the one hand, and the consolation which sustains him, on the other. He connects the two εἴτε . . . εἴτε. He joins this statement to the foregoing by a simple δέ, which in this instance is not adversative, nor purely progressive. The relation between the two statements may in English be conveniently expressed by a simple *now.* Εἴτε δὲ θλιβόμεθα, ὑπὲρ τῆς ὑμῶν παρακλήσεως καὶ σωτηρίας, εἴτε παρακαλούμεθα, ὑπὲρ τῆς ὑμῶν παρακλήσεως, *now, whether we are being troubled, (it is) on behalf of your comfort and salvation; if we are being comforted, it is on behalf of your comfort.* Behind all this lies, unexpressed, indeed, but plainly evident, the thought that Paul has but one interest in his life, and that he is sacrificing his very life in order to attain his purpose, namely, the advancement of his readers on the way to salvation.

The thought to which he had referred only in a veiled way by speaking of the sufferings of Christ he now draws into the discussion directly by adding to the comforting of the Corinthians the remark τῆς ἐνεργουμένης ἐν ὑπομονῇ τῶν αὐτῶν παθημάτων, *which becomes effective in the enduring of the same sufferings.* Yes, the Corinthians will need comfort, strong and effective comfort. They will be subjected to sufferings. The truth which Paul proclaimed so emphatically to the newly founded churches of Galatia still is in force also for the Corinthians: "We must through much tribulation enter into the kingdom of God" (Acts 14:22). There is no other way. Jesus asked them who would come after Him to take up their cross and follow

Him. The Corinthians, for the time being, may seem to enjoy exemption. But difficulties will come upon them when God so ordains. Then they will be in need of comfort. Therefore Paul assures them that the comfort which he experienced from the Father of all comfort will prove effective in their case also. Their afflictions may assume a different form from those which Paul experienced, but in essence they will be the same. His afflictions were extremely severe, as he will tell his readers in the next short section, but God's comfort was sufficient to carry him through, and he is certain that, no matter how severe the afflictions of the Corinthians may be, that comfort will be effective in their case also. Ἐν ὑπομονῇ τῶν αὐτῶν παθημάτων ὧν καὶ ἡμεῖς πάσχομεν, *in the endurance of the same sufferings which also we are suffering.* They will be enabled by the consolation to bear up under the load; they will not be crushed.

(7) Paul now sums up his thoughts and concludes the opening section of his epistle with the declaration: καὶ ἡ ἐλπὶς ἡμῶν βεβαία ὑπὲρ ὑμῶν, *and our hope is firm concerning you,* namely, εἰδότες ὅτι ὡς κοινωνοί ἐστε τῶν παθημάτων οὕτως καὶ τῆς παρακλήσεως, *knowing (for sure) that as you are partakers in the (our) sufferings, so also in our comfort.*

This first short section has something mysterious hanging over it. What is all this about bitter afflictions and the sweet comfort which follows and which in connection with those afflictions will bring forth rich fruit toward salvation, plus the broad hint that the Corinthians might expect tribulations which would place them in dire need of comfort? Were not the ailments in Corinth of an altogether different nature? One thing stands out most clearly in this section: Paul's warm interest for the welfare of the Corinthian congregation. He is willing, yes, happy to undergo tribulations, so that, when God comforts him, this places him in a position to pass on to the Corinthians a comfort both rich and powerful. But what particular thing he may have in mind is not immediately discernible. Nor does it become evident in the next short section.

2. 1:8-11

It is apparent from the foregoing that a comfort gains in importance with the severity of the affliction which it helps us to sustain. If the affliction is trivial, so will also the comfort be regarded that alleviates it. But should a comfort carry us through a very severe and dangerous affliction, then it would be appreciated accordingly and would be estimated more highly.

That is precisely Paul's case. His afflictions were not of the ordinary variety; they had been most harrowing.

(8) Paul begins this section by saying, Οὐ γὰρ θέλομεν ὑμᾶς ἀγνοεῖν, ἀδελφοί, For, brethren, we do not want you to be ignorant.

We feel from this opening that Paul attaches great importance to the point which he is about to make. There is not only the special address of endearment, ἀδελφοί, but the negative οὐ and the infinitive ἀγνοεῖν, holding the two emphatic positions in the clause, make a very strong positive: "We want you to understand well, to realize unmistakably." What? Ὑπὲρ τῆς θλίψεως ἡμῶν τῆς γενομένης ἐν τῇ Ἀσίᾳ, about our tribulation which happened in Asia. What was it? Ὅτι καθ᾽ ὑπερβολὴν ὑπὲρ δύναμιν ἐβαρήθημεν, that excessively above ability we were burdened. A heavy blow fell on us. It hit us hard, above our ability to take it. We could not evade it, nor could we parry it. Ὑπὲρ δύναμιν is a strong term in itself, but it seems too weak to Paul to describe the situation adequately; he adds καθ᾽ ὑπερβολήν: it was excessively over our ability, 'way beyond our strength.

How far it was beyond his strength Paul states in the following clause: ὥστε ἐξαπορηθῆναι ἡμᾶς καὶ τοῦ ζῆν, so that we despaired even of living. We gave up the hope of coming through alive. Note the aorist ἐξαπορηθῆναι, we were seized with despair; and the present infinitive ζῆν, to continue living.

(9) This negative statement Paul now turns into the positive: ἀλλὰ αὐτοὶ ἐν ἑαυτοῖς τὸ ἀπόκριμα τοῦ θανάτου ἐσχήκαμεν, yes, we ourselves had within ourselves the verdict of death. Ἀλλά is not really adversative, but rather heightening and intensifying the previous statement. The perfect ἐσχήκαμεν seems to be used here practically as the equivalent of a historical aorist, stating merely a past fact. If taken as a true perfect, it would imply that Paul still felt traces of that gruesome experience when he carried the verdict of death in his heart. There are similar instances of this use in 2:13 and 7:5. Blass-Debrunner, #343, 1.2, calls the ἔσχηκα in chap. 2:13 historical, but thinks that the forms in our present passage and in chap. 7:5 may be explained as true perfects.

To what event in his Ephesian ministry does Paul refer? Already in First Corinthians (15:32) he mentioned the fact that he fought with wild animals. It is debatable whether this remark is to be understood in the literal sense or figuratively. The latter is the more likely. That event, whatever it may have been, was past history about Easter time when Paul wrote his first letter. There he mentioned it merely to show by his own example that Christianity would be futile if there were to be no resurrection. Moreover, his remark leaves the impression that the event itself was well known to the Corinthians. In the present connection, where Paul is speaking about tribulations and God's relieving comfort, it would not serve his purpose any too well if he referred to an event of some distant past, an event with which the Corinthians were already familiar. The introduction, "We want you to know," points to some event about which the Corinthians did not yet have full information. The event more likely happened after First Corinthians, at a fairly recent date.

The riot stirred up by the silversmith Demetrius seems to be the answer (Acts 19:23-41). True, there was no martyr's blood spilled on that occasion; there were not even scourgings or imprisonments. But it would be a mistake to discount the ferocity of that riot. The mob was unpredictable, the craftsmen were enraged because their business was falling off as a result of Paul's preaching, and the coming May festival of Diana threatened to be a "flop" financially. Ordinarily it was the main source of their income. The Asiarchs (representatives supervising the festivals of Diana) were perturbed by the attitude of the mob, and some sent word to Paul, warning him not to show himself in the amphitheater. Nobody can tell what would have happened if Paul had ventured out on the street. He was ready to do so without any regard for the possible consequences to himself, but was prevented by some of the brethren. Because of the quiet, almost tragicomic end of the riot, people may have soon forgotten the whole affair, and particularly the instigators may have been only too glad to have it so; but while it was going on, it looked dangerous enough for Paul. And he wants the Corinthians to realize this.

The seriousness of the occasion will make the comfort stand out in bold relief. Paul does not immediately speak about the comfort itself, but about the lesson which the event with its accompanying comfort should inculcate, both negatively and positively. Negatively: ἵνα μὴ πεποιθότες ὦμεν ἐφ᾽ ἑαυτοῖς, *that we might not be people who have set their confidence on themselves.* Paul uses the periphrastic perfect, which brings out the tense idea more pointedly than does the regular perfect. The affliction was far beyond human ability to remedy it. No human resources, human strength or human ingenuity, were able to overcome it. Anyone having nothing but human means at his disposal was bound to incur dismal failure. Paul learned his lesson. He forgot all about self-reliance.

The positive lesson was: ἀλλ᾽ ἐπὶ τῷ θεῷ τῷ ἐγείροντι τοὺς νεκρούς, *but (that we should have our confidence) in the God who is the one raising the dead.* We note that Paul does not simply say that we should trust in God. That would be too general a statement. The relief which God provided demands a more specific designation for God. He calls Him the God whose outstanding characteristic is that He raises the dead; He is the Raiser of the dead. Paul had given up hope that he would ever come out of the affair alive; he himself had pronounced the death sentence on himself. Humanly speaking, he was already as good as dead, and anyone who would rescue him out of that extreme situation would be doing a work which for all practical purposes amounted to a raising from death.

Paul learned his lesson, and he wants the Corinthians always to remember that God is one who raises the dead; he wants them to remember in such a way as not only to say so occasionally, but to live that confidence in times of affliction.

(10) Paul expresses his faith in these words: ὃς ἐκ τηλικούτου θανάτου ἐρρύσατο ἡμᾶς καὶ ῥύσεται, *who rescued us out of so great a death and will (ever) rescue (us).* With a simple future, ῥύσεται, Paul expresses the confidence which he had learned out of this incident. But that is only a part of the lesson. From every benefit which God bestows on us we should learn that He is able and willing to bestow ever greater ones. For Paul to say that God will continue to rescue and preserve him, is not enough. For that reason he adds, εἰς ὃν ἠλπίκαμεν ὅτι καὶ ἔτι ῥύσεται, *on whom we have placed our hope that He will even yet rescue us.* Ἠλπίκαμεν is a regular perfect with the ordinary meaning of that tense: we have placed our confidence on God and there it is anchored, there it rests.—Ἔτι, 'yet,' is ordinarily used in the temporal sense of 'again'; but since Paul in the previous part of the verse already referred to the future, it would be tautological

if he did so here again. Ἔτι may also refer to degree, in the sense of 'more' or 'higher.' God rescued Paul in a wonderful way out of a terrible situation; Paul has the confidence in God that He will rescue him even out of even more dangerous situations in a more wonderful way.

(11) What all of this has to do with the situation in Corinth is not indicated as yet. We still wonder what Paul is driving at. In the first section, though he did not answer the question, he did show his intense love for the Corinthians and his concern for their well-being. He indicated that he feels himself as one with them. This feeling of oneness should be mutual. The Corinthians should cherish the same feeling toward Paul. By his suggestion in the following verse Paul tries to elicit in the Corinthians the consciousness that they really feel as one with him. He says that the expected increase in God's saving help will materialize συνυπουργούντων καὶ ὑμῶν ὑπὲρ ἡμῶν τῇ δεήσει, when also you assist (us) with your prayers for us. Paul thus points them to the power of prayer, particularly the prayer for others. In First Timothy he urges that Christians, in order to receive from God a "quiet and peaceable life," should include their government, "kings, and . . . all that are in authority," in their intercessions (I Tim. 2:1,2). Frequently he requests the prayers of his congregations for God's blessing on his work. Paul had experienced a wonderful help from God, but, he says, with the support of the Corinthians' prayers that help will be increased immeasurably. And why should they not do that? They are interested in the work of the Gospel. By supporting Paul with their prayers they will help to spread the Gospel, for, as he later wrote to the Philippians, to him to live means working for Christ.

In our text he approaches the matter from another angle. He does not mention mission work as the purpose to be achieved, but the praise and glory of God, ἵνα ἐκ πολλῶν προσώπων τὸ εἰς ἡμᾶς χάρισμα διὰ πολλῶν εὐχαριστηθῇ ὑπὲρ ἡμῶν, in order that the gift (coming) to us (as) from many persons may be thanked for by many on our behalf. Πρόσωπον, 'face,' is frequently used metonymically for person (pars pro toto). Frequently it is used so when a personal pronoun would suffice (cf. Col. 2:1; Luke 9:51,53).

Paul calls the rescue which he has experienced and which he is expecting in greater measure in answer to the Corinthians' prayers, a χάρισμα, a 'free gift' of God's grace. He is conscious of the fact, and he wants the Corinthians also ever to remain conscious of it, that our prayer is not a meritorious work, for which God owes us a reward; nor is it a sort of charm which forces God to do our bidding. It is an appeal to the love and mercy of God. The answer to our prayer is a χάρισμα. As such it will elicit our thanksgiving. The many who asked God for His gift will then also join in praising Him for it.

The answer to our question about Paul's aim in his peculiar approach has not yet appeared. Nor will it in the following section.

3. 1:12-14

(12) Paul introduces this section with γάρ, thus offering it by way of explanation, motivation, or further elucidation. His explanation he reinforces with an appeal to the testimony of his conscience and of Timothy's conscience as well: τὸ μαρτύριον τῆς συνειδήσεως ἡμῶν, (such is) *the testimony of our conscience.* Men do not know our conscience; only God does. And He will judge us if we disregard our conscience or falsify its testimony. An appeal to conscience is an appeal to the court of God. What, then, is the matter which Paul here affirms so solemnly? He calls it a boasting, ἡ καύχησις ἡμῶν. It is this ὅτι ἐν ἁγιότητι καὶ εἰλικρινείᾳ τοῦ θεοῦ . . . ἀνεστράφημεν ἐν τῷ κόσμῳ, *that we have conducted ourselves in holiness and sincerity of God in the world.*

'Αναστρέφω literally means to 'turn up' (upside down), 'to turn over'; then to 'turn hither and thither,' to 'walk,' to 'conduct oneself.' (Compare the German *wandeln,* literally to change, then, to conduct oneself.) Εἰλικρίνεια is 'purity,' 'sincerity,' 'without hypocrisy,' 'without ulterior motives,' 'without deceit.' In 2:17 Paul uses the word with reference to his handling of the Word of God: he handles it ὡς ἐξ εἰλικρινείας. In our text he presents it as a special manifestation of ἁγιότης, 'holiness.' Holiness is the general concept, of which εἰλικρίνεια is the aspect pertinent in the specific case of Paul's conduct in the world. He calls it holiness and sincerity τοῦ θεοῦ. In 2:17 he parallels ὡς ἐξ εἰλικρινείας with the phrase ὡς ἐκ θεοῦ, and underscores this with another phrase, κατέναντι θεοῦ, 'in the presence of God.' This suggests that the genetive τοῦ θεοῦ is to be understood as qualifying: a holiness and purity which will pass the inspection of God, which God demands, and which He supplies (ἐκ).

Paul emphasizes the fact that it is truly a God-given holiness and purity by adding, both negatively and positively, the connection in which it came to him and is practiced by him: οὐκ ἐν σοφίᾳ σαρκικῇ, ἀλλ᾽ ἐν χάριτι θεοῦ, *not in human (fleshly) wisdom, but in God's grace.* Human wisdom dictates a certain holiness and purity. Think of the Scout Oath and Law about being "reverent" and doing one's "duty to God." Or think of the common saying that "honesty is the best policy." At best this demand for holiness and purity is an outgrowth of the natural knowledge of God, which in the case of natural man is inextricably wrapped up in and intertwined with the *opinio legis.* Paul will have none of that. His holiness and purity is inseparably connected with the grace of God procured for us by the redemptive work of our Savior. Only in connection with that grace was it given to him, and only in connection with that grace does he practice it.

Paul conducted himself with God-given holiness and sincerity in the world in general. He is now writing to the Corinthians. How did he conduct himself in their midst? With his outward conduct they themselves were thoroughly familiar. As Paul could invoke the testimony of the people in Jerusalem for his conduct in his youth, which he spent in their city, so he could also assume that the Corinthians knew his conduct in their home city. Whether that conduct was a sincere expression of his heart, or was a sham put on for a purpose, was beyond their ken. Because of that, Paul from the very beginning appealed to the testimony of his conscience. He now adds, περισσοτέρως δὲ πρὸς ὑμᾶς, *more abundantly so, however, over against you.* Περισσοτέρως is an adverb in the comparative degree, derived from the same root as the adverb περισσεύω, which means to 'abound.' Paul was exceptionally careful to practice holiness and purity in their midst. Not for a moment did he lose sight of it. He seems to find it necessary to stress this point; and in that stress we may have a first hint of what was on his mind, and why he made so much of affliction and comfort, and his resulting ability to pass on the comfort to others. He will have more to say later.

(13) For the present Paul takes up a particular point, by way of explanation, as the conjunction γάρ indicates. Οὐ γὰρ ἄλλα γράφομεν ὑμῖν ἀλλ᾽ ἢ ἃ ἀναγινώσκετε ἢ καὶ ἐπιγινώσκετε, *For we are not writing*

other things to you but either what you read or also understand.—
The accents in the Nestle edition indicate that the second ἀλλ' is not,
as Lenski thinks, a pleonastic repetition of the first ἄλλα. Ἄλλα with
the accent on the first syllable is the indefinite pronoun, neuter plural:
'other' (things), while the ἀλλ' with the accent on the (elided) second
syllable is the adversative conjunction 'but.'

When Paul here refers to his letters (γράφομεν) and the treatment
which they apparently received in Corinth, he evidently has the matter
in mind which he corrected in I Corinthians 5:9-11. He had written
to the congregation in a letter which we no longer possess that they
should not συναναμίγνυσθαι πόρνοις, into which the Corinthians read
more than the expression could mean. Paul corrects their misunderstanding, telling them that, if their interpretation would stand, then
Christians would have no other alternative but ἐκ τοῦ κόσμου ἐξελθεῖν.
What he wrote meant no more and no less than a suspension of church
fellowship. In our present text he uses this incident as an illustration
that in all his dealings with them, and in his letters as well, he used
holiness and sincerity.

To this statement Paul attaches a sort of directive for reading his
letters, a principle which should govern all our Scripture reading.
He says: Do not try to read between the lines or even behind the lines,
but read just as it is written. The words have been chosen with
holiness and sincerity. The *Wortlaut* is decisive. Then he adds a second
directive, ἢ (ἃ) καὶ ἐπιγινώσκετε. Ἐπιγινώσκειν, in distinction from the
simple stem γινώσκειν, denotes a thorough understanding. The Corinthians had received a thorough instruction from Paul in the Gospel
truths. The 18 months which he spent in their midst gave him
the opportunity to deepen and to broaden their understanding, and to
develop in them the ability to recognize the truth and to distinguish
it from error. This stock of knowledge Paul could presuppose in his
letters. If anything in his letters was not immediately clear to them,
they knew at least that Paul would not contradict anything which he
had taught them orally. To the Thessalonians he wrote that they should
hold fast whatever doctrine had been delivered to them εἴτε διὰ λόγου
εἴτε δι' ἐπιστολῆς ἡμῶν, "whether by word, or our epistle" (II Thess.
2:15). Similarly he says here ἢ ἃ ἀναγινώσκετε ἢ καὶ ἐπιγινώσκετε.

The appeal to his conscience Paul now supplements with a reference
to the final judgment. Ἐλπίζω δὲ ὅτι ἕως τέλους ἐπιγνώσεσθε, *but I hope*

that you will completely understand. Paul will immediately mention a truth which he hopes that the Corinthians will never allow to slip out of their hearts. Ἔως τέλους, 'till the end,' means fully or completely. Thus there is room for improvement in the Corinthians' understanding; it is at best a partial knowledge (cf. I Cor. 13).

(14) Καθὼς καὶ ἐπέγνωτε ἡμᾶς ἀπὸ μέρους, (May you fully understand) *as you have also understood us in part.* Now the main thing. What is it that they should fully grasp and ever hold fast in their hearts? Ὅτι καύχημα ὑμῶν ἐσμεν καθάπερ καὶ ὑμεῖς ἡμῶν, *that we are your (chief and only) cause of boasting, just as also you (are) ours.* Paul is saying this with specific reference to the final judgment: ἐν τῇ ἡμέρᾳ τοῦ κυρίου ἡμῶν Ἰησοῦ, *on the day of our Lord Jesus.*

The ὅτι in this case is not a causal conjunction, 'because,' but introduces a dependent declaratory clause, stating the content of their understanding. The καύχημα stands emphatically forward. If on that great day you expect to have any cause for boasting, it is this. But this is a real cause, one that will avail even in the most severe trial, and secure a verdict of "Not guilty." Your one and only cause for boasting are ἡμεῖς. What were you before we brought you the Gospel? Only with fear and trembling could you look forward to that day of Judgment. Your philosophers might try to tell you otherwise, that such a day will never come, but your conscience persisted in its accusations, telling you that there is no escape. How is it that now you can look forward calmly, yes, cheerfully, to that day? We are your καύχημα. We brought you the announcement of the forgiveness of all your sins for Christ's sake.

Likewise you are our καύχημα. We were commissioned to preach the Gospel, and you are proof of the fact that we did as we were commanded. In view of your faith the Lord will say to us: Well done, good and faithful servants. You have been faithful over a little thing. Enter into the joy of your Lord.

4. 1:15-22

In this section we have the answer to the question that puzzles the reader in the previous part of chapter one. Paul touches the sore spot, something which did not really cause the difficulty, but which was seized upon by Paul's opponents as affording them a convenient excuse for casting suspicion on his work. In itself the matter might be considered as quite trivial, and it should not have caused the least difficulty or friction. That it was "blown up" all out of proportion clearly reveals the character of Paul's enemies. But we see how tactfully, under God's guidance, Paul handled the situation. Instead of sharply exposing his critics at once and setting the Corinthians right, he turned the difficulty into an occasion for presenting an unsurpassed discussion of the glory of the New Testament ministry. Then we admire Paul and thank God for having given us in him a model of dealing with Christians troubled by errorists and their devices.

(15) Paul connects this section to the foregoing with a simple καί, 'and.' Because of the fact that this is a very unusual way of beginning a paragraph, the simple connective arrests the reader's attention: 'and,' 'now,' 'to come to the point.'

With ταύτῃ τῇ πεποιθήσει, *in this confidence,* Paul reaches back to the previous section. There he had spoken about the witness of his conscience to the holiness and sincerity of his conduct in the world in general, and particularly over against the Corinthians; he had expressed the hope that, as they had understood him in part, they would also understand him completely, namely, that he through the Gospel had entirely changed their prospects regarding the future judgment of God. That was his confidence, and in this confidence he had acted. Would the Corinthians take the blame if this confidence deceived him? Should it be said that Paul had misplaced his confidence in them?

(16) What had Paul done in his confidence? We take a look at the various components of his action. First, he says, ἐβουλόμην πρότερον πρὸς ὑμᾶς ἐλθεῖν, *first I was planning to come to you.* Ἐβουλόμην, being an imperfect, indicates that Paul weighed various possibilities very carefully, that in doing so he came to consider one plan as suiting his purposes, that he then reached a decision to which he held and for the execution of which he was getting ready. The verb does not, like θέλω, stress determination, but rather deliberation. In one of the following verses he lifts out this factor by using the verb βουλεύεσθαι, 'to deliberate,' 'to take counsel.' The comparative πρότερον is in place because only two plans of Paul's came into consideration, the one which he now presents, and the second, modified plan, which he later carried out. The idea of πρότερον is expressed by the English 'first.'

Thus the first step in his first plan was πρὸς ὑμᾶς ἐλθεῖν. He planned to sail across the Aegean Sea from Ephesus directly to Corinth, for the purpose ἵνα δευτέραν χάριν σχῆτε, *that you might receive a second grace.* It is not necessary to modify the regular meaning of χάρις. To be sure, it would have to be considered as a favor which he was conferring on the Corinthian congregation by paying them a visit; but it would be a favor only because he would be bringing them again the proclamation of God's grace in Christ Jesus, deepening and widening their understanding of this grace. When he lived and labored in their midst for 18 months, he brought to them the first grace; the planned visit would mean a continuation, a second grace.—The aorist σχῆτε connotes the ingressive idea, 'receive.'

That was only the first step in his original plan. The second was καὶ δι' ὑμῶν διελθεῖν εἰς Μακεδονίαν, *and to pass through you on to Macedonia.* Evidently he did not plan a long stay in Corinth. Referring to this matter in First Corinthians, he calls it a seeing them "now by the way" (ἐν παρόδῳ). But even a visit of only a few days would have greatly enriched the Corinthians—had the conditions been different. Paul had written First Corinthians after having been informed by a letter and by a delegation (I Cor. 7:1; 16:17) of serious abuses which threatened the congregation, and to some extent had already infected it. In his letter he counseled them how to remedy the situation. Following with a brief visit might have greatly strengthened the forces for good. Paul took these matters into consideration and made his plans accordingly. But already before writing his first epistle he had again abandoned them. Very definitely he wrote: "Now I will come unto you, when I shall pass through Macedonia: for I do pass through Macedonia" (I Cor. 16:5).

He had to see the Macedonians. In chapter seven of our present epistle he describes the conditions in that province as such that they resulted for him in ἔξωθεν μάχαι, ἔσωθεν φόβοι, "without were fightings, within were fears." What the difficulties were in Macedonia, we are not told. In speaking about the collection for the needy brethren in Jerusalem, Paul has nothing but praise for the zeal of the Macedonians (see chap. 8), yet for the present he decided to visit those regions before going to Corinth. Luke, in recording this visit, uses the expression παρακαλέσας αὐτοὺς λόγῳ πολλῷ, "when he had given them much exhortation" (Acts 20:2).

In his original plan the next step was this: καὶ πάλιν ἀπὸ Μακεδονίας ἐλθεῖν πρὸς ὑμᾶς, *and to return from Macedonia to you.* Πάλιν . . . ἐλθεῖν, 'to come again,' or 'to come back,' may conveniently be rendered with 'return.' After this return he planned a longer stay in Corinth, lasting probably through the winter. He expressed the hope to spend χρόνον τινά (I Cor. 16:7) with them: τυχὸν καταμενῶ ἢ καὶ παραχειμάσω, he wrote: "It may be that I will abide, yea, and winter with you" (I Cor. 16:6).

The final step was: καὶ ὑφ' ὑμῶν προπεμφθῆναι εἰς τὴν 'Ιουδαίαν, *and by you to be brought on my way to Judea.* The word προπέμπειν is elegant in the Greek, but rather difficult to render into English. The latest attempt of the RSV is "have you send me on my way." Goodspeed has: "have you send me off"; and Moffat translates: "to be sped by you on my journey." Jerome's *deduci* says more than the Greek word, as would the English 'accompany,' or the German *geleiten.* Since no neat translation, apparently, can be found, it seems best to retain the wording of the King James: "to be brought on my way." Lenski's "to be sent on forward" distorts the picture. The Corinthians were not to do any "sending," but merely, to use a colloquial expression, to "see Paul off," to escort in departure, or assist him in his departure.

In Second Corinthians Paul is more definite about his destination than in First Corinthians. He says εἰς 'Ιουδαίαν, while in his first letter he spoke rather vaguely, οὗ ἐὰν πορεύωμαι, "whithersoever I go." Since Second Corinthians followed about six months after First Corinthians, the progress of the collection for Jerusalem could be estimated more accurately, and success was practically assured at the time of its writing. At the time of First Corinthians it had not yet definitely been decided whether the collection should be delivered by delegates of the congregations without Paul, or whether Paul should accompany them (I Cor. 16:3). That question seems to have been settled in the meantime.

Thus Paul outlines his first plans. These he later revised by dropping the short stopover in Corinth on his way to Macedonia, and rearranging his route so as to visit Macedonia first. This change of plan was seized on by the troublemakers in Corinth to discredit Paul. From Paul's reply we can gather what their insinuations were.

(17) He asks, τοῦτο οὖν βουλόμενος μήτι ἄρα τῇ ἐλαφρίᾳ ἐχρησάμην; *In making this plan, did I perchance use lightness?* Μή in our case is reinforced with τι and ἄρα. The word "perchance" does not reproduce

the thought precisely; the German *etwa* would. The question is, Do you really think that I perhaps, etc.? I do not suspect you of so preposterous an idea.—The definite article in τῇ ἐλαφρίᾳ is idiomatic. The thought is: that thing which is known as levity. Before abstract concepts of that sort the English usually omits the article.

By his negative statement that in making his plans he does not proceed lightly or carelessly, Paul is trying to impress on the minds of the Corinthians this positive thought: On the contrary, I am very careful; I seriously weigh all the pertinent factors known to me. If I change my plans, this is no indication that in making them in the first place I carelessly overlooked anything which, if it had been duly taken into consideration, would have at once directed my thoughts into other channels. To charge me with fickleness, or to cast suspicion on my sincerity, is doing me a gross injustice.

But if Paul so carefully considers all circumstances in making his plans, should he then not abide by his first decision, once he has announced it? Paul takes up this question next, formulating it so that the question itself carries its own condemnation: ἢ ἃ βουλεύομαι κατὰ σάρκα βουλεύομαι; *or what I resolve, do I resolve it according to the flesh?* While so far Paul has used the verb βούλομαι (which Jerome renders with the corresponding form of *velle*), he now uses βουλεύομαι (Jerome: *cogitare*). While the former centers on the final outcome of the planning process, the plan itself, the latter names the process of planning. Thus by the two verbs the attention is focused on two different aspects of the same act. Here Paul calls attention to this that while considering all pertinent factors, he bars all fleshly motives. A fleshly motive suggested by the criticism of his opponents would be: ἵνα ᾖ παρ᾽ ἐμοὶ τὸ ναὶ ναὶ καὶ τὸ οὒ οὔ, *so that with me the Yes might be Yes, and the No, No.* He stresses the copula ᾖ by placing it into the emphatic position at the head of the clause. To bring out the stress, I suggest the auxiliary verb "must." There are people who insist that to change a plan once announced would show a lack of character. Does it? Most frequently the unwillingness to yield to changed circumstances or to better judgment is a sign of stubbornness. Paul was not stubborn. Such an attitude he condemns with the phrase κατὰ σάρκα.

Paul frequently had to change his most thoroughly considered plans. When on his second journey he looked upon Ephesus as a most inviting field, he and his companions "were forbidden of the Holy Ghost to preach the word in Asia" (Acts 16:6). The same thing happened with respect to Bithynia (vs. 7). When, after his leaving, the young congregation in Thessalonica faced overwhelming difficulties, Paul planned to hurry to their assistance "once and again"—"but Satan hindered us" (I Thess. 2:18).

(18) But does not Paul's willingness to adapt himself to circumstances and to alter his course of procedure cast doubt on the reliability of his message? Not at all. His plans are his own, always subject to revision. The Gospel which he proclaims is God's. And God is unchangeable, and His word endures forever. Πιστὸς δὲ ὁ θεός, Paul says, *faithful and trustworthy is God,* particularly in this respect ὅτι ὁ λόγος ἡμῶν ὁ πρὸς ὑμᾶς οὐκ ἔστιν ναὶ καὶ οὔ, *that our message to you is not Yes and No.*

(19) The message which God sent to the Corinthians through Paul and his associates has an unshakable foundation in Christ: ὁ τοῦ θεοῦ γὰρ υἱὸς Χριστὸς Ἰησοῦς ὁ ἐν ὑμῖν δι' ἡμῶν κηρυχθείς, *for God's Son Christ Jesus, proclaimed among you by us.* Note the peculiar position of the explanatory connective γάρ. Ordinarily it would follow immediately after the definite article ὁ; but here the genitive noun τοῦ θεοῦ is advanced to that position and made to precede the γάρ. This lays a great stress on τοῦ θεοῦ. Jesus Christ is the Son of the true God, the very God who sent His message to the Corinthians. That message is not subject to revision because God is faithful, and the message rests on His own Son, who is the very εἰκών and express χαρακτήρ (imprint) of His Father, yes, who is truth personified, the way, the truth, and the life (John 14:6).

The name of Jesus Christ, God's Son, sums up the whole message which Paul brought to the Corinthians. He "determined not to know any thing among you, save Jesus Christ, and him crucified" (I Cor. 2:2).

Paul came to Corinth alone, but he did not work among them alone for long. Soon after his arrival he was joined by two of his associates. Hence Paul now can write that Jesus was proclaimed among the Corinthians δι' ἡμῶν. With the aorist κηρυχθείς Paul stresses the act of the proclamation as such. He does not say anything about the result, nor does he refer to the continuation of the proclaiming by others. The fact as such is undeniable that at that time Jesus Christ was proclaimed. Paul next mentions the very names of his associates, δι' ἐμοῦ καὶ

Σιλουανοῦ καὶ Τιμοθέου, *by me and Silvanus and Timothy*. The great solemnity of this remark is evident from the way the name of the first associate is spelled out. He was commonly known as Silas, but here Paul uses the full official form, Silvanus. All three men proclaimed the same Jesus; there was no wavering between Yes and No. In age and training and personal characteristics these three ambassadors of Christ may have differed widely, but they all proclaimed the same Christ, the Son of the true God. Now this Christ, the Son of God, preached by Paul and his associates, οὐκ ἐγένετο ναὶ καὶ οὔ, ἀλλὰ ναὶ ἐν αὐτῷ γέγονεν, *He did not turn out to be Yes and No, but Yes stands (unshaken) in Him.*

The verbs demand our attention, ἐγένετο and γέγονεν. They are the middle aorist and the second form perfect active of the verb γίνομαι, 'to become.' From the fact that the new *Bauer, Woerterbuch zum Neuen Testament,* devotes exactly five columns (two and one half pages) to a discussion of this verb, it will be readily gathered how frequently this verb is used and how varied may be its application. Quite frequently it denotes a coming into existence, or a change in the inner structure of a thing. There are many instances, however, where an inner change is not indicated, but where some present, though latent, inner quality becomes active and manifests itself in operation. That seems to be the case in Paul's present statement about Christ. Christ Himself did not undergo any change in His nature, but His nature manifested itself in a certain performance. The aorist may be taken in the constative sense: Christ's action showed no wavering between Yes and No. The perfect form γέγονεν is a true perfect, expressing a lasting condition: in Christ the Yes stands firm and unshaken.

(20) What does Paul mean by this? He explains: ὅσαι γὰρ ἐπαγγελίαι θεοῦ, ἐν αὐτῷ τὸ ναί, *as countless as the promises of God (may be) in Him is the Yes.* God, whose unwavering faithfulness Paul had stressed before (πιστὸς ὁ θεός)—He has given the world many promises, too numerous to be counted, yet He did not leave one of them unfulfilled. What is more, all of these promises point to Christ, and in sending Christ, His Son, God has redeemed them all. In Christ they have become reality; all the promised blessings are found in Him, and through Him handed to us. There is only one thing left, namely, that in faith we accept and enjoy them. And this vital point is also

given with Christ, as Paul indicates in the following clause: διὸ καὶ δι' αὐτοῦ τὸ ἀμήν, *accordingly, likewise through Him (there is) the Amen.*

The connective διό expresses a causal relation, not necessarily in the strict sense of cause and effect, but often in a somewhat looser sense of correspondence. All the promises of God are made with the understanding that He will also induce us to accept them, something which we of ourselves are unable and unwilling to do. God understood our condition when He made His promises. He did not make His promises *pro forma*, as a mere formality; He wants us to receive the blessings. Hence the very promises imply that He will put us into the proper frame of mind for receiving them, and the promises themselves carry also the power to do so.

He will do this καὶ δι' αὐτοῦ (Χριστοῦ), *also or likewise through Him (Christ)*, who is the fulfillment of God's promises.

The two expressions: ἐν Χριστῷ τὸ ναί and διὰ Χριστοῦ τὸ ἀμήν are by some taken to be synonymous; yet the different prepositions indicate a change in the meaning of the statements. Ἐν is local, διά instrumental. In Christ, in His person and His work, we find the ναί. All things in heaven and on earth come to a head in Him (cf. the ἀνακεφαλαιώσασθαι of Eph. 1:10); but the Amen is not presented as being found *in* Him, but rather as being effected *by* Him. From I Corinthians 14:16 we learn that in the services of that congregation it was customary for the hearers to voice their agreement to an εὐλογία spoken by the leader by responding with Amen. Apply this to God's promises. The Amen denotes our believing response, our grateful acceptance. This Amen was produced in the hearts of the Corinthians *by* the same Christ *in* whom they had found God's blessings.

Thus all glory belongs to God, and by acknowledging that He has faithfully fulfilled all of His many promises in Christ, and through Christ has conveyed the promised blessings to us and led us to a believing acceptance, we but render Him His due glory: τῷ θεῷ πρὸς δόξαν, *for glory to God.*

Paul ends the sentence with a significant δι' ἡμῶν, *through our service.* Here is the nub. God had chosen Paul and his associates to bring the message of Christ to Corinth. It may be assumed that the Corinthians remembered how Paul had come to their city some five years earlier. He had not planned it so. He had planned to work in Ephesus. The

Holy Spirit had forbidden him. He planned to go to Bithynia. God again intervened and called him to Philippi. Through persecution he was forced out of Philippi, then out of Thessalonica, then out of Berea. Thus God had directed Paul's way till he came to Corinth. Through Paul the Corinthians had heard the message of Christ— through Paul, who always took his orders from God and carried them out as God demanded. Do they now listen to defamers of Paul, who question his sincerity, and the reliability of his message, because he changed his plans of travel? Though they may not understand his action, they must at least recognize that he showed great firmness in bringing them the Gospel. He had always been ready to follow God's guidance, and was not dismayed when he met with fierce opposition and persecution on the very way which God led him.

(21) Paul does not seek credit for his unwavering firmness in carrying out God's assignment. He gives all credit to God: Ὁ δὲ βεβαιῶν ἡμᾶς . . . θεός, *the one who makes us firm . . . is God.* Paul is firm; he is neither fickle nor stubborn. But that is not his own achievement; it is a gift from God. It is also God who is preserving the gift for him.

This gift of firmness, however, includes much more than a personal blessing for Paul and his associates; it includes much more than the strengthening of their human character, human will power. To ἡμᾶς, the men who brought Christ to the Corinthians, he adds σὺν ὑμῖν, *in connection with you.* Paul and the Corinthians simply belong together. Separate them, and nothing remains. Neither Paul nor the Corinthians mean anything alone and by themselves. Paul was sent to preach the Gospel; the Corinthians were blessed to hear it. Jointly they enjoyed its blessings. Paul touched on this intimate association when he spoke about his tribulations and God's comfort which he then experienced. Through those experiences he was prepared to pass the comfort on to the Corinthians when tribulations, as was to be expected, would come upon them. He spoke very emphatically about it when he said that on the day of our Lord Jesus Christ he (Paul) was the boast of the Corinthians and they his. Here again he refers to that union with the preposition σύν.

This union is not a type with other associations on earth, it is εἰς Χριστόν, *directed to Christ.* Paul had stated just a little while before what Christ meant both for him and for the Corinthians, namely, the ναί to all of God's promises. He need not repeat. He can say sum-

marily εἰς Χριστόν, their union is in the direction of Christ and rests
in the enjoyment of His blessings.

The name Χριστός with its etymology suggests a new and very
specific approach, which Paul takes up with the phrase καὶ χρίσας ἡμᾶς,
and the one who anointed us. Since Paul at the beginning of the verse
joined himself and his associates together with the Corinthians (ἡμᾶς
σὺν ὑμῖν), the ἡμᾶς at the end of the verse naturally refers to this
entire group, the Corinthian congregation as well as Paul and his assistants, and vice versa. The καί connects the participle χρίσας with
the other participle ὁ βεβαιῶν. Both participles are made definite and
are substantivized by the same article ὁ, the Confirmer and Anointer.
Both actions belong closely together as phases of the same activity;
the difference is that the confirming continues (present participle).
How could Paul have expressed our union with Christ, and thereby
with one another, more vividly than by using the word χρίω? God
anointed Christ with the Holy Spirit and with power. Now we are
included in that anointment. We are made a royal priesthood that we
should show forth the excellence of Him who called us out of darkness
into His marvelous light. Our fellowship which we have among ourselves truly is with the Father and with His Son Jesus Christ. The
Father has anointed us together with His Son and given us the same
Spirit.

(22) Who can grasp the full meaning of this blessing? Paul lifts the
veil a little in the following by adding two participial modifiers to
the subject of his sentence, θεός, both of which are again united in
one by a single article: ὁ καὶ σφραγισάμενος ἡμᾶς, *who also did seal
us for Himself.* The definite article is missing in some manuscripts,
but is well enough attested to be retained. The one who is strengthening us and has anointed us is God, the one who also did the following.
God's activity of blessing us in Christ is so rich that one or two verbs
are not enough to express it adequately. With καί Paul adds a third
and fourth verb.

The first addition is the middle aorist participle σφραγισάμενος. God
affixed a seal to us, thereby marking us as His own. The middle voice
shows the intense personal interest which God has for us. The seal
is a clear "Hands off!" to our enemies: "Touch not My saints, I am
protecting them and I will avenge any harm that is done to them."
The seal is to us an authorization and encouragement to realize and

live our exalted position. God has sealed us. Do not fear any enemy; do not listen to any seducers; love God and trust in Him, and love and trust those whom He has sealed jointly with you.

The second addition is again an aorist participle, but this time in the active voice, καὶ δοὺς ... ἐν ταῖς καρδίαις ἡμῶν, and (who) gave in our hearts. The heart is the organ which controls our life. Also in the transferred sense the heart signifies the center of our spiritual life. Out of the heart are the issues of life. If the heart remains in its natural state, then evil thoughts, words, and actions proceed out of it. When it is reborn, then, in spite of the fact that the old nature has not yet been completely eliminated, the heart produces a rich and beautiful garland of holy, God-pleasing thoughts and deeds. It is the heart into which God has poured His gift. What is it?

Paul calls it τὸν ἀρραβῶνα τοῦ πνεύματος, He gave us a pledge which is the Holy Ghost. The word ἀρραβών (which seems to be derived from a Hebrew root ʻārabh—cf. Gen. 38:17-20—but occurs as a business term also in Greek and Latin) is defined by Thayer as "an earnest, i.e., money which in purchases is given as a pledge that the full amount will subsequently be paid." The genitive τοῦ πνεύματος is epexegetical, explaining in what the ἀρραβών consists, namely, in nothing less than the Holy Spirit of God Himself. In this way God has anointed us, in this way He is confirming us, in this way He has sealed us unto Himself: that He has given us His Holy Spirit into our hearts as a down payment, caution money (Kaufschilling, Haft-pfennig). As though it were not enough that He is πιστός, that He has given His own Son, in whom we have the ναί to the countless promises of God, He gives us also His Spirit as a pledge of fidelity. The Spirit will do His work in our hearts, strengthening and preserving the new life of faith which He Himself has created, bringing fruit to perfection.

5. 1:23—2:4

Verses 23 and 24 are transitional, leading over to the new thought which Paul will present and develop in the next chapter. As such, they also put some finishing touches on the matter treated in the previous section.

In the foregoing Paul assured the Corinthians that he made his plans not without thorough consideration nor, on the other hand, with

such rigidity that stubbornly he would insist on going through with
them, and that, when he changed his plans, he did so for valid reasons.
Now he divulges to them one consideration which, far from showing
indifference on his part toward the Corinthians, was born of the most
tender concern for their welfare.

Things had not been going as they should in Corinth. Think, for
example, of the way they had neglected the incest case. In his first
letter Paul had given them the necessary instruction, and then he had
sent some of his coworkers, Timothy and Titus, to counsel them.
What would have happened if Paul had appeared personally on the
scene before the corrective work was finished, or at least well on the
way toward completion? We can easily imagine the uncomfortable
feelings on all sides. Paul took this into consideration, and he now
speaks about it.

(23) He says, Ἐγὼ δὲ μάρτυρα τὸν θεὸν ἐπικαλοῦμαι ἐπὶ τὴν ἐμὴν
ψυχήν, *I call upon God as witness in addition to my own soul.* Paul
is speaking for himself only. Otherwise he always spoke in the plural,
"we," including his associates with himself, in vs. 19 even mentioning
their names. Now he says emphatically "I," excluding even Timothy,
the coauthor of the letter. He does not include anyone else, nor can
he, since this concerns a matter which he decided before his God alone.
On God he calls as a witness in addition to his own soul. God is the
only one, besides Paul, who knows about this phase of his planning.
Paul could not discuss it even with Timothy; it was too delicate.

What was it? Ὅτι φειδόμενος ὑμῶν οὐκέτι ἦλθον εἰς Κόρινθον, *that,
sparing you, I did not yet come to Corinth.* In First Corinthians he had
written, "What will ye? shall I come unto you with a rod, or in love,
and in the spirit of meekness?" (4:21.) The conditions in Corinth
still, more or less, called for a painful application of the "rod." By
changing his plans and bypassing Corinth for the present, Paul actually
spared the Corinthians some considerable embarrassment. If he postponed his visit, that would give them an opportunity to complete the
work of setting their own house in order.

(24) Paul does not even now like to speak about the matter because
of the danger of being misunderstood. If he asserts the power to
wield the rod, and if he shows leniency by avoiding the opportunity
to apply it, is he then not acting as an autocrat? Does he not degrade
them to the level of slaves? Any such desire is far from his heart. It

would be the ruin of his work. He hurries to ward off the misunderstanding: οὐχ ὅτι κυριεύομεν ὑμῶν τῆς πίστεως, *not that we have lordship over your faith.* To claim rule over faith is really a contradiction in terms. Faith spells freedom, indeed not licentiousness, but real freedom. "If the Son therefore shall make you free, ye shall be free indeed" (John 8:36). "Ye are not under the law, but under grace" (Rom. 6:14). What then does it mean to come with the rod? What does it mean to spare them by laying the rod aside for a while?

Paul answers, ἀλλὰ συνεργοί ἐσμεν τῆς χαρᾶς ὑμῶν, *on the contrary, we are helpers of your joy.* The joy of faith may require assistance in various ways. Under conditions as they happened to obtain in Corinth, where their joy in the Lord was threatened by inroads of worldly-mindedness of various shades, their joy could be saved only by a painful application of the rod. But it would be far less unpleasant if they practiced self-discipline and submitted to self-chastisement than if Paul had to come and apply the rod.

Were they capable of self-discipline? Paul says, τῇ γὰρ πίστει ἐστήκατε, *for you are standing in the faith.* Their faith was threatened; it had already suffered and become weak. But it had not been extinguished. If they were now driven to exercise their faith in self-discipline, their faith would emerge purified and strengthened without the unpleasantness connected with a situation in which Paul had to apply the chastising rod.

So would also their joy be purified and increased.

In 2:1 we have Paul's decision, which he reached before God alone, without consulting with his associates, or even informing them about his deliberations. He alone bears the responsibility; to his assistants he announced his plans only after he had made the decision to change his route of travel. Ἔκρινα δὲ ἐμαυτῷ τοῦτο, *Now I decided this for myself.* The general motivation for this change he stated in verses 23 and 24 of the previous chapter. Now he speaks more specifically about the χαρά: how it would have been affected adversely by a premature visit on his part.

He calls his visit a πάλιν . . . ἐλθεῖν, the same expression which he had used in 1:16. Here he substantivizes the infinitive by prefixing the definite article τό. He thus places the substantivized infinitive in apposition to τοῦτο, I decided this, namely, τὸ μὴ πάλιν ἐν λύπῃ πρὸς ὑμᾶς ἐλθεῖν, *the not returning to you in grief.* He wanted this visit to be one of pure χαρά, undampened by any trace of λύπη.

From First Corinthians we know that there were many things awry in the congregation of Corinth, things which could not be corrected in short order. Paul sent Timothy to help the Corinthians do this work (I Cor. 16:10). He had sent Timothy and Erastus ahead to Macedonia (Acts 19:22), instructing Timothy to proceed from there to Achaia. Then he had sent also Titus, apparently after Timothy's return. Timothy was with Paul when he wrote Second Corinthians (1:1); but he seems to have been on his way somewhere when Paul wrote First Corinthians (unless he was the carrier). Now Paul anxiously awaited the return—and the report—of Titus (II Cor. 2:13).

From the fact that Paul deliberately postponed his own visit—even at the risk of being misunderstood—and from the further facts that he wrote two lengthy letters, and that he sent two of his most trusted colaborers, we can see how Paul tried to train his congregations to stand on their own feet, to meet dangers that threatened their well-being themselves, and to correct errors that had infected some of their members. He thus turned the difficulties that confronted the Corinthians into an opportunity for training them in self-discipline. He could have gone there himself, and by virtue of his apostolic authority have given orders. That, no doubt, would have brought quicker results, but it would have retarded the spiritual growth of the congregation. They would have remained babes, clinging to the "apron strings of mamma."

We have taken the πάλιν . . . ἐλθεῖν simply in the sense of coming back, returning. Paul had been in Corinth for 18 months on his second mission journey when he founded the congregation. That was some five years before. He had written them a letter—now lost—before he wrote First Corinthians (cf. I Cor. 5:9). He had also made a short visit to Corinth from Ephesus. In our present epistle he speaks about coming to them now for the third time (cf. 13:1).

When was that second visit? We do not know. Luke does not mention it in Acts, and Paul himself says no more about it than that he had visited the congregation some time after founding it. It was a visit, but it has no bearing on interpreting either First or Second Corinthians. It must have been made some time before First Corinthians was written. The arrangements which we know from First and Second Corinthians, namely, that Paul sent Timothy to Corinth,

that Timothy returned before Second Corinthians, that Paul in the
meantime sent Titus, leaves no room for a personal visit between the
two letters.*

But some people pounce on the word πάλιν in our verse. Although
Paul very definitely calls it *the* coming back, a visit about which the
Corinthians knew, which had been planned, announced, and then
postponed, still some people think that πάλιν must refer to time, that
Paul had visited Corinth recently, and now was planning to come once
more. Then these interpreters talk about the λύπη. Drawing on their
imagination, they paint a lurid picture of what they think happened
at Paul's recent visit. He was a sick man, and was rather irritable.
He could not have his way, and was openly insulted. In disgust he
cut his visit short, a defeated man. The various arrangements mentioned definitely in the two epistles leave no room for a visit by Paul
between them. To stretch the time from six months to a year and six
months also does violence to the record of these arrangements as contained both in the two letters and in the Book of Acts.

Paul is not complaining that a recent visit—which in fact did not
take place—was marred by λύπη, but he is postponing a planned visit,
so that he might not, because of the unsettled disturbances in Corinth,
have to come with a heavy heart, might not have to come "with the
rod," might not have to treat them sharply. That is the meaning of
τὸ πάλιν ἐν λύπῃ πρὸς ὑμᾶς ἐλθεῖν. Although himself grieved by the conditions, on the planned visit it would be chiefly Paul who would be
meting out λύπη. He would hurt the Corinthians' feelings. He would
have to.

(2) This is evident from the next sentence, which is connected to
the foregoing with an explanatory γάρ. Εἰ γὰρ ἐγὼ λυπῶ ὑμᾶς, *For if
I on my part grieve or hurt you.* The person of the subject is indicated
not only in the verb ending, but the personal pronoun itself is used,
thus laying great emphasis on Paul as the acting one: yes, he, he on
his part, would be the one causing the λύπη. Paul offers no excuses,
as if thereby he would be overstepping the bounds of propriety. He
takes it for granted that under the circumstances he simply could not
do otherwise. He speaks about this in such a matter-of-fact way that

---

*) Compare the notes on chronology in the Introduction for the most likely time
of Paul's second visit.

it is clear he assumed that everybody, including the Corinthians, would readily understand his actions, even expect them. "For if I on my part cause you grief"—that is the self-evident thing for him to do under the circumstances.

But that is not a very pleasant thing to do, neither for the Corinthians nor for Paul himself: καὶ τίς ἐστιν ὁ εὐφραίνων με; and who then (will be there as) the one to gladden me? Corinth was a city of pleasures and amusements. But the Corinthians, not only the Christians but the outsiders as well, would know that these held no attraction for Paul. He was interested in just one thing: to bring sinners to faith in their crucified Savior. "I determined not to know anything among you, save Jesus Christ, and him crucified." If they slumped in their faith, then there was nothing, and no one, in all of Corinth to cheer up Paul. Would they want things in their midst to be in such a sorry state that Paul would be forced to use stern words and apply stern measures? They should rather thank Paul for postponing his visit, thus giving them more time to correct the evils themselves before his arrival.

Paul therefore answers his own question with εἰ μὴ ὁ λυπούμενος ἐξ ἐμοῦ, except the very one who is being grieved by me. Paul here does not use the regular ὑπό of agent with the passive, he substitutes ἐξ. He would be the apparent source, or the channel, out of which their grief would come; the real agent inflicting the pain would be someone else. But it would be conveyed to them by Paul. Let them realize that Paul is merely performing a painful, though necessary, part of his office in causing them pain.

(3) Καὶ ἔγραψα τοῦτο αὐτὸ ἵνα μὴ ἐλθὼν λύπην σχῶ ἀφ᾽ ὧν ἔδει με χαίρειν, And I am writing for this very purpose that I might not at my arrival receive grief (from them) from whom I ought to receive (cause for) rejoicing.—It may be questioned whether ἔγραψα here is the epistolary or the historical aorist. It is true, Paul had reached his decision not to see the Corinthians in passing, ἐν παρόδῳ, but to postpone his visit, before he even wrote First Corinthians. He had also mentioned it in that letter, so that with ἔγραψα he might now be referring to I Corinthians 16:5. But that had been misunderstood by the Corinthians or, rather, had been twisted all out of shape by Paul's detractors in Corinth, so that now he had to explain the real motive for his change of traveling plans. If he had not written the present letter,

the mistrust and suspicions of the Corinthians would hardly have been allayed. This is the point which Paul seems to have in mind with this ἔγραψα. With what he is now writing he wants to remove the last cause for embarrassment before he arrived. The aorist is epistolary.

When he says ἔδει, thus using an indicative of fact where we prefer the subjunctive, he follows the Greek idiom. The necessity as such is not supposed, but real. There was no one outside the Christian congregation in Corinth to gladden the heart of Paul. If he was to experience joy, it must come from them. And, furthermore, have they any reason to withhold that joy from Paul? He will rejoice if he finds them sound in the faith. If they fail to warm his heart with that joy, then there is something wrong with them: they are the losers, the sufferers. In order to give them an opportunity to correct all remaining flaws, Paul postponed his visit, and is now writing this explanation.

He is doing this in full confidence that they will understand, and will act accordingly: πεποιθὼς ἐπὶ πάντας ὑμᾶς ὅτι ἡ ἐμὴ χαρὰ πάντων ὑμῶν ἐστιν, *having this confidence toward you all that my joy is (that) of you all.* We take notice of the stress which Paul puts on *all.* Twice he uses the word in this participial phrase with its dependent clause. Paul is not biased toward any member of the churches to which he is writing. There are, of course, differences in spiritual understanding among them. There are differences in their progress of sanctification. But whether anyone is weak in one respect or another, Paul has confidence in every one of them. The confidence which he has he states in very wide terms. It is difficult to reproduce this inclusiveness in a simple translation. The genitive πάντων ὑμῶν can express the thought: My joy is the *concern* of you all, i.e., you are all interested in gladdening my heart. Or it may mean: My joy is your joy, i.e., it makes you happy to see me happy. Or it may mean that your joy and mine are of exactly the same kind. My joy is Jesus Christ, and so you seek no other joy than that which is found in union with our Savior. The Greek phrase expresses all these shades of meaning. Paul here in this way repeats the thought which he has voiced in various ways before: his union with the Corinthians, the spiritual communion of all believers.

Who are the "all" whom Paul is here addressing? We must look for the answer in the salutation of the letter: "the church of God which is at Corinth with all the saints which are in all Achaia." There was a congregation in Corinth; there was a congregation in Cenchrea (cf.

Rom. 16:1); there was a group of Christians in Athens (cf. Acts
17:34); and there may have been others, of whom we have no record
(cf. Acts 18:27, 28). Paul indicates that what he is saying now, and
what he still may have to say in this connection, concerns them all:
all will have to reach a conclusion, all will have to take the proper
action. Paul has full confidence in them all, whether they are members
of the Corinthian congregation or of that in Cenchrea, or whether
they belong to some of the smaller groups of Christians in Achaia.

(4) In the following, Paul mentions much tribulation and anguish
of heart in connection with his letter. That can hardly refer to the
present letter. He is writing from Macedonia. Titus has returned
to him from Corinth and brought a very good report, which he never
grew tired of repeating, so that Paul was richly comforted and filled
with great joy. His tears, as far as Corinth was concerned, had been
dried; they were a thing of the past. When he now mentions afflictions
and grief in connection with his writing a letter, he must refer to
First Corinthians.

He connects with an explanatory γάρ: ἐκ γὰρ πολλῆς θλίψεως καὶ
συνοχῆς καρδίας ἔγραψα ὑμῖν διὰ πολλῶν δακρύων, For I wrote to you
out of deep affliction and anguish of heart with many tears.

The situation in Corinth grieved him—and that pertained also to
the other Christians in Achaia—their factionalism, which cropped out
even in connection with the Lord's Supper, their laxity in connection
with the incest case, looseness of morals in general, their offensive
action over against weak brethren, their wavering with reference to
the doctrine of resurrection, to mention only a few, were symptoms
which let Paul fear the worst. Even before First Corinthians he sent
Timothy, and later Titus. He felt downcast when he wrote First Corinthians, fear choked him, and many a tear trickled down his fur-
rowed cheek.

Especially the incest case weighed heavy on his heart, not so much
the foul deed itself as the fact that the Corinthians were not concerned about it, did not in brotherly love rush to the rescue of the
offender, but rather gloated over the matter, boasting of their Christian
liberty. Paul used sharp words in condemning their attitude: "Your
glorying is not good" (I Cor. 5:6).

What was Paul's purpose in using sharp language? Was it that his
temper, his grief, ran away with him? Did he use words which he

would not have used had it not been for his grief, and which perhaps now he regretted? No, those words were not dictated by rancor, but by love; and their purpose was not to hurt the Corinthians. Paul assures them, οὐχ ἵνα λυπηθῆτε, *not in order that you might suffer pain.* Pain was inevitable, but it was not an end in itself. If Paul could have achieved his purpose in some other way, without inflicting pain, he would have been only too happy to choose that course. But there was no other way. His purpose was: ἀλλὰ τὴν ἀγάπην ἵνα γνῶτε ἣν ἔχω περισσοτέρως εἰς ὑμᾶς, *but in order that you might recognize the love which I have in a special measure for you.* Ἀλλά is strongly adversative. Inflict pain? The very opposite was Paul's aim. He uses a clause of purpose, but for the sake of emphasis he places the object, τὴν ἀγάπην, even ahead of the conjunction ἵνα. He loves the Corinthians, he knows them. He understands their weaknesses, understands their faults, and they hurt him—but he is ready to do anything, to bring any sacrifice, in order to help them. He does not like, does not approve, many things which they did, but by that very fact he is driven on to put forth every effort for helping them. Yes, he has ἀγάπη for them, even περισσοτέρως, in an exceptional measure. That love motivated him when he used the sharp language which he did. That love he now emphasizes with all the rhetorical means at his disposal. That love—he wanted the Corinthians to get a taste of it, to recognize it.

Such recognition does not come automatically. The Old Adam, with which the Corinthians also were burdened, resents the manifestations of ἀγάπη such as Paul had given them. It may take a Christian a long time and a strenuous struggle before he overcomes the resentment of his Old Adam at being rebuked for his faults, and before he really appreciates the love which motivated his benefactor in rebuking him. That was part of the reason why Paul postponed his visit to Corinth. He was sure that, once the Corinthians recognized his motive of love, they would understand and thank him all the more.

It remains true, as he had stated at the beginning of this section, that because he was sparing them, he had not yet come to them.

6. 2:5-11

It was the incest case which the Corinthians had at first so badly bungled. Later they had taken Paul's admonition to heart. They had proceeded properly in the matter. They had in ever-increasing numbers recognized the error of their laxity, and brought the offending young man to acknowledge and rue his fall. Now there was danger that they might make the mistake of going to extremes in the other direction. Paul warns them and instructs them how to proceed.

(5) Let them recognize where the greatest danger lies in the case. Εἰ δέ τις λελύπηκεν, *Now, if anyone is guilty of having caused grief.* With a simple δέ Paul connects this to the foregoing. It is not adversative, but merely serves the purpose of taking up the case which, as everyone realized, was on Paul's mind in the previous section. By saying εἰ, *if,* Paul does not cast doubt on the correctness of the report which he had received about the case. He knows that the young man's sin is a fact, and εἰ merely furnishes a convenient way of referring to it. He uses the perfect tense, λελύπηκεν, thereby stressing the result of the action: the young man committed the sin, and now he is burdened with the guilt of it. But what is the guilt? Whom did he hurt? Οὐκ ἐμὲ λελύπηκεν, *he is not guilty of having hurt me.*

Here some commentators allow their imagination a field day. They forget about the grievous incest case. They assume that Paul's visit had taken place recently, and that he is now referring to it. They assume a congregational meeting in Corinth. They assume that Paul was present, ill of health and irritable in disposition. They assume that he used provocative language in correcting the congregation's shortcomings. They assume that some member answered Paul in an especially insulting way, so that Paul left in a huff and sailed back to Ephesus. They assume that Paul was now trying to pass over the breach in silence.—All fancy, without a single fact on record to support it, and ignoring the facts so plainly set forth in the records!

Paul is speaking about the incest case and its significance. To be sure, it had caused Paul bitter heartache. But now he says that that is not the point to be considered. Οὐκ ἐμὲ λελύπηκεν. What then? Ἀλλὰ ἀπὸ μέρους, ἵνα μὴ ἐπιβαρῶ, πάντας ὑμᾶς, *but in part, lest I make an overstatement, you all.* Here we have the same "all" who were mentioned twice in verse 3. Paul is not sure that they were all involved, hence, in order not to make an overstatement, he adds ἀπὸ μέρους, *in part.* That was something which they had not realized. They had not been aware of the close spiritual bonds which unite the believers, so that, if one member suffers, they all suffer. But they had taken Paul's admonition to heart, and had acted on it.

(6) Now Paul continues, ἱκανὸν τῷ τοιούτῳ ἡ ἐπιτιμία αὕτη ἡ ὑπὸ τῶν πλειόνων, *sufficient for this (such a) one is this punishment (inflicted) by ever-increasing numbers.* Ἐπιτιμία is punishment in the sense of rebuke or reproof. Paul says that this was administered to the sinner ὑπὸ τῶν πλειόνων. This comparative often means the *majority,* the greater part of a group. But in this case that meaning would hardly harmonize with the πάντες about whom Paul spoke (though with a slight reservation). This comparative can also indicate that the number was increasing: first some, perhaps only a few, then ever more and more. Yes, the congregation had taken the proper steps, not all of the members at once, but in ever-increasing numbers.

The admonition which they administered had borne fruit. The sinner, such a one as he was, had been brought to repentance. Ἱκανόν, Paul says. Ἱκανόν cannot strictly be considered as the predicate adjective with the subject ἐπιτιμία; the gender does not agree. It has the nature of an adverb: in a sufficient way for the "such-a-one" was the ἐπιτιμία applied. The goal had been reached. Now what next? Paul continues with ὥστε, literally, 'and thus.' The statement that follows contains an inference or a conclusion, the result of the situation presented in the previous part of the sentence. What is it that now follows from the fact that the sinner yielded to the admonition of his brethren and came to repentance?

(7) Ὥστε τοὐναντίον μᾶλλον ὑμᾶς χαρίσασθαι καὶ παρακαλέσαι, *so that contrariwise you rather forgive and comfort (him).* Τοὐναντίον is a contraction of τὸ ἐναντίον. The accusative is used adverbially. The rebuking about the man's sin must now cease; the directly opposite procedure must begin. That will not consist in belittling the sin or in pointing the man to some good deeds in his behavior otherwise. No, the sin remains the same, and its damnableness remains the same. But the guilt has been wiped out by the sacrifice of Christ. Hence, comfort the sinner by announcing to him the forgiveness of his sin. Paul uses two infinitives in the aorist, the tense which stresses the action as such. He thus tells them that just this is the thing to do. He does not say anything else, neither by the verb form nor in some other way, either about the method or duration of the new procedure. He just stresses the forgiving and comforting, pure and simple. The danger is ever present that we give the sinner who is down and out an extra kick. Our Old Adam tries to meddle in the affairs which lie

strictly in the field of the Gospel. No, when a man is struck by the *terrores conscientiae,* the grace of God must be proclaimed to him; the unadulterated Gospel is the only word to apply to him, without any ifs and buts, without any conditions or reservations, without any admixtures of any kind.

Paul next points out the danger, if the Corinthians should fail to adopt this procedure: μή πως τῇ περισσοτέρᾳ λύπῃ καταποθῇ ὁ τοιοῦτος, *lest in some way the "such-a-one" be swallowed up by his (the) excessive grief.* Paul places the subject of the sentence, ὁ τοιοῦτος, into the unusual position at the very end of the sentence. Thereby, in addition to the word which he uses, he calls special attention to the spiritual condition of the man, such a one as he was, burdened with his guilt, ashamed of his sin, grieved about the offense which he had caused. He apparently was bordering on the brink of despair, doubting whether his sin might ever be forgiven. In him you could see an illustration of the Thirty-eighth Psalm. He stood in danger of being drowned in his excessive grief. Therefore, so Paul urges the Corinthians, comfort him with the assurance of forgiveness.

(8) Paul adds some practical advice on the mode of procedure: διὸ παρακαλῶ ὑμᾶς κυρῶσαι εἰς αὐτὸν ἀγάπην, *accordingly I urge you to ratify (your) love to him.*—Paul here uses the verb κυρόω, which he uses also in Galatians 3:15; and then in its compound form, προκυρόω, in Galatians 3:17. There he speaks of a man's testament as κεκυρωμένη, and then applies it to God's promises, calling them προκεκυρωμέναι. The verb means 'to confirm solemnly and officially.' A man's testament is probated, and God's promises were probated in advance. In our text the verb suggests the idea of confirming by solemn resolution, ratifying.

When Paul was informed that incest had been committed by a member of the congregation, he formulated a resolution to be adopted by the brethren in their meeting: "In the name of our Lord Jesus Christ ... to deliver such an one unto Satan for the destruction of the flesh, that the spirit may be saved in the day of the Lord Jesus" (I Cor. 5:4,5). The purpose of destroying the man's flesh had now been achieved. He had repented in deep sorrow. Now a different resolution was in place: the congregation must solemnly confirm love to the repentant sinner. This pertains not only to the local congregation in Corinth, but, as Paul had emphatically declared repeatedly above, he is speaking to all the addressees of his letter, to each and every one. It concerns them all, they all must act.

(9) The Corinthians had blundered seriously in many respects. Their conduct was an offense to the Church Universal. It is important for themselves and for the whole Church that they give unmistakable evidence of their unequivocal submission to the Gospel. Their action in the incest matter is a case in point. Εἰς τοῦτο γὰρ καὶ ἔγραψα, ἵνα γνῶ τὴν δοκιμὴν ὑμῶν, εἰ εἰς πάντα ὑπήκοοί ἐστε, *For this was also the purpose of my writing that I might get to know your proof, if you are obedient in all things.* Δοκιμή is a test successfully passed, a proof (German, *Bewaehrung*). Their obedience, which the test was to show, is not personal obedience to Paul—he had emphatically declined lordship over their faith (1:24)—it is obedience to the Gospel, something which had been dangerously dwindling in Corinth.

(10) As Paul had so far always stressed the close bonds that united him with the Corinthians, so he does here again. Ὧι δέ τι χαρίζεσθε. κἀγώ, *And to whom you forgive anything, I also.* Such full confidence has Paul in the Christian faith and judgment of the Corinthians that he practically hands them a blank check to fill in as they please. If they announce to an excommunicated sinner that he has been reinstated, Paul will go along with them. Not only will he raise no objections, he will rejoice with them in their action. Such is the tie that binds Christian hearts together. When they excommunicate, and when they reinstate, they do this as brethren and as representatives of Christ, in His name, as people who have been entrusted with the keys by Him. Paul states this principle by explaining how he exercises it personally: καὶ γὰρ ἐγὼ ὃ κεχάρισμαι, εἴ τι κεχάρισμαι, δι' ὑμᾶς ἐν προσώπῳ Χριστοῦ, *for also what I have forgiven, if I have forgiven anything, (it was) because of you in the person of Christ.*

(11) The matter was very serious in Corinth, and is serious in every case of disciplinary action by a church body. Both the admonition and the announcement of forgiveness must be carried out in the spirit of Christ. The devil is always busy, trying to worm his way into the picture. Paul says, ἵνα μὴ πλεονεκτηθῶμεν ὑπὸ τοῦ σατανᾶ, *that we may not become the victims of Satan's wiles,* that Satan may not take advantage of some weakness in our Christian armor.

This is something which the Corinthians had overlooked in their dealings with the incest case. The devil had "his fingers in the pie."

Paul had reminded them of this when, in I Corinthians 5, he suggested a resolution delivering the offender to Satan; he reminds them of it again now. It is something every congregation must remember. When they neglect to admonish a sinner, Satan is winning a victory. When they admonish a sinner in a legalistic way, Satan again is reaping the benefits. And when they refuse to proclaim forgiveness to a repentant sinner, Satan celebrates a triumph. Do not let him get an advantage.

Paul concludes this section with a remark the full meaning of which will not become apparent till we reach the third main part of the epistle. Οὐ γὰρ αὐτοῦ τὰ νοήματα ἀγνοοῦμεν, *for we are not ignorant of his devices.* What were the schemes of the devil, of which Paul was well aware? Paul does not say. We must leave the question open for the present. We shall return to it later.

B. THE GREAT TREASURE IN EARTHEN VESSELS
Chapter 2:12 to Chapter 5:10

1. 2:12-17

In the previous parts of chapters 1 and 2 Paul had time and again voiced his great interest in the Corinthian congregation, and had expressed his deep concern for their welfare. In the last verse of the previous section he had also referred to the schemes of Satan, of which he maintained he was well aware. He did not reveal what the deadly designs of Satan are, but left that for some later discussion. In our present section, in vss. 12 and 13, he cites an incident from his stay in Troas which illustrates his deep concern for the Corinthians, pointing out what effect it had on the Apostle's mission activities.

(12) Ἐλθὼν δὲ εἰς τὴν Τρωάδα, *Now, having come to Troas.* Δέ merely continues the narrative. There is no contrast between the present statement and the forgoing. The important thing is his stay in Troas. Paul is on his way to Corinth via Macedonia. The time is probably the end of May or the beginning of June, since he left Ephesus immediately after the riot stirred up by Demetrius, which took place in connection with the May festivals in honor of Diana. Troas was his last stopping place in Asia. From Troas he had set sail for Macedonia on his second mission journey, about five or six years before. As we

see from 7:5, his presence was required in Macedonia; the Gospel work needed his personal attention, but the situation was not really pressing. Paul planned to spend some time first in Troas. He came there εἰς τὸ εὐαγγέλιον τοῦ Χριστοῦ, *in connection with the Gospel of Christ*

We have no record of the Gospel work in Troas. It may be assumed that Paul preached there during his stop on his second mission journey before receiving the call to Macedonia, which came to him in a vision. On his journey to Jerusalem to deliver the collection which he was even now in the process of gathering, after he had visited Corinth, he preached to a large gathering in an upper room (Acts 20:7ff.). There was a congregation in Troas at that time. Paul mentions the place again in the last letter which we have from his pen (II Tim. 4:13).

En route to Corinth via Macedonia Paul came to Troas in the interest of the Gospel of Christ, evidently planning to spend some time in the city. The opportunity for preaching the Gospel was very good. He says, καὶ θύρας μοι ἀνεῳγμένης ἐν κυρίῳ, *and a door standing open before me in the Lord.* Ἀνεῳγμένη is the perfect tense, thus denoting a condition resulting from some completed action, the nature of which (punctiliar, repeated, durative) is of no further interest. The fact to be noted is that the door stood wide open, ready for Paul to walk in. This was the case ἐν κυρίῳ. The arrangement of the situation was clearly of the Lord's doing and promised rich blessings from the Lord.

Why did Paul not seize upon this golden opportunity?

(13) Paul answers, οὐκ ἔσχηκα ἄνεσιν τῷ πνεύματί μου, *I had no rest in my spirit.* In ἔσχηκα we have another case of a perfect tense which apparently lost its specific perfect tense meaning and degenerated into a mere statement of historical fact. It does not seem to mean that Paul still was feeling the effects of a certain disappointment which he experienced in Troas, but it seems to register merely the fact that Paul did experience a disappointment.

There was something about the situation in Troas which troubled his πνεῦμα. Are we going too far, or are we reading something into the word, if we assume that Paul was not only mentally upset, but that he actually felt a disturbance in his spiritual life, in his faith, as an Apostle of Jesus Christ? Physically he seems to have been well taken care of in Troas, and in view of the "open door" his mind might have felt very much satisfied. Yet his spirit was disturbed.

By what? and in what respect? Paul answers, τῷ μὴ εὑρεῖν με Τίτον τὸν ἀδελφόν μου, *by not finding Titus, my brother.* Titus was to meet him in Troas, to bring a report from Corinth. He did not arrive on time. What had happened? What had delayed Titus, so that he did not keep his appointment? Had his mission to Corinth been a failure? Were conditions in Corinth deteriorating? Were they improving, but too slowly, so that Titus' presence was still required? Were things turning hopeless? No wonder Paul was uneasy, since he might fear the worst. The uncertainty robbed his spirit of its rest. To know the worst would have been more tolerable than this suspense.

It was not ordinary curiosity, or purely human concern that troubled Paul. If it had been, then he might have felt more than compensated by the splendid mission opportunity which he found in Troas. But Paul seemed to think that if matters did not improve in Corinth, then that loss would by far outweigh any gains which he might make in Troas. From his experience in his mission work in general and in Corinth in particular, and from the Lord's announcement that He had much people in that city, Paul had learned to recognize Corinth as a key city in his work. As long as conditions in Corinth remained unsettled, he could not proceed beyond it. He was entertaining plans to go west, to visit Rome and to bring the Gospel to Spain. But with Corinth lost, there would not only be a basis of operation missing; rather, the city would have been turned into a stronghold for the enemy. The loss of Corinth might also have its repercussions on congregations in the east, the churches in Macedonia, in Asia Minor, in Galatia. The Judaizers and other detractors of Paul's work would be encouraged and strengthened by their success in that key city. Paul had no rest in his spirit. He left for Macedonia.

What impression would this procedure of Paul make on the Corinthians? It made them aware of the deep concern which Paul had for their well-being. He not only said so, but now they could see that this concern determined his decisions and actions; it had a far-reaching influence on his mission work. Healthy conditions in their midst would strengthen the hands of Paul, but by their default they would dampen his spirit and hamstring his efforts. By thus getting to feel Paul's deep concern they were reminded of their own responsibility.

Paul departed from Troas: ἀλλὰ ἀποταξάμενος αὐτοῖς ἐξῆλθον εἰς Μακεδονίαν, *but taking my leave from them I departed for Macedonia.* Ἀποτάσσεσθαι, literally, 'to set oneself away from,' 'to separate oneself,' 'to withdraw from,' is frequently, as in this case, used for formal leave-taking, bidding farewell. If we take Paul's farewell address to the Ephesian elders, which St. Luke records in Acts 20:17ff., as a pattern, we can easily imagine what Paul may have said to the brethren on this occasion, encouraging them to go through that "open door," something which he, because of circumstances, could not do; warning them to be on the alert against troublemakers who would come to them from without, and against ambitious teachers who might arise in their own midst; and commending them to the Lord and to the Word of His grace.

It certainly was not easy for Paul to take leave under such circumstances; but his concern for Corinth made it necessary.

Let us not get the idea that Paul was suffering from defeatism. Far from it. He was firmly convinced that the Gospel would come out victorious in any event, even though the Corinthians might squander its blessings for themselves. Both as a warning to the Corinthians, and at the same time as an encouragement for timid believers, he compared the course of the Gospel to a triumphal procession.

(14) Τῷ δὲ θεῷ χάρις τῷ πάντοτε θριαμβεύοντι ἡμᾶς ἐν τῷ Χριστῷ, *But thanks (be) to God, who always grants us a triumph in Christ.* Θριαμβεύω occurs but twice in the New Testament, besides our passage only in Colossians 2:15. It is not used in the same sense in both cases. In the Colossians passage it is applied to the defeated enemies. God, having stripped the princes and rulers of darkness of their armor through Christ Jesus, through Him also made a public show of them, leading them in a triumphal procession. In our passage the θριαμβεύειν is applied to Paul as the victorious general, meaning that he was granted a triumphal procession in recognition of his successful campaign. In fact, his whole mission work was one continuous triumph.

It is not pride when Paul compares his success in the Gospel work to a triumphal procession. He did not merit it by his own skill and ingenuity. With due modesty, yet true to fact, he adds ἐν τῷ Χριστῷ. It is Christ's victory and Christ's triumph, not Paul's. Paul was Christ's minister, but God granted him the triumph in and through Christ.

Having introduced the figure of a triumph, Paul now speaks about the successful work of the Gospel in terms borrowed from a triumphal procession, with which his readers were well acquainted. In a triumph garlands of flowers decorated the victors and their chariots, and quantities of incense would be burned. There would be a strong sweet odor tickling the olfactory nerves of all, participants and spectators, the victors as well as the defeated victims, in such a procession. Paul applies this aspect to his Gospel work in the following participial phrase: καὶ τὴν ὀσμὴν τῆς γνώσεως αὐτοῦ φανεροῦντι δι' ἡμῶν ἐν παντὶ τόπῳ, (God) who brings forth into the open the odor of His knowledge through us in every place. The course of the Gospel in the world is like a triumph because in it God spreads His sweet odor, namely, a knowledge of Him. Remember how Jesus in His high-priestly prayer connected the knowledge of God with eternal life: "This is life eternal, that they might know thee the only true God, and Jesus Christ whom thou hast sent" (John 17:3). That knowledge is a sweet odor which God spreads through the Gospel in every place where it is proclaimed.

(15) The odor in a triumphal procession was sweet to the participants and spectators only. To the victims, who were led in chains along the triumph, to be executed at its close—to them that same odor was a terrible one; for them it meant shame and certain death. The odor was the same in both cases. Just so it is with the Gospel: Ὅτι Χριστοῦ εὐωδία ἐσμὲν τῷ θεῷ ἐν τοῖς σωζομένοις καὶ ἐν τοῖς ἀπολλυμένοις, for Christ's sweet odor we are to God in those being saved and in those perishing.

(16) Christ's sweet odor remains unchanged, though its appreciation by different people varies immensely. Οἷς μὲν ὀσμὴ ἐκ θανάτου εἰς θάνατον, οἷς δὲ ὀσμὴ ἐκ ζωῆς εἰς ζωήν, to the ones an odor from death to death, to the others an odor from life to life. The Gospel always triumphs; it is never put to shame. In the case of those that are saved it appears as the glorious power of God unto salvation. No one is ever lost too deeply in sin; the Gospel is able to rescue him, and does rescue him ἐκ ζωῆς εἰς ζωήν. There is complete life, vigorous life, a happy life all along the line, with no trace left of death or weakness.

But the Gospel is just as triumphant in the case of them that are lost. Why are they lost? Because they refused to accept the Gospel. They would not have it; they relied on their own efforts. And now what have they? Perdition, ἐκ θανάτου εἰς θάνατον. The Gospel triumphs again. It stood ready with its salvation for all, also for the ones that rejected it. Outside of the Gospel there is no salvation. Those that declined the salvation of the Gospel, imagined they could have salvation without it; they relied on their own record. Their attempt was a complete failure. By their very failure the Gospel stands vindicated as the only power unto salvation.

Paul mentioned above that God grants *us* a triumph, and spreads the sweet odor of His knowledge *through us,* that *we* are the sweet odor of Christ. What have *we* to do with the matter? The matter seems too stupendous for our poor power.

Therefore he now asks the question: καὶ πρὸς ταῦτα τίς ἱκανός; *And who is sufficient for these things?* This is a real question, not a rhetorical one. Paul wants his readers to start thinking about the qualifications required to produce such results. This was necessary particularly over against his detractors, who posed as apostles far superior to Paul; who insinuated that Paul's Gospel could not be trusted because he had changed his travel plans. Now Paul said that his Gospel preaching is one grand triumphal procession, that his Gospel preaching means complete life to some of his hearers and inevitable death to the others. What qualifications can he show which enable him to produce such results? Yes, who is sufficient for these things?

(17) Paul answers: οὐ γάρ ἐσμεν, *for we are not.* Γάρ introduces a motivation. Before this motivation a thought must be supplied. The answer to the question, Who is sufficient? assumes and presupposes the thought that *we are*; then the answer continues, for we are not, etc. This thought that we, Paul and his associates, are sufficient is not foreign to the context; in fact, the context demands it. Had not Paul in the immediately preceding sentence spoken about himself and his associates as enjoying a constant triumphal procession, as being instrumental in spreading the odor of God's knowledge, yes, as being themselves Christ's sweet odor with its tremendous effect? The question, *Who* is sufficient? thus actually amounts to this: How is it that we, yes, we much-maligned, weak servants, can achieve such results? The answer now, in the first place, is negative: because we are not so and so, because we avoid a certain mistake.

Paul is sorry to say that the mistake is a very common one. We are not ὡς οἱ πολλοί, *as the many,* like the common run of false apostles. The Corinthians were at this very moment being disturbed in their individual as well as in their congregational faith-life by troublemakers who posed as superior apostles. Their methods were not exceptional; they have a certain appeal, and many are entrapped by them. These same alluring errors are surrounding us today, and threaten to ruin our Gospel work. We do well to let ourselves be put on guard by Paul's οἱ πολλοί, and to pay close attention to his description of their ruinous ways.

He uses the expression, καπηλεύοντες τὸν λόγον τοῦ θεοῦ. Here the pivotal word καπηλεύω demands our attention. It is derived from κάπηλος, 'an innkeeper,' 'a petty retailer,' 'a huckster,' 'a peddler.' Καπηλεία occurs in contrast to ἐμπορία, from which our English word emporium is derived. Thayer, Greek-English Lexicon of the New Testament, lists as meanings of the verb: 'to be a retailer, to peddle; to make money by selling anything, to get sordid gain by dealing in anything, to do a thing for base gain; also to corrupt, to adulterate'—the last particularly because of the habit some tavernkeepers had of diluting their wine with water. Compare Paul's parallel phrase in 4:2, δολοῦντες τὸν λόγον τοῦ θεοῦ, "handling the word of God deceitfully." Thus καπηλεύειν τὸ εὐαγγέλιον means to regard the Gospel as a commodity, to try to "sell" the Gospel, usually with the connotation of some "shady" dealings.

This abuse may assume different forms. The Judaizers of Paul's day did it by adding the observance of the Old Testament ceremonial law to the Gospel. To submit to circumcision and to observe the Jewish festival calendar and clean-food regulations was presented as an aid to making the blessings of the Gospel secure. In that sense people, particularly Jews, were more ready to accept the Gospel, seeing that thereby some credit accrued also to themselves for their salvation. The troublemakers in Corinth tried to sell their Gospel on a competitive basis, considering Paul as their rival, and denouncing his Gospel as inferior. Others may practice the abuse of καπηλεύειν by offering inducements together with the Gospel. Paul hints at such tactics when in I Corinthians 2:1 he says that he did not come "with excellency of speech or of wisdom."

All such and similar practices fall under the general head of καπηλεύειν. They are not harmless tricks of trade, but they affect the Gospel itself and corrupt it. Regarding the Judaizers' procedure, Paul says expressly in Galatians 1:6, 7 that they are bringing another Gospel, which may not be considered as just another brand, but which is no Gospel at all. Καπηλεύειν in any form deactivates and ruins the Gospel. Anyone who wishes to see the Gospel produce its divinely intended fruit must abstain from καπηλεύειν; otherwise he cannot qualify as ἱκανός .

After having stated, negatively, the abuse which must be avoided, Paul with a strong ἀλλά turns to a positive statement of the requirements. He lists four points. He says first of all λαλοῦμεν, we speak, ὡς ἐξ εἰλικρινείας, as from sincerity. The most commonly accepted etymology of εἰλικρινής is interesting. The second part clearly contains the stem κρίνω, 'to examine,' 'to evaluate.' The first part is from εἴλη, the bright sunlight. In order to be εἰλικρινής, able to pass the testing of the bright sunlight, the preaching of the Gospel must be done in perfect accord with its nature. According to Romans 1:17, the Gospel reveals the "righteousness of God." It addresses itself to a sin-laden world, assuring every guilty conscience that God Himself in Christ prepared a valid righteousness for every sinner, that in the resurrection of Christ He already proclaimed all sins of the world forgiven, and then in the Gospel invites the trembling conscience to accept His gracious gift in faith. Εἰλικρίνεια demands of the preacher that he present the Gospel just so, without additions, or subtractions, or alterations.

The second point which Paul stresses is that the preachers of the Gospel speak ὡς ἐκ θεοῦ, as from God. He prefixes this with a second ἀλλά, used by way of intensifying the thought: not only ordinary human εἰλικρίνεια, but such as has its origin in God. The ὡς naturally does not mean 'as if,' but has a causal connotation. With the prepositional phrase ἐκ θεοῦ Paul places himself and his assistants completely at the disposal of God. They speak only when and what God would have them speak, and are silent when God is silent. Their message is God's message; as Peter expressed it, they speak ὡς λόγια θεοῦ, "as the oracles of God" (I Pet. 4:11).

They speak, thirdly, κατέναντι θεοῦ, in the presence of God. This not merely refers to God's supervision: God has appointed us to preach, He has given us the message to deliver, and now He is ever with us, supervising our work to see that we carry out our assignment as He would have us. That is true, but κατέναντι θεοῦ means much more. Remember Jesus' last promise to His disciples: "Lo, I am with you alway, even unto the end of the world." Remember what Paul said to Agrippa in Caesarea: "Having therefore obtained *help of God,* I continue unto this day, witnessing both to small and great, saying none other things than those which the prophets and Moses did say should come" (Acts 26:22). A proof of God's ever-present help Paul had mentioned in 1:9,10: "That we should not trust in ourselves, but in God which raiseth the dead: who delivered us from so great a death, and doth deliver: in whom we trust that he will yet deliver us." In the presence of God Paul performed his apostleship, trusting alone in His aid and protection.

Closely connected with the preceding, practically embracing them all and giving meaning to them, is Paul's last prepositional phrase: We speak ἐν Χριστῷ. Paul's message is absolutely Christ-centered. Whatever Christ means to the world, that he will proclaim in full, and nothing but that; whatever is foreign to Christ, he will eliminate from his words. Christ is not a mere man; He is the Son of God. So Paul will proclaim Him. Christ was crucified for the sins of the world. Though this is a stumbling block to the Jews, and foolishness to the Greeks, Paul proclaims Christ crucified as the only One in whom we have redemption, and justification, and sanctification. He proclaims Christ as the One in whom our life is hidden. He proclaims Christ as the God-appointed Judge of the world. And he pronounces an anathema on any and every endeavor to mingle human works with Christ's righteousness. They are dung and a loss. Thus Paul speaks ἐν Χριστῷ, having determined not to know anything in his work as an Apostle save Jesus Christ and Him crucified.

That is his answer to the question, Who is sufficient for these things? That was the proper answer in his day; it is the only proper answer in our day. It breathes the spirit of εἰλικρίνεια and insures the purity of doctrine. It is not our own achievement, but is the spirit ἐκ θεοῦ. That spirit won the victory over character assassins and Judaizers in Paul's day; it will insure the triumph of the Gospel over unionism, over *Pro deo et patria* awards, and what have you, today.

2. 3:1-6

"Are we beginning to commend ourselves again?" Thus according to the RSV St. Paul begins the third chapter of his Second Epistle to the Corinthians. With these words he refers to the closing remarks in chapter 2, which we then must review in order to get the background for our present study.

In vs. 14 he compared his past mission work to one glorious triumphal procession. His present epistle was written from Macedonia in the summer of 57. About 10 years of mission activity lay behind him. He had worked in Cyprus and southern Galatia before 51; then in Macedonia and Achaia; then in the Roman province of Asia with Ephesus as his headquarters. Now he was on his way to pay Corinth a third visit. He had met with much opposition, especially on the part of the Jews. He had been maltreated and imprisoned (e.g., in Philippi); he had been stoned (in Lystra). There had occurred the riot of Demetrius in Ephesus. Paul showed in his own person that we must enter into the kingdom of God through much tribulation.

Does this look like a triumphal procession? Yet that is precisely what Paul calls it: "Now thanks be unto God, which always causeth us to triumph in Christ."

Carrying out the figure of a triumphal procession, Paul makes several applications to his mission work. In a triumphal procession there was a rich, sweet odor, coming from numerous garlands of flowers and from burning incense. Paul compares the knowledge of Christ to this "savor," which was made manifest in every place by his work.

In a triumphal procession leaders of the defeated enemy were dragged through the streets, chained to the victor's chariot, to be executed at the end of the triumph. The sweet odor of the flowers and of the incense reached also their nostrils; but to them it meant death. It was to them a terrible odor, while to the victors it assured the end of their past troubles and undisturbed security for the future. Paul applies these features to his Gospel work: "For we are unto God a sweet savor of Christ, in them that are saved, and in them that perish: to the one we are the savor of death unto death; and to the other the savor of life unto life" (vss. 15, 16).

That is a stupendous achievement. So Paul asks the question: "And who is sufficient for these things?" This is a real question, not a rhetorical one, or a thinly veiled exclamation. Paul is inquiring after the source of such work, after the qualification of a man who can achieve such results. Paul answers the question himself with words that merit our closest attention: "For we are not as many, which corrupt the word of God: but as of sincerity, but as of God, in the sight of God speak we in Christ" (vs. 17).

The word *corrupt* is not a literal translation of the Greek καπηλεύειν, which is derived from κάπηλος, 'an innkeeper,' 'a petty retailer,' 'a huckster,' 'a peddler'; and which according to Thayer means: 'to be a retailer, to peddle; to make money by selling anything, to get sordid gain by dealing in anything, to do a thing for base gain.'

Paul complains that there are "many" who so abuse the Word of God that their Gospel work may be called a καπηλεύειν. One is vividly reminded of Schiller's distich on *Wissenschaft,* saying that, while by some it is considered as an exalted, heavenly goddess, to another it is but *eine melkende Kuh, die ihn mit Butter versorgt.* Such καπηλεύοντες were the false apostles who had invaded Corinth. They supposed that godliness is a means of making a gain; and accordingly they resorted to all manner of questionable means for putting their message across and winning the favor of the people. They defamed Paul, whom they considered as their competitor; they added to the Gospel, or subtracted from it, in order to make it more acceptable to the people. — As far as the substance of the matter is concerned, the translation of the King James Version is correct: they "corrupted" the Gospel message.

Over against such methods, so Paul maintains, he and his associates are very careful to preach the Gospel ἐξ εἰλικρινείας from pure motives just as it came to them ἐκ θεοῦ. They preach it, always conscious of the fact that they are standing κατέναντι θεοῦ. And their entire message comes to a head ἐν Χριστῷ, and is centered in Him. As their motives are pure, so is their message the unadulterated Word of God.

This is the reason why Paul's work had such stupendous results. They were the fruit of the pure and unadulterated Gospel. But since he makes the emphatic statement that this is the manner and the spirit in which he performs his work, he anticipates that some of his detractors will raise the charge that he thereby in his turn is beginning to "commend" himself, in fact, is writing his own letter of recommendation.

(1) Paul counters by raising the question: "Do we begin again to commend ourselves? Or need we, as some others, epistles of commendation to you?" Do we really need such letters? Others may need them, but do we? A letter of introduction is in place over against strangers.

Paul's question thus really is an appeal to the heart of the Corinthians: Are we strangers? Am I a stranger to you?

His question means more. He does not merely remind them of the fact that they had met him personally, and had made his personal acquaintance some five years before; his question implies that his work in their city had brought them and him much closer to one another, had united their hearts in Christ. When at the end of the previous chapter he stressed that he preached the Gospel as of sincerity, as of God, in the presence of God, in Christ, he was not revealing any secret to them. That is the very way how they themselves had gotten to know him for 18 months. They knew his work in the Jewish synagogue. They knew the opposition of the Jews, and his separation from them. They knew how he had continued his work in the house of a certain Justus. They knew how he had been hailed, by the Jews, before the court of Gallio. They knew also how Paul in all those days had never asked for any remuneration. Day and night he had worked in the shop of Aquila to provide for his own maintenance and for that of his assistants.

Surely, all of these things were not forgotten in Corinth. Those false apostles, it is true, were working hard day and night underhandedly, trying to estrange the Corinthians from Paul. But had things really come to such a pass that he needed a letter of introduction to them? This is an appeal to the heart of the Corinthians, to bring them to their senses.

Paul deepens the thought by adding the question: Or do we need "letters of commendation from you?" Did his work in Corinth remain unnoticed? Were there no fruits in evidence? Was the case this that the Corinthians nominally accepted Christianity, but that otherwise things remained very much the same as they had been before? When the Thessalonians accepted the Gospel, their conversion was talked about everywhere. Did Paul's work in Corinth make less of an impression? Will nobody know about it unless the Corinthians record it in a letter of recommendation for Paul?

(2) Very emphatically Paul makes the statement: "Ye are our epistle." Our letter—why, that is *you*. You yourselves, you in your very person, you are our letter of recommendation.

Having said that, Paul can freely borrow expressions which refer to a letter of introduction, and he can be sure that the Corinthians will take those expressions as applying to themselves. They dare not be interpreted literally, but must be understood metaphorically as expressing some truth concerning living persons.

This applies to the very first statement which Paul makes about his letter of recommendation, which the Corinthian Christians are. He says: "written in our hearts." Ordinarily the heart must be considered as a very poor place for a letter of recommendation. What good would such a letter do if written in the bearer's heart? A letter of recommendation is for presentation. By handing it over to someone the bearer identifies and introduces himself. But how can a letter written in the heart serve that purpose? The difficulty disappears if we remember that Paul is speaking of persons. The Corinthians fill the heart of the Apostle. He is always thinking of them, and the deep concern for them motivates all his doings. Thus he can add that, because they occupy so prominent a place in his heart, his letter of recommendation is "known and read of all men."

This is true, not only because out of the abundance of the heart the mouth speaks, but in an even greater measure because out of the heart are the issues of life. Since the Corinthians are enshrined in the heart of Paul, since they are the object of his interest and his love, this will inevitably manifest itself in his conduct. If Paul's actions show no concern for the welfare of the Corinthians, or only a very small concern, then it will be evident to all that they are not very deeply engraved in his heart. Then the letter of recommendation will not make a very favorable impression. If, on the other hand, Paul's actions betray a deep concern for the Corinthians, then the writing will stand out in bold relief, so that everybody can read it without glasses—and get to feel its weightiness.

The latter was the case. In chapter 2:12, 13, Paul mentioned his visit to Troas. He stopped there to do mission work. The opportunity was excellent. He found a wide-open door. Yet he did not avail himself of the opportunity. Why not? He had expected to meet Titus in Troas, Titus, whom he had sent to Corinth to help the church there to overcome its difficulties and to solve its problems. He was anxiously awaiting a report from Titus. Titus did not reach Troas at the appointed time. Paul's composure was upset. His concern gave him no rest; he could not summon the calmness of spirit necessary to exploit the splendid opportunity for Gospel work in Troas. He took his leave and proceeded to Macedonia. Thereby everybody got to feel and to read the letter of recommendation written in the heart of Paul: his deep concern for Corinth. Does he need a letter of recommendation to Corinth, or even from Corinth? It was plain to everybody what a warm place the Corinthians occupied in the heart of Paul.

(3) Paul deepens the thought. The content of a letter of recommendation is of the utmost importance. What do the Corinthians show as Paul's letter? Paul still uses the figure of a letter to express what the Corinthians represent, and what it is that makes them so dear to him. He says that they are becoming manifest as a "letter of Christ." "Forasmuch as ye are manifestly declared to be the epistle of Christ." He adds by way of explanation that this letter was "written not with ink, but with the Spirit of the living God." There was a new life throbbing in the hearts of the Corinthians, a life which thoroughly revolutionized their outward conduct. To be sure, as Paul complained in his earlier epistle, the conduct of the Corinthians was far from perfect; it showed some alarming weaknesses. Yet it could not be denied that there was a new life, a life which the Spirit of the living God had produced in them. Paul widens the figure, at the same time introducing some terms which will serve as a transition to his next part. He says, this letter is written, not on stone plaques, but on plaques which are human hearts.

Paul's interest in the Corinthians, however, is closer than that of a mere fellow believer, closer than that of brother to brother, based on the fact that both he and they were reborn by the Spirit of God: Paul had had a hand in the conversion of the Corinthians. They became a letter of Christ through the instrumentality of Paul, διακονηθεῖσα ὑφ' ἡμῶν. If Paul had not come to Corinth with the Gospel, they would never have become a letter of Christ; they would still be serving dumb idols. Paul was used by Christ to bring about that change in the lives of the Corinthians. This fact joined his heart still more closely to them and deepened his concern for them.

Paul needs no letter of recommendation to the Corinthians; he does not need any from them. Hence, when he mentions the sincerity with which he had proclaimed the Gospel to them and had achieved those extraordinary results, he does so, not in order to commend himself;

far from it. He does so to remind the Corinthians of the nature of
his work.

(4) After warding off the misunderstanding of his question concerning the qualification necessary to produce the result: sweet odor
to God both in them that are saved, ἐκ ζωῆς εἰς ζωήν, and in them that
perish, ἐκ θανάτου εἰς θάνατον, he takes up the main thought concerning
that sufficiency. He speaks about his "confidence," which is indeed
a very great and special confidence, τοιαύτην. He first states very summarily that it is a confidence which he has through Christ toward God.

(5) Negatively stated, his sufficiency does not spring from himself.
He places the ἀφ' ἑαυτῶν emphatically at the head. Paul was by nature
gifted with a keen mind and a strong will, who readily grasped a
situation, held to his purpose with vigor and perseverance. He had
developed his mind in the schooling which Gamaliel administered
and in the opportunities which his hometown Tarsus offered. After
his conversion he had retired into Arabia. Was it this natural endow-
ment plus thorough training and application that had made him sufficient? Emphatically Paul says, *not of ourselves,* namely, not with
ourselves considered as the starting point, as the source. We are not
the soil from which such sufficiency will spring.

In eliminating any thought of self-sufficiency, Paul adds the infinitive
λογίσασθαι. This verb means to 'reckon, count, compute, calculate, count
over.' The RSV is correct in translating: *to claim.* The infinitive is
adverbial, showing in what respect or to what extent Paul declines
any self-sufficiency. It reaches to the absolute zero point. Paul cannot
credit himself with anything, not with the least, as having the source
of his strength in himself, ἐξ ἑαυτῶν. There is sufficiency, but its source
must be sought entirely outside of Paul. Positively stated: "our sufficiency is of God," ἐκ τοῦ θεοῦ.

(6) The next verse leads to a climax, καί, 'even,' *sogar.* Yes, God
has endowed us with sufficiency to be administrators of the New Testament, καινῆς διαθήκης. The genitive is qualifying: New Testament
ministers. We translate: *testament,* not as the RSV has, *covenant.*
Διαθήκη is the LXX translation of the Hebrew *berith.* But as Genesis
15 already clearly indicates, God's covenant is very one-sided. God
is the only active partner; Abraham and all his fellow believers are
purely receptive. They are the beneficiaries of the blessings which God
in His covenant obligates Himself to bestow. This idea of one-sidedness

is better expressed by *testament.*—God made Paul sufficient to be a New Testament minister. This testament is one of life-giving Spirit, in contrast to the death-dealing letter of the Old Covenant.

With the words *Spirit* and *letter* Paul is not referring to two ways of approaching the same testament, two ways of handling it, one superficial and mechanical, the other truly spiritual; no, he is speaking of two distinct testaments, as is clearly seen from the characterization given of both in the following section, vss. 7-11. The RSV rather beclouds the issue by substituting *written code* for *letter.*

When Paul speaks about the stupendous results which he achieved in his ministry, he is not doing so in order to commend himself to the Corinthians, much less to elicit a letter of recommendation from them: they by their faith in the Lord Jesus, by the radical change in their attitude and conduct as a result of Paul's work among them—they are a living monument to the dynamic of his work. They are his letter of recommendation. But do they realize to what ministry and to what sufficiency they are bearing testimony? It is the ministry of God's New Testament.

3.   3:7-11

(7, 8) The two parts just treated, vss. 1-3, and vss. 4-6, belong together very closely, really forming only a single unit. The part which we begin now cannot be so subdivided. It is a closely knit entity. Paul compares, contrasts the two testaments which he briefly introduced in vs. 6.

They have one thing in common, they are *glorious.* And yet, how vastly different even on this score!

Paul leaves no room for doubt to which διαθήκη he is referring in contradistinction to the New Testament. It is not the promise given by God to Noah, or to Abraham. It is the one ἐν γράμμασιν ἐντετυπωμένη λίθοις. This description points to the Law of Moses. This testament is not that portion of the Bible which we call the Old Testament, nor does it mean the condition in which the Old Testament people stood in relation to their God. The *letter* simply does not affect the promise given to Abraham. The *letter* is that thing which was added 430 years later because of sin, the thing which was ordained by angels in the hand of a mediator (Gal. 3:19, 20). It was the διαθήκη engraved in letters on stone tables. The administration of this διαθήκη Paul calls an administration of death.

By way of contrast he calls the New Testament an administration of the Spirit. While the one inflicts death, the other conveys the Spirit. That is the Spirit whom he had mentioned before, the life-giving Spirit of the living God. By phrasing the contrast in this way, substituting the word Spirit for life, Paul at once indicates that he is not referring to physical life and death, nor to a condition of our natural mental faculties. He is speaking about our relation to our God: whether we are united with the Fountain of Life, or are separated from Him. Without going into details, Paul simply states that the Law of Moses with all its demands, its threats, its promises cannot bring us a hair's breadth closer to God; rather, it has only the opposite effect: it kills. The conditions which the Law imposes are impossible of fulfillment for a sinner. No letter of recommendation which a preacher of the Law may carry can change the matter.

Before taking up the question of the glory connected with both testaments, we briefly consider a second difference which Paul points out. The Law is the administration of κατάκρισις, the New Testament is the administration of δικαιοσύνη. Κατάκρισις is the act of condemning. It is the function of the Law to condemn. It may also acquit, declare innocent and righteous, but only in the case of one who has perfectly kept all commandments. Among sinners there is not one found who can qualify. All have come short of the glory of God. So the Law condemns.

(9) By way of contrast, the New Testament administers δικαιοσύνη. A direct opposite to the verbal noun κατάκρισις would be δικαίωσις, the act of declaring righteous. But Paul at once goes deeper. A few chapters later he will tell us what δικαιοσύνη means. God "hath made him to be sin for us, who knew no sin; that we might be made the δικαιοσύνη of God in him" (5:21). Δικαιοσύνη is a righteousness prepared for us by Christ, and credited to us by God, in the death and resurrection of Christ. In the administration of the New Testament this δικαιοσύνη is announced to us for our appropriation and enjoyment.

Now as to the glory. Paul asks the question, since already the administration of death and condemnation manifested itself in glory, if then the administration of righteousness and of the life-giving Spirit would not excel in glory. He presents the matter in two forms: (1) If the one *manifested itself* in glory, will not the other rather *be* in glory? and (2) If the one was with glory, the other will much more *excel* in glory. Concerning the one he merely predicates the presence of glory, while in the case of the other, glory is a part of its essence.

(10) Concerning the glory of the Law there can be no doubt. When Moses came down from Mount Sinai, his face shone with such splendor that the Children of Israel, including even Aaron, were afraid to come near him. He called them, and they had to face as best they could the blinding rays from his face. They had to blink their eyes or shade them with their hands. This dazzling light was not natural to the face of Moses. His face was glorious because it had been glorified. But just as this glory had come to the face of Moses from without, so it also went away again. It is different with the glory of the New Testament. This is inherent, hence a lasting characteristic. Paul says καὶ γάρ, that is, strictly speaking, the thing that had been glorified was not actually glorious in this respect, on account of the surpassing splendor of the New Testament.

(11) The next verse has no finite verb. It must be supplied in both members. Lenski insists that the verbs must be taken from the two participles found in the two parallel members of the sentence. He reads: "If the passing thing κατηργεῖτο . . . much more the permanent thing μένει." This leads to a difficulty concerning the preposition διά. This preposition means *through,* locally, temporally, instrumentally. Lenski maintains that in this instance it must mean 'in spite of': The passing thing passed in spite of its glory. But this meaning of διά has not been established. Moreover, the resulting thought veers away from Paul's argument. Paul's point is not that the Law passed away in spite of its glory, but rather the other way around, it had glory although it was only a passing thing. The simplest way is to supply the verbs from vss. 7 and 8, thus: For if the passing thing manifested itself through a period of glory, much more will the permanent thing ever be in glory.

Such is the New Testament, a thing of lasting glory. And God has made Paul sufficient to administer this New Testament.

4.   3:12-18

Before entering upon a discussion of this part, it will be well to review briefly the events at Mount Sinai to which Paul refers. The

RSV is correct in this case, and gives a much clearer picture than does the KJV, especially in the translation of Exodus 34:33. The KJV says: "*Till* Moses had done speaking with them, he put a veil on his face." According to the Hebrew text, the situation was not that Moses wore a veil while delivering God's message, till he had done speaking, but rather, while he was speaking, the Children of Israel were forced to look at his uncovered face with all its blinding glory. Only after he had delivered God's message, then he covered his face. The RSV says: "And when Moses had finished speaking with them, he put a veil on his face." This was repeated every time Moses was called into the presence of God to receive further instructions.

(12, 13) The typical meaning of this procedure Paul now explains to the Corinthians. All that he had said about the operation of the New Testament he now sums up in the one word *hope*: "Seeing then that we have such hope." Then he continues: "We use great plainness of speech, and not as Moses, which put a veil over his face." The KJV has the correct idea, but its expression is cumbersome; the RSV gives a wrong shading to the words. What Paul says is that in administrating the New Testament he uses complete frankness, without hiding or covering anything. In this respect he is totally different from Moses, who veiled his face when he was through speaking.

The significance of this procedure is stated in these words: "that the children of Israel could not steadfastly look to the end of that which is abolished." The RSV changes this to "might not see," thereby coming closer to the preposition πρός, but losing some of the force of ἀτενίσαι. The first use of πρός with an infinitive is to express purpose. Lenski says that the grammarians are reluctant to admit that it ever means result, an interpretation which he favors in our passage. Yet Paul seems to be using πρός in the primary sense of purpose, as the strongly adversative ἀλλά in the next verse indicates. The purpose of Moses was one, but the actual result was something altogether different.

(14) What was the purpose? That the Children of Israel should not be forced to look intently to the end of the passing thing. 'Ατενίσαι is difficult to translate. It means to 'look straight at a thing, to gaze at it.' The Children of Israel were forced to look into the brightness of Moses' face while he was delivering God's message to them. But

since that brightness was a passing thing anyway, Moses veiled his face even before the glory had faded completely. The Children of Israel were to gather from this that the Law is not the final word of God. It has indeed a definite purpose in God's economy, but its function is solely preparatory. Its glory is a passing thing. When the Law has struck terror into the consciences, it has done its work. It can do no more. It makes way for the life-giving message of the New Testament. But the Israelites failed to grasp this grand truth. Their hearts and minds were hardened. They had been impressed by the glory of the Law, and they assumed that the Law was to be a permanent institution. They became set in their opinion and did not grasp the meaning of Moses' veil. They may have assumed that it indicated a mitigation of some sort, but they were convinced that the Law itself was permanent and final.

In this respect, Paul says, his ministry differs radically from that of Moses. Moses spoke openly only for a time; then he veiled his face. His message was not final. Paul never uses a veil. He speaks with complete frankness and openness all the time. His ministry is not a passing thing, it is not preparatory. It conveys to the hearer the final verdict of God, the sure mercies of David, the everlasting covenant, the New Testament.

(15, 16) To the present day, Paul says, the hardness of the Jewish mind shows itself in this that the same veil, which symbolized the passing of the glory, and at the same time hid its end from the eyes of the people, remains unlifted as they read the Old Testament. They still read the Old Testament as though the Law were God's final word. They do not realize that in Christ the veil has been abolished and "is done away," because the Old Testament with all its laws stands fulfilled in Him. Paul repeats: "But even unto this day, when Moses is read, the veil is upon their heart." The statement is not really a contrast to the foregoing, it is rather an emphatic repetition. Ἀλλά should therefore not be rendered with *but,* rather, as the RSV does, with *yes.* Paul here does not say that it is the same veil, as he had said in vs. 14. That veil has been abolished in Christ. Here he says *a veil,* a veil of their own making, but a veil effectively hiding the truth from their hearts. Is there then no way of removing that veil? Paul says: "Nevertheless, when it shall turn to the Lord, the veil shall be taken away."

(17) Paul now turns back to the starting point. He had called the New Testament the ministration of the *Spirit* (vs. 6). In vs. 16 he invited Israel to turn to the *Lord*. He now shows that his end and his beginning do not thereby drift apart; they meet and match beautifully. "Now the Lord is that Spirit." With these words Paul does not identify the person of the Spirit and the person of the Lord in Sabellian fashion. They are two distinct persons in the Deity. But he does emphasize their close connection. This use of the copula is easy to understand. For an example let us look at a word of Jesus. When He says to Martha: "I am the resurrection," He means to say that there is no real resurrection, a resurrection unto life, without Him and His redemptive work. About the Spirit, Jesus had said: "If I go not away, (into suffering and death) the Comforter will not come unto you; but if I depart, I will send him unto you" (John 16:7). On the strength of that statement Paul can say: "The Lord is that Spirit." He adds: "Where the Spirit of the Lord is, there is liberty"—liberty from death; liberty from the condemnation of the Law; liberty of access to the Father; liberty of the children of God.

(18) With one grand thought Paul now brings this chapter to a close. "We all, with open face beholding as in a glass the glory of the Lord." *Open* face, Paul says, no veil interfering. The translation of the RSV is more appropriate, both more literal and more meaningful: with *unveiled* face. The verb translated with *beholding,* κατοπτρίζειν, has for its original meaning to 'reflect.' This thought may well be retained. The Jews bar the truth by putting a veil over their hearts. We permit the glory of the New Testament to shine on us, and we begin to reflect it as does a mirror. However, much more than this happens. The Children of Israel were blinded by the blaze on Moses' face. That glory was but a passing thing and far inferior to the glory of the New Testament. What effect will this superior brightness have on us, if the Children of Israel could not even bear the lesser glory? Paul says: We "are changed into the same image from glory to glory, even as by the Spirit of the Lord." The glory of the New Testament does not kill. It has a healing, a vitalizing effect. We are transformed by it. We not merely reflect it; we absorb it and are ourselves made glorious with the same glory that issues from the Lord, into a copy of the Lord. That is the work of the Spirit.

God has made us sufficient to be ministers of this New Testament.

5. 4:1-6

"This ministry," Paul says. This is the administration of the New Testament of God, a testament of justification; a testament of the life-and-liberty-granting Spirit procured for us by Christ's redemptive work; a testament the administrators of which employ complete frankness because it is not a passing, temporary thing like the testament of the γράμμα, which has only a preparatory function to perform in God's economy of salvation, as a testament to be superseded by the new testament which is God's final word; a testament which with its glory does not blind and kill but permeates the hearts and transforms them into the same image of glory. What effect will it have on us to have received this ministry?

This is the question which Paul now takes up, thus linking chapter 4 to chapter 3. He uses for a connective the phrase διὰ τοῦτο, 'because of this,' 'therefore.'

(1) Before Paul proceeds to illustrate the effect which so exalted a commission must have on the administrators of this new testament, he inserts the remark that he and his associates received the high office out of the pure mercy of God, which they did not merit and of which they were not worthy, yes, in order to receive which they must first be rescued out of their miserable condition. He says καθὼς ἠλεήθημεν, *as we have been granted mercy.* He uses the term *mercy,* not *grace.* Think of the blind people who prayed to Jesus for help, the Syrophoenecian woman, the father of the lunatic, the rich man in hell: they all called ἐλέησον. It was the compassion of God that made Paul (and his associates) what they were. Unfit though Paul was by nature and more so by his early training in Pharisaism, God had pity on him and made him what he now is.—We note also that Paul uses a passive form of the verb. Our KJV loses some of the force of this voice by translating: *"we have received mercy,"* the RSV still more by reducing the clause to a phrase: "by the mercy." Luther is far better, saying: *nachdem mir Barmherzigkeit widerfahren ist,* i.e., we were granted mercy. The clause contains a terse summary of what Paul had stated more fully in the previous chapter: "Not that we are sufficient of ourselves to think (i.e., claim) anything as of ourselves; but our sufficiency is of God" (vs. 5).

What effect did this fact have on Paul and his colleagues that he, the absolutely unworthy one, was entrusted with so exalted an office?

Paul sums this up in the brief statement: οὐκ ἐγκακοῦμεν, 'we do not faint,' 'we do not lose courage,' 'do not grow tired.' There was no defeatism in Paul. Take the double negative as a reinforced positive: we are confident, with a firm, unshaken, and unshakable confidence; we do our work with cheerful determination and unquenchable, invincible hope. No matter what discouraging situations may confront Paul, no matter what indifference or opposition he may encounter, he will continue to do his work with zeal unabated.

Paul was human like us; success cheered him and apparent failure grieved him, but he did not permit these human reactions to influence his endeavors.

(2) To set forth more vividly the full force of ἐγκακεῖν, Paul contrasts the spirit and the methods that might suggest themselves to one less confident. In a summary statement he declares that "we have renounced (once and for all) the hidden things of shame (or disgrace)"—introducing this statement with a very strong ἀλλά: no ἐγκακεῖν, 'rather,' 'on the contrary.'

We note the aorist ἀπειπάμεθα, stressing the action, the definiteness and decisiveness of the action, without hesitation or possibility of reconsideration. We have renounced, and that's that.

More important is the question: What has he thus definitely and with finality ruled out? He says: "the secret things of shame." Here the KJV translates the Greek word αἰσχύνη with "dishonesty," the RSV turns the genitive into an adjective, "disgraceful" (which is permissible), while Luther renders τὰ κρυπτὰ τῆς αἰσχύνης with *heimliche Schande*. The KJV stands in need of correction. Paul is not speaking about a scandalous life, of indulging in shameful vices secretly; he is speaking about methods of preaching the Gospel. He means to say that you can introduce methods into your Gospel work which on the surface do not appear as shameful, but which in reality disgrace the Gospel. He is harking back to 2:17, where he spoke about καπηλεύειν, about "selling" the Gospel. To use a coarse illustration: Some ministers, in their eagerness to bring the Gospel to the people, resort to entertainment to attract the crowds, in order to get an opportunity to preach to them. If you would tell such ministers that they are ashamed of the Gospel and that by their methods they disgrace it, because they manifest a lack of trust in its efficacy, they would resent the charge. Are they not doing all in order to promote the Gospel? The disgrace their methods bring upon it does not appear on the surface; that is why Paul speaks of secret things of shame. The disgrace is, nevertheless, very real, as will become evident from Paul's further remarks.

In the following Paul elucidates by using more specific terms. A method which he conscientiously avoids he describes as περιπατοῦντες ἐν πανουργίᾳ, he and his associates are not *walking about in craftiness.* Περιπατεῖν is here used figuratively, referring to conduct or method of procedure. Πανουργία, compounded of πᾶν plus ἔργον, corresponds very closely, both in etymology and meaning, to our German expression *zu allem faehig,* "capable of anything." A πανοῦργος will not shrink from any means that to him seems to hold out the promise of success; he will stoop to apply it. Words like "trickiness," "craftiness" express the idea.

The type of minister to which we referred above as using entertainment in order to lure the people is employing πανουργία, and is therefore guilty of committing secret things of disgrace. The Gospel is the word of *Truth.* To resort to ruses in proclaiming it, even though with the best of intentions, is heaping shame on the Truth. Not only are truth and lures incompatible in their nature, but to use lures in connection with the Gospel ministry treats the Truth, the eternal Truth of God, as though it were inefficient, not attractive enough in itself.

For a second specific manner of disgracing the Gospel ministry, while apparently promoting it, Paul refers to people: δολοῦντες τὸν λόγον τοῦ θεοῦ, (he is not) *adulterating the Word of God.* Δολοῖ occurs as a variant reading to ζυμοῖ in I Corinthians 5:6: "A little leaven leaveneth (adulterates) the whole lump." In extra-Biblical Greek it is used with τὸν οἶνον as object. In Paul's day the chief danger of such δολοῦν stemmed from the Judaizers, although also the morbid fancies of Gnosticism already had begun to rear their ugly head. The Judaizers were not satisfied with the plain Gospel of justification and salvation through Jesus Christ's vicarious work alone; they insisted on adding to it the observance of the ceremonial ordinances, particularly circumcision, of the Mosaic Law. Not only additions to the Word of God, also omissions would constitute a δολοῦν.

It is difficult to determine just where the gravest danger lurks today. It is present both in the field of practice and of doctrine. Masonry has its appeal. There is ever present with us the temptation to tone

down our testimony against the Christless lodge. The same applies
to our testimony against Scoutism. Government is invading the realm
of the Church by appointing chaplains in various of its agencies,
naturally defining also their functions and duties. The temptation is
that in order to get the "advantages" which the system offers we
condone its infringements on Christ's prerogatives. In the interest of
the Gospel we tone down the Gospel — craftily: a κρυπτὸν τῆς
αἰσχύνης. Remaining still in the field of practice, we refer to the slogans
of the day: about a united front against the corruption rampant in
the world, about the strength that lies in unity, etc. In the interest
of outward unity of organization we are subtly tempted to sacrifice,
or at least compromise, the unity of faith and confession.

This leads directly to the field of doctrine. Here we register a twofold danger. There is, on the one hand, the danger of confessing the
truth in ambiguous terms, which may readily be understood as stating
the truth correctly, while at the same time also the opposing error
may conveniently find cover under the same words. When a doctrine
is not in controversy there may be no offense involved in using the
words which are actually used; but when a document so drawn up
is presented as a settlement of past controversies, then the use of words
which do not definitely exclude the known error constitutes a δολοῦν,
for, though not expressly proclaiming an error, it grants the opponent
license to hold his erroneous views as before.

The other danger is that of legalistic rigorism. After an error has
been irrefutably pointed out with cold logic, in "doubtful disputa-
tions," the demand is made of the erring brother that he signs on
the dotted line. Love, which "believeth all things, hopeth all things,"
demands that weakness on the part of a brother be taken into consideration, and, when he pleads for further instruction, that a reasonable
opportunity be granted. To determine when the limit has been reached
is a matter of Christian judgment, which may differ considerably
among devout Christians because of differences in temperament, in
experience, in closeness to or remoteness from actual participation in
the controversies. Just as it would be a δολοῦν of the Word of God
if we agreed to disagree in doctrine and granted an allowable and
wholesome area where it is neither possible nor necessary to agree,
or conducted our doctrinal discussions on such a basis: just so it would
be a δολοῦν of the Word of God to insist on absolute uniformity of

judgment, and to leave a body if the majority is not yet ready to accept our judgment.

Having from the mercy of God received the glorious ministry of the life-and-liberty-giving Gospel, Paul is extremely careful to avoid everything that conflicts with its nature.

So far Paul has been speaking in negative terms, with a strong ἀλλά. He now turns to the positive side of the action and attitude which conforms to the nature of the Gospel. He says τῇ φανερώσει τῆς ἀληθείας συνιστάνοντες ἑαυτοὺς πρὸς πᾶσαν συνείδησιν ἀνθρώπων ἐνώπιον τοῦ θεοῦ, by the revealing of the truth commending ourselves to every conscience of men before God.

The important term in this sentence is συνείδησις, conscience. Paul makes some specific statements about conscience in Romans 2:15. The Gentiles, who do not possess the written Law of Moses and yet do the things contained in the Law, thereby show that the work of the Law is inscribed in their hearts. It is inscribed in such a fashion that their conscience gives them strong testimony, the result being that a storm of conflicting thoughts rages within them, accusing and excusing. Conscience operates on the basis of the inscribed law and stirs up the accusing and excusing thoughts.

The main function of conscience is to testify. Testify to what? In the following verse of Romans 2, Paul places the whole matter into relation and connection with God's judgment on the Last Day. Conscience testifies to the divine origin of the inscribed law and to the fact that God, who is the author of the inscribed law, will also be the judge, and His judgment will be final. Conscience, thus, is not a merely intellectual function, evaluating the comparative merits of men's actions; it is not a merely ethical function, establishing the moral right or wrong of men's behavior: it is a religious function, weighing men's lives in their relation to God.

Paul speaks of accusing thoughts which conscience stirs up and of feverish attempts to find excuses. The history of nations bears out this statement. Everywhere we find an uneasy fear of the gods, and restless attempts to appease their wrath and to buy their favor. Dread and despair is in evidence among the peoples.

To the troubled consciences, Paul says, he commends himself: "to every conscience of men," he says, or, as we would put it, to the conscience of all men. He addresses himself to conscience; he makes his appeal to conscience; he has something to offer for conscience. What he has to announce is not designed to lead men to a deeper understanding of nature, it is not science; nor to train them in the rules of hygiene, to produce a more healthy population; nor to teach them to procure greater wealth, or to get more satisfaction and enjoyment out of life; it is not even to elevate them to more idealistic views and to morally cleaner habits. No, he addresses himself strictly to the troubled consciences, promising them relief and peace.

He has a real remedy to offer. He has the Truth, God's Truth, the Truth which came by Jesus Christ. This Truth is something which eye has not seen, nor ear heard, and which has not entered into man's heart; it is a deep and hidden mystery. Paul will make his appeal to the troubled consciences by revealing the Truth, a Truth which not merely lets them forget their despair momentarily, but which gives them rest in the presence of God.

Because such is Paul's ministry, he cannot, on the one hand, stoop to trickery or an adulteration of the Word, to practice the hidden things of shame; nor can he, on the other hand, ever grow weary of administering so wholesome and glorious an office.

(3) Since Paul has so glorious a life-and-liberty-conveying office, and since he is untiring in devoting his best efforts to the administration of that office, might it not be expected that all troubled consciences will receive him with joy? The evidence shows the opposite. He not only meets with widespread indifference; he often faces violent opposition. Will this not have a depressing effect on him? Paul takes up that question and shows that this negative result not only does not detract from the glory of his office but serves, on the contrary, to spur him on to more determined service.

When he begins the next statement with a conditional clause εἰ δὲ καὶ ἔστιν, *but even if it* is *the case,* he thereby plainly admits that it actually is so, thus making the meaning of the clause concessive: although even this happens. What? Κεκαλυμμένον τὸ εὐαγγέλιον ἡμῶν, *that our Gospel is hidden.* By saying *our* Gospel he does not make a distinction between various forms of the Gospel, among which his particular one meets with especially vehement opposition: he speaks about the Gospel which has been committed to the Church and which he has in common with the Corinthians.

He says that the Gospel often is κεκαλυμμένον. In the previous chapter he had spoken about a special κάλυμμα, one hanging before the hearts of the Jews in the reading of Moses. Here he is speaking more generally, although he uses a verb of the same stem. We note, however, that he uses the perfect tense in its periphrastic form, thus setting forth the meaning of the perfect more emphatically, viz., the state or condition resulting from the completed action: the Gospel is (to some) a veiled thing.

Why does such an unfavorable result not dampen his zeal? He answers: ἐν τοῖς ἀπολλυμένοις ἐστὶν κεκαλυμμένον, *in the case of those on the way to perdition is it a veiled thing*. He places the ἀπολλύμενοι in the emphatic position at the head of the clause, thereby indicating that by their own fault they deliberately, and hence inexcusably, remain on their lost course. It is no fault of the Gospel that they are not saved. They refuse to accept the proffered salvation. They yield themselves to the very enemy from whose clutches the Gospel would set them free.

(4) Paul says about this: ἐν οἷς ὁ θεὸς τοῦ αἰῶνος τούτου ἐτύφλωσεν τὰ νοήματα τῶν ἀπίστων, *in whose case the god of this world did blind the minds of the unbelievers*. These words are clear in themselves and require no detailed discussion. Ἐτύφλωσεν is an aorist, thus stressing the action as such. As 2:11 shows, where νοήματα indicates the wicked designs of Satan, νοήματα does not refer to a purely intellectual activity of the heart, but to one that is tinged with ethical quality and includes a kind of striving. The metaphorical use of "blinding" is easily understood: Satan has deceived and led astray the minds and plans of the unbelievers regarding their salvation and the course of action which they should follow. The figure is retained by Paul when he now continues to discuss the extent and the degree to which Satan has succeeded in his attack on the "unbelievers," a word here used proleptically, since unbelief really is the result of Satan's work.

A word that arrests our attention is the name "god" for the devil. Jesus once called the devil the "prince of this world" (John 14:30). The appellation "prince" suggests power and control, such as may be wielded by a tyrant ruthlessly. While the appellation "god" apparently implies even greater power and control, it also connotes a certain willingness on the part of the people. Compare Luther's words in the Large Catechism: "A god means that from which we are to expect all

good and to which we are to take refuge in all distress, so that to have
a God is nothing else than to trust and believe Him from the heart.
. . . That . . . upon which you set your heart and put your trust is
properly your god" (Trgl. p. 581). This is the position which the
world accords to Satan, a position which he obtained when our first
parents succumbed to his temptation in Paradise. It is not against its
will that the world is blinded by Satan. Yes, from Satan's lies it even
expects salvation.

To what extent does Satan blind the minds of the unbelievers? Here
Paul becomes very profuse, piling term upon term in his explanation:
εἰς τὸ μὴ αὐγάσαι τὸν φωτισμὸν τοῦ εὐαγγελίου τῆς δόξης τοῦ Χριστοῦ,
ὅς ἐστιν εἰκὼν τοῦ θεοῦ. Before we attempt any reproduction of Paul's
thoughts in English, two of his terms demand a little closer inspection.
They are εἰκών and αὐγάσαι.

Εἰκών means an image. Hebrews 10:1 draws a comparison between
two synonyms which both refer to some representation of an original.
The two words are εἰκών and σκιά. "The law having a σκία of good
things to come, and not the very εἰκών." Σκιά is a shadow picture. Christ
is called by Paul in our text the εἰκών of God, similarly in Colossians
1:15, the εἰκών of the invisible God, expressing about the same thought
as the one for which the Epistle to the Hebrews uses the word
χαρακτήρ (1:3). Latin, figura. As opposed to a shadow picture it indicates something substantial, about like a copy or a duplicate.

There is considerable controversy about the proper rendering of
αὐγάσαι. The verb occurs only in our present passage. A noun from
the same root, αὐγή, also occurs only once, in Acts 20:11. The meaning
of the noun is clear. It refers to daybreak, to dawn. Besides there
is the compound ἀπαύγασμα. In extra-Biblical Greek other words from
the same root occur, as, αὔγασμα and αὐγασμός, αὐγέω, αὐγήεις, αὖγος,
αὐγοειδής. They all contain the idea of glowing, or radiating light.
Accordingly, the common meaning of our verb αὐγάζω is 'to shine.' The
form in our text, being aorist, would then convey the idea of a beginning of light, of dawning. Several poets used the verb in the sense
of 'to see.' Now some translators and commentators, among them the
RSV, insist that that is the meaning of the verb in our passage. But
there seems to be no compelling reason for departing from the regular
prose meaning of the word.

Now we note the piling up of terms which Paul employs. He begins with φωτισμός, *illumination*. It is the light τοῦ εὐαγγελίου, which is connected with δόξα. This is the glorious Gospel τοῦ Χριστοῦ, who is no less than the εἰκών of God. What a glorious, what a powerful light! Yet the blinding of the minds of the unbelievers by Satan is so thorough that not even this glorious light gets a chance to dawn on them, let alone that it should illumine them.

Such being the case, does Paul grow weary of performing his ministry? If anything, it would stimulate him to redouble his efforts.

Paul began this short section with the concessive remark: "though really his Gospel was veiled to certain people." Thus he implied his ardor would not be dampened. Why not? He answers this question in the next short section.

(5) Such lack of success would be discouraging if Paul were seeking personal advantages by his work. But that is not the case. It is not even his own work which he is doing. He is merely the tool in the hand of God: οὐ γὰρ ἑαυτοὺς κηρύσσομεν ἀλλὰ Χριστὸν Ἰησοῦν κύριον, *for we are not proclaiming ourselves but Christ Jesus as Lord.*

The title "Lord" was claimed by the Roman emperors of Paul's day as rulers and benefactors of the empire. It implied both ideas, that of ruling and that of providing for. Tertullus, in flattering Felix the governor in Judea (Acts 24:1ff.), does not call him directly by that title (that would have been an insult to the emperor), but in hinting that he really is worthy to hold a higher position than that of a governor he speaks about the πολλὴ εἰρήνη which the province is enjoying under his governorship (*pacator provinciae*), about the many διορθώματα (reforms) which he instituted, and about his πρόνοια (*providentia Caesaris*). From this overdone *captatio* we can gather what is meant when the Roman emperor was addressed as Κύριος.

In our sentence the word κύριος is found in the predicative position. Paul is proclaiming Christ Jesus *as* Lord (not as the KJV has it: Christ Jesus *the* Lord. The RSV is correct in this case.) Christ Jesus is Lord, not in the political application of the word. In vs. 2 Paul had said that he is addressing himself and is making his appeal to the *consciences* of men. It is Jesus who brings peace and hope to the hearts of men, so that, being assured of their proper standing before God and of His favorable disposition toward them, they are in a position to undergo the tribulations and injustices of this curse-laden earth in the proper spirit. Thus Christ Jesus is the One whom Paul proclaims as Κύριος.

The word κύριος should be applied as predicative also to the negative part of Paul's statement: we are not proclaiming ourselves, namely as κύριοι. Philosophers, in advertising their systems, claimed that they had found a solution, and they were ready to introduce their pupils to a remedy for the evils of this world. They thus announced themselves as κύριοι. Paul is not proclaiming his own wisdom. He is not a κύριος. If he were proclaiming his own inventions, then any lack of success might have a depressing effect on him. But since he is not proclaiming himself but Christ Jesus as Lord, the cause which he represents is not his own but that of his Lord. And he is sure that the Lord will know how best to deal with any unfavorable response of the people to His offer.

Paul throws a still stronger light on the situation: ἑαυτοὺς δὲ δούλους ὑμῶν διὰ Ἰησοῦν, *but* (we announce) *ourselves as slaves to you for Jesus' sake.* The word δοῦλος does not have the unpleasant connotation which our English word has, both as noun and particularly as a verb. It merely indicates that Paul has no own choice in the matter; as δοῦλος he is one taking orders and carrying them out to the best of his ability. It does not imply that he has no interest in the work. No, he is doing that "heartily" just as he admonished all slaves to be doing their work. See his Epistle to the Colossians (3:23). He is doing his work "because of Jesus." This is saying more than just "by the command of Jesus." Paul feels himself under obligation to Jesus because of what Jesus did for him; he has also imbibed the spirit of Jesus, His love for sinners; and thus he does his work for Jesus because of what Jesus means to him.

These remarks will help us to understand the genitive ὑμῶν. It is not strictly possessive. The Corinthians do not own Paul as a master owns his slaves. It is in a sense objective. Paul is working in the interest of the Corinthians; he is a slave to them.

(6) These truths Paul now illustrates and deepens by a reference to God's work on the first day of creation: ὅτι ὁ θεὸς ὁ εἰπών, ἐκ σκότους φῶς λάμψει, *because the God who* (once) *said, Out of darkness light shall shine,* etc. The future λάμψει is the future of command, very common in the wording of laws. This was a creative command. There was as yet no light; all was impenetrable darkness. But when God's

order was issued, the light, so far nonexistent, began to shine—out
of the midst of darkness.

Paul is speaking about this God who in the beginning by a mere
word of His mouth brought forth light out of darkness. What he
now wishes to set forth is a glorious parallel to the creation of light.
And it is the same God who is performing this second wonder. Paul
continues, ὃς ἔλαμψεν ἐν ταῖς καρδίαις ἡμῶν, (is He) who started light in
our hearts. The spiritual darkness in our hearts was no less intense
than was the cosmic darkness in the beginning of creation. And the
God who replaced darkness with light in the beginning has again
done so in our case. He is the God of light, and has taken it upon
Himself to spread light and its blessings.

He created light in our hearts for this very purpose, not merely
that we ourselves might enjoy its blessings, but that we as children
of light might also be instrumental in spreading it. Paul says, πρὸς
φωτισμὸν τῆς γνώσεως τῆς δόξης τοῦ θεοῦ ἐν προσώπῳ Χριστοῦ, for the
illumination (which consists in) the knowledge of the glory of God
in the person of Christ. The genitive τῆς γνώσεως is epexegetical, explaining the meaning of the metaphorical term "illumination." Paul
is not speaking about a physical light. If anyone has the γνῶσις of
the glory of God in the person of Christ, then he is enjoying the illumination of which Paul is speaking. We bear in mind that γνῶσις
is not a knowledge obtained through information; it is a knowledge
based on experience. It is a tasting. In this case: tasting what? The
glory-of-God-in-the-person-of-Christ is one compound concept. It is the
same as the one expressed above in vs. 4 with the words: the glory
of Christ who is the image of God. Christ is God's glory. When we
see Christ, see His condescending love for sinners, when we see Him
suffering and dying in order to redeem sinners, when we see Him
rejoicing over a lost soul which He found: then we see the glory of
God. When Christ comes to our conscience with His saving love, then
we get a taste of the glory of God. God's glory appears in the πρόσωπον,
in the person of Christ. Christ in His glory is an εἰκών, a duplicate of
God. When we begin to taste this glory of God, then the φωτισμός
has produced its intended result, in fact, that is the φωτισμός.

God's one great interest is this φωτισμός. Paul is instrumental in
conveying this φωτισμός, in fact, he is a δοῦλος, taking his orders exclusively from the God who manifests His glory in this φωτισμός.

Can Paul grow weary of administering this office? Can any apparent failure discourage him? Can he stoop to trickery of any sort in bringing this φωτισμός to despairing consciences? Having this ministry, he said in vs. 1, we do not grow weary.

6.　4:7-15

Paul in this section intensifies the thoughts which he presented in the foregoing. So far he spoke about cases which might be construed as failures in his office. In the present section he proceeds to cases of open opposition and hostility. He speaks of tribulations which he reaps from administering his office, and of the meaning which they have for his ministry.

(7) The truth which he is going to unfold he presents in summary form: ἔχομεν δὲ τὸν θησαυρὸν τοῦτον ἐν ὀστρακίνοις σκεύεσιν, *but we hold this treasure in vessels of clay*. Something which brings peace and hope to despairing consciences is certainly a great treasure; none greater than that. Would it not be proper that so great a treasure be deposited in exceptionally strong containers in order to add security? God did the very opposite: He chose vessels of the most fragile material.

There is a purpose in God's action. If this treasure were applied through implements which are firm in themselves, some of the credit for success might be attributed to the vessels. But if the vessels are weak, needing protection rather than adding strength, then it will become apparent that the treasure itself is the all-powerful agent. Paul had to learn this truth the hard way. When he was buffeted by a messenger of Satan, he implored God to relieve him. When God did not answer at once, he repeated his petition. He evidently was of the opinion that if he were relieved of his suffering, he could proclaim the Gospel more efficiently. But what was the answer which God gave him? "My grace is sufficient for thee: for my strength is made perfect in weakness" (12:9).

Paul was comforted by this instruction and became bold in his weakness. He conveyed the instruction which he had received to his readers by adding the explanation in the passage under discussion: ἵνα ἡ ὑπερβολὴ τῆς δυνάμεως ᾖ τοῦ θεοῦ καὶ μὴ ἐξ ἡμῶν, *that the super-abundance of power may be (plainly) God's and not (as springing) from us*. Paul is here changing the modifiers of δύναμις in a significant way. First he uses the genitive: it is simply God's power. Then he continues with a prepositional phrase, ἐξ ἡμῶν, thereby referring to the source of the power. The genitive is all-inclusive: God possesses, God generates, God applies, God directs and controls that power, in fact, God is that power in person. Then this power is not simply omnipotence, it is the power of love, of grace and mercy, the power of the Truth. The preposition ἐξ presents the power as springing from some fountain. If the power which is manifest in our work were in any sense springing from us, in whole or in part, then some credit would be due us for the results, and a lack of success would reflect on us and tend to make us weary. But since it pleased God to apply His most excellent power by means of implements which, if not preserved by His special protection, would long ago have crumbled to pieces, we can rest assured that God has matters well in hand. The very fact that we, being such cheap and fragile implements, continue in our service unbroken is proof of the excellency of God's power, and is an incentive to renewed cheerful efforts on our part.

(8, 9) Paul now graphically presents the preserving power of God as it gloriously shows itself in the protection of His "earthen vessels." He does so in four pointed contrasts. Ἐν παντὶ θλιβόμενοι ἀλλ' οὐ στενοχωρούμενοι, *afflicted in every way but not cornered.* Afflictions is a very general term, embracing sufferings of every description, as Paul indicates by adding ἐν παντί, in every respect. Such afflictions have a tendency to hamper him in the fulfillment of his ministry, but they never did stop him. He was never στενοχωρούμενος, squeezed into a corner. Στενός means narrow, or close and tight. The Greeks used the expression εἰς στενὸν καθίστασθαι, German, *in die Enge getrieben werden, in die Klemme kommen.* The same idea is expressed by στενοχωρεῖσθαι. All afflictions which Paul endured never stopped him from preaching the Gospel. Rather, God turned every affliction into a golden opportunity for reaching some conscience which otherwise would not have been contacted.

Paul continues, ἀπορούμενοι ἀλλ' οὐκ ἐξαπορούμενοι, *being at a loss but not in despair.* The Greek play on words cannot well be reproduced in English, though Lenski makes a noteworthy attempt: "being at a loss, but not having lost out." Again the second part may well be taken in the sense of a litotes: every perplexity turned into a golden opportunity.

The third contrast is, διωκόμενοι ἀλλ᾽ οὐκ ἐγκαταλειπόμενοι, *being pursued but not forsaken*. How often did not God turn the tables on the pursuers of Paul, so that they became uneasy and worried, being pricked in their conscience by Paul's words! The last of the four pointed contrasts is, καταβαλλόμενοι ἀλλ᾽ οὐκ ἀπολλύμενοι, *thrown down but not perishing*. Down, but not down and out. Stoned and dragged away for dead, but returning to strengthen the brethren.

Earthen vessels indeed, but filled with insuperable power! "When I am weak, then am I strong" (12:10).

(10) In vs. 5 Paul had assured his readers that his ministry is to proclaim Christ Jesus as Lord. In vs. 6 he stated that the illumination, the creation of peace, hope, and joy in troubled consciences, is connected with the person of Christ. Naturally, then, the weakness of the vessels holding the rich treasure is not any weakness in general; it is a weakness in connection with Christ, and the support and preservation which God shows in His weak vessels again stands in relation to Christ. Πάντοτε τὴν νέκρωσιν τοῦ Ἰησοῦ ἐν τῷ σώματι περιφέροντες, ἵνα καὶ ἡ ζωὴ τοῦ Ἰησοῦ ἐν τῷ σώματι ἡμῶν φανερωθῇ, *always carrying about in our body the putting to death of Jesus, in order that also the life of Jesus might become evident in our body*.

In this statement some terms require a special study. There is the word νέκρωσις. Greek nouns ending in σις denote action. Hence the translation of the RSV, "death," is too indefinite. Νέκρωσις is a killing. Unlike this English word, the Greek νέκρωσις may be used either in the intransitive or in the transitive sense. In our passage it is the putting to death, while for example in Romans 4:19, the νέκρωσις of Sarah's womb indicates a ceasing in the functioning of the organ. In the sufferings which Paul underwent (vss. 8 and 9) he recognizes an echo, a reflection of the sufferings and death to which Jesus submitted at the hands of His enemies.

The word ζωή means more than either βίος or ψυχή. Βίος is never used in the New Testament in reference to Jesus. In fact, it usually occurs in combinations like the following: the poor widow threw her whole βίος into the temple treasury; the father of the prodigal son divided his βίος to his sons; and the Prodigal squandered his βίος (used interchangeably with οὐσία, Luke 15:13 and 30); there are the pleasures of βίος, the affairs of βίος, the pride of βίος; and we may lead a quiet and peaceable βίος..

According to the commandment of His Father, Jesus laid down and gave His ψυχή for the sheep, as a ransom for many. His ψυχή was not left unto hell. Jesus never laid down His ζωή. As the Father has ζωή in Himself, so has He given to the Son to have ζωή in Himself. He is the resurrection and ζωή. Although they killed the Prince of ζωή, they could not touch that ζωή. Rather in His very death His ζωή won the complete victory over death, so that everyone who believes in Him has eternal ζωή, and anyone who refuses to eat His flesh and to drink His blood thereby excludes himself from ζωή. In fine, think of John 1:4: "In him was ζωή; and the ζωή was the light of men." That is the connotation of ζωή when predicated of Jesus.

Twice the prepositional phrase occurs ἐν τῷ σώματι (ἡμῶν). There is no indication that σῶμα is here used with special emphasis on the contrast to psychic life; rather in the four pointed contrasts of vss. 8 and 9 the psychic life of Paul was included in the afflictions to which he was exposed and in which the Lord preserved him. Nor was the νέκρωσις of our Lord limited to the physical part of His being. There is thus no reason why σῶμα here should not be taken in a way in which it occurs quite frequently, namely, emphatically pointing to the very being of something that is mentioned: thus here, our very being. Our very being was summed up by Paul in the word "earthen vessel." Now, while he might say "in us" (the life of Jesus becomes evident), he uses a more emphatic formula, "in our being," such fragile vessels as we are. That we should be able to carry the putting to death of Christ about in our weak being is indeed wonderful enough, though this point easily escapes our notice, but that we weak and fragile vessels should manifest the ζωή, the salvation-bringing life of our Savior, is beyond conception. That power certainly does not spring from us; it is God's.

(11) This thought bears repetition, to impress it indelibly on our heart: ἀεὶ γὰρ ἡμεῖς οἱ ζῶντες εἰς θάνατον παραδιδόμεθα διὰ 'Ιησοῦν ἵνα καὶ ἡ ζωὴ τοῦ 'Ιησοῦ φανερωθῇ ἐν τῇ θνητῇ σαρκὶ ἡμῶν, *for all the time we the living ones are being delivered into death because of Jesus, in order that also the life of Jesus might appear in our mortal flesh.* We the living ones, we in whom the life of Jesus is being manifested, we are in reality undergoing a constant death, our entire career is one of continuous death—on account of Jesus, on account of our connection with Him, because we proclaim Him as the Κύριος. Thus

what appears before men's eyes is not the victorious life of Jesus, what appears makes the impression of being nothing but θνητὴ σάρξ, weakness and death. Σάρξ itself underscores the idea of weakness; this is brought out with double strength by the addition of the modifier θνητή; our flesh, weak in itself, is subject to death. In spite of all this there radiates from us in all our weakness a hope-and-cheer-producing, an invigorating light.

(12) Briefly Paul says, ὥστε ὁ θάνατος ἐν ἡμῖν ἐνεργεῖται ἡ δὲ ζωὴ ἐν ὑμῖν, thus death is operative in us, but life in you. It is Paul's purpose and mission to bring life to the Corinthians. Even if they shamefully misunderstood and falsely accused him, he does not grow weary in performing his ministry, although for him it means a constant tasting of death.—How is this possible?

(13) Paul answers the above question by pointing to Psalm 116. He quotes vs. 10: ἐπίστευσα, διὸ ἐλάλησα, I have believed, accordingly I have spoken.

When Paul quotes from the Old Testament he does not do so exactly in the same manner as we quote proof passages. He, rather, chooses statements which briefly summarize the content of a whole section. In the present case the Psalmist is speaking about great afflictions which he is undergoing: "The sorrows of death compassed me, and the pains of hell gat hold upon me: I found trouble and sorrow" (vs. 3). He mentions his "tears," his "falling" feet, his being "greatly afflicted." At the same time he speaks about the grace and mercy of the Lord who helped and preserved him: "For thou hast delivered my soul from death, mine eyes from tears, and my feet from falling" (vs. 8). Then the Psalmist speaks about his gratitude to the Lord and the thanks which he will offer Him: "I will offer to thee the sacrifice of thanksgiving, and will call upon the name of the Lord. I will pay my vows unto the Lord now in the presence of all his people" (vss. 17, 18). All of these experiences the Psalmist sums up in the verse which Paul quotes: "I believed, therefore have I spoken: I was greatly afflicted" (vs. 10).

This verse causes some difficulty in the Hebrew original. Paul adopts the translation of the Septuagint. Since Paul thus puts his stamp of approval on this rendering of the original as expressing a God-intended truth, we need not at this time investigate any further what exactly may be the meaning which the words have in their original setting. Paul uses them in the form: "I have believed, therefore have I spoken."

Paul stresses the fact that the same Spirit is present in him and is activating him which manifested itself in the Psalmist. It is the Spirit of faith and trust: ἔχοντες δὲ τὸ αὐτὸ πνεῦμα τῆς πίστεως, *but having the same spirit of faith.* Since that is the case, naturally, also the manifestation of the Spirit will be the same in both instances, in the case of Paul and that of the Psalmist. The manifestation in the case of the Psalmist is recorded in the Scriptures, κατὰ τὸ γεγραμμένον, *according to that recorded statement.* Now καὶ ἡμεῖς πιστεύομεν, διὸ καὶ λαλοῦμεν, *also we believe, accordingly we also speak.*

Thus Paul marks a parallel between himself and the Psalmist. Both had to suffer deep afflictions; both called for help upon the Lord; both experienced the salvation of the Lord; both were confirmed in their faith. And as a result, just as the Psalmist spoke for the glory of God, so does Paul, and he does not grow weary of proclaiming the Gospel.

(14) While the Psalmist sings of help in temporal troubles, Paul carries the thought through to the very end. He speaks of the hope of resurrection: εἰδότες ὅτι ὁ ἐγείρας τὸν κύριον Ἰησοῦν καὶ ἡμᾶς σὺν Ἰησοῦ ἐγερεῖ, *knowing that He who raised the Lord Jesus will raise also us jointly with Him.* We note that Paul uses the preposition σύν, which denotes intimate union, a union which is much closer than a mere grouping together as expressed, for example, by μετά. We are joined with Christ in His death; His death is our death; when Christ died, we all died. The same holds true of the resurrection. Christ's resurrection is our resurrection; He is the "firstfruit of them that slept" (I Cor. 15:20), the "firstborn from the dead" (Col 1:18). With reference to time, our resurrection may be separated by centuries from the resurrection of Christ, yet in reality it is contained in it.

We note how Paul's eyes are fixed on his resurrection, and how he directs the attention of his readers to the Resurrection. It is instructive to see how Paul, whenever comfort is needed to bear the cross, turns to the hope of resurrection. When the Thessalonians worried about their loved ones who had fallen asleep, he pointed them to the resurrection, in which neither the living nor the dead will have any advantage over each other. In our present passage, where he is coping with his own afflictions, we again see him lifting up his eyes toward the day of resurrection. It is important for an understanding of Paul's words in the following verses to bear in mind that his heart is lingering in a contemplation of that last day with the events that will transpire in it and with the glory which it will usher in. Let us look ahead a little to the 10th verse of the next chapter: "We must all appear before the judgment seat of Christ, that every one may receive the things done in his body, according to that he hath done, whether it be good or bad." His eyes are there still glued on the importance of that great day, and all the arguments which he elaborates from 4:14 to 5:10 can be understood correctly only if we bear this fact in mind. The assurance of his resurrection gives him the courage and the strength to bear up under his heavy load of afflictions and to carry out his ministry without fainting.

Paul, who in his afflictions for the Gospel is facing death every day, bases his hope for his own resurrection on the resurrection of the Lord Jesus: God raised up Jesus. When Paul speaks about the supreme significance of Jesus' resurrection, he bears in mind the nature of Jesus' death. Jesus is He who was in the form of God, who might have lived on an equal footing with God, who, instead, emptied Himself and bore our curse, being made a curse for us. The Son of God succumbed to death because He was laden with the sins of the whole world. The great question is: Will even the death of God's Son be sufficient to wipe out so enormous an amount of guilt? The resurrection of Jesus is the answer. It establishes the righteousness of every sinner in the sight of God. In it God proclaims peace to the world. Warfare is at an end; hostilities have ceased; a status of peace has been declared. "The wages of sin is death" still remains as true as ever, but it no longer applies to us. Though we still suffer affliction and ultimately die, that is no real death, it is an empty form. It belongs to the πρόσκαιρα, as Paul calls them in vs. 18. It is not final, it is transitory, a passing condition. In the resurrection of Jesus our own resurrection is assured.

It will be a glorious resurrection, Paul continues, καὶ παραστήσει σὺν ὑμῖν, *and will present (us) jointly with you.* Jesus will present us to the Father who sent Him, present us as redeemed through His blood; and the Father will acknowledge and welcome us as His own, receiving us into His heavenly mansions.

This, however, is not something special for Paul and his colaborers. No, it is something which he will receive only in conjunction with his readers. His resurrection unto glory is closely knit together with that of the Corinthians.

(15) This close union between Paul and his readers he now proceeds to unfold a little in the following verse. He says, τὰ γὰρ πάντα δι' ὑμᾶς, for all these things on your account. Throughout this entire section of the epistle, beginning in 1:3, Paul has stressed the intimate ties that unite him with the Corinthians. Whatever he does, he has the welfare of the Corinthians in mind, and whatever he must suffer he endeavors to turn to their advantage, their spiritual advancement and edification. So also here: All things because of you.

Our theologians are accustomed to distinguish the *finis ultimus* as one *absolute talis* and one *ultimus secundum quid*. The salvation of the Corinthians, which St. Paul so far has set forth as the final purpose of all his actions and all his sufferings is such really only *secundum quid,* the *finis absolute ultimus* is the glory of God. Paul finishes this part by saying, ἵνα ἡ χάρις πλεονάσασα διὰ τῶν πλειόνων τὴν εὐχαριστίαν περισσεύσῃ εἰς τὴν δόξαν τοῦ θεοῦ, *in order that grace, growing by the increasing number, may increase the thanksgiving to the glory of God.*

The comparative πλεῖον may be used in different ways. Two groups of things may be compared, with the result that one is found to be greater in number than the other. With the definite article, οἱ πλείονες, it may indicate the majority within a group. In our verse the idea of a majority does not seem to fit the situation. It would be a rather peculiar thought that the thanksgiving is increased by a majority. The idea of growth is mentioned twice in the verse, in the participle πλεονάσασα and in the finite verb περισσεύσῃ. The comparative, διὰ τῶν πλειόνων, readily lends itself to the same idea: the people enjoying the grace of God are ever becoming more and more in number.

It is easy to understand that by an increase in number the thanksgiving will be increased, but it is a bold stroke to say that grace itself grows by an increase in the number of recipients. But that is what Paul says. The grace of God is inexhaustible, and the more people get a share in its enjoyment, the greater the amount of grace in the Church may be said to become.

The verb περισσεύειν in by far the majority of cases occurs as an intransitive verb: 'to abound'; in our text it is transitive: by an increase in number grace *increases* the thanksgiving, for the glory of God.

7. 4:16—5:10

(16) Paul connects this section to the foregoing with διό, *according-ly*. He had carried out the thought that his faith impels him to speak even under the most adverse circumstances in order that an increasing number of believers might increase the praise and thanksgiving rising to the throne of God, proclaiming His glory. How then can he faint and grow weary of performing his ministry? Rather the opposite is the case. He continues with a strong ἀλλ', *on the contrary*. Εἰ καὶ ὁ ἔξω ἡμῶν ἄνθρωπος διαφθείρεται, ἀλλ' ὁ ἔσω ἡμῶν ἀνακαινοῦται ἡμέρᾳ καὶ ἡμέρᾳ, *even though our outward man be destroyed, yet our inner (one) is being renewed day and (i.e., after) day.*

His life, as he had outlined it in vss 8 and 9 above, and his experiences, which he had summarized in vs. 10 as a constant being put to death, may well be called a process of destruction; διαφθείρεται is a present tense expressing an action in progress, which may some day lead to complete destruction. Paul says εἰ καί: though this is going on, what of it? It is only his outer man who is perishing. They are only outer conveniences, outer pleasures that he is losing, only outer pains and hardships that he is enduring. They cannot touch his real, his inner life, his πνεῦμα τῆς πίστεως, and his vigorous ζωή from Jesus. Rather, in spite of all hardships and, as the next verse will present it, by means of the hardships, the inner man of Paul experiences a daily rejuvenation. The outward hardships are an efficient means in the hand of God for preparing Paul for eternal glory.

(17) A few expressions in the following verse call for some preliminary remarks before we study the meaning of the sentence as a whole.

There is first the word τὸ ἐλαφρόν. This is an adjective, neuter singular. In the New Testament this form is often used to express an abstract idea. So here. The word here does not mean something light in weight, but lightness itself. In our verse this is clear from the contrast: the ἐλαφρόν produces a weight, βάρος. Βάρος is an abstract noun, such then must also its counterpart be, τὸ ἐλαφρόν, 'lightness.'

Then there is the repetition of ὑπερβολή with the prepositions κατά and εἰς. They together form one concept, excess in excess, "beyond all measure," as Lenski translates.

With an explanatory γάρ Paul joins vs. 17 to vs. 16. Τὸ γὰρ παραυτίκα ἐλαφρὸν τῆς θλίψεως καθ᾿ ὑπερβολὴν εἰς ὑπερβολὴν αἰώνιον βάρος δόξης κατεργάζεται, *the momentary lightness of the affliction produces beyond all measure an eternal weight of glory.*

In vs. 14 Paul had pointed to our resurrection as marking the day on which God will present both Paul and his readers, in fact all believers, before Himself and will receive us into His heavenly mansions. The θλίψις, including the hardships of this life plus our death, precedes that glorious event. We easily yield to the thought that this θλίψις is a heavy burden and of long duration, but Paul calls it a momentary lightness, as compared with the endless weight of the heavenly δόξα.

Though it is of such short duration and of such slight significance in itself, yet in the hand of God it becomes an instrument for working out that grand eternal glory. Κατεργάζεται, Paul says. He certainly does not mean that by our afflictions we *merit* the glory of heaven: that was accomplished by our Savior in His suffering and death. The glory of heaven is a ready blessing which, in addition, has already been awarded to us in God's judgment, so that Paul, in 5:1, can say that we *have* it. It is ours. But they who are to inherit the glories of heaven must for a time pass through tribulation. That is God's way of preparing them. "We must through much tribulation enter into the kingdom of God" (Acts 14:22).

(18) God prepares the eternal glory ἡμῖν, *for us,* Paul says. Then he continues with a participle describing us for whom all this is done. But he does not simply join the participle to the dative ἡμῖν, as he might easily have done, he makes the participle more prominent by changing to a genitive absolute, μὴ σκοπούντων ἡμῶν, *we not looking at.* In this way the fact that we do not look for and pay no attention nor attach great importance to certain things is made to stand out more prominently.

Which are the things to which we give only slight attention? Paul says τὰ βλεπόμενα, and adds emphatically that contrariwise, ἀλλά, we devote all our attention to τὰ μὴ βλεπόμενα. The βλεπόμενα are the things that appear on the surface, that lie open before men's eyes. In Paul's case they were the hardships which constantly beset him, and his daily exposure to a violent death. These are the things which appear, but to which Paul attaches no importance. These he called the momentary lightness of affliction. The μὴ βλεπόμενα are: that beyond-all-measure eternal weight of glory. He keeps his eyes glued on these things.

As a motivation for his conduct he now mentions summarily: τὰ γὰρ βλεπόμενα πρόσκαιρα, τὰ δὲ μὴ βλεπόμενα αἰώνια, *for those visible things are transient, but the invisible, permanent.* With the word πρόσκαιρος he repeats the idea previously expressed with παραυτίκα, while in the other member of the comparison he uses αἰώνιος both times.—Yes, all our sufferings, including temporal death, are transient; with our resurrection from death the permanent and unchangeable things will begin.

The permanence and unchangeableness is a thought worthy of further consideration. Paul takes up the matter in the next chapter under the figure of a residence.

(5:1) Paul continues with an explanatory γάρ, for further elucidation of the two ideas last mentioned, namely, πρόσκαιρος and αἰώνιος.

He begins by saying emphatically οἴδαμεν, *we know.* He does not use the verb γιγνώσκειν because as yet we have no experience in this matter. We know because God has given us some information. Yet, though we lack experience, our knowledge is for that reason not less certain. God has told us, and that makes us sure, so sure that we may base our entire conduct on this knowledge. On the strength of God's assurance we are ready to dismiss as unimportant the entire θλίψις, and to concentrate on the unseen δόξα.

Now for the new figure under which Paul presents the matter. Our present life he calls the ἐπίγειος ἡμῶν οἰκία τοῦ σκήνους, *our earthly tent-house,* while he describes our life in heaven with the following words: οἰκοδομὴν ἐκ θεοῦ, οἰκίαν ἀχειροποίητον αἰώνιον ἐν τοῖς οὐρανοῖς, *a building from God, a non-handmade eternal house in the heavens.* It is apparent at a glance that Paul with these words stresses the permanence and the spiritual character of our life in heaven. He says *eternal* and *non-handmade.* By way of contrast, then, the description of our life on earth must presuppose, at least, something material and transitory. This should dispose of the question whether σκῆνος is a figurative expression for our body. It is not; it refers to our restless mode of living, which resembles a tenting rather than living in a permanent residence.

Just by the way, if σκῆνος referred to our body, what then about the resurrection? The permanent house in heaven is certainly not presented in a way to suggest our resurrected body.

Our life on earth may be compared to the unsettled tentlife of a wandering nomad. "Here have we no continuing city" (Heb. 13:14). Therefore Paul speaks in our text about the prospect that our present unsteady life καταλυθῇ, will be dissolved. But that does not worry us, for we have, ἔχομεν, that permanent non-handmade residence from God in heaven. We *have*, Paul says; it is ours, it has been adjudged to us. We hold a clear title.

(2,3) With a second γάρ Paul continues the explanation. *And we groan in this respect, desiring to put on our dwelling from heaven.* At first glance it might appear as a badly mixed metaphor to speak about "putting on" a "habitation." But if we remember that Paul under the figure of a dwelling is presenting a mode of living, then "putting on" the heavenly mode of living will not seem so awkward.— Yes, our looking at the unseen glory means an eager longing for it. Paul now states the motivation with the words, εἴ γε καὶ ἐνδυσάμενοι οὐ γυμνοὶ εὑρεθησόμεθα. Εἰ with the emphatic γε introduces a condition about which there is no doubt. We translate with *since: since we shall not be found naked on putting it on. Not naked* is a litotes, meaning fully and permanently dressed. Yes, when the great changeover will be made on resurrection day from this unstable, tentlike form of living to a form becoming the heavenly surroundings, then we shall be found provided for completely and forever.

But, does not such anxious longing for our life in heaven make us unfit for our work on earth? It would under certain circumstances. It would if under the present hardships we became impatient, unwilling to leave matters to God and to follow cheerfully His guiding. Such is not the case. True, we are burdened, and we feel it. We moan and groan under our load; but we do not impatiently look for an exit. That on which we fix our attention is the glory of heaven which awaits us; and that braces us in our tribulations.

(4) Paul adds the following explanation regarding our present attitude, καὶ γὰρ οἱ ὄντες ἐν τῷ σκήνει στενάζομεν βαρούμενοι, *yes, we who are in this present tentlife, we groan (as people who are) burdened.* In Philippians 1:23,24, Paul gives expression to a similar feeling: "For I am in a strait betwixt two, having a desire to depart,

and to be with Christ; which is far better: nevertheless to abide in the flesh is more needful for you." He further says, "What I shall choose I wot not" (vs. 22). In our text he expresses his motivation (ἐφ' ᾧ, meaning ἐπὶ τούτῳ ὅτι, *because or since*) in the following: οὐ θέλομεν ἐκδύσασθαι ἀλλ' ἐπενδύσασθαι, *we do not desire to put off, but to put on.* To put off, to get rid of this present θλίψις, that is not the thing on which we have set our mind. The time and the manner of our departure we leave entirely to God to determine. The grand thought which Paul has been unfolding since 4:1, namely, that we do not grow weary, applies also here to the fullest extent. We are not maneuvering for a departure from this life. But we do have our eye set on the heavenly life, which, according to 4:18, is the hope that really sustains us under our present afflictions.

What does that putting-on mean for us? The answer is given in a ἵνα clause: ἵνα καταποθῇ τὸ θνητὸν ὑπὸ τῆς ζωῆς, namely, *that mortality be swallowed up by life.* This is only another way of describing the events on resurrection day. In I Corinthians 15:54, Paul said, "Death is swallowed up in victory." Both expressions mean about the same, and both refer to the time when death will be finally overcome, when it will be forced to disgorge its victims which it had swallowed. Death thus is the last enemy that shall be destroyed. In view of this, Paul says in I Corinthians 15, that death shall be swallowed up *in victory,* while in our passage, where the thought of a combat, of victory and defeat, is absent, Paul says that mortality shall be swallowed up *by life.*

(5) This certainly is a μὴ βλεπόμενον, all appearance being completely to the contrary, namely, that our outward man must perish, that everything ultimately will be swallowed up by death. How then can we make that remote eventuality the guiding principle of our life, which upholds us so that we do not grow weary? That spirit is not of ourselves; it is a gift from God. Paul continues, ὁ δὲ κατεργασάμενος ἡμᾶς εἰς αὐτὸ τοῦτο θεός, *He who prepares* (*or has prepared*) *us for this very thing is God.* Κατεργασάμενος is the aorist participle, thus stressing the action as such without any further reference to time or effect. The work of preparation is God's. The source of our disposition to make the future glory, though unseen, the guiding principle of our present unstable life is not found in us. All credit belongs to God alone.

How does God perform this miracle? Paul explains, ὁ δοὺς ἡμῖν τὸν ἀρραβῶνα τοῦ πνεύματος, *who is the giver (the one giving, or having given) to us the earnest, namely, the Spirit.* In δούς again we are dealing with an aorist participle. The fact that we have God's Spirit is plainly due to a gift, pure and simple. But the Spirit now serves as a pledge, as an earnest. It is a first installment of our life eternal. It is this Spirit of God through whom God makes us what we are.

Thus in this section, by using the figure of an unstable tentlife for our present state, and of a permanent residence for our future state, Paul has elucidated in various ways his previous declaration about the temporary lightness of affliction and the future eternal weight of glory.

(6,7) With the following verses Paul concludes that portion of the first chief part of the epistle in which the leading thought is that he does not grow weary in his ministry of the glorious Gospel of Christ. In this short final section his cheerful confidence holds the prominent place: θαρροῦντες οὖν he says, and again θαρροῦμεν.

Our confident hope is unlimited; πάντοτε, Paul adds. Nor is our cheerfulness dimmed by the knowledge that ἐνδημοῦντες ἐν τῷ σώματι ἐκδημοῦμεν ἀπὸ τοῦ κυρίου, *while present in the body, we are absent from the Lord.* With the phrase ἐν τῷ σώματι Paul repeats the idea which above he had presented as a perishing of our outer man, as a short time of affliction, as leading a tentlife. This form of our existence is burdened with the fact that in it we are absent from the Lord. This latter expression, of course, refers merely to the outer form of our existence, as Paul hurries to explain διὰ πίστεως γὰρ περιπατοῦμεν, οὐ διὰ εἴδους, *for we live by faith, not by sight.* Εἶδος, from the same stem as εἶδον, the second aorist of ὁράω, occurs only five times in the New Testament, but in at least three different applications. In Luke 3:22, the Holy Spirit is reported to have descended on Christ in the εἶδος of a dove; in the transfiguration the εἶδος of Jesus' countenance was altered, Luke 9:29; John 5:37, speaks of both the voice and the εἶδος of the Father; then we have the passage in I Thessalonians 5:22, where Paul cautions us to abstain from every εἶδος of evil. In each one of these four cases the English word "form" may serve as a translation, however with a slightly different connotation: while in the first three "shape" might serve as an alternate expression, in the fourth passage εἶδος seems to point to a subdivision, a class of evil, a species.

In our passage, εἶδος being compared with πίστις, and placed in contrast to it, the original meaning of the root is in evidence; εἶδος here means "sight." In our present state of tenting we are joined to our Lord by faith, but as far as any visible contact is concerned, we are still absent from Him. Yet we are cheerfully confident.

(8) Paul repeats the verb, now in the indicative, θαρροῦμεν. Yes, we are really cheerful in our present mode of living, and are not at all continually brooding about some way of escape—οὐ θέλομεν ἐκδύσασθαι, Paul had said in vs. 4. We are not wasting our time in self-pity, although it is true that we εὐδοκοῦμεν μᾶλλον ἐκδημῆσαι ἐκ τοῦ σώματος καὶ ἐνδημῆσαι πρὸς τὸν κύριον, *we much prefer to be absent from the body and to be present with the Lord*. We do not forget that in vs. 6 Paul introduced the expression "to be in the body" as an alternate for our present tentlife with all that this implies, and that "to be present with the Lord" refers to our state after mortality has been swallowed up by life.

(9) Paul continues with a διό, *accordingly*. Far from making us impatient and despondent, our longing for heaven has among others also (καί) this wholesome effect that we φιλοτιμούμεθα . . . εὐάρεστοι αὐτῷ εἶναι, that *we strive earnestly to be pleasing to Him*. Φιλοτιμεῖσθαι is a very strong expression, meaning 'to be actuated by a love of honor,' 'to be ambitious.' Paul uses it here to bring out how devoted we are to our Lord and His cause and how earnestly we strive to please Him.

Into this sentence Paul inserts the phrase εἴτε ἐνδημοῦντες εἴτε ἐκδημοῦντες, *whether present or absent*. We might paraphrase: whether present or absent is neither here nor there. That is a matter which we leave entirely to the Lord; we have something else to consider, namely, to please the Lord. If the Lord is for us, who can be against us? But if the Lord is dissatisfied with us, then even the whole world could not offset our loss. The Lord's attitude toward us, our status before the Lord, that is the all-important thing; that is the only matter of concern for us.

(10) This leads quite naturally to the thought of the final judgment, with which Paul now brings the present point and the entire section on his irrepressible cheerfulness in the execution of his office to a close.

He speaks about various aspects of this final judgment which we will consider separately.

One of the first things he mentions is the inescapableness of this judgment. He uses the word δεῖ. Try as you may, you cannot obviate it. God has appointed a day in which He will judge the world, and that appointment stands. The exact time may be unknown, unknown to men so that some begin to fear as though God were slack concerning His promise, and others openly scoff at the idea of a judgment. It may be unknown to the angels, even to the Son of Man Himself in His state of exinanition. Yet the day will come inescapably. There stands that rugged and stern, forbidding δεῖ. Paul does not fear any contradiction from any side when he pronounces that δεῖ, for even the conscience of natural man testifies to its truth.

Another phase which Paul mentions is that this judgment is universal; he says τοὺς πάντας ἡμᾶς, we all must appear. That includes the just and the unjust, both the living and the dead. An appeal to the mountains to fall on us and to the hills to cover us will be to no avail. All, every individual, must appear.

The most important thing about that final judgment is the question of who the judge is to be, and according to what standards the verdict will be rendered. Paul answers this question by saying that we must appear ἔμπροσθεν τοῦ βήματος τοῦ Χριστοῦ, before the tribunal of Christ.

That is the same person who laid down His life as a ransom for us; the same person who, though He knew no sin, permitted Himself to be made sin for us, that we might be made the righteousness of God in Him, who by His act of substitution procured for the whole world, for every individual sinner, the verdict of "not guilty" from His Father. He is the same one who sent His apostles into all the world with instructions to proclaim the message of a re-established peace between God and man.

By what standards will He conduct the final judgment? Will He who devoted His entire life and work to the redemption of sinners and to the establishment of the Gospel reverse Himself on the last day and apply the Law to every case? The same Law which in His person was nailed to the cross, blotted out and taken out of the way? No, the judgment has been committed to Him for this reason that He is the Son of Man. The judgment is the final phase in His act of mediation. He announced His verdict in advance when He declared: "He that believeth and is baptized shall be saved; but he that believeth not shall be damned." If anyone's name is found written in the book of life, that will obviate all further investigation; only in case a name was not entered in the book of life, will the record books of his deeds be consulted.

The way in which Paul describes the judgment itself may seem a little involved for us who do not use Greek as our mother tongue. We begin with the simpler problem. Paul clothes the outcome of the judgment in the form of a purpose clause, which reads in its simplified form, ἵνα κομίσηται ἕκαστος . . . εἴτε ἀγαθὸν εἴτε φαῦλον, *that each one may receive* (*carry off for himself*) . . . *either good or evil.*—The relative clause has several difficulties. The phrase τὰ διὰ τοῦ σώματος, is placed ahead for emphasis. The σῶμα, our present tentlife, is the decisive thing. It is the time of grace, it is also the time of testing and of either approval or failure. The fact that this important phrase is thus taken out of its ordinary position within the relative clause caused another alteration, the use of the definite article instead of the demonstrative pronoun. If we write out the relative clause in full we must replace the τά with ταῦτα, πρὸς ταῦτα ἃ ἔπραξεν διὰ τοῦ σώματος, *in proportion to those things which he practiced through his body* (*throughout his tentlife*).

Paul is here not proclaiming work-righteousness. He does not mean to say that the good deeds and the evil deeds of a man will be counted and checked off one against the other. He has in mind the practice and attitude of a man, whether he was motivated by faith, or by the *opinio legis.* Paul is well aware that a Christian's life of sanctification is never perfect. Paul, who admits that he has not yet attained and is far from perfect, who bitterly complains that he is unable to do the good which he wants to do, and who sighs, "Who shall deliver me from the body of this death," finds consolation in the redemptive work of his Savior: "I thank God through Jesus Christ our Lord." A ἔπραξεν does not refer to the individual good or bad deeds, but to the spirit in which a man's life is conducted.

The question may be raised whether εἴτε ἀγαθὸν εἴτε φαῦλον refers to the life of the defendant in Christ's final court, or to the verdict. I take it in the latter sense. Both adjectives are in the singular, while all words that refer to our life are in the plural, τὰ διά, etc., and πρὸς ἅ. It offers some difficulty to combine those singulars with these plurals; ἀγαθά and φαῦλα would come more naturally. This difficulty is removed if ἀγαθόν and φαῦλον are understood as referring to the verdict.

The thought that Paul conducts his whole life with a view to the coming resurrection and judgment was voiced by him also in his trial before the governor Felix: "(I) have hope toward God . . . that there shall be a resurrection of the dead, both of the just and unjust. And herein do I exercise myself, to have always a conscience void of offense toward God, and toward men" (Acts 24:15,16).

The reference to the final judgment and the new life in glory which it will usher in not only concludes Paul's presentation of his cheerfulness in conducting his office, but also forms a transition to the next part in which he presents the basic facts of his Gospel preaching and pleads for a wholehearted acceptance.

C. PAUL'S CAREFULNESS IN AVOIDING ANY OFFENSE

Chapter 5:11 to Chapter 6:10

In the section just concluded Paul presented, from various angles, the fact that he does not grow faint in proclaiming the Gospel. He prefaced the section with remarks extolling the glory of the New Testament ministry. Similarly in the new section, in which he will present the attitude toward the ministry becoming to both a preacher of the Gospel and the hearers of the message, he prefaces his remarks with a summary statement of the pivotal facts of our salvation. Since a correct understanding of these basic truths is of vital importance, we shall do well to devote a little more extended attention to them.

1. 5:11-17

(11) Εἰδότες οὖν τὸν φόβον τοῦ κυρίου: *knowing then the fear of the Lord.* With οὖν Paul connects the new section to the previous one, immediately to his last remark on the coming final judgment of the world, and indirectly to the truth as he had presented it in the entire preceding part of the epistle. Such being the case, as outlined above, what effect does it have on our work and, furthermore, in what spirit ought the hearers to receive our work?

For a summary expression Paul uses the concept τὸν φόβον τοῦ κυρίου. The fear of the Lord does not merely mean a due regard in thought and conduct for the coming judgment. It embraces all that Paul had said, e.g., about the glory of the New Testament in contradistinction from the old condemning and killing letter of the Law; about God's manner of handling the wonderful treasure by means of frail earthen vessels; about the certainty of the Gospel, which is not affected by Paul's inability always to carry out his own plans as he had conceived them; about the complete rescue from danger, which he had experienced when he carried the death sentence in himself. All these and other experiences which Paul had he sums up in that one concept: the fear of the Lord. It is the attitude of the heart for which the German language has the word *Gottesfurcht,* a childlike, confident, loving awe and reverence for God.

Paul takes the concept from the Old Testament, where, e.g., Psalm 111 sings the praises of the Lord, His works, and His redemption, concluding with the statement that "the fear of the Lord is the beginning of wisdom."

Applying this term to his own case, Paul uses the word εἰδότες, a perfect participle from the verb οἶδα. He does not use a form of γιγνώσκω, which word always implies some experience as the source of knowledge. Paul certainly had a rich experience on which he could draw, but that is not the point he wishes to stress in this case. In fact, to mention his experience might weaken the idea which he wants to put across. He uses the verb οἶδα, which concentrates the attention on the knowing itself, its certainty, and the bearing it may have on the case in hand. What Paul here wants to say is that he is ever aware of the fear of the Lord, that in all his work he has the fear of the Lord constantly before his eyes, that he performs the task assigned to him with a constant view to the fear of the Lord.

He underscores this idea by placing the word εἰδότες into the most emphatic position at the head of the whole sentence. Misled by the disparaging suspicions and sneers of false apostles on the basis of Paul's changes in his announced plan of travel, the Corinthians had begun to waver in their attitude toward Paul. Now they should consider that Paul does all his work with the fear of God ever before his eyes; also that he had made those misunderstood changes in no other spirit.

What is the nature of Paul's work which he is thus performing in the fear of the Lord? He does not need to make lengthy explanations. The Corinthians had observed him in their midst for 18 months. But Paul does want to impress upon them the spirit, the true nature of his work. He says, ἀνθρώπους πείθομεν, *we are engaged in winning (persuading) men.* The present indicative must not be stressed as expressing a conative idea: we are *aiming* to win men. The conative idea is contained in the verb itself. To counsel, to advise, to persuade, always implies an effort to gain a point. The present tense serves to point out in what work Paul is regularly engaged: it is the persuading, the winning of men. He does not have to say for whom or for what he is trying to win men, but it was important to stress that the spirit of his work is an attempt to win—not money, not personal recognition, but men for salvation through faith in Christ Jesus.

Just why does Paul say that? He answers this question in the rest of the verse: θεῷ δὲ πεφανερώμεθα, ἐλπίζω δὲ καὶ ἐν ταῖς συνειδήσεσιν ὑμῶν πεφανερῶσθαι, *Now to God we are manifest, but I hope that also in your consciences (we are) manifest.*

Commentators here spend much labor to find an acceptable contrast between the persuading of men and the being manifest to God; but no matter what solution they offer, it never really satisfies. The clause θεῷ πεφανερώμεθα does not seem to belong to the first part of the verse at all, but, rather, to begin a second thought. The statement that, with the fear of the Lord constantly before their eyes, the Apostles are engaged in winning men, is complete in itself, calling for no "but." Moreover, the idea of being manifest applies to two interested parties, from which these two statements about πεφανερῶσθαι should not be separated. The first δέ apparently is not adversative; it leads over to a special thought, somewhat like our English *now.*

When Paul says that he and his assistants are manifest to God, he naturally has reference to the work which they are doing and the spirit in which they are doing it. They are manifest as engaged in winning men, and doing it with the fear of the Lord constantly before their eyes.

Why does he make this statement? Not merely as a confirmation of his claims, in order to convince the Corinthians as with an oath. He rather uses it as an introduction to an appeal which he is about to address to their consciences. About his manner of winning men, he had said before (4:2) that he is directing his efforts to the consciences of men. Consciences of all men are by nature troubled about their status before God. They have the inscribed Law. They know that it is divine in its origin. They know that God will hold them to strict accountability. And they realize that they have transgressed God's Commandments and must plead guilty before His court with nothing to make atonement for themselves. They are without excuse.

To the despairing consciences in Corinth Paul had addressed his Gospel of salvation. His Gospel proved its power in their hearts. The message of Christ's vicarious suffering and death kindled a spark of faith and hope in them. They found peace to banish their fears.

Thus the Corinthians knew from experience in what the πείθειν of the Apostle consisted. They knew from experience how serious Paul had been in his work. His was more than human faithfulness. His faithfulness gave evidence of springing from the fear of God. If they only stopped to think for a moment what Paul's work among them meant for their spiritual health, they could not but agree: "Don't we know that Paul is winning men for Christ in the fear of the Lord?" That is what Paul means to say when he declares: "Now to God we are manifest, but I hope that we are manifest also in your consciences." "I hope," he says; for if such were not the case, what was there left of Paul's work? Must he then not register an egregious failure? But that cannot be the case. Did not God Himself encourage him to continue his work in Corinth, assuring him: "I have much people in this city" (Acts 18:10)? Paul can say with full confidence: "I hope that we are manifest also in your consciences."

(12) Why is he so insistent that his work be properly evaluated in Corinth? Certainly, not as though he were jealous of his personal glory. In doing his work he was ready to pass through honor and dishonor, through evil report and good report (6:8). He was concerned about the Corinthians. Their faith was in danger of wavering, of faltering, because false apostles were at work trying to undermine their confidence in Paul's integrity and in the reliability of his message. And they, the Corinthians, did not know how to ward off these attacks. To strengthen and fortify their faith, Paul directs their attention to their own consciences and to the blessed change they experienced as a result of his work in their midst. His message proved itself as a power of God unto salvation. In this sense Paul can say: οὐ πάλιν ἑαυτοὺς συνιστάνομεν ὑμῖν: *We are not again commending ourselves to you.*

The purpose of his seeming self-recommendation he states in these words: ἀλλὰ ἀφορμὴν διδότες ὑμῖν καυχήματος ὑπὲρ ἡμῶν: *but giving you an incentive for a boast on our behalf.*

Ἀφορμή literally means 'a starting-point,' 'a basis of operation,' 'a springboard,' then 'an occasion,' 'an inducement.' It was really up to the Corinthians to do some boasting about Paul, seeing how much he had done to bring peace, a peace which passes all understanding, to their restless hearts. They had enough material at their disposal to formulate an impressive boast, but they were bluffed by the glib arguments of the false apostles, so that they no longer could clearly see what great things Paul had done for them; and though many had the feeling that the false apostles were doing Paul an injustice, they did not exactly know how to go about the task of exonerating him. Therefore Paul gives them an ἀφορμή. His statement about the character of his work thus is not meant as a self-recommendation; it is merely setting the sights right for the Corinthians.

Paul uses the participle, διδότες, because this statement is not co-ordinate, as being on the same level, with the statement συνιστάνομεν; the thought is subordinate, somewhat like this: We are not saying this in the sense of self-recommendation, but rather in the sense of providing you with an ἀφορμή.

What, then, must be the chief point in the boast of the Corinthians about Paul, in order to be an effective defense against the scurrilous maligning by the false apostles and a telling counterattack against their raids on Paul's character? Paul states it in these words: ἵνα ἔχητε πρὸς τοὺς ἐν προσώπῳ καυχωμένους καὶ μὴ ἐν καρδίᾳ: *that you may have (it) over against those who boast in connection with appearance, and not in connection with the heart (of the matter).*

The false apostles are boasters. But if you analyze their boasting just a little, you will soon find that it concerns the πρόσωπον of things only, and does not touch the καρδία. Πρόσωπον is the face, the surface. And there their boasting stops. It is superficial. What some of these externals were, about which the false apostles boasted, we may learn from chapter 11:22, 23 and 11:6. But they carefully avoided such questions as : What dangers did the fear of God impel you to face? What hardships to endure? How much were you concerned about the consciences of men? What comfort did you bring them in their terrors?

Paul has provided the Corinthians with the material for confronting the false apostles with some very uncomfortable questions, and for completely unmasking them.

(13) How will a man proceed who in the fear of the Lord is engaged in "winning people"? What would be a superficial view of the matter? What would it mean to go to the heart? In vs. 13 Paul gives an illustration. He connects the verse to the foregoing with an explanatory γάρ. In the explanation he mentions two methods of procedure which, according to the πρόσωπον, seem to be miles apart.

Εἴτε . . . ἐξέστημεν, . . . εἴτε σωφρονοῦμεν: *If on the one hand, we went to excess . . . if, on the other, we are moderate.* On the use of the middle and intransitive forms of ἐξίστημι, cf. Mark 3:21; also Matthew 12:23; Mark 5:42; 6:51; Luke 2:47; Acts 10:45; also Acts 3:11.—By saying εἴτε ἐξέστημεν, Paul admits that, superficially considered, he and his assistants did go beyond bounds. He had, e.g., written the Corinthians a very sharp epistle, about which he himself worried for a time that he might have been too severe (7:8). He had used some very cutting words regarding their attitude in the incest case (I Cor. 5:1,2,6). This gave the false apostles, who judged only according to the outward appearance, an opportunity to make some caustic remarks about Paul's "weighty and powerful" letters (II Cor. 10:10).

But such criticism did not go to the heart of the matter. Was it not a very grievous offense that had been committed against a holy order of God? Was not the attitude which the Corinthian church took in the case bordering on blasphemy? Even if one considered it as only a little leaven, would not the results be most far-reaching and disastrous? Would they be harming only themselves by their flippant attitude? Would not the whole Church of God suffer most severely from their action, the Church of God for which Christ shed His holy blood? Should Paul tread softly when the Corinthians thus ruthlessly trod the honor of God under foot? He had to speak sharply, the honor of God was at stake. Εἰ ἐξέστημεν, θεῷ.

In the present letter he had been very moderate so far; he would soon become vehement when he would take up the case of the false apostles and their adherents. The Corinthians were far from perfect, and the matters that had been awry in Corinth were far from having been adjusted completely. But the attitude of the Corinthians had undergone a change. They regretted their former carelessness and negligence. The fact that Paul had grieved them severely had led them to repentance. They were still weak. All the more a mild and moderate treatment was indicated. The superficial detractors of Paul could not understand; but if anyone went to the heart of the matter, he could readily grasp Paul's statement: εἰ σωφρονοῦμεν, ὑμῖν.

(14) Such a one would, moreover, be impressed by the fact that Paul in all these seemingly so contradictory actions is motivated by a peculiar type of love. He formulates it in these words: Ἡ γὰρ ἀγάπη τοῦ Χριστοῦ συνέχει ἡμᾶς, For the love of Christ constrains us. The connecting γάρ marks this statement as explanatory of the foregoing.

What is the love of Christ? In other words, what is the function of the genitive Χριστοῦ? The first possibility which suggests itself will likely be that it is either the subjective or the objective genitive, meaning either the love which Christ has toward us, or the love which we entertain toward Him. Now, certainly it is the love which we have toward Christ that motivates us in our entire behavior; all our thoughts, words, and deeds should be expressions of our love toward Him. And again, our love for Christ is only the response to His love for us. We love Him because He first loved us.

True as it is that our love for Christ provides the motivation for our whole Christian conduct, yet, since Paul is here speaking about some very specific actions of his, which, superficially at least appear as contradictory and incapable of coordination, the remark that he is motivated by his general love for Christ seems too banal for so serious a discussion. Something more pithy, more directly to the point in hand, seems to be required.

There is an understanding of the genitive which meets these requirements: τοῦ Χριστοῦ may be understood as a qualifying genitive: a Christlike love. The same love, or at least the same kind of love, which was evident in Christ's conduct toward sinners is permeating Paul's heart and dictating his mode of procedure in the individual cases. When Christ called the Pharisees hypocrites, it was His Savior-love that prompted Him to use that ugly word. With that word He hoped to rouse them out of their smugness. On the other hand, that same Savior-love led Him to eat with publicans and sinners, to say to the grief-stricken mother at Nain, "Weep not," and to the adulteress, "Thy sins are forgiven." Paul had learned that love from his Savior, and now he imitated Him in His methods; and that love constrained him in all his dealings with sinners, as in the fear of the Lord he engaged in the work of winning them.

Of course, this is not a special kind of love. It is not generically different from the common love of Christians both toward their Savior and toward their brethren; rather, it is only a special manifestation, which, however, has its root in our common faith, which Paul now proceeds to set forth.

He forcefully pronounces the basic truth of the Gospel, God's principle of substitution, of vicariousness, and of imputation. This principle may seem utterly unfair to our natural reason. It is unfair to charge Adam's transgression against his unborn children; it is the height of unfairness to punish the holy Jesus so mercilessly for sins which He never committed—yet this "unfairness" of God is the principle which made our redemption possible.

Paul says, κρίναντας τοῦτο, ὅτι εἰς ὑπὲρ πάντων ἀπέθανεν, ἄρα οἱ πάντες ἀπέθανον, judging this, that one died for all; well, then they all died. We begin our study of these words with a brief look at ὑπέρ. This preposition originally had a local meaning, referring to a place over or above some other place. In this sense it does not occur in the New Testament, where it is found only in the metaphorical sense: 'for the benefit of.' This general sense, as the papyri indicate, developed into the very particular meaning of substitution. To substitute for someone is in the highest sense benefiting him. In many passages both the general and the particular meaning would make good sense. Then it will be impossible to determine with certainty, whether substitution was in the mind of the writer; yet since, as the evidence indicates, the development was strong in the direction of the particular meaning of substitution, we dare not be too hesitant about reading the word in that sense.

There is one passage in the New Testament where the meaning *instead* is beyond any question, Philemon 13. There Paul says to Philemon, he would like to retain Onesimus that ὑπὲρ σοῦ he might serve. Onesimus would serve Paul in his Gospel work, not for the benefit of, but instead of Philemon, who was living in distant Colosse. When Paul says in Galatians 3:13, that Christ purchased us free from the curse of the Law by becoming a curse for us, the situation (buying, redeeming) turns about a substitution, the price in place of the purchased object, vice versa. In our present passage also the idea of substitution is dominating the situation.

When Paul says that we *judge* in this matter, he does not have an opinion of our natural reason in mind. This is a judgment of faith. The judgment of faith stands firm: One did die in the place of all men, for the Lord laid on Him the iniquity of us all. The second also stands: Then they all did die. We note that Paul here uses the aorist, thus stressing the action as such. Our KJV is not exact when it renders the aorist with "then *were all dead.*" The RSV is better: "therefore *all have died.*" The process of dying and its agony is credited to all men when the One suffered it in their stead.

(15) This is only the beginning. If we went through the process of dying, what is there left of us? But the One who died in our stead did not remain dead. The Lord did not deliver His soul to hell, nor did His flesh see corruption. Just as He had died in our stead, so also He rose again from death as our champion, becoming the firstfruits of them that slept.

Since through Him we have paid the penalty of death, and through Him have again received life, it is evident that we now belong to Him. As far as we were concerned, we were doomed sinners; but since His death is counted as ours, we through it were freed from our guilt. And since He as our Representative rose again from death, we also have life in Him. We are not the former people anymore; we are a new creation.

Paul expresses this thought in vs. 15: καὶ ὑπὲρ πάντων ἀπέθανεν ἵνα οἱ ζῶντες μηκέτι ἑαυτοῖς ζῶσιν ἀλλὰ τῷ ὑπὲρ αὐτῶν ἀποθανόντι καὶ ἐγερθέντι, *And He died for all that the living ones no longer live unto themselves but to Him who died for them and was raised again.* Paul uses the passive voice, ἐγερθέντι, to direct our attention to the agent. The One who raised our Savior from death was the Father. The death of Jesus was sacrificial, it was a ransom price for our sins. Was the price sufficient? Did the death of Jesus remove our guilt? The Father Himself raised Him from the dead. Thereby He declared Him free from all our sins which had been imputed to Him. Paul pointed out before that in *His* life we also have life. Our guilt was declared liquidated by the death of Jesus. The acquittal of Jesus in His resurrection is our acquittal. The Father raised up Jesus.

The main thought in this section is that, although according to appearance we, the living ones, are the same people that we always were, yet according to God's principle of imputation we are counted as having died, and as living a borrowed life, sharing the life of Him who died for us and was raised again.

This thought Paul will develop more fully in the following verses, first in a transitional way.

(16) The thought in this verse and the following is linked to the foregoing with ὥστε: *and so, therefore*. Thus the effects are to be shown in some detail: the real meaning of the transaction will be pointed out more fully.

The first result to which Paul calls attention is that in sizing up people, and in dealing with them, we must use an altogether new approach. The idea is not that on the whole we retain the old approach, but modify it a little, re-enforce it a little here and there; the idea is that the approach must be new in the sense of being the direct opposite of the former. Ὥστε ἡμεῖς ἀπὸ τοῦ νῦν οὐδένα οἴδαμεν κατὰ σάρκα, *Therefore we* (I Paul and my assistants) *from now on recognize no man according to* (*the*) *flesh.* When evaluating the importance of a man κατὰ σάρκα, you take into consideration his social, political, financial standing, his education, his age, his health, his nationality, his sex, and many other things. These things, important though they may be κατὰ σάρκα, regarding the affairs of the present life, do not come into consideration for Paul in his work. True, he will adapt his work to people's special needs. In true sympathy he will place himself into their position and fight their special battles in his own heart. He will adapt the Gospel message to their special difficulties (see I Cor. 9:19-23); but the heart of his work will always be that in them he recognizes people who according to God's judgment have died with Jesus, and to whom belongs the life of Jesus.

This meant for Paul, first of all, a re-evaluation of Christ Himself: εἰ καὶ ἐγνώκαμεν κατὰ σάρκα Χριστόν, ἀλλὰ νῦν οὐκέτι γινώσκομεν, *If also we have known Christ according to* (*the*) *flesh, but now we know him* (*thus*) *no more.*

The question whether Paul ever met Jesus personally is beside the point here. It is possible that Paul was in Jerusalem at the time of Jesus' death, pursuing his studies under Gamaliel. And if he was there, then it is more than probable that he saw Jesus (cf. Cleopas' remark in Luke 24:18). Paul is here not speaking about meeting Jesus, he is speaking about his former evaluation of the Christ. It was a false evaluation; for that reason alone the verb οἶδα would have been out of place, a verb which always stresses the element of certainty. Paul is recording the false impression which he formerly held of the Messiah. It was the conception of a temporal savior, then current among the Jews. This misconception had induced him to persecute Christ as a blasphemer. Now he has learned to view Christ, His work, and His message in an altogether different light.

(17) Repeating ὥστε, Paul in this verse further unfolds the result of God's principle of imputation and substitution, which he had tersely stated in vs. 14. It is this: εἴ τις ἐν Χριστῷ, καινὴ κτίσις, *If anyone is in Christ, he is a new creation.* To be in Christ means the subjective appropriation of the grand deed of God performed in Christ's death. That means a new creation, a being that is new from the bottom up. It does not mean a being that has been overhauled, that has been improved, that has been developed a little more fully. To be sure, the old material is still there, the same body with its physical properties, the same soul with its mental faculties: but the attitude, to be specific, the attitude regarding the person's relation to his God, has been completely transformed.

Objective and Subjective Justification

In the foregoing Paul has spoken about God's judgment based on substitution and imputation objectively without any reference to any man's faith. One Man died for all. That means that all died. And then he spoke about the subjective appropriation of this judgment by the faith of individuals: "If any man be in Christ." Before we proceed to study Paul's further elucidation of the matter, we may do well to look a little more closely at the two terms *objective* and *subjective,* specifically, *objective* and *subjective justification.*

The *Brief Statement* offers the following very clear presentation of the matter, stating both the objective justification and the subjective justification and their mutual relation in a single sentence: "Scripture teaches that God has already declared the whole world to be righteous in Christ; that therefore not for the sake of their good works, but without the works of the Law, by grace, for Christ's sake, He *justifies,* that is, *accounts* as righteous, all those who believe in Christ, that is, believe, accept, and rely on, the fact that for Christ's sake their sins are forgiven." Here we have three clear definitions, first, one concerning a declaratory act of God in respect to the whole world, performed on Good Friday and Easter; secondly, one concerning a daily declaratory act pertaining to individual believers; and thirdly, one concerning the relation of the latter act to the former, being its personal application in specific cases.

With the above clear presentation of the *Brief Statement* compare the following definition:* "By His redemptive work Christ is the Propitiation for the sins of the whole world; hence *forgiveness* of sin has been *secured* and *provided* for all men. (*This* is often spoken of as objective justification.) . . . God *offers* this propitiation and reconciliation freely to all men through His means of grace. . . . God justifies the sinner solely on the basis of Christ's righteousness, which He imputes to the sinner through the Gospel *and* which the sinner accepts by faith." (Emphasis mine. M.) The three points so clearly set forth in the *Brief Statement* have here become vague and hazy. By a wide stretch of the imagination, and by putting a rather loose construction on the words, a correct view of objective justification may be read into them; but in their natural sense the words confuse objective justification and redemption.*

A confusion inadvertently crept into the English translation of F. Pieper's *Christliche Dogmatik*: "When the sinner comes to faith in Christ or in the Gospel, he is at once justified before God by his faith. Since the Gospel offers him the forgiveness of sins gained by Christ for the whole world (objective justification), the acceptance

---

*) This definition is found in the **Common Confession**, Part I, adopted by The Lutheran Church—Missouri Synod and by the American Lutheran Church, 1950. In 1956, however, The Lutheran Church—Missouri Synod declared that the **Common Confession**, Part I, together with Part II, was not to be regarded or employed as a functioning basic document toward the establishment of altar and pulpit fellowship with other church bodies.

*) This fact the Index to the **Common Confession** underscores by referring to a statement in the paragraph on Redemption: "God by raising Christ from the dead proclaimed to the world that He accepted the atonement for man's sin as completed and that Christ, the risen and exalted God-Man, shall reign as Lord forever." Thus God proclaimed two things: the completeness of **redemption** and the eternal rule of our exalted Savior; but nothing about a declaration of forgiveness.

of this offer, by faith, is all that is needed to accomplish his subjective justification. . . . Subjective justification is meant when Paul says: 'Therefore we conclude that a man is justified by faith.'" (Vol. II, p. 503.) Note: To what does "objective justification" stand in apposition, to "forgiveness gained by Christ" or to the whole statement about the Gospel's offer?

Compare the German text: *In demselben Augenblick, in welchem ein Mensch an Christum oder an das Evangelium, das heisst, an die von Christo erworbene und im Evangelium dargebotene Vergebung der Suenden, glaeubig wird, wird er* durch diesen Glauben *vor Gott* gerechtfertigt. *Dies ist die sogenannte* subjektive *Rechtfertigung im Unterschiede von der sogenannten* objektiven *Rechtfertigung, die vor dem Glauben vorhanden ist.** (Vol. II, p. 606 — Emphases in the original.) The conciseness and perspicuity of this statement is lost in the English translation.

An unmistakable statement on Objective Justification is imperative in view of the position voiced, e.g., by the former Ohio Synod: *Wir glauben und bekennen: Durch die durch Christum geschehene Versoehnung ist der heilige und gnaedige Gott uns* entgegengekommen, *so dass er uns nun die Suende vergeben und rechtfertigen* kann; *die Rechtfertigung selbst geschieht aber nicht eher, als bis durch Gottes Gnade der Glaubensfunke im Herzen des armen Suenders angezuendet worden ist;* dann *vergibt Gott dem Suender die Suenden.** (Quoted by Grosse from *Kirchenzeitung* for June 17, 1905. Emphasis mine. M.)

The danger of losing Objective Justification and with it *den realen Inhalt des Evangeliums** (Hoenecke) cannot be shrugged off when voices are heard deploring the fact that "a clean break has not yet been made with Objective Justification. But it *must* be made," adding

---

*) At the same moment that a man comes to faith in Christ or in the Gospel, that is, in the forgiveness of sins won by Christ and offered in the Gospel, he is **justified** before God **through this faith.** This is the so-called **Subjective** Justification in distinction from the so-called **Objective** Justification, which is present **before** faith.

*) We believe and confess: Through the reconciliation effected by Christ the holy and gracious God **made an approach** to us, so that now He **can** forgive us our sin and justify us; justification itself, however, does not take place until the spark of faith is kindled by God's grace in the heart of the poor sinner; **then** God forgives the sinner his sins.

*) the real content of the Gospel

that a dangerous situation prevails "as long as we do not *frankly disavow* Objective Justification, as Sola Scriptura requires of us."

Our theologians clearly taught Objective Justification without using the term, as quotations from Gerhard and Calov will show:

In Christi resurrectione a peccatis nostris sumus absoluti, ut non amplius coram Dei iudicio nos condemnare possint* (Disputationes theol.—quoted in Hoenecke III, p. 354.) —*Ut punivit Deus peccata nostra in Christo, quae ipsi ut sponsori nostro erant imposita atque imputata, ita quoque excitano eum a mortuis ipso facto absolvit eum a nostris peccatis ipsi imputatis, ac proinde* etiam nos in ipso absolvit* (Biblia III ad Rom. 4:25).

Enumerating among the blessings of the Gospel this in the first place: *dass ein armer suendiger Mensch vor Gott gerechtfertigt, das ist, absolviert, los und ledig gesprochen werde von allen seinen Suenden und von dem Urteil der wohlverdienten Verdamnis,* the Formula of Concord continues: *Welche Gueter uns in der Verheissung des heiligen Evangelii durch den Heiligen Geist vorgetragen werden, und ist allein der Glaube das einige Mittel, dadurch wir sie ergreifen, annehmen und uns applizieren und zueignen** (Trgl. p. 918).

In the Apology we read the terse remark: *Evangelium arguit omnes homines, quod sint sub peccato, quod omnes sint rei aeternae irae ac mortis, et* offert *propter Christum remissionem peccatorum et* justificationem, *quae fide* accipitur* (Trgl. p. 138). Justification is offered as a ready blessing to be received in faith.

----

*) In Christ's resurrection we were absolved from our sins, so that they can no longer condemn us before the judgment seat of God.

*) As God punished our sins in Christ, which sins had been laid upon Him as our Surety (or: Substitute) and had been imputed to Him, so also in raising Him from the dead, He by that very deed absolved Him (Christ) from our sins which had been imputed to Him, and **consequently He also absolved us in Him.**

*) that a poor sinner is justified before God, which is to say, is absolved, is declared free and quit of all his sins and from the verdict of a well-deserved damnation. . . . Which blessings are offered to us in the promise of the holy Gospel, and it is faith alone which is the one means through which we grasp and accept them, and appropriate and apply them to ourselves.

*) The Gospel convicts all men that they are under sin, that they are all subject to eternal wrath and death, and it **offers** to them, because of Christ, remission of sins and **justification,** which **is received** by faith.

We conclude this brief survey by adding two quotations from Luther which show that also he considered justification as a ready blessing (Objective Justification) prepared for us by Christ and brought and applied to us in the Gospel, to be accepted and enjoyed by us in faith (Subjective Justification).

First, a quotation from a sermon on Matthew 9:1-8. *Die Summa dieses Evangelii ist der grosse, hohe Artikel des Glaubens, der da heisst: Vergebung der Suenden.* After speaking about civic righteousness (*menschliche Froemmigkeit*), Luther develops three thoughts.

1. *Unsere Froemmigkeit vor Gott. Das ist nun die, so man heisset Gottes Gnade, oder Vergebung der Suenden.* 2. *Daher kommt sie, dass Jesus Christus, Gottes Sohn, vom Himmel kommen und Mensch worden, fuer unsere Suenden gelitten hat und gestorben ist.* 3. *Wie oder wodurch wird uns nun solche Gerechtigkeit heim gebracht, dass wir den Schatz, durch Christum erworben, empfahen?* After developing these thoughts very vividly in detail, Luther summarizes: *Siehe, da hast du alles, so zu diesem Artikel gehoert, von der christlichen Gerechtigkeit, die da stehet in der Vergebung der Suenden, durch Christum uns geschenkt und mit dem Glauben durch und in dem Wort empfangen** (E.A. 14, 175-189). Our righteousness before God, the forgiveness of our sins, is conveyed to us ready-made through the means of grace.

The second quotation is taken from Luther's lectures on Genesis (1536-1545), chapter 15:6, concerning the verb *chaschabh. De verbo* CHASCHABH *non valde repugno, sive id pro reputare sive cogitare accipias; nam res eodem redit.* Cum enim divina maiestas de me cogitet me esse iustum, *mihi esse remissa peccata, me liberum esse a morte aeterna, et ego cum gratiarum actione in fide hanc cogitationem*

---

*) The sum and substance of this Gospel is the great, sublime article of faith which bears the name: Forgiveness of Sins. . . .

   1. Our righteousness before God. Now this consists in what we call God's grace, or forgiveness of sins. 2. It came about in this way that Jesus Christ, God's Son, came down from heaven and became man, (and) suffered and died for our sins. 3. How or by what means is such righteousness conveyed to us, so that we obtain the treasure won by Christ? . . . You see that here you have everything that comprises this article of Christian righteousness: it consists in the forgiveness of sins; it is given us through Christ; it is received by faith through and in the Word.

Dei de me apprehendo, vere sum iustus, non meis operibus, sed fide, qua apprehendo cogitationem divinam* (E.A. III, p. 300).

Die Hervorhebung der allgemeinen Rechtfertigung (Objective Justification) *ist noetig, um den realen Inhalt des Evangeliums zu bewahren** (Hoenecke, III, p. 355).

2. 5:18-21

We permitted ourselves a brief digression to study the terms *objective* and *subjective* as they are applied to God's act of justification. The study was suggested by some remarks of Paul on the vicariousness of Christ's death. A correct understanding and use of these terms, as Hoenecke cautions, is essential for the preservation of the real content of the Gospel in our theology. In our study of Second Corinthians it will help us to follow Paul's line of thought more easily in the following presentation of the nature of Christ's achievement. — We return to the text.

In vs. 14 Paul stated the basic fact of the Gospel message in the following words: *If one died for all, then they all have died.* The idea that underlies this fact is that of substitution. The one holy One, the Son of God, volunteered to take the place of all sinners. He suffered death and experienced its agony. By virtue of the substitution His death with all its excruciating pain and terror is credited to all sinners. God considers them all such as have now paid the penalty for their sins in full — not, indeed, in their own person, but by proxy.

Paul then, in vs. 17, turned to the individual sinners, saying: If anyone is in Christ, he is a new creation. Objectively speaking, without any reference to an individual sinner's attitude toward Christ's sacrifice, purely on the basis of God's verdict, every sinner, whether he knows about it or not, whether he believes it or not, has received

---

*) In regard to the verb CHASCHABH, I do not strongly object whether you take it in the sense of 'to count for' or of 'to judge'; for the matter comes out to the same thing. **Since the divine Majesty does indeed judge concerning me that I am righteous,** that my sins have been forgiven me, that I am free from eternal death, and since I on my part in faith, with the giving of thanks, lay hold of this judgment of God concerning myself, I verily am righteous, not by my works, but by faith, **through which I lay hold of the divine judgment.**

*) The stressing of general justification (Objective Justification) is necessary in order to retain the real content of the Gospel.

the status of a saint. What will be his reaction when he is informed about this turn of events? Will he accept, or will he decline? Paul for the present disregards the possibility of rejection; he takes up the case of one who accepted the good news. He describes him as one "in Christ," and sums up the situation by calling him a "new creation."

In the section of Paul's epistle which is up for consideration now, the word καταλλάσσω occupies a very prominent place, making it imperative that we devote some special attention to it. Furthermore, the study of the matter itself which Paul here presents will make it necessary that we study it in the light of Romans 5:1-11, particularly vss. 8-11, where Paul discusses the same truth.

Κατ-αλλάσσω is a composite verb, compounded of the following two elements: the preposition κατά with its perfective idea, and the verb ἀλλάσσω, from ἄλλος, meaning to change, to alter.

The simple verb ἀλλάσσω occurs six times in the New Testament, in five different passages.

One, being a quotation from the Old Testament, is found in Hebrews 1:12, quoted from Psalm 102:26. Here the everlasting unchangeableness of God is presented on the background of the instability even of heaven and earth, which ἀλλαγήσονται, which grow old like a garment and will be rolled up and discarded.

In Acts 6:14, St. Stephen is charged with the statement that "Jesus of Nazareth shall destroy this place, and ἀλλάξει the customs which Moses delivered us." Ἀλλάσσω is here coupled with καταλύω, conveying approximately the same idea.

The idea of a radical change for the worse is present also in Romans 1:23: In their vanity men "ἤλλαξαν the glory of the incorruptible God into an image made like to corruptible man, and to birds, and to four-footed beasts, and creeping things." Of course, the glory of God itself cannot be touched by sinful man, but men's inexcusable ignorance and arrogance becomes evident in their sacrilegious attitude over against God.

A decided change for the better is indicated in I Corinthians 15:51 and 52. Paul is speaking about the resurrection of the believers: "It is sown in corruption; it is raised in incorruption: it is sown in dishonor; it is raised in glory: it is sown in weakness; it is raised in power: it is sown a natural body; it is raised a spiritual body" (vss. 42-44). Adam was from the earth, earthy; Christ is the Lord from heaven.

"And as we have borne the image of the earthy, we shall also bear the image of the heavenly" (vs. 49). It is a wonderful change which the believers will undergo in their resurrection. But what about those who shall survive till Judgment Day? Paul says, "We shall not all sleep, but we all ἀλλαγησόμεθα" (vss. 51, 52).

There is one more passage in which the simple verb stem ἀλλάσσω occurs, Galatians 4:20. There Paul expresses the wish to be personally present with the Galatians, so that he might ἀλλάξαι, modulate, his voice as the circumstances would indicate.

Thus ἀλλάσσω simply denotes a change — ranging from a slight modulation to a wonderful glorification or to practical destruction, as the case may be, and from a change which affects the object itself to a change in the estimation and treatment accorded to it.

Besides the compound καταλλάσσω there are four other compounds of the simple verb stem, plus one double compound. They are ἀπ-αλλάσσω, δι-αλλάσσω, μετ-αλλάσσω, συν-αλλάσσω and ἀπο-κατ-αλλάσ-σω. We may add that a compound noun formation also occurs, ἀντ-άλλαγμα (Matt. 16:26; Mark 8:37).

The meaning of ἀπαλλάσσω may be seen from the following three passages: "When thou goest with thine adversary to the magistrate, as thou art in the way, give diligence ἀπηλλάχθαι from him" (Luke 12:58). — From Paul's body handkerchiefs and aprons were brought to the sick so that the diseases ἀπαλλάσσεσθαι from them (Acts 19: 12). — Jesus assumed human nature "that through death he might destroy . . . the devil and ἀπαλλάξῃ them who through fear of death" were held in bondage (Heb. 2:15). In each case the riddance from some evil is meant.

In Matthew 5:23ff., Jesus speaks of a man who, while bringing his sacrifice, suddenly remembers that he has given his brother cause to have something against him. Jesus tells him to go at once and "διαλλάγηθι to thy brother." Note the passive. The man is the offender, and he must be reconciled. This does not mean that he must change his mind or attitude toward the offended brother, but he must see that he is cleared of the offense which he has committed; he must see that his status is cleared before his brother, and an unsullied relation re-established.

After Paul had said in Romans 1:23 that men ἤλλαξαν the glory of the incorruptible God, he says in vs. 25 that they "μετήλλαξαν the truth of God into a lie." They twisted or contorted the truth into its very opposite. He uses the same verb in the next verse: "Their women μετήλλαξαν the natural use into that which is against nature" (vs. 26). By a judgment of God they turned into sex perverts.

Συναλλάσσω occurs only once. When Moses found two Israelites quarreling, he συνήλλαξεν them, he "would have set them at one again" (Acts 7:26). He tried to compose their differences.

We reserve a study of the double compound ἀπο-κατ-αλλάσσω till we have investigated the meaning of καταλλάσσω from our present text and from the other passages in which it occurs, particularly Romans 5.

Καταλλάσσω

The very first verse of the section to be studied gives prominence to the concept of καταλλάσσειν. It traces the effecting of a new creation and everything that is connected with it to God as the καταλλάξας, and it sums up all the work of a Gospel herald in the word καταλλαγή. Paul then himself gives us a definition of καταλλάσσειν in the following verse. He announces his explanatory remarks as such by ὡς ὅτι: the whole matter took place *in this way that*. For the present we disregard other remarks and concentrate on the one which describes the nature of καταλλάσσειν. Paul uses a participle to do so. God performed His καταλλάσσειν of the world μὴ λογιζόμενος αὐτοῖς τὰ παραπτώματα αὐτῶν, not imputing their trespasses unto them. The καταλλάσσειν is basically an act of accounting, of imputing, of charging. The world had trespassed. Every individual found in that group of beings which are summarily called the world transgressed the commandments of God, and thereby burdened himself with a heavy load of guilt, if his trespasses were to be charged against his account. But God in His mercy decided not to do that. He did not impute their trespasses to the sinners. To whom God imputed them, Paul does not state at once in express words. He does not leave us in doubt, however, saying that God performed this καταλλάσσειν through Christ and in Christ. In vs. 21 he will tell us directly that God made Christ to be sin for us.

We thus see that καταλλαγή does not denote a change in the nature of the sinner, in the attitude of his heart. That change will take place when he is led by the Spirit to accept in faith the offered καταλλαγή. The change occurred in the standing of the sinner before his Judge.

Before Christ's intervention took place God regarded him as a guilt-laden, condemned culprit. After Christ's intervention and through Christ's intervention He regards him as a guilt-free saint. The *nature* of the sinner has not been changed. *God* did not undergo a change, did not experience a change of heart. The *status* of the sinner was changed.

A few remarks from Hoenecke bear repeating. *Es ist nach allem gewiss, dass* θεὸς κόσμον καταλλάσσων ἑαυτῷ *als versoehnende Taetigkeit Gottes nicht heisst, die Welt in eine befreundete Herzensstellung mit ihm bringen, aber auch nicht, eine veraenderte Stellung seines Herzens der Welt geben, sondern das* Verhaeltnis *zwischen Gott und ihr so aendern, dass die Welt nicht mehr als die nach Gerechtigkeit durch Suende von ihm geschiedene und verdammliche erscheinen muss. Das* καταλλάσσειν *ist von seiten Gottes das* in Christo geschehende Aufheben der Suende- und Schuldzurechnung an die Welt. . . . *Das* καταλλάσσειν *als Tat der Versoehnung Gottes ist sachlich in Wahrheit die* objektive, allgemeine Lossprechung oder Rechtfertigung der ganzen Welt in Christo von Suende und Schuld, *welche eine subjektive, spezielle durch den Glauben werden muss und wird* (Dogmatik III, p. 191f.).

In our passage Paul clearly indicates that καταλλάσσειν means a change of status. This fact is supported by the use of the same verb in the case of a woman who deserted her husband (I Cor. 7:11). Paul says, Let her remain ἄγαμος, single. She stepped out of her married state by deserting her husband. Now let her remain in the unmarried state. Or let her καταλλαγήτω to her former husband, return to her former state as his wife.

When Paul in our text uses a passive imperative, καταλλάγητε, it is a little more specific than the same imperative in I Corinthians 7. There nothing is said concerning the manner in which the καταλλαγή is to be brought about; the demand is simply raised that the woman re-enter her previous status. In our passage the invitation expressed by the imperative has been prepared most thoroughly. On the basis of the καταλλαγή which God perfected for the whole world in Christ and through Christ by not imputing their trespasses unto them, He now through His Apostle pleads with sinners: καταλλάγητε τῷ θεῷ. The meaning, as Paul himself paraphrases the expression in Romans 5, is:

καταλλαγὴν λαμβάνειν, to receive, to appropriate the ready-made καταλλαγή.

(18) With τὰ δὲ πάντα Paul sums up everything which he had said before about Christ's substituting for us by His death, and about our becoming a new creation by being in Him. All of this, every phase of it, has its source in God, flows ἐκ τοῦ θεοῦ. But not in a general way, as from His love, His wisdom, His power; but from God in so far as He performed a very specific deed, τοῦ καταλλάξαντος ἡμᾶς ἑαυτῷ, who reconciled us unto Himself, who took us out of our former state of being guilty and condemned sinners and placed us into a position before Himself where He regards us as having been purified from our sins, as spotless, unrebukable saints. All of this διὰ Χριστοῦ. If God finds us outside of Christ, He sees us as people who are not only covered over and over with sin, but who are permeated through and through with this poison. But as soon as Christ intervenes, and God looks at us through Christ, then all our sins are screened and blocked out. His all-searching eye finds none, and He pronounces us righteous.

Paul does not need to say more here than just διὰ Χριστοῦ. He explained before what that means: Christ went through the process of dying in our stead. He exposed Himself to the attacks of our death and wrestled with it in bitter agony till His sweat became heavy drops of blood that fell to the ground. He suffered the torments of hell, being forsaken of God on the cross. By thus tasting the bitterness of death in our stead He blotted out our guilt. God reconciled us to Himself διὰ Χριστοῦ.

No particular stress seems to attach to ἡμᾶς. Paul had said before in a very sweeping way that Christ in His death substituted for all. He had said that thus, if anyone is in Christ, he is a new *creature*. With another all-inclusive expression, τὰ δὲ πάντα, he proceeded to the further development of the great truth. Keeping all of this in mind, it does not seem likely that with ἡμᾶς Paul should wish to refer to some special group. He does not use the word in contrast to some other group, not even with any noticeable emphasis.

With a second participle modifying θεοῦ Paul adds another thought on how all the above-named blessings flow from God as their fountain: καὶ δόντος ἡμῖν τὴν διακονίαν τῆς καταλλαγῆς, *and giving to us the administration of the* καταλλαγή. God performed the καταλλαγή through Christ. Now the καταλλαγή is present as a ready blessing. All that remains is that it be administered. God establishes the administration. It is God's act alone that does this, and that is an act of giving. We do well to pay attention to this word. When God instituted the administration of His καταλλαγή, this was a gift of His, pure and simple.

Who are the ἡμῖν, to whom the administration was given? In a general way we may say: to men, to them to whom the καταλλαγή applies. When Jesus had healed the paralytic, cheering him with the forgiveness of his sins, the multitude glorified God who "had given such power unto *men*" (Matt. 9:8). On a later occasion Jesus stated that the power to forgive sins is vested in His Church. Paul could say that to him, being a called Apostle of the Lord, this administration had been given in a special sense.

(19) With ὡς ὅτι Paul announces a more specific explanation of the matter. Ὡς is a relative adverb, but while the Greek language very readily connects a new independent clause to the foregoing one by means of a relative, English idiom prefers a demonstrative. Thus instead of translating: *in which way that,* we say, *in this way that,* or briefly, *that is.*

Above we have taken note of the fact that Paul defines καταλλάσσειν as an imputative act: μὴ λογιζόμενος αὐτοῖς τὰ παραπτώματα αὐτῶν. We need not repeat.

We take up the first part of the statement: θεὸς ἦν ἐν Χριστῷ κόσμον καταλλάσσων ἑαυτῷ, which the King James Bible translates: *God was in Christ reconciling the world unto himself.* We note first of all that Paul extends God's act of καταλλάσσειν to cover the whole world. No sinner is excepted. The sins of everyone were laid on Jesus, were imputed to Him. Forgiveness of sins was not only secured and provided for the sinners, it was pronounced over them. Their sins were nonimputed to them; they were imputed to Christ. This applies to the whole world, to every individual sinner, whether he was living in the days of Christ, or had died centuries before His coming, or had not yet been born, perhaps has not been born to this day. It applies to the world as such, regardless of whether a particular sinner ever comes to faith or not.

How did God perform this stupendous task? St. Paul says, He was in Christ reconciling the world unto himself. The translation of the King James Bible seems to be clear, following the Greek word order. But there are some who question its correctness. They contend that the meaning is not: God was in Christ, but: God was reconciling. They combine ἦν with καταλλάσσων as a periphrastic imperfect tense, thus emphatically making a continued action of the καταλλάσσειν: God was in the course of history reconciling one individual after the other in an unbroken succession.

If that combination should stand, then it would almost be inevitable that the meaning of καταλλάσσειν undergo a change; it would come to signify something like bringing to faith. But no matter what meaning might eventually be given to καταλλάσσειν, what about the tense that God *was* doing it? We rather should say that He *is* doing it. The difficulties are obviated if we retain the combination as the KJV understood it, that when Christ won the new status for the world, God was in Him doing it. (Compare also Luther.)

This understanding of the construction is supported by a statement of Paul in Colossians. In speaking about the redemptive work of Jesus, he there explains: ὅτι ἐν αὐτῷ εὐδόκησεν πᾶν τὸ πλήρωμα κατοικῆσαι, *because in Him all the fullness (of the Godhead) decided to dwell* (Col. 1:19). Add to this that Paul thus not only would express the same thought in the two passages, but also in a very similar connection. For it is precisely in this passage of Colossians that Paul twice uses the double compound ἀποκαταλλάσσειν, of which we shall speak a little later. God was in Christ, and in this way, by the personal union of the divine with the human nature in the God-Man, the stupendous task of changing the legal status of the whole world was achieved.

The second statement of vs. 18, viz., that God gave to us the administration of the καταλλαγή, is explained by Paul in the last part of vs. 19 as meaning that God was in Christ θέμενος ἐν ἡμῖν τὸν λόγον τῆς καταλλαγῆς, *establishing in us* (in our midst) *the message of the* καταλλαγή. The administration of the καταλλαγή is carried out by means of the Word. The Word is made the vehicle for conveying and applying the καταλλαγή to the world. There is no other way of administering it. This Word is a very definite thing. God has placed it firmly; He has established it. It is not something that we should develop, find by observation or self-inspection, and clarify by study and speculation. No, God established it, and thus it stands, for us to proclaim without addition or subtraction or alteration. It is the Word which God established through which the καταλλαγή is brought to us and through which we bring it to the world. In these short words Paul gives us a terse presentation of the doctrine concerning the function of the Means of Grace.

A fact that has troubled some exegetes considerably is the change of tense in the two participles which Paul uses, first the present καταλλάσσων, and then the aorist θέμενος, the present denoting duration of the action. Yet the clash is more apparent than real. It is readily accounted for by the different nature of the two acts. God was in Christ refers, of course, to the historical appearance of Christ in the flesh. The whole life of Christ on earth was occupied in working out our καταλλαγή, His entire state of exinanition being devoted to the task. Hence the present participle, καταλλάσσων. But the ἦν ἐν Χριστῷ throws this tedious work into the past; the present participle, though denoting duration, does not predicate a continuation of the work beyond the earthly career of our Savior. The establishing of the message of the καταλλαγή, in contrast to the working out of the καταλλαγή, was a single act, completed in a moment; hence the aorist, θέμενος.

Καταλλάσσειν in Romans 5

Before continuing a study of our text to see how Paul applies the basic truths which he has just presented to himself and to his ministry, it may not be out of place to check our findings against Paul's presentation of the same matter in his Epistle to the Romans.

The starting point is different in the two cases. In our present epistle Paul had the task of leading the Corinthians to a proper evaluation and appreciation of his ministry, since his detractors were trying, and had succeeded to some extent, to warp their views. In Romans, Paul had no such difficulty. He was planning a visit to Rome, and thus took the opportunity of introducing himself by letter, presenting to them a summary statement of the Gospel which he preached.

Paul opens the fifth chapter with the statement that to have been granted justification means to "have peace with God."

How did it come about that God declared peace through justification? In 5:5 he answers the question by referring to the love of God which "is shed abroad in our hearts." Paul is not speaking of a *caritas infusa,* although his expression sounds familiar. He is speaking of the love which God so richly bestowed on us. That Paul is thinking of an attitude of God's heart toward us, a favorable disposition of His, is evident from vs. 8, where he mentions God's ἀγάπη εἰς ἡμᾶς.

It is important to note that Paul traces the entire matter of justification, peace, etc., to God's love as its source. God's love is present and productive at the very beginning. It is the motivating cause of our καταλλαγή. There are some who assume that καταλλάσσειν points to a change in God, that during the process He changed from an irate into a placated God, that some sort of appeasement took place.—But no, not the least change took place in the heart of God. It was His love which was active during the entire process of καταλλάσσειν. The change was effected in our status before our Judge.

Now let us take up Paul's development of the truth in vss. 6-11.

He begins by making the statement that Christ died for us (ὑπὲρ ἡμῶν, i.e., in our stead) when we were yet ἀσθενεῖς, weak in every respect, completely worthless. In order to set forth the unprecedented paradox of Christ's procedure, Paul calls attention, in the next verse, to the fact that one will scarcely die for "a righteous man." Paul may have had the case of Aristides in mind, whom the Athenians surnamed the Righteous, only to ostracize and exile him later. But if people as a rule are loath to give up their life for a righteous man, how much more will they refuse to die for some worthless person?

Paul admits that ὑπὲρ τοῦ ἀγαθοῦ some will be ready to risk death. The definite article of τοῦ ἀγαθοῦ, while δικαίου was anarthrous, indicates that Paul is not thinking of a good *person*; the adjective is neuter, meaning the common good. We Americans may think of Nathan Hale in the history of our own country, who regretted that he had but one life to give for his country. We may think of Arnold von Winkelried, sacrificing his life in the battle of Sempach in order to make a way for liberty. Paul certainly knew of the self-sacrificing bravery of the 300 Spartans at Thermopylae, and possibly their epitaph went through his mind as he penned these words.

Ὦ ξεῖν', ἀγγέλλειν Λακεδαιμονίοις ὅτι τῇδε
Κείμεθα τοῖς κείνων ῥήμασι πειθόμενοι.*

But what about Christ, who died for us when we were absolutely worthless? Paul answers in the next verse, replacing the somewhat vague term ἀσθενεῖς with the very concrete and specific word ἁμαρτωλοί,

---

* O stranger, tell all Spartan men that here
Lie we who did their will and command revere.

taking this word in its widest and deepest sense. God commends His love, lets His love shine forth in its brightest luster, in that Christ died in our stead when we were putrid with sin. No parallel can be found to that love anywhere.

Paul does not stop to explain the matter, he proceeds on the assumption that everybody is familiar with the sacrificial character of Christ's death. Paul had spoken about His death as an ἀπολύτρωσις (Rom. 3:24), had said that in His blood Christ is our ἱλαστήριον (vs. 25); he had said that Christ was delivered into death because of our παραπτώματα, and was raised because of our δικαίωσις (4:25). He can now presuppose all this and state the meaning of Christ's death in terms of justification, and proceed from this with a *conclusio a maiore ad minus* or, perhaps better, *a peiore ad melius*. He says, "Much more now, our justification having taken place in His blood, etc." We note that Paul uses the participle of the aorist, not of the present nor of the perfect. The present would point to the action as being in progress, and the perfect would stress the result of the completed action, viz., that we are righteous by virtue of our justification. The aorist stresses the fact that justification actually took place, it took place in the blood of Jesus. This being the case, we shall be saved from God's wrath. Paul had spoken about the wrath of God as being revealed from heaven on all godlessness and unrighteousness of men (1:18); he warned that they who despised the call to repentance which issues from God's goodness were treasuring up for themselves wrath on the day of wrath (2:4,5). He now draws the conclusion that, since justification was performed by the blood of Jesus, we shall be saved from wrath in every form (ἀπὸ τῆς ὀργῆς).

So far Paul has spoken in terms of justification. He now illustrates what he has said by substituting the term καταλλάσσειν. Thus: For if we, being enemies, were reconciled to God through the death of His Son, much more, our reconciliation having been achieved, shall we be saved in His life.

In determining the meaning of the last phrase ἐν τῇ ζωῇ αὐτοῦ, it would seem best to remember 4:25: that Christ was delivered for our offenses, but raised again for our justification. If the death of Jesus accomplishes great things for us, how much more His resurrection and life? *Vivit,* Luther wrote on the wall of his room, to have the fact constantly before his eyes for his own consolation.

Since Paul is speaking of καταλλάσσειν, instead of δικαιοῦν, he changes, with the figures, also the name which he applies to us. When he spoke of justification, he called us sinners, for as sinners we stand in need of justification. When he changes over to καταλλάσσειν he calls us ἐχθροί, enemies.

In what sense is the word enemy here to be taken, in the active or in the passive sense? Does Paul want to say that we hated God, or that we were hated by God? It is true, we were ἀσεβεῖς by nature, godless, we were ἁμαρτωλοί, sinners; we were ἀσθενεῖς, worthless, contemptible. We deserved God's wrath and should be hated by God, should be His enemies in the passive sense of the word. Yet that is not what Paul has in mind. He rather views the enmity as a state or condition. As in vs. 1 of this chapter he had said that, our justification having been achieved, we now have peace—not a feeling of relaxation, but peace as an actual state of affairs, as the cessation of hostilities— so now, going back to the time before peace was declared, he speaks of us as being enemies. That was our status before God. Though it is true that we by our sins showed hostility to God and His holy will; though it is likewise true that by our sins we forfeited the fatherly love of our God and incurred His wrath; yet Paul is here speaking of objective conditions, both of peace and of enmity.

A καταλλαγή took place. It was brought about by the death of God's Son. This does not mean a change in our personal attitude towards God, nor a change in His personal attitude toward us. In spite of the fact that we by our sins had aroused His righteous wrath, He had never wavered in His love toward us; and the more we burdened ourselves with sin and guilt, the more we displayed our aversion to His holy will, all the more His pitying love rose to ever greater heights in its efforts to save us, and finally brought the unbelievable sacrifice of His own Son. Thus the status of enmity was changed into one of peace. That is the καταλλαγή.

The objective nature of the καταλλαγή is beautifully set forth by Lenski in his commentary on Romans. We quoted his words some 15 years ago; they will bear repeating. They are as pertinent today as they ever were.

"Reconciliation . . . signifies that *through Christ's death God changed our status.* By our enmity, our sin, our ungodliness (all synonymous) we had gotten ourselves into the desperate status that deserved nothing from God but wrath, penalty, damnation; and unless God did something *to change this our status,* it would compel him to treat us thus. By means of Christ's death (*dia*) God changed this into an utterly different status, one that despite our enmity, etc., enabled him to go on commending to us his love, this very love that changed our status, this love that impelled Christ to die for us hostile enemies of God.... A change had to take place in our case, and we could not make it ourselves, God had to make it. It took the sacrificial death of his Son to do it. . . . Being enemies we were reconciled to God. *This is the objective act.* It wrought a change with or upon these enemies, not within them. It as yet did not turn their enmity into friendship, did not make the world the kingdom. *It changed the unredeemed into the redeemed world.* The instant Christ died the whole world of sinners was changed completely. It was now a world for whose sin atonement had been made, no longer a world with sins unatoned" (pp. 351ff.—Emphasis mine. M.).

How anyone with this grasp of the objective nature of the καταλλαγή can still refuse to accept the objective nature of the justification of which Paul is here speaking is difficult to understand. Yet Lenski transcribes δικαιωθέντες νῦν ἐν τῷ αἵματι αὐτοῦ (in 5:9) as we "who now already are justified in connection with Christ's blood" in contradistinction from "all who will yet be justified, as we already have been" (p. 353).—Paul introduces his remarks on our καταλλαγή as ἐχθροί with an explanatory γάρ. But what of the explanation if the καταλλαγή and the δικαίωσις, which it is supposed to elucidate, do not refer to the same thing? A logical *quaternio terminorum* confuses and deceives. In order not to charge Paul with one, we must treat δικαιωθέντες and καταλλαγέντες as covering the same case and understand the former as objective just as the latter admittedly is.

There is a subjective way of speaking about καταλλαγή, as Paul does in the second half of the following verse. Δι' οὗ (Χριστοῦ) νῦν τὴν καταλλαγὴν ἐλάβομεν; through whom we have now received the καταλλαγή. The καταλλαγή is a ready blessing, prepared for the whole world, for every individiual member of the world, brought to every one by means of the Word. Through faith we receive, we appropriate, this blessing. We enjoy the reconciliation as we become subjectively reconciled. Καταλλαγὴν λαβεῖν of Romans 5 equals the καταλλαγῆναι of II Corinthians 5.

This seems to be a convenient place for inserting a brief study of the double compound, ἀποκαταλλάσσω, as used in the New Testament. It occurs twice in the Epistle to the Colossians.

The Colossian congregation, not founded by Paul himself, most of whose members had never met Paul personally, was troubled by a peculiar error. From remarks in Paul's epistle we may infer that it consisted to a great extent of Judaistic elements and contained also some elements which look like incipient Gnosticism. With their smooth talk, πιθανολογία, the errorists made an impression on the Colossians. How does Paul meet the situation? He does not with keen dialectic refute the errors of the Judaistic-Gnostic falsifiers of the Gospel; he begins by fortifying the shaky faith of the Colossians. He makes Christ great before their eyes. He calls Him the εἰκών of the invisible God, the πρωτότοκος before all creation, through whom and with reference to whom all created things exist. He also calls Him the Head of the Church.

In unfolding this thought Paul uses the word ἀποκαταλλάσσω, the first time in a parenthetical remark inserted in the following statement: "Who (Christ) is the beginning, the First-born from the dead, that he might be in all things the pre-eminent leader . . . having made peace by his cross-shed blood" (Col. 1:18,20). Into this statement Paul inserts the explanatory remark: "Because all the fullness pleased to dwell in Him and through Him ἀποκαταλλάξαι all things to Him" (Col. 1:19,20). If all fullness dwelled in Him, not accidentally but by deliberate choice, then nothing is left outside Him. God was in Christ, so Paul says in Second Corinthians. In Colossians he repeats the thought later: "For in him dwelleth all the fullness of the God-head bodily" (2:9). This fullness determined not only to dwell in Him, but to achieve its lofty purpose through Him, namely, ἀποκαταλλάξαι τὰ πάντα εἰς αὐτόν. The meaning of the verb may be gathered from the participle which Paul uses in the main clause, εἰρηνοποιήσας, Christ definitely establishing peace by His blood which He shed on the cross. By establishing the relation of peace between God and man Christ achieved the ἀποκαταλλάξαι.

The manner of this transaction Paul now carries out with greater detail and special application to the Colossians. Why should an ἀποκαταλλαγή be necessary? Because they were ἀπηλλοτριωμένοι (a perfect participle, denoting a state of alienation) and ἐχθροί. This state was brought about by their mind in their wicked works. (The dative διανοία does not modify the noun ἐχθροί, but states the reason for the situation.) But now Christ ἀποκατήλλαξεν them by giving His very flesh into death, to present them as holy and blameless and unrebukable in His judgment by the sacrifice of Himself. (Col. 1:21.)

It appears that the meaning of the double compound is the same as that of the simple compound with the idea added that this *brings them back, restores* them to a former position.

(20) Ὑπὲρ Χριστοῦ οὖν πρεσβεύομεν, *for Christ we then serve as ambassadors*. With οὖν Paul connects this thought to the foregoing discussion and makes his application. It was God, and God alone, who brought about the decided change in our social standing, in our status before Him, particularly before His tribunal. He achieved it through Christ, to whom He imputed the sins of the world, and in whom all divine fullness dwelt bodily. God alone, through Christ alone. In what spirit will those whom He appoints to administer the καταλλαγή perform their work?

Ὑπὲρ Χριστοῦ, Paul says emphatically. They will consider it throughout as Christ's work, being careful neither to add, nor to omit, nor to alter one iota. They will discharge their task with awe and reverence. Did Christ offer Himself as a sacrifice, Himself who is none less than the Son of God, to achieve the καταλλαγή? Then the called ministers will tremble at handling so costly, so dearly bought a treasure. They will be constrained by a Christlike love in administering the blood-bought καταλλαγή, careful that the treasure itself be preserved unsullied, anxious that no one for whom the καταλλαγή has been prepared be prevented from enjoying it, either by a falsification of the message, or by a crude handling on the part of the administrant.

We note that the verb πρεσβεύομεν, being the present tense, here does not refer to a specific act performed at the present moment, but indicates an activity in which Paul and his associates were regularly engaged. To serve as ambassadors of Christ was their occupation, about which Paul has been speaking all this while in this epistle, and about which, since 4:1, he has been pointing out that they do not grow weary. How can anyone who is aware of the terrible consequences of sin for his own person, of the state of hostility which exists between him and his violated God, and has then heard the heart-cheering, soul-reviving news that through Christ's sacrifice his status has been changed, his guilt has been canceled and peace declared—how can such a one grow weary of hearing, of proclaiming, of living the καταλλαγή? How can he, even in the face of insusceptibility and indifference, in the face of opposition and apparent failure?

An ambassador of the καταλλαγή will perform his mission, as Paul now phrases it, ὡς τοῦ θεοῦ παρακαλοῦντος δι᾽ ἡμῶν, *as though God did beseech you by us.* He realizes that it is God Himself who is channeling His appeal through us. He will remember that God stretches out His hand beckoning the people to come; He draws them to Himself with loving-kindness; in seeming slackness He may defer punishment, "not willing that any should perish, but that all should come to repentance" (II Pet. 3:9). Yes, He even endures with much long-suffering, with oft-repeated strenuous attempts at rescue, the vessels of wrath which are already ripe for destruction.

This God is proclaiming His καταλλαγή through us. Can we do other than what Paul now states: δεόμεθα ὑπὲρ Χριστοῦ, καταλλάγητε τῷ θεῷ, *we plead in Christ's stead, be ye reconciled to God?*

The thought which Paul here expresses with the aorist passive of καταλλάσσειν is the same for which he used two words in Romans 5: καταλλαγὴν λαμβάνειν. The καταλλαγή is an accomplished fact, a ready blessing, achieved through the death of Christ, administered by heralding the message (λόγος) of the καταλλαγή. Now by the God-appointed heralds the invitation is extended to all, καταλλάγητε, or καταλλαγὴν λάβετε. Must the glorious, blood-bought blessing go begging among those who are to enjoy its inestimable benefits? Yes! Yet the God-appointed heralds do not grow weary of pleading, begging.

(21) In this last verse of the chapter, St. Paul rises to unprecedented heights, in a ringing statement of the lofty truth of the Gospel. Τὸν μὴ γνόντα ἁμαρτίαν ἡπὲρ ἡμῶν ἁμαρτίαν ἐποίησεν, ἵνα ἡμεῖς γενώμεθα δικαιοσύνη θεοῦ ἐν αὐτῷ, *the One who knew not sin He made (to be) sin in our stead, so that we on our part might become God's righteousness in Him.*

"The One who knew not sin"—this does not merely mean that Christ never committed a sin in thought, word, or deed; that every thought which He ever conceived, every pleasure that He ever felt, every desire that ever stirred in His heart, was absolutely without stain of sin, sweet and pure; not merely that He was free from every stain of original sin: it means that He was the One whom sin could not

reach, the One who could not be tempted with sin, as St. James expresses it (Jas. 1:13), the One who was "holy, harmless, undefiled, *separate from sinners,* and higher than the heavens" (Heb. 7:26). Only God is such a One. Man was tempted in Paradise, and succumbed. The holy angels, although now *confirmati in bono,* were in the beginning subject to temptation, and a great number of them fell away. God alone is ἀπείραστος κακοῦ, so far removed from sin, so antagonistic to sin, that sin can do nothing but nauseate Him. Such a One was Christ.

True, the Word was made flesh, and as such it became subject to temptation. The temptation which Jesus endured in the flesh was no shadowboxing; it taxed His powers of resistance to the utmost. He was exhausted in body and mind when the Tempter left Him in the wilderness. In spite of the fierce struggle, sin had not seared His conscience in the least. He did not learn to know sin. He knew no sin. The temptations were repeated with a vehemence that staggers our imagination, particularly in the last hours of His life. He shuddered to drink the cup, and wrestled with death till He sweat blood which fell to the ground in heavy drops; on the cross He was forsaken of God and cruelly mocked and tortured by His enemies. Yet He never wavered; He prayed, Not My will, but Thine be done; in faith He clung to His Father, and prayed for His enemies that God would not lay their sins on them, but on Him. He thus clearly demonstrated that He was One who knew no sin.

Yet He was made to be sin for us. Paul has stated above that this was done by imputation. He need not repeat. But the immensity of the matter is brought home to us by the expression that God *made* Him to be sin.

The planned fruit of all this is that we might be made God's righteousness, about which Isaiah prophesied, which Paul extolled in Romans 1:17, as being revealed in the Gospel from faith to faith, so that God is both just and justifier in one. Paul speaks about δικαιοσύνη in many places in Romans, and especially do we compare 3:9 of our present epistle, where the διακονία τῆς δικαιοσύνης stands in contrast to διακονία τῆς κατακρίσεως. Δικαιοσύνη is a righteousness established and pronounced in a court proceeding.

In Christ we have God's δικαιοσύνη, established and declared in God's court, the validity of which dare be questioned by no one.

3. 6:1-10

In the closing words of the previous chapter, Paul rose to unprecedented heights in describing the work which God did for us: "He made Him who knew not sin to be sin for us, that we might become God's righteousness in Him." This work of God he called the καταλλαγή.

Paul and his associates have been called to administer this blessing which God prepared at so stupendous a cost. Paul and his associates are ambassadors of God; God through them is urging the people, His former enemies, the curse-laden sinners, to accept the offered καταλλαγή.

This is for Paul a trust of the highest kind. On the one hand, it fills him with exquisite joy that he was "allowed (i.e., approved) of God to be put in trust with the gospel" (I Thess. 2:4); on the other, he trembles because of the responsibility. It was from the bottom of his heart, on the basis of his own inner experience, that he exhorted the Ephesian elders: "Take heed therefore unto yourselves, and to all the flock, over the which the Holy Ghost hath made you overseers, to feed the church of God, *which he hath purchased with his own blood*" (Acts 20:28). Paul as an ambassador of God was deeply concerned, on the one hand, that he deliver the glorious message of God unsullied, unadulterated, unabridged, in a manner becoming its grandeur, and on the other, that it reach and benefit all consciences, for which it is intended.

What impressions must these thoughts make on the Corinthians? They had listened to false apostles who cast suspicion on Paul's sincerity and on the reliability of his message. Will not all their doubts and suspicions have to melt away when they realize how grand an office God has entrusted to Paul, and how conscientiously he administers it? Will they not perhaps begin to feel ashamed of themselves to such a degree that they forget the blessed message which Paul had brought to them with its comforting meaning for their conscience?

Such a result would be defeating Paul's purpose. At the end of the first chapter he described his work as that of "helpers of your joy." Then he had to use sharp language in dealing with their faults—to be "beside ourselves" he called it in vs. 13 of the previous chapter. He had to hurt them, make them sorry, cause them grief. But this was not an end in itself; it was, just as when God does His *opus alienum* in applying the Law to us, to lead them to repentance.

These considerations we must bear in mind if we are to appreciate properly the thoughts and feelings which fill the heart of Paul and the words in which they overflow from his heart in the next section.

A Special Note on the Structure of 6:1-10

The structure of the section under consideration arrests our attention. It is unique. It is one long sentence, yet not at all involved. It contains a parenthetical remark which demands our special attention. Verse 2 is parenthetical.

In vs. 1 Paul states the nature of his work, and by means of a participial construction adds in vss. 3 and 4a his aim of keeping his ministry blameless, beyond reproach. So far there is nothing unusual in the construction. But now begins a long list of modifiers, and we must take a look at their grouping.

First we find a group of 10 in vss. 4b and 5. But these 10 are not simply an enumeration; there is system in their arrangement, a grouping according to content of the terms, and subordination of some to others. While nine of the terms are simple nouns, the first one of the 10 stands out from the rest by having an adjective modifier: "much patience." A little closer look will readily reveal that each one of the nine following ones names something which furnishes Paul an opportunity to practice much patience. Thus we really have a group of nine held together by the concept of much patience. If we look at these nine, it will appear that they fall into three smaller groups of three members each. The first three speak of afflictions in a general way: "afflictions, necessities, distresses." The second three consist of rather specific afflictions: "stripes, imprisonments, tumults." While Paul had no choice in these six—they were inflicted on him and he was purely passive in the matter—the last three were, in part at least, assumed by him more or less voluntarily in the interest of the Gospel: "labors, watchings, fastings."

Paul continues with a group of four nouns, each one consisting of a single word prefixed by the preposition ἐν. Since the first two denote an inner quality, while the second pair denotes one which manifests itself in a transitive way, terminating on some object outside itself, the four terms are easily arranged as a square, with "purity" and "knowledge" on the one side, and "patience" and "goodness" on the other.

This group of four is followed by another of the same number, each member, however, consisting of two words: a noun with its modifier, each compound term preceded by the preposition ἐν. These four terms again readily fall into two pairs, the modifiers of the first two being adjectives, those of the second two, genitives: "in a holy spirit, in un-feigned love; in a word of truth, in power of God."

This again is followed by a square of four ideas, however, not of uniform size. The fact that they are to be considered as belonging together is marked by the preposition δία, in the sense of 'by means of' in the first case, then as 'passing through' something in the other. The first speaks of the implements which Paul employs, which are those of δικαιοσύνη exclusively, since they are found on the right hand and on the left. The second consists of two pairs of opposites arranged chiastically: "through glory and shame, through evil report and good report."

While this group showed some artistic manipulation to bring out the number four, the next one shows this artifice in a still more pronounced degree. Moreover, the members of the three groups men-tioned have been constantly increasing in size: first a single noun, then a noun with a modifier, lastly pairs of contrasting concepts. The idea of contrasts is continued in the final group, where each member is introduced by ὡς. Paul is acting as such and such a character in his work.

This group consists of seven members, which are divided into three and four respectively. Paul marks this division by changing the con-struction in the third member, following a participle with an indicative introduced by ἰδού. Thus we have: "as deceivers and true, as unknown and becoming well known, as dying and, behold, we live."—This triad is followed by: "as chastised and not killed, as grieved but always rejoicing, as beggars but making many rich, as possessing nothing and controlling all things."

Once the structure of this unique sentence has been visualized the separate expressions, as a rule, are readily understood, and do not call for any lengthy discussion.

We shall take up the main statement first, as it is contained in vss.. 1, 3, and 4a; then the parenthesis of vs. 2; then the groups of modifiers in vss. 4b-10.

Verses 1, 3, and 4a

Now as helpers we also urge you not to receive the grace of God in vain, (we) giving no occasion for stumbling to anyone, in order that the (our) administration be not blamed, but in every respect showing ourselves as God's ministers.

Συνεργοῦντες, 'helpers,' 'assistants,' laboring jointly with someone. With whom? In the foregoing Paul had carried out the idea that God in preparing the καταλλαγή for the world had also established the message of the καταλλαγή, and thus had given to us the administration. Then he said that he and his colaborers were serving as God's ambassadors and God was urging (people) through them. Bearing this in mind, we see Paul as laboring jointly with God.

But then Paul had addressed the Corinthians in particular. He had offered them the καταλλαγή and had pleaded with them to accept it. Plainly, he was a helper to them also.

He now places this idea emphatically at the head of the sentence, at the head of the whole paragraph. "Helpers" is the controlling concept. Because Paul is dominated by the idea that his position is that of a helper, assisting God in carrying out His great work, and helping the Corinthians to appropriate and enjoy God's reconciliation, he does what he is doing and in the manner in which he is doing it. It is not his own enterprise; it is a trust.

It is important that we take note of the word χάρις. Paul has been called to administer a divine blessing. In the previous chapter he had called it a διακονία τῆς καταλλαγῆς, which is carried out by delivering a message, as an ambassador of God earnestly pleading for the acceptance of the καταλλαγή. He now calls it an administration of χάρις. It was χάρις which moved God to make Him who knew no sin to be sin for us, to make Him to undergo the agony of death in our stead, so that we might be considered as having undergone this agony ourselves, so that what we are now through Christ's sacrifice might unmistakably appear as a new creation, all stemming from the fact that we were made the righteousness of God in Christ. We recall the classical definition which St. Paul gives us of χάρις in Romans 11:6: "If by grace, then is it no more of works; otherwise grace is no more grace."

As a helper of God, Paul endeavors to bring home to his hearers this grace of God, urging them to accept it by opening their hearts in faith to the message which he proclaims. And as a helper of God he continues his work by urging them not to receive this grace in vain, making of the grace an empty, meaningless thing (εἰς κενόν). This could happen in various ways, not only by considering it lightly and neglecting it, but also by attempting to add one's own merits to God's grace. This latter error was very rampant in Paul's day. The Judaizers taught the Christians that, in order to secure God's grace, they must fortify, reinforce, it with their own merits by observing circumcision and the other ceremonial laws of Moses. According to Paul's definition in Romans 11, God's grace and human merits do not mix. Any attempt to add human merits in any form or degree to God's grace will utterly ruin it and lead to its loss. In that case grace had been received εἰς κενόν.

This imposes certain obligations on Paul as a helper of God. He expresses it thus: μηδεμίαν ἐν μηδενὶ διδόντες προσκοπήν, *scrupulously avoiding in every respect to give the slightest occasion for stumbling.* The double negative, μηδεμίαν ἐν μηδενί, does not produce a positive, but reinforces the negative idea. Paul is most anxious and apprehensive lest he cause offense in any respect. For "offense" he here does not use the strong word σκάνδαλον, but a milder term, προσκοπή. While σκάνδαλον would indicate a complete loss of faith in spiritual death, προσκοπή indicates a stumbling, a momentary disturbance of faith. Paul is careful to avoid giving even the slightest offense.

His aim is: ἵνα μὴ μωμηθῇ ἡ διακονία, *that our ministry be not blamed.*

Paul had changed his plans of travel. Originally he announced to the Corinthians that he would visit their church first. From them he would go up to Macedonia, and then return to them, before he would go up to Jerusalem to deliver the collection which he was gathering. For certain very good reasons he changed his plans, and went to Macedonia first. This change his detractors in Corinth construed as fickleness, and from this jumped to the conclusion that Paul's Gospel was unreliable. They attached a blame to his ministry and tried to make it stick. Paul now reminds the Corinthians how careful he is to keep his ministry clear. With this he is not telling them anything new. He had spent 18 months in their midst, where they could observe him at close range. They ought to know from their extended observation how Paul lived only for his ministry, that he steered clear of fickleness as well as of stubbornness (cf. 1:17).

Having stated negatively the pitfalls which he is most careful to avoid, he now turns to a positive expression, stating that in every respect he and his associates present themselves as God's ministers. What this means in detail he will carry out in vss. 4b-10. We here note only that ὡς θεοῦ διάκονοι is the nominative case. He might have used the accusative. That would have made the phrase predicative, and the meaning would have been: we present ourselves to be the ministers of God. The nominative makes the statement stronger: We, being servants of God, present ourselves in the manner to be described in the following verses.

The Parenthesis in Verse 2

Lenski thinks that to assume a parenthesis in vs. 2 is derogatory to the style of Paul. "Why let grammar become pedantic and wooden? ...Paul *used* grammar, used it for what it is intended, a flexible and a beautiful medium for expressing thought."* Exactly. But a parenthesis is a legitimate and frequently a highly effective form for expressing a thought. In its form it usually interrupts the regular construction of a sentence. It injects a thought which may be presupposed in the regularly constructed part of the sentence, but might be overlooked if not expressly stated. The parenthesis effectively guards against such loss by oversight, without hindering the easy flow of the main sentence. Think of the highly effective way in which Jesus made use of a parenthesis in His discussion with the Jews: "If he called them gods, unto whom the word of God came—*and the scripture cannot be broken*—say ye of him, whom the Father hath sanctified, and sent into the world, Thou blasphemest; because I said, I am the Son of God?" (John 10:35, 36.)

In the part of our text now under consideration, a truth which is tacitly assumed in the whole discourse and which makes the words of Paul so very weighty is inserted parenthetically into his discourse, in vs. 2, namely, that now the time has come of which the prophets spoke of old, and that Paul's work among the Corinthians is a part of the fulfillment of their prophecy.

---

*) R. C. H. Lenski, **Interpretation of I and II Corinthians** (Wartburg Press, Columbus, Ohio, 1946), p. 1061.

Paul quotes from the Book of Isaiah, 49:8. When Paul quotes from
the Old Testament, he does not look for a word that may serve as
a convenient proof text for some of his statements; he usually selects
a verse which briefly summarizes the thoughts developed in a lengthier
section. In our case we must consider vss. 1-13 of Isaiah 49. Here the
servant of the Lord complains: "I have labored in vain, I have spent
my strength for naught, and in vain" (vs. 4). But he receives the assurance from the Lord: "In an acceptable time have I heard thee, and
in a day of salvation have I helped thee" (vs. 8). His work is outlined in the following words: "It is a light thing that thou shouldest
be my servant to raise up the tribes of Jacob, and to restore the preserved (rather: the desolations; Luther: *das Verwahrlosete*) of Israel:
I will also give thee for a light to the Gentiles, that thou mayest be
my salvation unto the end of the earth" (vs. 6). The section closes
with a shout of rejoicing: "Sing, O heavens; and be joyful, O earth;
and break forth into singing, O mountains: for the Lord hath comforted his people, and will have mercy upon his afflicted" (vs. 13).
Isaiah clearly refers to the times of the New Testament. Simeon borrowed from Isaiah's language in his *Nunc Dimittis*: "A light to lighten
the Gentiles, and the glory of thy people Israel" (Luke 2:32).

Paul could well say: *"Behold, now is the accepted time, behold,
now is the day of salvation"*—and those remarks served wonderfully
to reinforce his exhortation not to squander the grace of God or to
let the grand opportunity slip away. At the same time his extreme
caution in avoiding every kind of offense appears in a new, impressive light.

Verses 4b-10

We have studied the general structure of this section above; it
remains that we now look at a few details.

'Υπομονὴ πολλή, *full endurance,* is required of God's διάκονοι, if
they wish to encourage their hearers not to receive the grace of God
in vain, and at the same time guard against the danger that, because
of their conduct or some neglect on their part, a blame were with
some show of right attached to their ministry. They must show by
their ὑπομονή that the grace of God which they proclaim has fortified
their hearts sufficiently so that they will cheerfully endure any suffering which the enemies may inflict on them, θλίψεις, ἀνάγκαι, στενοχωρίαι,

no matter what concrete form they may assume, whether πληγαί, such as Paul and Silas endured in Philippi, or φυλακαί, such as happened to the same two men in the same place, or ἀκαταστασίαι, such as brought a stoning to Paul in Lystra. Πολλή endurance is required if, in the face of such sufferings, the strenuous labors of bringing the Gospel to the people are to be kept up under dire privations for lack of food and lack of sleep.

Ἐν ἁγνότητι, *in purity*. If any impure motive can be suspected in the διάκονοι of God, this would at once cast a shadow on the message which they carry. The purity of God's grace must be reflected in the purity of the ambassadors' conduct. Their conduct must show also γνῶσις, a *knowledge* based on experience and coupled with interest and confidence. Else they might rightly be told: "Physician, heal thyself." A bald-headed barber's recommendation of some hair restorer does not carry much conviction. In keeping with God's patience and His kindly way of dealing with sinners also His διάκονοι must display μακροθυμία, *long-suffering* and χρηστότης, *kindness*.

In the next group of four the first term, ἐν πνεύματι ἁγίῳ, arrests our attention. All terms used so far denote some characteristic manifested by the διάκονοι of God in their work. Those following do the same. To list the Holy Ghost among them seems incongruous. But does πνεῦμα ἅγιον necessarily mean the third Person of the Trinity? Scripture often speaks of the spirit of a man. May not Paul here be speaking of the spirit in which he performs his work? A διάκονος of God must certainly evince holiness of spirit in his work, a holiness of spirit which is coupled with ἀγάπη ἀνυπόκριτος, a *genuine, understanding love*. A Christlike love must constrain him. Zeal of spirit is not sufficient for a minister's work. It must be a holy zeal, the zeal of a holy spirit, which will proclaim the χάρις of God in the manner dictated by unfeigned love. That is the spirit in which our Savior Himself performed His ministry, and that is the type of work which pleases Him in His διάκονοι. In all sincerity he will employ only the λόγος ἀληθείας, of which the Yea and Amen is in Christ, use it without trickiness or deceit, without resorting to the methods of a καπηλεύων. And himself being an earthen vessel, he will perform his work ἐν δυνάμει θεοῦ.

He will use only the implements of δικαιοσύνη. This is the δικαιοσύνη of which Paul spoke in the last verse of the previous chapter. He said that we are made the righteousness of God in Christ, since

God made Him who knew no sin to be sin for us, by imputing our trespasses to Him and having Him undergo the agony of death in our stead. It is the δικαιοσύνη which Paul had placed in contrast to κατάκρισις, as denoting a declaratory judgment of God, acquitting us of our sins. A διάκονος of God will operate with the implements of δικαιοσύνη, and with them only, on the right hand and on the left. If he added anything to them, that would be conclusive evidence of his secretly being ashamed of the Gospel. Troubled consciences will honor him for bringing them the unadulterated message of God's δικαιοσύνη, while men of a Judaistic bent of mind will heap shame on him. Like the false apostles, they will "smear" him with evil reports, while the true believers will speak well of him. A διάκονος of God will not let any of these things throw him off his straight course of employing only implements of righteousness in his ministry.

The double reception which the Gospel has in the world is given picturesque expression by Paul in a group of seven contrasts, which we may transcribe in a free translation: "As deceivers and true, as misunderstood (*verkannt*) and understood perfectly, as dying and behold, we are very much alive; as chastened and not put to death, as being grieved, but always rejoicing, as abject beggars, but making many rich, as having nothing and controlling all things."

If anyone conducts the Gospel ministry in such spirit of confidence, can he grow weary of it? Can that spirit of confidence remain hidden from his hearers? It is in agreement with the nature of the Gospel, by which in fact it is produced, which is a power of God unto salvation, and proves itself as such on both the preacher and his hearers.

D. PAUL'S PLEA FOR UNDERSTANDING

Chapter 6:11 to Chapter 7:16

Chapter 6:11-7:16 forms the last section of the first main part of Second Corinthians (chapters 1-7). It consists of several subdivisions, all closely linked to each other and closely connected with the body of the entire first part, so that it often is most difficult to draw a clear line of demarcation, as well as to group various smaller parts into larger thought-units.

1. 6:11—7:1

(11) Paul indicates in 6:11 that he is beginning a new section by using the arresting expression: Τὸ στόμα ἡμῶν ἀνέῳγεν πρὸς ὑμᾶς, Κορίνθιοι, *our mouth is open before you, Corinthians.*

To what does Paul refer with these words? Are they an announcement of what he is now about to say, or do they indicate that the previous line of thought has now been completed? In answering this question, a closer look at the tense of the verb may be helpful. The aorist of this verb is frequently used to mark the beginning of an address; e.g., in Matthew 5:2, ἀνοίξας τὸ στόμα . . . ἐδίδασκεν, marks the beginning of the Sermon on the Mount. Similarly the future is used in Matthew 13:35, ἀνοίξω ἐν παραβολαῖς τὸ στόμα μου; also the present infinitive, Acts 18:14, μέλλοντος τοῦ Παύλου ἀνοίγειν τὸ στόμα. In cases of this kind it is clear that the opening of the mouth serves the purpose of uttering the words which are to follow. But in the passage under consideration we have a perfect tense; it is the second perfect active, used intransitively: the mouth has opened itself and now stands open. The act of opening lies in the past and is completed; the result of the action continues in the present. It is difficult to understand such a statement as referring to the beginning of an address. It rather seems to point to an address now completed. Roman orators would indicate that they had come to the end of their speech by saying, *Dixi,* I have spoken. Similarly Paul here writes, τὸ στόμα ἡμῶν ἀνέῳγεν. The new Bauer *Woerterbuch* paraphrases: *Ich habe frei und offen geredet;* similarly even the old Schirlitz: *Wir haben freimuetig zu euch gesprochen;* so also Thayer, "We speak freely to you, we keep nothing back." (The last expression is a good rendition of Wilke-Grimm's *nihil reticemus, verschweigen.*)

We are keeping nothing back, *wir verschweigen nichts*—that is a thought which fits the situation excellently. Some of the trouble in Corinth started from the fact that Paul had changed his travel plans. At least, his detractors made this change an excuse for questioning his sincerity, and then also for casting suspicion and doubt on his Gospel message. Paul did not brush this aside as too childish. He took up the charge, and in a very friendly way explained the matter. He does not make his plans in a careless way, nor does he, on the other hand, stubbornly stick to a plan once he has made it. He is serious in making his plans; but they are always subject to revision by God's overruling providence. In this case he had changed his plans out of consideration for the Corinthians, to spare them (and himself) some very embarrassing moments. Moreover, his personal plans have nothing whatsoever to do with the Gospel which he proclaims. The Gospel is the faithful Word of the faithful God, resting on the unshakable foundation of Christ's redemption.

The fact that he changed his plans is only a minor point anyway; far greater weaknesses may be found in connection with his person. He is an earthen vessel; but this very fact will serve to set forth with all the more compelling force the divine power of the Gospel of Christ. In bringing the Gospel to the people Paul does not, and does not have to, resort to trickery. He is not "selling" the Gospel for personal gain or glory; he is bringing it as healing balm to mortally wounded consciences. If it does not save them, that fact is their own fault because they permitted the "god of this world" to utterly blind their hearts. But this will not induce Paul to change his methods or to supplement the Gospel message in some way in an endeavor to make it more palatable to the people: No, he does not grow weary—an understatement—rather, all the more strenuously, under a constraining Christlike love, will he labor untiringly that the glorious grace of God be not received in vain.

Is he holding back anything? Τὸ στόμα ἡμῶν ἀνέῳγεν πρὸς ὑμᾶς.

The statement receives additional appeal from the address by name, "Corinthians." He is not using words like φίλοι or ἀγαπητοί or τέκνα. An address of that type would be in place if the point were to assure them of his good will toward them. But since he is assuring them of having made a frank statement of his case without keeping anything back, such designations might not seem quite appropriate; a name was in place which would call for their candid evaluation of the facts presented by Paul. The simple Κορίνθιοι admirably achieves that purpose.

(12) On the basis of these facts which Paul frankly discussed in his letter so far, he can now say, ἡ καρδία ἡμῶν πεπλάτυνται, *our heart is wide (expanded, roomy)*. The Corinthians may have felt that Paul had little room for them in his heart; that other people came first and held the first place in his interest and in his affection; that if the Corinthians wished to get into his heart at all, they would find rather

cramped conditions. But Paul assures them that there is "lots of room" for them in his heart. Οὐ στενοχωρεῖσθε ἐν ἡμῖν, *you are not crowded in us.* It simply is not true that you can barely squeeze into our heart, if indeed you can get in at all. The facts which Paul presented in the foregoing chapters rather showed what a warm and vivid interest he took in the Corinthians. His concern for them not only caused him to plead with them not to receive the grace of God in vain; it not only made him postpone his visit in order not to cause an embarrassing situation; nor did it merely make him pass up a splendid mission opportunity in Troas. It also gave him the fullest confidence in them in the most difficult and serious case of discipline which they had on their hands: If ye forgive anyone, I am with you in the name of Jesus.—No, you are not cramped in our heart.

The shoe is on the other foot: στενοχωρεῖσθε δὲ ἐν τοῖς σπλάγχνοις ὑμῶν, *you are cramped in your own feelings.* You imagine that we lack interest in you because you yourselves have allowed other interests to occupy your heart, and thus to crowd into some corner the interest in the Gospel and therewith a correct evaluation of our work and of our concern for your welfare. In other words, our attitude towards you did not change, but your attitude toward the Gospel has become contaminated. You are receiving into your heart some elements which vitiate the Gospel and crowd it and its true messengers out of your heart.

(13) Paul's mouth is wide open; he is holding back nothing. His interest and concern regarding the welfare of the Corinthians is as fervent as ever. Now Paul asks them for a return favor. He motivates the expression by explaining that he is talking to them as to his children, ὡς τέκνοις λέγω. They are his spiritual children. It was he who through the Gospel effected a new birth in them. "Though ye have ten thousand instructors in Christ, yet have ye not many fathers: for in Christ Jesus I have begotten you through the gospel" (I Cor. 4:15). He is now speaking to them as his children in the language of children; and as children they will understand when he asks them for a return favor, τὴν αὐτὴν ἀντιμισθίαν. The word ἀντιμισθία has so far been found only in ecclesiastical literature. In the New Testament it occurs, besides our passage, only in Romans 1:27: "Men with men working that which is unseemly and receiving in themselves that ἀντιμισθία of their error which was meet (ἔδει)." The Second Epistle

of Clement speaks about the sufferings of Christ, and then asks the question: "What ἀντιμισθία shall we give Him, or what *fruit* (κάρπος) worthy of His gift?" (chap. 1:3.) In chapter 9:7,8, Clement calls repentance from a sincere heart the proper ἀντιμισθία which we should give to God who healed us. In chapter 1:5, Clement has the combination μισθὸς ἀντιμισθίας: "What praise, then, or what μισθὸς ἀντιμισθίας shall we give Him (Christ) in return for what we received?" This is the word which Paul here uses when asking his "children" for the fruit or return favor for what he has done for them. He adds the modifier τὴν αὐτήν. Their ἀντιμισθία shall consist in this that they copy him and walk in his footsteps, that they conduct themselves over against him and his Gospel just as he conducted himself over against them. They were not cramped in his heart, crowded into some corner; so he asks them: πλατύνθητε καὶ ὑμεῖς, just as ἡ καρδία ἡμῶν πεπλάτυνται.

(14) In order to achieve this, namely, that Paul with his Gospel have an uncramped position in the hearts of the Corinthians, they will have to throw out some things which they have admitted to a greater or lesser degree by listening to Paul's detractors. Μὴ γίνεσθε ἑτεροζυγοῦντες ἀπίστοις, *do not become mismatched yoke-fellows with unbelievers*. The word ἑτεροζυγοῦντες is easy to understand, but difficult to translate. Lenski's cumbersome rendering is: "heterogeneously yoked up with," while Beza has: *impari iugo copulari*. Wilke-Grimm suggests: *impar vel diversum iugum subire*. In my suggestion above I tried to express the idea of the present participle, which denotes the action of the verb as a characteristic quality of the subject, by translating *yoke-fellow*, while applying the idea of ἕτερος to the situation in the word *mismatched*. The RSV has simply *mismated* for the whole word, thus losing the idea of a yoke; while the Goodspeed Bible says: "Do not get into close and incongruous relations."*

Paul takes the figure of a mismatched yoke-fellowship from one of the Old Testament ceremonial ordinances: "Thou shalt not plow with an ox and an ass together" (Deut. 22:10). The ox was considered as clean, and its meat could be used for food, while the ass was forbidden as unclean. Paul here shows what ethical principle God tried to impress on the hearts and minds of His children by this ceremonial

---

*) The NEB has: "Do not unite yourselves with unbelievers; they are no fit mates for you."

injunction. He will tolerate no unionism of any kind. In itself there may be no wrong in having an ox and an ass join their efforts under the same yoke, but since God had declared the one to be clean and the other unclean, this separation must in no way be ignored or obliterated.

If believers and unbelievers are yoked together in some common venture, it will always be at the expense of the truth. If the unbeliever would accept the truth, he would cease to be an unbeliever. He may vary the shade of his error, but no matter whether it is an error of the deepest dye, or whether it shows only faintly, it remains an error, and error by its very nature is hostile to the truth.

In speaking about unbelievers, Paul does not have in mind some weak brother. The minds of true believers may be tinged with deep and dangerous delusions, but since they are in all humility, prayerfully seeking the truth and are willing to be instructed by the Word of God, they are not unbelievers. The Corinthians knew what to do in the case of weak brethren; Paul had devoted several chapters in his first epistle to this problem. Here he has in mind unbelievers, men who take a firm stand on some error of theirs.

Were they out-and-out unbelievers, men who rejected the Gospel in toto? Paul will deal with the disturbers of the peace in Corinth at length in the last main part of this epistle, chapters 10-13. Thus a more detailed investigation of their particular case must be deferred to some later time. One thing may be mentioned now. In comparing himself with them, Paul points out that they claim to be "ministers of Christ" (11:23). Yes, in their own estimation their work for Christ was superior to that of Paul. Ironically, Paul calls them superfine (ὑπερλίαν) apostles (11:5). They pretended to preach the Gospel in a more perfected form than Paul. But the warning which Paul addressed to his Galatian churches would apply in the present case also: they preached another (ἕτερον) Gospel which is not another (ἄλλο— Gal. 1:6, 7). Paul does not question their sincerity when they claim to preach Christ—they were deceivers who themselves had been deceived—nor does he question their general ability. He does not call them theological nincompoops, but because of the error with which they adulterated the pure Gospel, he calls them unbelievers in spite of the fact that they professed allegiance to Christ.

We can well imagine how difficult it must have been for the Corinthians to swallow this pill. There had come to them men who were devout, who devoted themselves to the cause of the Gospel, who would present the Gospel in an attractive, fascinating way. They themselves felt that they had been greatly enriched spiritually and edified by the warm and eloquent presentation of these excellent apostles. And now Paul bluntly calls them unbelievers, and warns his readers against cooperation with them, not even making an exception for cooperation in externals. Of course, he is not speaking about business affairs, social, economic, or political projects. He is speaking about church work and things that have to do with church work, about which he had said in the previous section that, if offense is to be avoided, then, among other things, it must be done in a holy spirit, with the word of truth, with the implements of righteousness. Hence, any cooperation with adulterators of the Gospel of justification or with violators of the Holy Spirit of the truth must be avoided. Not to do so would result in a mismatched yoke-fellowship with unbelievers.

That Paul is here not ranting against persons, but in holy indignation is denouncing the treacherous errors which they espouse, is clear from his statement of the reasons with which he motivates his warning, vss. 14b-16a. We take them up one at a time.

Τίς γὰρ μετοχὴ δικαιοσύνῃ καὶ ἀνομίᾳ, *what (have) righteousness and lawlessness in common?* Μετοχή, from its etymology, indicates a share in some possession held jointly by several parties: 'to have something in common.' The two states or conditions which, as Paul emphatically indicates by his rhetorical question, have absolutely nothing in common, are δικαιοσύνη and ἀνομία. The δικαιοσύνη is the same about which Paul has spoken repeatedly in his epistle before. It is the righteousness which the New Testament brings us in contrast to the condemnation (κατάκρισις) of the Law. It is the righteousness which we possess by God's imputing the righteousness of Christ to us, whom He has made to be sin for us. It is the righteousness which, in God's estimation, we acquired when in the person of Christ we suffered the agony of eternal death as a punishment for our sins, and yet, under those trying conditions, again in the person of Christ, preserved a perfect faith in God and love to Him. Christ is our righteousness without spot or blemish. There is not a speck of lawlessness or any violation of the Law in Him.

'Aνομία is the direct opposite of Christ's righteousness. Christ with His blood-bought δικαιοσύνη came to abolish ἀνομία. Just as there is not a speck of ἀνομία where Christ's δικαιοσύνη holds the field, so there is not a trace of δικαιοσύνη in ἀνομία. They are mutually exclusive opposites, with nothing in common. If anyone attempts to establish a community between the two, he will only spoil Christ's δικαιοσύνη and increase the ἀνομία.

What if someone insists that the work of Christ must be supplemented in some way, be that, as the Judaizers insisted in the days of Paul, that Christians must submit to Mosaic circumcision in order to secure the righteousness of the Gospel, or be it, as some insist today, that faith must be present before justification can take place, that the requirement of faith, a totally God-created faith, must be met as a term for God to pronounce the forgiveness of our sins on us? He is an advocate of ἀνομία; he assumes that Christ's righteousness is not complete, that the declaration of our righteousness in Christ is not an accomplished fact, ready to be appropriated and enjoyed by us in faith. He insists that something, be it ever so little, is still lacking. Since God declared every sinner righteous in the resurrection of Christ, anyone who maintains that justification does not take place until the moment that faith is kindled, is an unbeliver in the pointed sense in which Paul here uses the word, and he is advocating unbelief, no matter how highly he may otherwise extol Christ.

This is the first point which Paul makes, the incompatibility of Christ's blood-bought δικαιοσύνη and ἀνομία. Inexhaustible patience, ὑπομονὴ πολλή, toward weak brethren, yes, but no mismatched yokefellowship with persistent exponents of even a scintilla of unbelief!

The second reason Paul mentions is: Τίς κοινωνία φωτὶ πρὸς σκότος, *what communion (has) light with respect to darkness?* We notice a little change in the construction. The first question contained two subjects, both in the dative with ἐστίν supplied. The second question has only one subject so expressed, and instead of the second subject it has the prepositional phrase πρὸς σκότος, *in the direction of, with respect to.* The κοινωνία which light offers does not reach out to include darkness. If light reaches out toward darkness, it will do so for battle only, to expel the darkness, but never to give it a share of itself, or to accept a share of it. In this direction there is no κοινωνία.

Light and darkness are metaphorical expressions for life, hope, and joy on the one hand, and death and despair on the other. Christ is the light of the world, and there is no darkness in Him. The devil is the prince of darkness, blinding the eyes of his victims so that even the bright light of the Gospel of Jesus Christ, the Son of the living God, who lives in an exquisite, unapproachable light, cannot even begin to dawn in them. Satan keeps his victims bound all their lifetime by the fear of death, dragging them down into outer darkness, where there is wailing and gnashing of teeth.

What communion, what sharing, either active or receptive, is possible for light and darkness? The Christians through faith in Jesus Christ enjoy the light. And if anyone tells them that they themselves must supplement that light, and if it were only by an infinitesimal fraction of a candle power, he is fusing darkness into their light. But since these are mutually exclusive opposites: light and darkness, life and death, hope and despair, then by an attempt to combine the two the light will be put out and the darkness intensified. There is no yoke-fellowship possible.

(15) As a third reason Paul poses this question: Τίς δὲ συμφώνησις Χριστοῦ πρὸς Βελιάρ, *what harmonious speech of Christ (is there) toward Beliar?* Paul retains the πρός phrase as in the second question, but instead of saying what συμφώνησις has Christ toward Beliar, he changes the dative case to a genitive: what συμφώνησις of Christ is there toward Beliar? The word here used as a name for the devil is a Hebrew word meaning literally *dominus silvae.*

Christ has a very definite φώνησις. He proclaims the Gospel of salvation. And though at times He sounds forth the Law in decisive, piercing tones, He does so in the interest of His Gospel, to reduce the haughty hearts and to prepare them so that His comforting, life-giving Gospel may enter. His word is the word of truth. He never spoke anything else, and even laid down His life in order to establish the Truth. Beliar, on the other hand, is a liar from the beginning. There is no truth in him. The lie is his invention, and when he speaketh a lie, he speaketh of his own.

What harmonious speech is there possible between the two? Can the truth be adjusted to the lie without losing its very nature? If only the slightest ambiguity be introduced into the truth, the latter is thereby corrupted; its very nature is lost.

A yoke-fellowship between truth and error, between Gospel and legalism, would be a thorough mismatch. No joint work is possible, not even joint speaking. There can be no harmony, only shrill dissonance.

Paul started out by denouncing an attempted yoke-fellowship of the Corinthians with confirmed representatives of any form of unbelief as a thoroughly mismatched association, and he supported his verdict so far by three pointed questions. Now he brings the very concepts of faith and unbelief into his next question: ἢ τίς μέρις πιστῷ μετὰ ἀπίστου, *or what share does a believer hold together with an unbeliever?* As citizens of this earth, a believer and an unbeliever may hold many temporal blessings in common, may pursue many interests jointly, but when it comes to the blessings which are specifically apprehended by faith, the situation changes. What faith possesses, unbelief rejects, in whole or in part. What then about a yoke-fellowship under such conditions? If it is attempted, there will result a pulling in opposite directions, because the believer does not hold any share together with an unbeliever.

(16) Paul concludes with the question: Τίς δὲ συνκατάθεσις ναῷ θεοῦ μετὰ εἰδώλων, *what (approving) agreement has God's shrine with idols?* Think of a shrine in which God dwells; think of the service which His people render to Him; think of the rules according to which He demands to be served, and which are in force in His temple. Imagine that people would try to serve the true God in the same fashion as they served their idols. The Athenians tried it and erected an altar to the Unknown God. Although Paul gave them credit for being very religious, yet he denounced their attempted service as one of gross ignorance (Acts 17:23). When Israel in Old Testament times committed similar errors, the Lord rebuked them: "They (their celebrations) are a trouble unto me; I am weary to bear them" (Isa. 1: 14). God's temple has no approving agreement with idols; it stands in irreconcilable, condemning antithesis to them.

We recall once more that Paul uses these sharp questions not against such people as stood in outright opposition to the Gospel, but against such who posed as especially devoted ministers of Christ.

The last question concerning the shrine of God and of idols serves Paul as a translation leading over to a positive statement of a Christian's position before God, with Paul borrowing his language from some Old Testament prophets.

'Ημεῖς γὰρ ναὸς θεοῦ ἐσμεν ζῶντος, *for we are (the) living God's temple.* Paul places a double emphasis on the pronoun 'we,' first by adding the personal pronoun to the pronominal idea expressed in the verb ending, and then by placing this pronoun into the prominent position at the head of the statement: *We,* the believers in the Gospel in marked contrast to all others, *we* the believers as a separate class. There is nothing boastful about this emphasis, as the enemies are wont to insinuate. By pride and boastfulness we would automatically drop out of the class. There is no merit or worthiness in us. We may not even claim that little credit as though we had suppressed our resistance to the Holy Spirit and kept it on the level of natural resistance, not permitting it to boil over into willful resistance. We did not go, as it were, into a neutral position by a proper use of the prevenient grace of God, thereby giving God a chance to see what He could do with us. The emphasis on the 'we' is one of humility and gratitude. We are never to forget what God has made out of us in spite of ourselves, so that we carefully guard against defiling His handiwork.

Since God made us what we are through the Gospel, and since we are blessed as His new creation, can we in any form cooperate with unbelievers of any shade? Can we admit legalism in any degree? Can we toy with darkness, as though it would not destroy our light? Can we expect a symphony if we let a note from Beliar, even though coming from a distance, creep into the Gospel music of Christ? Belief and unbelief have no joint possession, and there is no common ground for God's temple and idols. We as believers are isolated. God has isolated us. We are not of the world because Jesus chose us out of the world.

Humbly and gratefully recognizing the miracle which Jesus performed on us, shall we not most carefully avoid every form of contamination? The very emphasis which Paul lays on the word 'we' tends to make us humble and grateful.

What did God make of us? Paul answers with the word ναός, a shrine, a sanctuary. The tabernacle which Moses erected in the wilderness contained a part called the Holy of Holies, and Solomon's Temple retained this arrangement. This part is the real ναός. In it Jehovah was enshrined (symbolically). It contained the ark of the covenant, covered by the mercy seat, on which stood the cherubim. There God resided for Israel. "There I will meet with thee, and I will commune

with thee from above the mercy seat, from between the cherubim"
(Exod. 25:22). Now Paul says that we believers are the ναός of God,
and adds, of the *living* God, who in contrast to the dumb idols, in
contrast to all creatures, in contrast to heaven and earth, has life in
Himself and is the only source of life, of all life.

With this statement Paul motivates the seriousness of the previous
questions, and now substantiates it by referring to various passages of
the Old Testament. He introduces them with the remark καθὼς εἶπεν
ὁ θεος, *exactly as God said*. Paul quotes from different books of the Old
Testament, but he does not mention the human authors as his witnesses; he ascribes their words to God. It was He who made those pronouncements, using the human authors to record them.

As we noted before, it is not one passage from the Old Testament
which Paul quotes, but he weaves a number of them into his statement, adapting their form to the structure of his sentence. The first
part is taken from Leviticus 26:11, 12, which reads: "I will set my
tabernacle among you: and my soul shall not abhor you. And I will
walk among you and will be your God, and ye shall be my people."
This is part of an exhortation from God in which He reminds His
people that it was He who set them free from their bondage in Egypt,
and on that basis promises them blessings and warns them of a curse
if they violate His covenant. In using this promise Paul does not
specifically mention the tabernacle, nor does he speak of God's pleasure
in His people ("not abhor" is a litotes). Long before Paul the great
Prophet Ezekiel had made use of the same thought in a similar connection: "My tabernacle also shall be with them: yea, I will be their
God, and they shall be my people. And the heathen shall know that
I the Lord do sanctify Israel, when my sanctuary shall be in the midst
of them for evermore" (Ezek. 37:27, 28).

(17) With a διό, *accordingly*, Paul connects his next quotation to
the first one. If God dwells and walks in them, being their God, and
they are His people, this fact must leave a definite mark on their
conduct. Their conduct must reflect their intimate union and communion with their God. If it does not, if they are in the least careless
in their mode of living, they will defile the gracious and glorious
creation of God. The great promise of God will be lost and will be
turned into its opposite.

Borrowing his expressions from Isaiah and Jeremiah, Paul tells his readers some things which they must avoid. First, Isaiah prophesies the salvation of Zion in words like these: "Break forth into joy, sing together, ye waste places of Jerusalem: for the Lord hath comforted his people, he hath redeemed Jerusalem. The Lord hath made bare his holy arm in the eyes of all the nations; and all the ends of the earth shall see the salvation of our God." Then the Prophet continues: "Depart ye, depart ye, go ye out from thence, touch no unclean thing; go ye out of the midst of her; be ye clean, that bear the vessels of the Lord" (Isa. 52:9-11). Paul abbreviates this exhortation into the form: Accordingly the Lord says, "Come out from among them and be ye separate, and touch not the unclean thing." Again Paul stresses the absolute separation.

He says, ἀφορίσθητε. This word may be easily checked. It occurs only 10 times in the New Testament in nine different passages, among them Matthew 25:32, speaking about a separation as absolute as that between heaven and hell. The Judge will divide the people who are gathered before His tribunal and will separate (ἀφορίσει) them from one another as a shepherd separates (ἀφορίζει) the sheep from the goats. In connection with the parable of the net and the fishes, Jesus said that at the end of the world the angels shall come forth and sever (ἀφοριοῦσιν) the wicked from among the just (Matt. 13:49). With this same word Paul now admonishes the Corinthians to separate themselves from the various unclean things which he had mentioned in vss. 14-16a, no matter where such an unclean thing may be found, or to what slight degree it may have contaminated the whole body.

In a similar way Jeremiah had warned the Israelites who were living as captives in Babylonia: "My people, go ye out of the midst of her, and deliver ye every man his soul from the fierce anger of the Lord" (Jer. 51:45).

Paul's chief thought in his motivation for the demand of separation is the truth of God's overwhelming goodness. He placed it at the head of his quotation from the Old Testament, before he introduced a quotation which speaks about separation; and now he concludes the list with a reference to several Old Testament passages which proclaim God's love.

The first is taken from Ezekiel 20:34, which reads in our King James Version: "And I will bring you out from the people, *and will gather you* out of the countries wherein ye are scattered, with a mighty hand, and with a stretched out arm, and with fury poured out." He selects only the second announcement in the words as the Septuagint had rendered it: κἀγὼ εἰσδέξομαι ὑμᾶς, *and I will receive you.*

(18) The second statement Paul adapts from the message of Nathan to David concerning his plan to build a temple. God there speaks about the Son of David, the Messiah. Paul applies the words to the Christians, changing the third person 'his' to the second person plural ὑμῖν, and adding θυγατέρας (from Isa. 43) to υἱούς. II Samuel 7:14 reads: "I will be his father, and he shall be my son." — Not only is the Messiah our Substitute, representing us, so that we are made the righteousness of God in Him, and His blessings become ours, but there are numerous passages in the Old Testament which describe the relation between God and the redeemed believers as that between father and children. We list a few. Jeremiah 31:9: "For I am a father to Israel, and Ephraim is my firstborn." Isaiah 43:6: "I will say to the north, Give up; and to the south, Keep not back: *bring my sons* from far and *my daughters* from the ends of the earth." Hosea 1:10: "It shall come to pass, that in the place where it was said unto them, Ye are not my people, there it shall be said unto them, Ye are the sons of the living God."

As Paul began these promises with a statement from Nathan's message to David, so he concludes with an emphatic declaration from the same message (II Sam. 7:8): "Thus saith the Lord of hosts," which he quotes in the translation of the Septuagint: λέγει κύριος παντοκράτωρ.

(7:1) This verse is connected to the foregoing with οὖν, *now then.* It urges the Corinthians, whom Paul addresses with a winsome ἀγαπητοί, to ponder God's rich promises and to join Paul and his colaborers and all Christians in applying them in their daily life of sanctification.

Ταύτας οὖν ἔχοντες τὰς ἐπαγγελίας, ἀγαπητοί, *having then these promises, friends.* The stress is on *these* and *promises.*

Καθαρίσωμεν ἑαυτοὺς ἀπὸ παντὸς μολυσμοῦ σαρκὸς καὶ πνεύματος, *let us concentrate on cleansing ourselves from every defilement of flesh and spirit.* The verb is in the aorist; hence the stress is on the action as such. The stress is heightened by the emphatic position which the verb here holds at the head of the sentence. By saying σαρκὸς καὶ πνεύματος,

Paul means more than just "outside and inside." Πνεῦμα refers to the spiritual life of the Christians. Also this life may become spotted and stained. A defilement, which apparently affects only the flesh, cannot thus be localized; it will affect the spirit also and defile it. Hence, let us cleanse ourselves from every (παντός) defilement. Only in this way will progress in sanctification be possible.

Paul concludes: ἐπιτελοῦντες ἁγιωσύνην ἐν φόβῳ θεοῦ, *bringing sanctification to its goal in the fear of God*. Ἐπιτελεῖν contains the root τέλος, 'end' or 'goal.' Our sanctification is never completed this side of the grave. It is a constant process, a strenuous struggle with many a setback. But keeping those wonderful promises of God in mind, we shall not despair of our own sanctification, nor pounce on an erring, but struggling brother. We shall continue our endeavors ἐν φόβῳ θεοῦ, in *Gottesfurcht*.

2. 7:2-16

In 6:11f. Paul had assured the Corinthians that they were not cramped in his heart, rather, that he granted them much room. They held a prominent place. He thought highly of them, had a warm love for them, and a deep concern for their well-being. He then asked them for a return favor, that they widen their hearts for him.

In 7:2 he continues the theme: χωρήσατε ἡμᾶς, *receive us*.

Before we take up a study of the special angle of approach from which Paul here treats the relation between himself and the Corinthian congregation, we must take a look at the function which the previous section, 6:14-7:1, has in the presentation of his argument. If this section were omitted altogether, and our present verse, 7:2, were joined directly to 6:13, there would be no apparent break in the continuity of the argument. One might feel, perhaps, that χωρήσατε of our verse is somewhat weak after the strong term πλατύνθητε in 6:13, but otherwise the progression would seem quite natural. This fact has induced some exegetes to consider 6:14-7:1 as a later insertion.

They try to strengthen their theory by pointing to an apparent incongruity. They say that since Paul in the larger section is pleading for understanding and harmony, it is difficult to see how he can in a very unconciliatory, condemning way speak about certain disagreements. Therefore the section must be dropped as an interpolation.

Let us grasp more clearly that it is most proper for Paul, at this place, to warn most sternly against certain forms of "harmony." We bear in mind that he is not pleading for peace and unity as such, as do the unionists of all ages; nor is he pleading for harmony as a personal favor to himself and his associates. We remember that he emphatically told his readers that he is not preaching himself to them, but is only and always preaching Christ to them as the Savior. Thus, in asking for a roomy place in their hearts, Paul has himself and his assistants in mind only in so far as their Gospel message is concerned. He is pleading for Christ.

As far as Christ is concerned, it is always either all or nothing. Christ wants the whole heart; He will not share it with Beliar, nor with any idol. Christ, who came to destroy the works of the devil, will not, and cannot, admit any part of the devil's works to occupy the same heart with Himself. To admit Christ into one's heart means a death struggle against the devil and all his works and all his ways. Hence the section about the mismatched yoke-fellowship of believers with unbelievers is not misplaced. Nor is the case merely such that it may be tolerated where we find it—it is essential. The truth about the unity would not have been set forth with full force and clarity without this antithesis against false unionism, which includes every defilement of flesh and spirit.

(2) Paul resumes the subject which he discussed in the previous section with the plea: χωρήσατε ἡμᾶς, *receive us*. We bear in mind that this is not a request for a personal favor. It is a plea for receiving his message, in fact, a plea for receiving Christ.

The verb χωρεῖν occurs in the New Testament as an intransitive in several shades of meaning (cf. Matt. 15:17; Mark 2:2; John 8:37; II Pet. 3:9). In our passage it has a direct personal object. We briefly list the other passages in which a direct object is found. Matthew 19:11: οὐ πάντες χωροῦσιν τὸν λόγον τοῦτον, ἀλλ' οἷς δέδοται. Christ is here speaking of a Christian's self-control with regard to the sex impulse. It is a special gift of sanctification. He concludes: ὁ δυνάμενος χωρεῖν χωρείτω. Here χωρεῖν is clearly used in a figurative sense (metaphor). A second passage uses the verb in the literal sense, John 2:6, where, speaking about the water jugs, John says they were χωροῦσαι ἀνὰ μετρητὰς δύο ἢ τρεῖς, they *held* about so much. In a sense hanging somewhere between the strictly literal and the metaphorical, John uses the verb in chapter 21:25 of his Gospel. If all things that Jesus did were to be written, then not even the world would be able itself χωρήσειν τὰ γραφόμενα βιβλία (contain and absorb).

This is the verb which Paul uses in his plea to the Corinthians: χωρήσατε ἡμᾶς. He uses the aorist, thus laying stress on the action as such. They simply must receive his Gospel into their spiritual system. In this they must not let anybody or anything stand in their way. What does *receive* mean? The thought is about the same as the one expressed by Jesus in another figure with the word "to eat." He told the Jews: You must *eat* Me, eat My flesh and drink My blood, else you will have no life in you. My flesh is meat indeed, and My blood is drink indeed (John 6:50-55). In the same sense Paul asks the Corinthians to absorb his Gospel message. Let us enter your heart, as food enters your physical system. (In Matt. 15:17 the verb is used of this physiological process.)

Naturally, Paul and his Gospel message cannot be separated. Paul not only proclaimed the Gospel by word of mouth; he lived the Gospel before the eyes of the Corinthians. Hence, instead of merely saying, Receive the Gospel, Paul can say, Receive *us*. And in pointing out the benefits which the Gospel brought the Corinthians, Paul can say that he and his associates brought them these blessings. He reminds the Corinthians of these blessings in the following.

Three points are enumerated by Paul: οὐδένα ἠδικήσαμεν, οὐδένα ἐφθείραμεν, οὐδένα ἐπλεονεκτήσαμεν, *we have wronged no one, we have corrupted no one, we overreached no one.* These are understatements, the double negative in each case making a very strong positive statement to which the Corinthians will agree on the basis of their experience.

We have wronged no one, have done no one any injustice. The Corinthians had the incest case in their congregation. Paul used some very strong language in the matter, both regarding the one who had committed the sin and regarding the congregation, which failed to take steps in order to rescue the erring brother. He roused the congregation to action, to deliver the sinner to Satan. Did he thereby commit an injustice against anyone, or lead the congregation to commit an injustice? The sinner was induced to repent, and in the members of the church faith and love were deepened and strengthened.

It need not be assumed that anyone in Corinth felt as though Paul had wronged them, whether he raised the charge openly or felt only in his heart that Paul's action was an injustice. Paul is not defending himself against any false accusation. He is supporting his plea to the Corinthians for receiving him by reminding them of the treatment which they had received from him, which always had been anything but an injustice.

We have corrupted no one. Against Socrates the Athenians raised the charge that he had corrupted the morals of their youth—and he had to drink the hemlock cup. Paul's work in Corinth had had no corrupting or damaging influence on anyone. Far from it. The Corinthians, even many outside the congregation, well realized what an uplifting in heart and spirit and in conduct the believers had all experienced from Paul's preaching.

We have overreached no one, have not taken an undue advantage of anyone. Paul pointed out to the Corinthians what honor and what financial support they owed to them who ministered the Gospel in their midst. It is the Lord's arrangement that a laborer is to be considered worthy of his hire, and that they who serve the altar also live off the altar. But Paul personally had never availed himself of this rule of God. He had sought neither honor nor financial gain. He had devoted himself to serving them for Christ's sake without remuneration.

On the basis of such experience should they not be willing to receive Paul and his associates, receive them with open arms, with an open, roomy heart?

(3) Paul's effort would be frustrated if anyone in Corinth understood the motivation of his plea as a veiled accusation that the Corinthians had falsely raised such against him, or even had merely suspected him of such dealings. He wards off such misunderstanding of his words by assuring the Corinthians: πρὸς κατάκρισιν οὐ λέγω, *I am not speaking (this) for the purpose of condemnation.* If Paul finds anything to criticize, he will do so frankly and openly, without recourse to underhanded insinuations. Both his plea and its motivation are completely above board; they are to be taken in their natural sense, without reading anything between the lines. He is not condemning the Corinthians, which by way of a litotes means that he is trying to help them, to encourage them.

The real meaning of this litotes Paul points out by referring to something which he already said and which still stands: προείρηκα γάρ. Πρό shows that this is something which Paul has said already at an earlier time; the perfect tense implies that what he said then is still exactly what he means now. In order not to misunderstand his plea as a covert accusation, they merely have to remember his former statements.

He now summarizes: ὅτι ἐν ταῖς καρδίαις ἡμῶν ἐστε, *that you are in our hearts*. Yes, we have you in our hearts, and there you occupy a prominent place; you are not crowded into some corner, as it were. Think of what he had said in 1:6: "Whether we be afflicted, it is for your consolation and salvation . . . or whether we be comforted, it is for your consolation and salvation." Think of his worry in Troas, which prevented him from taking advantage of some splendid mission opportunities (2:12ff.). Think of 4:12 and 15: "So then death worketh in us, but life in you. . . . For all things are for your sakes." And of the last concise statement: "Our heart is enlarged, ye are not straitened in us" (6:11, 12). Paul's heart is filled with love for the Corinthians, with sympathy for their difficulties, with admiration for the Spirit's work in their midst.

You are in our hearts; and this union is a most intimate one: εἰς τὸ συναποθανεῖν καὶ συνζῆν, *in a joint death and joint living*. Here we have to take note of two things, one pertaining to the forms, the other to the position. Συνζῆν is the present infinitive, which connotes duration; the joint living is a continued process, over against the aorist συναποθανεῖν, which merely denotes death as something which takes place, or has taken place, without any reference to duration or to result. Thus death is a momentary, a transitory act, while living is a permanent process. But in both, the momentary act and the continuing process, Paul says, we are inseparably joined together. The second point which we note is that death precedes life. Our joint death has taken place already; our joint life is still going on. We have died with Christ. When the One, Christ, died for us all, then we all died. By believing in Christ's substitutionary death our old self has passed away; we have become new creatures who are now leading a new life in Christ.

Can any union be closer and more intimate than this union which our common death and our common life in Christ has produced in us?

This union is not a beautiful idea only; it is a very real and powerful actuality.

Above, in 6:14, Paul had warned against a mismatched yoke-fellowship with unbelievers. A yoke-fellowship brings two animals very closely together, both in respect to their bodily presence and their efforts in a joint endeavor. Yet, in spite of all that, the union remains an external one. Here, however, we have a union which begins with, not a merely simultaneous, but an essentially identical death, and continues in an identical life. We are all one body, Paul says in another place.

(4) Since Paul and the Corinthians thus are one mind, one spirit, Paul does not have to use veiled language. In fact, to do so would violate the community of death and life which unites him with the Corinthians. He continues: πολλή μοι παρρησία πρὸς ὑμᾶς, *I use much (complete) frankness toward you.* To use veiled language would indicate a lack of confidence on the part of Paul. He, in spite of all protestation to the contrary, would show that he does not feel safe in telling them openly what he thinks, that he fears that both praise and warning or rebuke might be misunderstood. On the other hand, the use of veiled language would arouse suspicion in the hearts of the Corinthians. Where there is a common spiritual life in a common faith and mutual love, there complete frankness is in place; and only there is it possible. Thus Paul asserts and strengthens the community of spiritual life which he shares with the Corinthians and they with him, by calling attention to the complete frankness which he uses in speaking to them.

When we preface something which we are about to say with the remark that we will be frank, we usually mean to prepare our hearer for something unpleasant, for words that will have a rather sharp and cutting edge. We sometimes add an adverbial modifier and say *brutally* frank. Not so Paul. His heart was filled with joy over the fruits of the Gospel in Corinth. Just at that time, as these lines were being written, fruits of a signal Gospel victory were maturing in Corinth, as the whole previous part of the letter up to this point indicates. Paul still had some sharp words to say about the troublemakers, but the congregation had come to its senses. Its spirit had been stirred up to a righting of conditions, as Paul will carry out in the following brief section of the first main part of this letter. His heart was filled with joy, which he could not hold back from breaking forth in strains of triumph.

He says, πολλή μοι καύχησις ὑπὲρ ὑμῶν, I have rich occasion to boast about you, and I am doing much boasting. This boasting naturally concerns the fruits which the Gospel has produced in Corinth, and it is elicited from Paul by the comfort and joy which the recent report by Titus had brought to his heart. Καύχησις is a verbal noun denoting action. It does not stress the cause for boasting or the content of the boasting (καύχημα) but the act of boasting as such. Paul sees so many wonderful fruits which the Gospel has produced in Corinth far above his fondest hopes, that he simply cannot help himself, he must speak about them. He speaks about them before God in his prayers of thanksgiving and before the brethren for their joy and encouragement.

What motivates him in this ceaseless boasting, Paul states in the following: πεπλήρωμαι τῇ παρακλήσει, I am filled (to overflowing) with the comfort. Πεπλήρωμαι is a perfect tense, thus stressing the present condition of his heart. There are no empty spaces left in his heart, as it were, waiting to receive some comfort. No, the comfort which Titus brought to him was so rich and plentiful that his heart is saturated. Since Paul before the arrival of Titus had been troubled by great anxiety and fear, παράκλησις is here best translated with comfort and encouragement.

Paul adds a sentence in which he uses the word χαρά, joy: ὑπερπερισσεύομαι τῇ χαρᾷ ἐπὶ πάσῃ τῇ θλίψει ἡμῶν, I abound beyond measure in the (my) joy above all our tribulation. The simple verb περισσεύω already expresses the idea of exceeding a certain measure. The compound with ὑπέρ reinforces the idea. What a joy it must have been that filled Paul's heart, a joy so overwhelming that only a verb like the compound ὑπερπερισσεύω seemed capable of conveying an approximately adequate idea.

Paul speaks about θλίψις. Remember what he said about it in chapter 1. It was a θλίψις so severe that "we were pressed out of measure, above strength, in so much that we despaired even of life; but we had the sentence of death in ourselves" (vss. 8,9). There must have been various things that troubled Paul and his colaborers, but they were all linked together and formed an unbroken chain, so that Paul here sums up everything in the comprehensive expression πᾶσα ἡ θλίψις. His life, outwardly considered, was one line of never-ceasing tribulations. Remember the section on the "earthen vessels." But the joy caused by the good news from Corinth by far outweighs the tribulation.

(5) With complete frankness Paul in the following verse states the most recent tribulation which he experienced. Καὶ γὰρ ἐλθόντων ἡμῶν εἰς Μακεδονίαν οὐδεμίαν ἔσχηκεν ἄνεσιν ἡ σὰρξ ἡμῶν, *For when we came to Macedonia, our flesh found (had) no rest whatever.* Καὶ γάρ is explanatory. Paul left Troas when he failed to find Titus there. His concern for Corinth drove him on. But coming to Macedonia brought no immediate relief. Apparently Titus had not yet arrived with news from Corinth, and conditions in Macedonia do not seem to have been quite satisfactory. Paul does not mention any details in his brief reference to his arrival, but states summarily that his flesh had no rest.

Note. About the form ἔσχηκεν I am not quite clear. It is a perfect tense, which ordinarily denotes that the action was completed in the past, but that the result of the completed action continues in the present. But it does not seem to be the implied sense in this passage that Paul is still trembling from the shock which he experienced on his arrival in Macedonia. Some manuscripts read the aorist, ἔσχεν, which would fit better. However, there are other cases where the perfect of ἔχω seems to be used as a historical tense, e.g., 1:9; 2:13. Blass-Debrunner, #343,1.2, calls the ἔσχηκα in 2:13 historical, but thinks that the forms in 7:5 and 1:9 may be explained as true perfects. The commentators also differ.

Paul had used "our flesh" as the grammatical subject, which, for all practical purposes, means the same as the pronoun "we." He continues the sentence as though he had written "we": ἀλλ' ἐν παντὶ θλιβόμενοι, ἔξωθεν μάχαι, ἔσωθεν φόβοι, *but being troubled in every respect, battles without, fears within.* What these "battles" were, is impossible to say. In writing about the collection for the needy brethren in Jerusalem (chapters 8 and 9), Paul merely mentions the utter poverty of the Macedonians. Luke, reporting on Paul's visit to Macedonia (Acts 20), sums up his activity in the brief statement that he gave them "much exhortation" (παρακαλέσας αὐτοὺς λόγῳ πολλῷ), but we are left in the dark as to the specific occasion and the nature of the situation. In the verse now under discussion Paul uses the strong word μάχαι.

Paul had left Troas greatly perturbed. He found no immediate relief upon his arrival in Macedonia. His fears continued unabated. If anything, they became more intense, ἔσωθεν φόβοι. There was hardly room for anything else in his heart but fears, fears of the worst kind about conditions in Corinth. We bear in mind that, when Paul went to Macedonia from Troas, his first stop would naturally be in Philippi. That was the first city of Europe in which the Church had been planted. Paul had suffered severe beatings from the Roman lictors and then painful imprisonment in the innermost dungeon. In this city he had also achieved most wonderful victories by his Gospel work. Typical and prophetic was the casting out of the spirit of divination from a maiden. There was the assurance of God's presence in the peculiar earthquake. There was above all the warm reception of the Gospel by Lydia and by the jailor and his house. The relation between Paul and the Philippian congregation had been most intimate from the beginning. This little church was very close to his heart. One might be inclined to think that in such congenial surroundings and company Paul would soon forget his worries about Corinth. No, on his arrival in Macedonia: ἔσωθεν φόβοι. From these remarks the Corinthians had to realize Paul's deep concern for their welfare. What a strong support for his plea: "Receive us"!

(6) Paul's fears were soon to be dissipated. God Himself did it: ἀλλ' ὁ παρακαλῶν τοὺς ταπεινοὺς παρεκάλεσεν ἡμᾶς ὁ θεός, *but God, the Comforter of the lowly, comforted us.* Comforting the lowly is a characteristic of God. Oh, that we would always remember! In the Greek the present participle is used to express the same idea as does the English noun formation in -er: ὁ παρακαλῶν is the Comforter. By the peculiar arrangement of his words Paul stresses both ideas, on the one hand, that God is the only true Comforter, there is no comfort outside of Him; and on the other, that it is characteristic of Him to dispense comfort. He will not leave His children comfortless, but will pour real, effective comfort into their hearts. He is ὁ παρακαλῶν ὁ θεός.

To show how intense was his anxiety Paul speaks about two stages in God's comforting act. First he mentions ἐν τῇ παρουσίᾳ Τίτου, *in the arrival of Titus.* The very fact that Titus finally arrived was in itself a source of comfort for Paul. It meant a relief from the nigh unbearable tension of uncertainty. If things had gone wrong in Corinth,

Paul now at least would get the facts. To know the worst would be a relief compared with the torture of hanging in doubt.

(7) But the arrival of Titus was only the first step and, by comparison with the following, a rather minor and insignificant one. Οὐ μόνον δὲ ἐν τῇ παρουσίᾳ αὐτοῦ, ἀλλὰ καὶ ἐν τῇ παρακλήσει ᾗ παρεκλήθη ἐφ᾿ ὑμῖν, but not only in his arrival, rather also in the comfort with which he had been comforted concerning you. Ἐπί with the dative, in the transferred sense, very commonly denotes the basis on which something rests. In our sentence the pronoun ὑμῖν is not limited to a mere designation of the persons as such, as distinguished from other persons (you, not they or someone else), but includes particularly their attitude, their response to the evangelical admonition of Paul, supplemented by the work of Titus. The reaction of the Corinthians had been a very favorable one. They, with their expressions of repentance and faith, which came from their lips and were confirmed by their conduct, were a rich source of comfort for Titus, and at the same time a secure basis on which his comfort rested. He was comforted concerning them, because of them.

Titus reported about the comfort which he had experienced in Corinth. He evidently could not say all he had on his mind and in his heart in one session. His heart was filled to overflowing. He reported about his happy experience, but there was always more to add. Paul uses the present participle, which always denotes repeated or continued action (compare above on God as ὁ παρακαλῶν). Titus was ἀναγγέλλων, reporting. It was not a cold formal report, purely factual; it was the heart of Titus which was doing the reporting; it was a report saturated with joy and bubbling over with joy.—The nominative of the participle need not trouble us. It is a constructio ad sensum, much more vivid, and much more correct, than if the participle had been stiffly joined to the genitive αὐτοῦ.

Three points stand out in Titus' report: first, τὴν ὑμῶν ἐπιπόθησιν, your longing. After what the false apostles had done in Corinth, the disparaging rumors they had spread about Paul, after the sharp letter which he had written to the Corinthians, Paul could fear that the Corinthians would, at least, be rather cool toward him and his announced visit. No, Titus reported, the opposite was true. They were anxiously awaiting his coming. They were ashamed of their gullibility in regard to his detractors, and they realized that with his warm interest for their spiritual welfare he would give them what they needed most. They were now eagerly looking forward to the opportunity of seeing him again.

This was, indeed, comforting, encouraging news for Paul. He was not catering to anyone for personal popularity. The fact that some of the Corinthians called themselves after his name, he had branded as evidence of fleshly-mindedness (I Cor. 3:3,4). Their longing for him now was a spiritual longing, a desire for the Gospel which he represented and which they had belittled in maligning his person.

Titus reported secondly, τὸν ὑμῶν ὀδυρμόν, *your lamentation*. 'Οδυρμός is used by Matthew in conjunction with κλαυθμός in quoting Jeremiah's prophecy concerning Rachel's wailing about her lost children (Matt. 2:18), while, according to the Nestle text, he omits the third synonym which Jeremiah used in this connection, θρῆνος. Deep grief was felt and was given free expression by the Corinthians about their insulting attitude over against Paul—and, inseparably connected therewith, the loss of the Gospel, a loss which was happily, though narrowly, averted for them by the untiring efforts of the same Paul's self-sacrificing love. Paul will have more to say about their grief in the next section.

The third point which stands out conspicuously in Titus' report is: τὸν ὑμῶν ζῆλον ὑπὲρ ἐμοῦ, *your zeal on my behalf*. Ζῆλος in itself is neutral. It may denote an eagerness either in the direction of good or of evil. To illustrate the latter use, we look at Philippians 3:6. There Paul says of himself: "concerning zeal, persecuting the church." Picture Paul to yourself dragging Christians before the Jewish Sanhedrin, traveling to distant cities to accomplish his purpose of forcing them to renounce their faith and to blaspheme. There we feel the impetuous zeal of Paul's implacable hatred toward the Gospel. To visualize zeal in the direction of good, we picture to ourselves Christ as He cleansed the Temple. This act vividly reminded the disciples of a word in the Psalms: "The zeal of thine house hath eaten me up" (John 2:17).

With their emotions stirred to their deepest depths, the Corinthians concentrated on giving Paul a hearty welcome at his arrival. The Galatians once showed a zeal for Paul when he brought them the Gospel. They were ready to pluck out their eyes for him (Gal. 4:15). The Corinthians now matched the Galatians' zeal.

These are reports which Paul heard time and again from Titus. Did he grow tired of listening to them? Or did their effect gradually begin to wear off? Perhaps at first he listened eagerly, but gradually he merely listened—politely, and eventually he became bored? Not at all. Every day he heard the reports with the same rapt attention and joy. The same? No, with increased joy. Ὥστε με μᾶλλον χαρῆναι, *so that I rejoice the more.*

Ὥστε with an infinitive in the time of the Koine expressed not only a conceived, a possible result, but a result actually produced. Thus Paul here says more than that Titus' report was of such a nature that joy might follow; he says that it actually produced joy in Paul's heart. And he adds μᾶλλον, *more.* The comparative degree points to an increase in the joy. The oftener Paul heard the report, the greater grew his joy. He heard the report with increasing joy.

Will the Corinthians hesitate to receive Paul and his Gospel into their hearts? Will they grant him only a cramped position? Will they expect him to share their hearts with unbelievers? Will they not, just as Paul's heart is wide open for them, in turn open their hearts wide to him?

It seems that Paul is ready to close this part of his letter. But no, he has not yet reached the climax. He has one more point to discuss.

3. 7:8-13a

The content of this section might be summed up under the head:

A painful grief leading to refreshing joy.

Here many questions are raised by commentators as to the nature of the case and the time when it happened. To anyone who is at all familiar with First Corinthians the incest case treated in chapter 5 will readily come to mind. But this does not satisfy a certain type of commentators. A number of them assume a visit of Paul in Corinth some time after he had written his first letter to the Corinthians. They assume that in a meeting during this visit some member of the Corinthian congregation had become exceptionally insulting and abusive toward Paul. This, they say, is the case to which Paul here refers, and to which he had already referred in chapter 2.

This assumption is a pure guess. Nothing of such an incident is recorded in the Book of Acts, nor is there anything mentioned in Paul's letters. Moreover, the sponsors of this assumption do not agree among themselves, so that frequently the hypothesis of one cancels out that of another.

The theory does not affect the exegesis of our passage very seriously, since neither the person nor his offense are mentioned directly, but it does derange the time schedule. If this special visit actually took place, then the six months from Easter (the time of First Corinthians) till the fall of the year (Paul's arrival in Corinth) will hardly be sufficient for all the events that must be crowded into them. Hence the half year is stretched into a year and a half, a procedure which raises more questions than it proposes to solve. Instead of accepting unproven guesses, it will be safer to abide by the assured facts as given in Acts and in Paul's letters.

In vs. 7 Paul closed with a note of increasing joy at the report of Titus. Is that joy now to be marred by a reference to a very unpleasant event which had caused great grief all around? No, even this unpleasant event in its fruitful development and with its happy ending will serve to increase and secure the joy of the Apostle.

(8) Ὅτι εἰ καὶ ἐλύπησα ὑμᾶς ἐν τῇ ἐπιστολῇ, οὐ μεταμέλομαι, εἰ καὶ μετεμελόμην, *For if I also grieved you in my letter, I do not feel bad about it, although I even was feeling bad.*

Paul had rebuked the Corinthians very severely for the way they had acted in the incest case. Instead of grieving over a sin which was frowned upon even by Gentiles, they had been puffed up and had gloried boastfully. Instead of trying to help the sinner to overcome his fault by true repentance, they miserably failed in their Christian duty of love. Paul had told them bluntly: "Your glorying (your boast, καύχημα) is not good"—with a strong emphasis on the "not good."

This rebuke hurt the Corinthians' feeling. Paul says ἐλύπησα. Had he been too severe? Had he, as he expresses it in 5:13, overstepped the bounds of propriety (ἐξέστημεν)? For a time he felt rather uneasy about the tone of his letter, μετεμελόμην. This imperfect is a real imperfect denoting duration. Although it occurs in the prothesis of a conditional clause, it is not the imperfect of irreality. Nowhere does Paul state what would happen if he were still regretting his letter.

What he wants to convey to the Corinthians is the fact that his heart is at the moment filled with joy, although he must admit that for a time he was troubled about his letter. Οὐ μεταμέλομαι he says; and then repeats the statement with νῦν χαίρω.

How does this statement agree with the doctrine of inspiration? If Paul wrote what he wrote, and in the manner in which he wrote it, by inspiration of the Holy Ghost, why should he feel worried about it? If inspiration consisted in this that Paul mechanically took down a dictation from the Holy Ghost, then Paul's worries would have been uncalled for. But Paul's case illustrates the fact that also under inspiration the Apostles never ceased to be what Jesus called them, namely *witnesses* of Him, who were ever to testify the things which they had experienced themselves. They were, as Peter expressed it, φερόμενοι ὑπὸ πνεύματος ἁγίου. The Holy Spirit took them as they were, with all their limitations, with their peculiar vocabulary and grammar, with their knowledge and with their feelings, and thus carried them along to deliver His message. Although the Holy Spirit was the true author of Paul's letters, Paul himself felt fully responsible—and rightly so—for every word he wrote and for the manner in which he wrote it. Let us remember that inspiration is a supernatural process which escapes our intelligence and analysis.

Paul continues: βλέπω (γὰρ) ὅτι ἡ ἐπιστολὴ ἐκείνη εἰ καὶ πρὸς ὥραν ἐλύπησεν ὑμᾶς, *for I see that that epistle grieved you, even though only for a moment.* The γάρ is not found in all manuscripts, but the thought evidently demands it, as is indicated in other manuscripts which changed the βλέπω into a participle, βλέπων. Paul states the reason why his letter had made him feel bad for a time. He is realizing that with that letter he grieved them. It had been only a momentary grief, yet in that moment the welfare of the Corinthian congregation, yes, the future success of Paul's mission work hung, as it were, in the balance. Had Paul's letter been too severe, perhaps just a little too severe, so as to tip the scales on the wrong side? Severity was called for in the case, if the Corinthians were to be brought to their senses, but the danger was that, instead of repenting, they might resent Paul's admonition and become hardened. The admonition was taken in the proper spirit and produced the result at which Paul had aimed, produced it in such abundant measure that the nasty case which had caused all the anxiety was turned into a source of increased joy.

The proper punctuation causes some difficulty. Some publishers inclose the clause βλέπω γὰρ . . . ἐλύπησεν ὑμᾶς in parentheses. Yet it seems to belong more directly into Paul's line of thought. The colon which the Nestle text has seems to separate the conditional clause εἰ καὶ μετεμελόμην too much from the main statement, which it appears to modify. Does the first statement come to an end with the ὑμᾶς, which would be the case if the conditional clause is joined to the preceding μεταμέλομαι? Then νῦν χαίρω would stand there without any connective; and an asyndeton sounds a little harsh. Yet on closer inspection it may appear to be the most satisfactory arrangement of the various statements. The thoughts presented in vs. 8 are grouped about the οὐ μεταμέλομαι as their center. They form a complete unit, and a period should be placed after ὑμᾶς. Then Paul begins a new statement asyndetically. The νῦν χαίρω in a positive way takes up the thought expressed negatively in οὐ μεταμέλομαι. The Greek asyndeton has about the force of our English "I say." Now then, I say, I rejoice. Then follows the explanation: Why does Paul not regret that he grieved the Corinthians? Why does he rejoice?

(9) Οὐχ ὅτι ἐλυπήθητε, ἀλλ᾽ ὅτι ἐλυπήθητε εἰς μετάνοιαν, *Not because of the fact that grief was inflicted on you, but because grief was inflicted on you towards repentance.*

We must pay close attention to the tense of ἐλυπήθητε. It is the aorist, which always stresses the action as such. without any reference to duration or result. In the previous verse we had the statement that Paul's letter caused grief to the Corinthians. Here the active statement of the previous verse is turned into the passive, again with the action as such receiving the attention: grief was inflicted on you. The person who inflicted the grief is clear from the previous verse: it was Paul with his letter. Thus it is not the *grief in itself* about which Paul is writing, but the *inflicting* of the grief. That inflicting of pain had to be done, but it was not done for its own sake; it was not an end in itself. It was done by Paul with an ulterior purpose in mind. That purpose was to lead the Corinthians to repentance, to open their eyes, to bring them to a recognition of the grievous sin into which they had been entrapped, and to extricate them from the snare of the devil.

Now Paul was happy that his method, which is God's method, had not miscarried, neither by a refusal of the Corinthians to be corrected, nor by any inept handling of the case on his part. Repentance had been achieved.

In reading the next remarks of Paul in explanation of his procedure, this fact must be kept in mind that he started with a stress *on the act* of inflicting pain, not on the state or condition of pain, *on the motive* that prompted the act, not on the nature of the resultant pain. This will help us to get a clearer focus on the expressions which Paul uses, and on the lesson which he would inculcate.

Ἐλυπήθητε γὰρ κατὰ θεόν, ἵνα ἐν μηδενὶ ζημιωθῆτε ἐξ ἡμῶν, *For you were grieved in God's fashion, so that you might suffer loss in no respect from us.*

By mentioning the active subject of ζημιωθῆτε expressly, ἐξ ἡμῶν, Paul reminds his readers who the acting subject is also of ἐλυπήθητε. Paul and his associates inflicted pain on them, but in such a way that no harm or loss might result. Pain, yes, but no damage. When Paul inflicted pain on the Corinthians he did so in the spirit and manner of God. In the next verse he will explain what he means by this. Here he merely introduces the new idea with κατὰ θεόν, *according to, along the lines of God.* The chief feature of God's fashion of inflicting pain is the fact that any idea of harm or damage is completely absent. The double negative may be read as an emphatic affirmative: the sole purpose is to rescue them from damage and to safeguard their well-being.

(10) What is ἡ γὰρ κατὰ θεὸν λύπη, specifically, what is the meaning of λύπη in this connection? Γάρ shows that this statement is made by way of explanation. That presupposes that the idea stated in the foregoing, to which an explanation is now to be added, is taken over exactly in the sense in which it was used in the foregoing. Any alteration of the concept itself would spoil the explanation. It would be misleading. Now in the previous verse we have ἐλύπησα, I caused grief, ἐλύπησεν, my letter caused grief, and three times ἐλυπήθητε, you suffered the inflicting of grief. The action stood in the foreground in bold relief. This is the idea which Paul now takes up with the noun λύπη. From the previous verse he also takes over the prepositional modifier. He had spoken about inflicting pain κατὰ θεόν, now he speaks about that κατὰ θεὸν λύπη. Λύπη, then, does not mean a state or condition of the heart of the Corinthians; it refers to an act performed by Paul, its manner, its motivation.

About this manner of inflicting inward pain Paul now says μετάνοιαν εἰς σωτηρίαν ἀμεταμέλητον ἐργάζεται, *it works to produce an unregrettable repentance toward salvation.* Soreness and anguish is not the final aim toward which an inflicting of pain in divine fashion works, though it is a necessary step in attaining it. The aim is repentance, a change of heart, in the direction of salvation. True repentance over a sin, especially a sin such as burned the conscience of the Corinthians, cannot be achieved without grief over the sin. The pain itself has no positive value. When Paul was not sure whether his efforts had perhaps resulted in nothing but pain, he was troubled in his mind. But when the pain is followed by true repentance, then every cause for regret has been removed, μετάνοια is ἀμεταμέλητος.

There is another way of inflicting pain, that is ἡ τοῦ κόσμου λύπη, *the grief of the world.* While in the previous statement Paul had described the λύπη as being κατὰ θεόν, he now shortens the expression to a plain genitive, τοῦ κόσμου. The meaning remains the same, the λύπη of the world is the λύπη inflicted in the fashion of the world. The world inflicts pain for the sake of pain. Hence that sort of λύπη— θάνατον κατεργάζεται, *it effects death.* Note that Paul here uses a compound of ἐργάζεσθαι, formed by prefixing the perfective κατά.

(11) The results of the λύπη κατὰ θεόν, which Paul so far had sketched in very general terms, he now pictures in detail, as they stood out in the action of the Corinthians. He calls attention to the importance of the development, which in the excitement might have been overlooked by the Corinthians. He introduces his remarks with an emphatic ἰδοὺ γάρ, *for see and consider.*

In enumerating the various phases of the process he connects the several terms with ἀλλά. This word here does not express a contrast, but denotes progress. In English we may express the idea with *yes.* The next mentioned result is always greater and more important than the preceding one. For look, αὐτὸ τοῦτο τὸ κατὰ θεὸν λυπηθῆναι, *this very fact of having been grieved in a godly fashion,* πόσην κατειργάσατο ὑμῖν σπουδήν, *what great earnestness it has effected for you.* You were at first very slack in the incest case; now you have dealt earnestly in the matter. Ἀλλὰ ἀπολογίαν, *yes, defense.* You have cleared yourselves in the matter. Ἀλλὰ ἀγανάκτησιν, *yes, indignation,* which now replaces your former unconcern and inattention. Ἀλλὰ φόβον, *yes, fear,* whether you had now done the proper thing properly. Ἀλλὰ ἐπιπόθησιν, *yes, longing,* a true spiritual longing for Paul, to help you if you should happen to be still deficient in some respect. Ἀλλὰ ζῆλον, *yes, zeal,* renewed zeal to hear and live the Gospel.

We notice that the first three steps, earnestness, defense, and indignation, belong together; and so do the second three, fear, longing, and zeal. These two groups of three members each Paul now brings to a head in a seventh step: ἀλλὰ ἐκδίκησιν, *yes, rectifying.* The things in which the Corinthians were remiss before, have now been set right, i.e., not merely amended or corrected, but actually righted in every way.

What Paul means to say by ἐκδίκησις and the six terms that precede he now sums up in the following statement: ἐν παντὶ συνεστήσατε ἑαυτοὺς ἁγνοὺς εἶναι τῷ πράγματι, *in every respect you have established yourselves to be pure with regard to the case.* Ἁγνός is usually followed by a genitive, τοῦ πράγματος, *pure or clean of the case.* But that is not the thought which Paul here wishes to express. They were all involved in the incest case in one way or another. Now that case has been settled completely and properly. The situation is not so much this that they are clean of the case, but rather this that they have become clean with respect to it. Hence the dative τῷ πράγματι. Their handling of the case, after Paul had inflicted some severe pain on them, was highly commendatory: συνεστήσατε ἑαυτούς, *you have commended yourselves.* Your action recommends you as true followers of Christ, since you have so satisfactorily cleared yourselves with respect to that disgraceful case.

(12) From the foregoing Paul now draws a conclusion, introducing it with ἄρα. In classical Greek this illative particle is postpositive, as a rule. In the New Testament several instances are found where it is placed at the beginning of a sentence. Our passage is one such. The meaning is *so then, accordingly, consequently.* Ἄρα εἰ καὶ ἔγραψα ὑμῖν, *so then, although I wrote to you.* This ἔγραψα is not the epistolary aorist, but refers to the letter which was mentioned in vs. 8, and earlier in 2:3. The reference is to the chapter dealing with the incest case and the failure of the congregation to handle it properly in the spirit of the Gospel.

Paul states the purpose of that sharp chapter, first negatively. The Corinthians might think that Paul's chief concern had been either with the guilty offender in the case, or the innocent sufferer, that the one be made to atone for his tort and the other receive some recompense. Paul says, No, that was not his chief concern. Naturally Paul had an interest in bringing the offender to repentance and in adjusting the claims of the one who had been wronged. But these are comparatively minor considerations, far greater stakes were involved: οὐχ ἕνεκεν τοῦ ἀδικήσαντος οὐδὲ ἕνεκεν τοῦ ἀδικηθέντος, *not (chiefly) because of the offender, nor because of the offended one.*

What, then, was his main purpose in writing that stern letter, which caused such painful feelings? Ἀλλ᾽ ἕνεκεν τοῦ φανερωθῆναι τὴν σπουδὴν ὑμῶν, *but that your eagerness be brought out into the open.* Paul assumes that in reality the Corinthians are, and always were, very eager in the Gospel spirit, but that this is not as public as it should be. In what terms he is thinking of this matter will become evident immediately as we hear him explain to what eagerness he is referring, and to whom it should be made manifest. He says, your eagerness τὴν ὑπὲρ ἡμῶν, *your eagerness for us.* Paul is, of course, not looking for a personal partisanship on the part of the Corinthians, in fact, he took them sharply to task when the first traces of that type of "eagerness" appeared in their midst. "Was Paul crucified for you? or were ye baptized in the name of Paul?" (I Cor. 1:13). He is speaking of their eagerness to hear and live the Gospel, which Paul preached.

It is somewhat startling to read to whom that eagerness of theirs was to be shown. Paul says πρὸς ὑμᾶς, *to yourselves.* This is so startling a statement that some manuscripts transpose the ὑμῶν and ἡμῶν above. Instead of reading "your zeal for us" they read "our zeal for you." Yet it is as the Nestle text has it: your zeal for us should become known to you yourselves. In their disturbances and squabbles the Corinthians themselves lost sight of the zeal which in the bottom of their heart was still aglow for the Gospel. It seemed overgrown and stifled by their various entanglements. Paul's sharp letter roused them to their senses so that they became aware of where their true interests lay. If Paul had not written as sternly as he did, they might have kept on in their fumbling, bungling ways until it was too late to make amends. Now they had been set straight, and that ἐνώπιον τοῦ θεοῦ, *before God.*

Paul can conclude this section with the jubilant assertion, διὰ τοῦτο παρακεκλήμεθα, *for that reason we stand comforted.* With the report of Titus about the present attitude of the Corinthians Paul's anxiety was completely relieved, the tension of his heart eased. His fears had given place to a serene peace of heart. Here recall what Paul said in 1:3-7, about παράκλησις.

4. 7:13b-16

(13) The climax has not yet been reached with the παρακεκλήμεθα. Another factor must be mentioned, one which even heightens Paul's joy still more. Ἐπὶ δὲ τῇ παρακλήσει ἡμῶν, *in addition to our comfort, over and above this comfort.*

Paul connects this paragraph to the foregoing with a simple δέ, which, however, is not adversative, nor merely progressive. It introduces a thought which is different from the foregoing in degree. Great was the experience of Paul's heart as presented in the foregoing, but now a still more inspiring aspect of the case must be mentioned, one which carries the aforementioned παράκλησις to still greater heights.

It is this: περισσοτέρως μᾶλλον ἐχάρημεν ἐπὶ τῇ χαρᾷ Τίτου, *more exceedingly (still) we were cheered at the cheer of Titus.* The report of Titus was comforting in itself. But to hear him make his report, to feel the warmth with which he spoke, greatly added to the comfort. Titus did not report in a calm, matter-of-fact way. His heart was in his report. His report bubbled over with the joy which filled his heart and with which he was able to deliver it. Although the content of Titus' report was cheering in itself, the cheer with which he delivered his report added immensely to Paul's cheer, περισσοτέρως μᾶλλον. There is a double comparative in this phrase: περισσοτέρως in itself denotes an unusually great degree, which is here reinforced by another comparative μᾶλλον, *exceeding great by far.* Paul is not exaggerating. His heart was filled with joy, and these apparently hyperbolic expressions just flow naturally from his pen.

He adds a remark about the attitude of Titus: ὅτι ἀναπέπαυται τὸ πνεῦμα αὐτοῦ ἀπὸ πάντων ὑμῶν, *for his spirit is completely at rest from (with respect to) you all.* About himself Paul had said that, when he came to Macedonia, his σάρξ had no rest; regarding Titus he now mentions his πνεῦμα. The conditions in Corinth had deeply affected the spiritual life of Titus. Is the Gospel really the power of God unto salvation? Did the Corinthians so soon harden themselves against the Gospel? Had God rejected the Corinthians and abandoned them to error because they did not receive the love of the truth? His own faith, his spiritual life had received a jolt. But now his spirit was completely at ease. This peace of mind came to him from the Corinthians, from what he had seen and heard and experienced in their midst. 'Aπό indicates the source of Titus' joy, while we prefer to say "with reference to."

(14) Now Paul with a peculiarly tactful turn takes the minds of the Corinthians off their past failures, and thus strengthens them in their present return to sound Christian life. Ὅτι εἴ τι αὐτῷ ὑπὲρ κεκαύχημαι, οὐ κατῃσχύνθην, *For if I have boasted in anything to him about you, I have not been put to shame.* Paul had given Titus the assurance that the Corinthians at heart were sound in their faith, and in spite of their momentary disturbance would without great difficulty find their way back. Paul had said such things and, naturally, could be held responsible for his remarks. That is the thought which he expresses by using the perfect tense, κεκαύχημαι. Now the report of Titus fully vindicated him: οὐ κατῃσχύνθην, *I was not put to shame.* This has the force of a litotes: I have been fully vindicated.

The form of a negative statement, which Paul had employed, gives him an opportunity to continue with an ἀλλά, and at the same time to expand the thought. 'Aλλ' ὡς πάντα ἐν ἀληθείᾳ ἐλαλήσαμεν ὑμῖν, οὕτως καὶ ἡ καύχησις ἡμῶν ἐπὶ Τίτου ἀλήθεια ἐγενήθη, *But just as we spoke all things to you in truth, so also our boasting before Titus turned out to be true.*

Two formal matters must be mentioned here: γίγνομαι often does not refer to an inner change in the nature of a thing, but rather to its outward behavior or appearance, meaning: to conduct oneself. What Paul had said to Titus about the Corinthians did not change its nature from error to truth, but on the basis of the developments in Corinth it manifested itself as the truth. 'Eπί is used with the genitive Τίτου. This makes a judge of Titus. The preposition in such cases means: *before the court of.*

Paul had preached the Gospel to the Corinthians. All that he ever said to them centered in Christ crucified. The false apostles, who had of late come to Corinth, made disparaging remarks about Paul's Gospel as though it were not trustworthy. Paul can now emphatically say that all of it, every word of it, was spoken in truth. And almost as by way of additional evidence he can refer to his boasting before Titus, which had turned out to be true.

(15) Another thing Paul adds to indicate the complete joy of Titus. Καὶ τὰ σπλάγχνα αὐτοῦ περισσοτέρως εἰς ὑμᾶς ἐστιν, *and his heart is* (*goes out*) *to you exceedingly.* Here is that περισσοτέρως again. For the general term σπλάγχνα, *intestines,* the English language prefers the more specific *heart.* The heart of Titus goes out, longs for, and rejoices in the Corinthians, ἀναμιμνησκομένον τὴν πάντων ὑμῶν ὑπακοήν, *as he remembers the obedience of you all.* The obedience of the Corinthians to which Paul refers is their obedience to the Gospel, not submission to Titus (or Paul) personally. It means the faith of the Corinthians. Ὑπακοή is by itself a neutral term which receives its specific meaning in the individual case from the object to which the ὑπακοή is directed. If it is to a commandment, then ὑπακοή means doing what the commandment prescribes; if it is a promise, then it means accepting in faith what the promise offers. Ὑπακοὴ τοῦ εὐαγγελίου is faith in the Gospel message.

The faith of the Corinthians is very sincere. Titus remembered ὡς μετὰ φόβου καὶ τρόμου ἐδέξασθε αὐτόν, *how with fear and trembling you received him.* This was not a cringing before the person of Titus, it was the qualms of conscience because of their recent conduct over against the Gospel. It showed the sincerity of their repentance.

Now Paul is ready for the conclusion. Χαίρω ὅτι ἐν παντὶ θαρρῶ ἐν ὑμῖν, *I rejoice that in every respect I have confidence in you.* He does not say, that I *can* have confidence in you, he says, that I *have.* Confidence is the basic tie that binds hearts together. Where confidence is lacking, there is alienation of hearts. Without confidence true love is impossible.

This confidence fills Paul's heart with joy.

We bear in mind that this is not a natural confidence in man, in his innate or established goodness and reliability. It is a spiritual confidence resting on the power of the Gospel and on God's promise concerning the effectiveness of the Gospel. It is a confidence resting on the faith of people which the Holy Ghost effects, and is itself a gift of the Holy Ghost through the Gospel. Without this confidence all Gospel work would be tedious drudgery indeed, but with this confidence it becomes the source of exquisite joy.

Again: *I rejoice that in every respect I have confidence in you.*

II. THE COLLECTION

Chapters 8 and 9

When Paul met with the pillars of the Jerusalem church to discuss with them the Law-free Gospel as he had preached it among the Gentiles, and when they acknowledged it as in full agreement with their own, then, on the basis of that agreement and in view of the special gift of Paul for the work among the Gentiles, they divided the field. They assigned to Peter the work among the Jews and to Paul that among the Gentiles. Their idea was not to organize two separate churches or church bodies, as is clearly shown by the request which they added that Paul "should remember the poor" (Gal. 2:10). Paul did not have to be told twice; he was very eager to carry out the request. From the experience at the Council in Jerusalem it was evident that forces were at work, though repressed for the time being, which tended to rend the Church in two. The Judaizers kept up their nefarious efforts in the churches which Paul had founded, and the minds of the Christians in Jerusalem were poisoned against him by false reports which were peddled against him. Even his solicitous care for the needy Christians in Jerusalem, the great collection which he had gathered, and the personal presence of representatives from the various Gentile-Christian congregations of his field, could not completely neutralize those reports, as he was soon to see (cf. Acts 21: 20, 21).

In the two chapters from Second Corinthians, 8 and 9, which we are now to consider, we get a clear picture of Paul's warm interest in this part of his ministry, of the evangelical manner in which he conducted the collection, of the goal which he hoped to achieve.

A. ASSISTANCE FOR THE CORINTHIANS IN RAISING THE COLLECTION
Chapter 8

Paul had been busy for some time organizing a collection for the needy brethren in Jerusalem. In I Corinthians 16 he had instructed the Corinthians how to systematize their work. At the same time he had informed them that the churches in Galatia were observing a similar system. In the present section of Second Corinthians he mentions the progress of the work in the Macedonian churches. From the list of representatives of the various churches who later accompanied Paul to Jerusalem to deliver the collection, we see that also the churches in and about Ephesus took part in the collection (cf. Acts 20:4).

In Corinth the troubles which intruders had caused had not only disturbed the relation between the congregation and its founder, but had also seriously hampered the progress of the collection. Indeed, it bogged down badly. If it was not to be a complete failure, then no time dared now be lost in reorganizing it. That is the task which Paul aims to achieve by his plea in these two chapters, and by the measures which he here reports that he has taken.

As long as the disrupted confidence of the Corinthians in their founder was not restored, there was no point in trying to revive the lagging collection. Chapters 1-7 serve to seal the restored relation. Hence Paul is now ready to tackle the second task.

1. 8:1-6

(1) He does so by emphatically calling the attention of the Corinthians to the success of the collection in Macedonia. The verb γνωρίζομεν stands at the head, not only of the sentence, but of the entire section: Γνωρίζομεν δὲ ἡμῖν, *We make known to you*. Δέ is merely transitional. The important thing is that Paul has great news, good news, impressive news for the Corinthians. He calls them ἀδελφοί. This news concerns them, not as interesting items about some strangers, but as of people who are involved in the same business, as of members of the same spiritual family.

Paul is beginning to report on the progress of the collection in Macedonia. It was to be a joint endeavor in the nature of a service rendered by the Christians to needy brethren. Yet the word διακονία,

or some similar expression, does not occur until verse 4. Paul opens
the discussion by placing the whole section under the head of χάρις,
grace. The collection, the participation in the collection, must be
viewed as part and parcel of the grace of God which the Christians
had experienced and were continuing to experience. The success of
the collection is not produced by their personal effort; it is God's
grace alone which does it. Paul does not even say that it is the Christians' response to the grace of God; grace itself is the active factor.
The Christian donors are really on the receiving end.

Paul underscores this thought by calling this grace a gift, τὴν δεδομένην. He does not use a word like ἐργατικός, 'effective,' 'operative.'
He does not intend to report on God's grace as a productive force,
but as a gift. Were the Corinthians aware that by taking part in the
collection they were really becoming the beneficiaries of a gift from
God? We may safely assume that their Old Adam was as wise in such
matters as is our own. They figured that they were doing something;
they were imposing a loss on themselves. They may well have been
startled when they read τὴν δεδομένην. But once they assimilated this
truth, it made them desirous of ever more grace, even though it came
to them in the form of a request for a donation. It is God's nature
to give; and by His grace His children have the same nature.

(2) In the next verse Paul paints, in a few bold strokes, a vivid
picture of God's grace which was found as a gift in the congregations
of Macedonia. Ὅτι ἐν πολλῇ δοκιμῇ θλίψεως ἡ περισσεία τῆς χαρᾶς αὐτῶν
καὶ ἡ κατὰ βάθους πτωχεία αὐτῶν ἐπερίσσευσεν εἰς τὸ πλοῦτος τῆς ἁπλότητος αὐτῶν, *that in a full test of tribulation the abundance of their
joy and their bottomless poverty overflowed into a rich development
of their singleness (of purpose)*.

The high point of this statement is ἁπλότης. The King James Version
translates "liberality," while Luther correctly has *Einfaeltigkeit*. The
original meaning of the word is "simplicity," and it is very difficult
to trace a line from that starting point to the idea of "liberality." No
one, to my knowledge, has so far succeeded in doing it. Moreover,
it will be extremely difficult to find a passage in the New Testament
which forces that understanding.

First of all, let us look at our own text. Paul is extolling the grace
of God, which was present as a gift in the churches of Macedonia,
and which manifested itself in connection with the collection. Later in

this section he will also have something to say about the amount of everyone's contribution; but then he uses a different word, εὐλογία, 'a blessing,' in contrast to πλεονεξία, 'stinginess.' When speaking about the amount, he compares the collection to a sowing for a harvest, and speaks of sowing ἐπ' εὐλογίας, in contrast to sowing φειδομένως, 'sparingly' (9:5, 6). In our present passage he speaks of ἁπλότης, without any hint that he is deviating from its original meaning. Christians have but one aim in life, and on the achieving of that aim their heart is set.

Moreover, Paul is speaking of a richness, a rich development of this ἁπλότης. Does that thought force us to abandon the original meaning of ἁπλότης? Not in the least. Rather, it would seem to agree better with the idea of singleness of purpose.

And when we look at the two factors which, with their combined force, served to produce that wonderful increase of ἁπλότης, it may strike us as peculiar that the one of them should be mentioned at all as a source of liberality. Paul refers to the bottomless poverty of the Macedonians. From the joy in the Gospel, which they experienced in their hearts along with deep poverty, and from that poverty—and, shall we say, from their victory over its temptations?—the Macedonians learned the lesson that "One thing is needful." They discarded all doubts, all double aims, all divided interests, and concentrated on the one thing needful. They, or better, the grace of God, developed in them this singleness of purpose.

The new *Greek-English Lexicon of the New Testament* (Arndt-Gingrich) lists, besides our passage, also 9:11, 13, as using ἁπλότης in the sense of liberality. The verses occur close to the end of our present section. A detailed study must be deferred to a later time. Only one remark at present. There Paul says that the Christians in Jerusalem, the recipients of the present collection, will glorify God because of the ἁπλότης of the Corinthians' fellowship towards them and *toward all*, καὶ εἰς πάντας. Did the Corinthians take up a collection for all Christendom? But this collection demonstrated the fact that all Christians are of one heart and of one soul, so that when one member suffers, all members suffer with it.

One more passage is adduced, Romans 12:8: "He that giveth, let him do it with simplicity." The new Lexicon suggests "liberality." St. James has a word on God's giving, which we may well compare here:

"God giveth to all ἁπλῶς, and upbraideth (ὀνειδίζω, *reproach*) not" (James 1:5.—Cf. Luther's translation: *Gott . . . gibt einfaeltiglich und ruecket es niemand auf.*) When anyone is elected to administer the alms of a congregation, he should simply give to the needy without "rubbing it in" to the recipient, or making him feel that he is a burden on the congregation. The King James translation of ἁπλῶς, 'liberally,' is not called for by the context. The St. James passage is the only one where the adverb ἁπλῶς occurs in the New Testament.

We now take a brief look at the other terms used in vs. 2. Paul speaks about a δοκιμή through which the Macedonians passed. Δοκιμή means more than a mere testing. The new *Greek-English Lexicon* has this definition in single quotes: 'the quality of being approved.' The German word *Bewaehrung* conveys about the same idea as the Greek δοκιμή. It means that a test is imposed and that the person, or thing, that was subjected to it passed it successfully, demonstrating his (or its) genuineness. The Macedonians won their laurels in πολλὴ δοκιμή. It was a severe test which they passed with flying colors.

It had been a test of θλίψις, *affliction*. We are not told in what the affliction consisted. About the Thessalonians we know that the Christians there suffered from their own unbelieving relatives (I Thess. 2:14); and Philippi was a Roman colony, settled by Roman ex-soldiers, where the citizens frequently out-Romed the Romans. But since we have no direct information on the nature of the θλίψις, we can say no more than that it was very severe, and that thus in a grand way it proved the character of the Macedonian Christians.

In this δοκιμή two characteristics stood out prominently, one was ἡ περισσεία τῆς χαρᾶς, *the abundance of their joy*. The peace of heart and the happiness which they enjoyed on the basis of their justification proved stronger than the severe θλίψις; their θλίψις merely served to clarify and strengthen it, and to set forth its real character. Their θλίψις set off the chain reaction which Paul describes in Romans 5: "Tribulation worketh patience; and patience, experience; and experience, hope; and hope maketh not ashamed" (vss. 3-5).

The other characteristic which stood out in bold relief in their affliction, and probably was greatly intensified by it, was ἡ κατὰ βάθους πτωχεία, *their bottomless poverty*. Κατὰ βάθους literally: 'down to the depth.' Πτωχεία by itself means the poverty of a beggar. A πένης is a poor man who owns no property, but must support himself by his labors, living from hand to mouth; but a πτωχός has not even that much. He is forced to beg, and is dependent on alms for a living. That was the kind of poverty which the Macedonians experienced, and in their case there was no bottom to it.

This poverty, however, did not interfere with their χαρά. Rather, both their πτωχεία and their χαρά were welded into one to produce a wonderful result. Note the singular of the verb ἐπερίσσευσεν with the double subject of χαρά and πτωχεία. This combination helped the Macedonians to concentrate their hearts and minds on the one thing needful.

(3) How did this singleness of purpose manifest itself in the matter of the collection? The verb of the main clause in the sentence beginning in vs. 3 is ἔδωκαν (in vs. 5). It is an aorist, summarizing the action of the Macedonians: *they gave*. Yes, they gave to the collection, but that was not the first thing they did. It was preceded by a far more important act of giving. Paul uses the adverb πρῶτον. The first thing they did was to give ἑαυτούς, *themselves*. They gave themselves τῷ κυρίῳ, *to the Lord*. This is a graphic description of faith. They gave themselves to the Lord with all their sins for justification. They also gave themselves, in the same act, to the Lord with all their thoughts, their emotions, their desires for sanctification. They did this in their ἁπλότης, without any reservations, without any division of loyalty.

They were not perfect in this. What Paul confessed of himself: "Not as though I had already attained," could be said of them also. Nor were they spared the difficulties of which Paul complains in Romans 7. We remember what Paul said in the previous chapter of the present epistle about his arrival in Macedonia: "Our flesh had no rest, but we were troubled on every side: without were fightings, within were fears" (vs. 5). There was no perfection.

There is another angle to this giving of the Macedonians. Paul says that they gave themselves to the Lord καὶ ἡμῖν διὰ θελήματος θεοῦ, *and to us by the will of God*. This was not a second act of giving, it was done in one and the same act with the giving of themselves to God. It was not an act of personal allegiance. Paul never sought a personal following; in fact, he severely rebuked the Corinthians for using his name as a party label: "For while one saith, I am of Paul; and another, I am of Apollos: are ye not carnal?" (I Cor. 3:4).

In recommending the Macedonians for giving themselves to Paul and his associates, Paul has his office in mind, as he indicates by the phrase διὰ θελήματος θεοῦ. They gave themselves to Paul because they recognized in him a God-appointed representative and administrator of the Gospel. They could not give themselves to God if they ignored Paul; nor could they give themselves to Paul under these conditions without giving themselves to the Lord.

Paul leads up to this grand statement by a number of steps which, grammatically considered, are modifiers of the verb ἔδωκαν. The first is κατὰ δύναμιν, μαρτυρῶ, καὶ παρὰ δύναμιν, *according to ability, I testify, and beyond ability.* This phrase calls for no further elucidation. The second modifier is αὐθαίρετοι, in predicative apposition to the subject. The word is composed of αὐτός and a form of αἱρέομαι, meaning that they themselves did the choosing; they took the initiative, acted entirely by their own choice, quite voluntarily.

(4) The third modifier even hints that Paul or his associates did some dissuading: μετὰ πολλῆς παρακλήσεως δεόμενοι ἡμῶν, *with much urging, begging of us.* Note that not the collectors but the contributors did the begging, δεόμενοι. Note that they were insistent, μετὰ παρακλήσεως. Note that their pleading was repeated and very solemn, πολλή. How did they regard the thing for which they were pleading? Paul repeats the word which he used at the very beginning, τὴν χάριν. They realized that in doing their giving, even under the adverse conditions imposed on them by their extreme poverty, they were not imposing a burden on themselves; they were enriching themselves spiritually, being steeped deeper into God's grace. It would mean for them a new experience of grace.

Grace is a general term. The specific grace for which they pleaded in this case meant τὴν κοινωνίαν τῆς διακονίας τῆς εἰς τοὺς ἁγίους, *the fellowship of this service to the saints.* The needy Christians in Jerusalem are called saints, not as though they constituted a special class of Christians by themselves; but because the whole Church is composed of people whose sins have been forgiven, whom God embraces as His holy children for the sake of Christ, whom they have put on in faith. To be permitted to minister to people to whom God Himself has already rendered the greatest service by sacrificing His only-begotten Son for them—that is grace indeed.

What is the κοινωνία τῆς διακονίας? Superficially considered, κοινωνία might here be translated with participation, a taking part. A gift is being served to the Christians in Jerusalem, and the Macedonians ask to be let in on it, to participate in the giving. This διακονία was not common relief work; it was very pointedly directed to fellow believers (in Jerusalem). A fellowship, created by the Holy Ghost, existed between Christians everywhere, whether they lived in Macedonia, or in Achaia, or wherever it might be, with those in Jerusalem. The present collection was a manifestation of that fellowship. By taking part in the collection, whether on the giving or on the receiving end, this fellowship was in evidence. Some gave their gift as an expression of the existing bond, and the others accepted the gift in the same spirit.

(5) Paul adds one more modifier. The attitude of the Macedonians by far exceeded his fondest expectations, καὶ οὐ καθὼς ἠλπίσαμεν, *and not as we had hoped*. Paul knew how firmly the Philippians, one of the Macedonian churches, were rooted in the Gospel. In his letter to them he speaks about their κοινωνία εἰς τὸ εὐαγγέλιον from the very first day (Phil. 1:5). The struggle with the problem of irregularities in Thessalonica (the second church in Macedonia) cannot but have had a beneficial influence on the spiritual understanding of both the leaders and the membership of the group. The Bereans, the third Macedonian congregation, had been very "noble" from the beginning. Paul knew that he could expect much from these churches. Yet his fondest hopes were left far behind by the spirit which he now actually found.

(6) What was Paul's reaction? And why did he write all these things to the Corinthians? He wanted the Corinthians to share the blessed experience. They should be enriched with the same grace; their ἁπλότης should be confirmed and deepened. Though not at present passing through the same test of affliction and extreme poverty, but emerging from a terrific spiritual struggle, their appreciation of the blessings afforded by the fellowship with the saints should be stimulated by this novel experience.

Thus his immediate reaction was εἰς τὸ παρακαλέσαι ἡμᾶς Τίτον, *that we urged Titus*. Titus had just returned from Corinth, where Paul had sent him to help the church rectify the sorry situation which the false apostles had caused. Titus never grew tired of repeating his rosy report. Titus may have undertaken the trip to Corinth with a heavy heart, but the response which he met had set his mind completely at ease, ἀναπέπαυται τὸ πνεῦμα αὐτοῦ ἀπὸ πάντων ὑμῶν (7:3).

The work which Titus had done in restoring the Corinthian congregation was of a general nature, repairing the damage which had been done and getting the Corinthians back on a straight course. Although the matter of the collection, which had suffered along with other church work, had been corrected in a general way with the help of Titus, it had not been given special attention. Now time was running out fast, and something special had to be done if the collection in Corinth was not to be a failure. Titus had done good work in Corinth. He was trusted and respected by the Corinthians; his heart was filled with glowing enthusiasm for the Corinthians. It was natural for Paul to think of Titus as the logical man for the task. He urged him to return to Corinth.

What was his special assignment? Ἵνα καθὼς προενήρξατο οὕτως καὶ ἐπιτελέσῃ εἰς ἡμᾶς καὶ τὴν χάριν ταύτην, that, just as he had already begun, so he should also complete for you also this grace. The groundwork for the collection had been done in the previous year, and in a general way the collection had gotten under way again during Titus' stay in Corinth. This is contained in the προενήρξατο. What remained was that the collection be brought to a speedy and successful finish. This is contained in the καί, also, before the ἐπιτελέσῃ. The καί before τὴν χάριν singles out this grace as the object of special attention, that he also finish particularly this grace.

Is not the sending of Titus for this special task actually implying a lack of confidence on the part of Paul both in the reliability of the Corinthians and in the thoroughness of the work of Titus? And will not such an attitude of Paul doom the new mission of Titus to failure even before it gets under way? Paul explains the meaning of Titus' visit in the following section.

2. 8:7-15

The meaning of Titus' mission is not that the Corinthians were not able or willing to carry out the collection themselves, or that Paul had to order them to do the proper thing. The thought of being lord over this or any part of their sanctification was as foreign to Paul's mind as was the thought that he was lord over their faith (cf. 1:24).

(7) He reminds them first of their spiritual riches. 'Αλλ' ὥσπερ ἐν παντὶ περισσεύετε, *But just as you abound in every respect.* Paul begins with ἄλλα. To what do the thoughts which he will now present form a contrast? The best assumption seems to be: against a possible misunderstanding of Paul's motives, as briefly indicated above. There is no lack of confidence implied in Titus' mission; the purpose is rather to aid the Corinthians in a certain point in which special help may be needed just now, and thus would be welcomed by the Corinthians.

The Corinthians abound in every respect. Paul enumerates five points, naming first three spiritual blessings in singular nouns without any modifiers, then points four and five in increasingly longer phrases. (Ἐν) πίστει καὶ λόγῳ καὶ γνώσει. The Corinthians have faith. Their faith had been threatened by the work of false apostles, and they had been wavering, on the verge of yielding to the ingratiating words of the seducers. But the danger was averted, their faith has been reestablished. Τῇ γὰρ πίστει ἑστήκατε, Paul had said at the close of the first chapter (1:24).

They abound also in λόγος. They know how to confess their faith, and they are willing to do so. They abound in this point. We remember how highly they prized the gift of tongues. They had not shown proper judgment in the evaluation of the various gifts of the Spirit. The special glamor that attached itself to the somewhat spectacular gift of tongues had warped their minds and had led to an overuse, if not abuse, of this gift. But that mistake now seems to have been corrected. They abound in the proper confession of their faith.

And they abound in γνῶσις, not only in the correct understanding with the intellect, but in the actual living experience of the heart. When they confess their faith, this is not a confession of the mouth only, but an expression of the blessings which their heart has found in the Gospel.

To these three Paul now adds as the fourth (ἐν) πάσῃ σπουδῇ. There is not only a willingness, but complete eagerness to live their faith. From First Corinthians we see that there were many flaws in the Corinthians' conduct, both in their personal lives and in their church practice. This had been changed. Their practice certainly was not yet 100 per cent clean, but they were striving for improvement in every way with all eagerness.

In the fifth point the Nestle text does not seem to be correct. A variant reading, which also Jerome used for the Vulgate, seems preferable. The corrected text would read: καὶ τῇ ἐξ ὑμῶν ἐν ἡμῖν ἀγάπῃ, *and in the love from you on us.* In the previous four parts it was always some characteristic of the Corinthians which Paul mentioned, it was *their* faith, *their* confession, *their* gnosis, *their* eagerness: why should he in the last point suddenly speak about the apostles' love? Moreover, it was the Corinthians' love toward Paul that had become shaky. The Corinthians may have unjustly doubted Paul's love momentarily; but by that very act their own love had come under a cloud. But that had been remedied. They had dropped their suspicions, and their hearts were again filled with warm love toward their apostle. It was ἀγάπη, an understanding, purposeful love. They again acknowledged Paul as their God-sent apostle, and were ready and happy to receive his instruction.

Since they abound in these five important basic points, Paul is now sending Titus to them for the purpose ἵνα καὶ ἐν ταύτῃ τῇ χάριτι περισσεύητε, *that you may also abound in this grace.* We quoted and translated this ἵνα clause as a clause of purpose. In reality that is not quite correct. In form it is a clause of purpose, but this here takes the place of an imperative. Paul's meaning is: As you abound in faith, etc., so abound also in this grace. But why then did he not write just so? The Greek sentence would have been subject to misunderstanding. The imperative would be περισσεύετε. But that form could also be read as the indicative, and might easily be read so in line with the previous five indicatives. His words would then be understood to say: As you abound in faith etc., so you also do abound in this grace. In order to insure the understanding of an exhortation, Paul chose the form of a ἵνα clause (used for commands in colloquial Greek; Blass-Debrunner, 387, 3. Compare the German form of a command: *Dass ihr mir aber, usw.*) Paul again uses the term χάρις, and he is concerned to see the Corinthians abound in it.

(8) The somewhat brusque form of a command must not be misunderstood. It is not meant as an order from a master, but as an expression of Paul's concern for the Corinthians. He continues, Οὐ κατ' ἐπιταγὴν λέγω, *I do not say this by command.* In what sense, then, is he speaking? He answers, δοκιμάζων, *testing* your love and giving you a chance to prove its genuineness. In connection with δοκιμάζων we

must repeat what was mentioned above about δοκιμή, vs. 2. Paul does not say that he is putting their *love* to a test, but says, τὸ τῆς ὑμετέρας ἀγάπης γνήσιον. Τὸ γνήσιον is the neuter of the adjective, here used for the abstract idea: *the genuineness*. This Paul is putting to a test in order to give the Corinthians an opportunity to prove it, and in the sure expectation that they will welcome the opportunity and will pass the test with flying colors.

(9) He is using the rich experience of the Macedonians as a touch-stone, as an incentive. Διὰ τῆς ἑτέρων σπουδῆς, *by the eagerness of others*. The Macedonians found great joy in Christ, which even their bitter afflictions could not dim, which rather became all the more intensive in their victory over their trials. The Corinthians have the same Christ, and have tasted His love, though their trials outwardly were different from those of the Macedonians. Γινώσκετε γὰρ τὴν χάριν τοῦ κυρίου ἡμῶν, Ἰησοῦ Χριστοῦ, *For you know the grace of our Lord Jesus Christ*. The grace of our Lord Jesus Christ had been pro-claimed to them, and they had found peace and joy in the message. And although this heavenly rest in their hearts had been seriously disturbed, and they had passed through bitter spiritual struggles, they had found their way back to the knowledge of Christ and His grace. The Sun of Righteousness was again beaming on their hearts "with healing in his wings." Yes, they knew the grace of our Lord Jesus Christ.

Paul now pictures this grace of Christ in words suggested by the topic under discussion, the collection for needy saints: ὅτι δι᾽ ἡμᾶς ἐπτώχευσεν πλούσιος ὤν, *that for your sake He became (beggarly) poor although He is rich*. Christ became poor. This does not refer to the incarnation as such; that was merely a preparatory step en-abling Him to become poor. Even after the incarnation He was in the form of God; but because He did not consider it as ἁρπαγμός, some-thing to be displayed jealously at all times, namely, to live on an equal footing with God, He emptied Himself and took on the form of a servant (Phil. 2:6, 7). The fact of the exinanition Paul here expresses with the word ἐπτώχευσεν. The Macedonians experienced a κατὰ βάθους πτωχεία, but that was nothing by comparison with the πτωχεία to which Christ lowered Himself. That took Him down to death, yes, the death on the cross, to the πτωχεία of being forsaken by God (Phil. 2:8).

Why did Christ do it? Δι' ὑμᾶς, *because of you, for your sake.*
We may say, In your stead. Paul continues, ἵνα ὑμεῖς τῇ ἐκείνου πτωχείᾳ
πλουτήσετε, *in order that you (yes, you) by means of His poverty
should become rich.* By using the personal pronoun ὑμεῖς Paul stresses
the fact that the redemption procured by Christ is not a thing merely
made ready for us, to which we then help ourselves; it is not a redemption procured for the world in a lump payment, but it is a very
personalized, individual affair. Christ took the poverty of every individual sinner upon Himself, and with His grace bought back and
brought back the riches of heaven for every individual sinner.

We might ask the question, When is the ingressive aorist, πλουτήσετε,
to go into effect? In other words, Do we become rich in the moment
we come to faith? In the moment a sinner comes to faith he becomes
aware of his riches, but his riches were a fact, and were declared in
the moment when Jesus cried, "It is finished."

Paul introduces this sentence with γάρ, *for, since, because.* Because
you are tasting the saving grace of Christ and are rejoicing in its
riches, namely, the full pardon which He has won for you, you will
welcome the opportunity of exercising and proving the sincerity of
your love.

When Paul saw the unexpected success of his collection for the
needy Christians in Jerusalem as it developed in the churches of Macedonia, and remembered how this same collection had bogged down
in Corinth because of the disturbance stirred up there by the troublemakers, he immediately dispatched Titus to Corinth to "finish in you
the same grace also." In explaining this move to the Corinthians, Paul
very carefully warded off the false impression as though he were
giving orders to them. He is not speaking κατ' ἐπιταγήν; he is merely
δοκιμάζων the genuineness of their love, giving them in this way an
opportunity to prove its genuineness in action.

(10) In the subsection which is before us now he adds καὶ γνώμην ἐν
τούτῳ δίδωμι, *and in this I am giving (you) an opinion.* He is here
adding a new thought, yet one that pertains to the same matter which
he discussed in the previous verses. While he had stated his first
motive in a participle, δοκιμάζων, he elevates the present point to a
main clause. There is no specific, easily recognizable antecedent to
τοῦτο. It may refer to Paul's action as just outlined by him, or perhaps
to the whole matter of the collection as far as the Corinthians are

concerned. For practical purposes both assumptions come out to the same thing, since Paul's present action is concerned specifically with the collection. Thus τοῦτο points to the collection and to Paul's sending of Titus with respect to it.

In all this he is giving them his γνώμη. This word occurs several times in the New Testament. We look at a few cases. In I Corinthians 1:10 Paul urges the congregation, which stood in danger of a rupture into a number of splinter groups, to be joined together in the same νοῦς and in the same γνώμη. As νοῦς denotes an attitude of the mind, so must γνώμη, which is added to complete the concept. When Paul in Corinth became aware of a plot of the Jews against his life, who intended to assassinate him as he boarded his ship for Syria, then he ἐγένετο γνώμης to travel by way of Macedonia (Acts 20:3). Here γνώμη indicates a planning, a decision. Paul desired to keep his convert Onesimus with him as his assistant, but since Onesimus was still the slave of Philemon, he would not do it χωρίς his γνώμης, without his express consent (Philemon 14). In I Corinthians 7:25 we find the same combination which we have in our text: γνώμην διδόναι, to render an opinion, or, as Jerome translates in both instances, *consilium do,* I give you a piece of advice.

Paul's action, which might easily be misunderstood as a command, but was intended as an assistance in a welcome test of their genuine love, really is of such a nature that it must be called a counsel or advice. Paul points this out by connecting the next sentence to the foregoing with γάρ, 'since,' or 'for.' Τοῦτο γὰρ ὑμῖν συμφέρει, *For this is helpful to you, profitable, advantageous.* Paul wants to say that he is aware of a certain aim of the Corinthians in regard to the collection, and by sending Titus to them at this time he will help them to achieve it more readily. The form of the relative which he uses is meaningful and revealing: οἵτινες. The antecedent is ὑμῖν. A plain relative, οἵ, would have done no more than link the following statement to the Corinthians (ὑμῖν) as being the grammatical subject, while οἵτινες adds the thought that the new statement flows from the fact that the Corinthians are people of a certain type, having certain objectives in mind, being activated by certain motives. Paul's γνώμη and his sending of Titus should be welcomed by the Corinthians, since it is in line with their own plans, and will help them to carry them out.

What were their plans? Οἵτινες οὐ μόνον τὸ ποιῆσαι ἀλλὰ καὶ τὸ θέλειν προενήρξασθε ἀπὸ πέρυσι, (you) *who have made the beginning not only of doing but also of willing already last year.* Προενήρξασθε, the aorist of προενάρχομαι, is a compound in which ἐνάρχομαι, 'to make a beginning,' is reinforced by the prefix πρό, 'in advance,' 'already.' The groundwork for the collection has been finished some time ago. It is now merely a matter of carrying out their plans.

What was the situation? The words of Paul may startle us: The Corinthians had been ready not only for the ποιῆσαι but for the θέλειν. At first reading we may feel that the order should be reversed: they were ready not only with the willing but also for the doing. But Paul meant exactly what he said. The aorist infinitive ποιῆσαι refers to the action as such of taking part in the collection. The matter was brought before the congregation, and the congregation adopted an enabling resolution. Paul goes deeper. Behind this action there was a real θέλειν, 'a readiness,' 'a determination.' The collection was not begun in a half-hearted, haphazard way, as an affair that might be dragged out indefinitely. They were determined to carry it through promptly, and to make a success of it. And they would have done so if the false apostles had not disturbed them and interrupted the work. All the more would they now welcome any help that might expedite the collection.

They were ready ἀπὸ πέρυσι. When was that? Already in his first epistle Paul treated the matter of the collection as something with which the Corinthians were thoroughly familiar. There he did not explain the situation at length; he did not plead with the Corinthians to participate. Anything that might have been necessary along these lines seems to have been settled completely before Paul took up his pen to write the letter. He merely suggests something regarding the mode of procedure: "Upon the first day of the week let every one of you lay by him in store" (I Cor. 16:2). Thus the ἀπὸ πέρυσι must lie farther back than First Corinthians. On the other hand, it can not well be more than a year. The First Epistle was written about Easter of 57, and the second in late summer of the same year. Also the intrusion of the troublemakers, which had temporarily delayed the collection, must have started a little prior to First Corinthians, because already then Paul announced that he had changed his travel plans. He made this change, as he explains in the first chapter of the present epistle (1:26), φειδόμενος, sparing the Corinthians, giving them a chance to rectify matters themselves.

(11) Things now having become more normal again, Paul sends Titus to assist the congregation in speeding the collection and making up for lost time. Νυνὶ δὲ καὶ τὸ ποιῆσαι ἐπιτελέσατε, *now, however, complete also the doing.* The two aorists indicate that now they must concentrate all efforts on this one project, so that the execution of the collection will match their readiness, ὅπως καθάπερ ἡ προθυμία τοῦ θέλειν, οὕτως καὶ τὸ ἐπιτελέσαι.

To this Paul adds the modifier ἐκ τοῦ ἔχειν, *from the having.* Carry out the collection according to each member's ability to contribute. Paul had mentioned, in vs. 3, the self-sacrificing efforts of the Macedonian Christians, who had contributed beyond ability. He does not want the Corinthians to get the impression that similar superhuman efforts were expected from them. The attitude of the Macedonians is praiseworthy; it shows their great devotion to the cause of the Gospel. However, their manner is not to be regarded legalistically, as an absolute standard. Rather, ἐκ τοῦ ἔχειν, everyone as God has prospered him.

(12) Paul develops this thought in the following: Εἰ γὰρ ἡ προθυμία πρόκειται, καθὸ ἐὰν ἔχῃ εὐπρόσδεκτος, οὐ καθὸ οὐκ ἔχει, *for if (as is a fact in your case) the willingness is plainly evident, (then) according as (one) may have, not as he does not have, he is acceptable.*

Since Paul had testified in the previous verse that the θέλειν was present in Corinth as long as a year before, the conditional clause in the present verse does not express an element of uncertainty, but the εἰ can correctly be rendered with "since." For the simple θέλειν Paul now substitutes the more formal προθυμία, with little difference in meaning, if any. For the reference to their preparatory work (προενήρξασθε) he now mentions the result of those efforts, πρόκειται: their readiness lies there in the open for all to see. Such being the case, let each one determine the amount of his contribution according to whatever he may have (ἐάν with the subjunctive ἔχῃ), not according to what he does not have (the plain indicative ἔχει).

Let not a man who is poor, and who because of his poverty can contribute but little, imagine that because of his small gift he is less acceptable, less pleasing to God. God does not measure the value of a gift by its size, but by the genuineness of the προθυμία. Else, what about the poor who not only are unable to give, but find themselves in the predicament that they must ask for and accept gifts?

Grammatically, προθυμία may be considered as the subject of the predicate εὐπρόσδεκτος; but then it would almost have to be considered as the subject also of ἐχῃ and οὐκ ἔχει, which would sound a little harsh. But the sense would not be affected. There is neither a copula in the sentence, nor a personal or an indefinite pronoun before the ἔχειν. Paul tersely brings the main concepts to the fore, and his whole statement is perspicuous.

At this point Paul takes the occasion to speak about another concept pertaining to the collection. In the beginning he mentioned χάρις as the great factor. Then the presented ἁπλότης, the singleness of purpose in a Christian's life; also the κοινωνία, as it finds expression and is cultivated in the collection. Now he adds ἰσότης.

(13) Οὐ γὰρ ἵνα ἄλλοις ἄνεσις, ὑμῖν θλίψις, ἀλλ᾽ ἐξ ἰσότητος, *For not that others may have rest, (and) you, distress, but as a matter of equality.* This ἰσότης is really a phase of κοινωνία. Κοινωνία is not a one-way process, but is reciprocal. It would be a caricature of κοινωνία if some would sit back and twiddle their thumbs, while others had to labor with sweat and blood. Paul says that such is not the idea of the collection. The idea rather is a sort of equalization.

(14) Paul immediately applies this truth to the case in hand: ἐν τῷ νῦν καιρῷ τὸ ὑμῶν περίσσευμα εἰς τὸ ἐκείνων ὑστέρημα, ἵνα καὶ τὸ ἐκείνων περίσσευμα γένηται εἰς τὸ ὑμῶν ὑστέρημα, *on the present occasion, your abundance toward their lack, that also (or, on the other hand) their abundance may (be-)come to your want.* Καιρός, a word which really denotes a measure, does not mean time as such, but always connotes a special relation, conditions or circumstances, connected with a given period of time. Thus it may mean opportunity or occasion. Ἐν τῷ νῦν καιρῷ may conveniently be translated: "in the present case." The remarks which Paul will now make about ἰσότης are to be applied directly and are to be limted to the collection which he was just then administering for the needy believers in Jerusalem. His remarks refer strictly to the case in hand, the νῦν καιρός. There is a certain περίσσευμα which the Corinthians enjoy, and a corresponding ὑστέρημα in Jerusalem; and there is a certain περίσσευμα in Jerusalem with a corresponding ὑστέρημα in Corinth. An exchange will be helpful to both congregations and bring about an approach to ἰσότης.

Some commentators think that Paul is urging the Corinthians to give liberally to the needy Christians in Jerusalem now, because possibly at some time in the future the tables might be turned, the Corinthians might encounter misfortune and poverty, while the people in Jerusalem lived in plenty. And then the people in Jerusalem would feel under obligation to return the present favor. *Hodie tibi, cras mihi.* That idea not only represents a peculiar type of ethics, which Jesus condemned as characteristic of sinners (cf. Luke 6:34), but it directly violates Paul's statement, who is speaking about the νῦν καιρός, the present case. The Christians in Jerusalem were in physical need, and would welcome some help from the Corinthians, while the Corinthians, after the grueling spiritual troubles through which they had passed, would be greatly benefited by this exercise of the Christian fellowship with the people in Jerusalem, and by the prayers of thanksgiving and intercession which it would evoke from them.

(15) God is a friend of ἰσότης. Paul refers to an incident in connection with the gathering of the manna in the wilderness. God had given orders that an omer of manna per person would be the right amount. Now some families among the Children of Israel were large; some were small. But when they went out to gather the manna, God directed matters so that each one found exactly the quantity which he needed for his family: "He that gathered much had nothing over, and he that gathered little had no lack" (Exod. 16:18). The manner in which the ἰσότης was brought about is not the point. In the wilderness God brought it about in His own way; in the collection for the needy in Jerusalem the Christians should bear in mind and recognize that, if the collection was carried out in the proper spirit, the givers would at the same time be recipients, and vice versa. This could easily be overlooked by the givers.

Paul quotes the words from Exodus 16: Καθὼς γέγραπται, Ὁ τὸ πολὺ οὐκ ἐπλεόνασεν, καὶ ὁ τὸ ὀλίγον οὐκ ἠλαττόνησεν.

3. 8:16-24

(16) Paul is eager to have the Corinthians experience the rich grace of God, as had the Macedonians. He is confident that the Corinthians have the same desire, and that they will, therefore, welcome any assistance which Paul may give them. And he knows that Titus, whom

he is sending, has the same concern for the Corinthians. Paul gives thanks to God for this. Χάρις δὲ τῷ θεῷ τῷ διδόντι τὴν αὐτὴν σπουδὴν ὑπὲρ ὑμῶν ἐν τῇ καρδίᾳ Τίτου, *Thanks (be) to God, the Giver of the same eagerness for you in the heart of Titus.* Δέ simply connects this statement with the foregoing; it is not adversative but transitional. It may be omitted in the translation.

The interest which Titus takes in the Corinthians is not one of mere human friendship; it is one which God has planted and keeps alive in the heart of Titus. Paul was sending him, yes, but Titus himself was not unwilling to go. It did not take much coaxing on the part of Paul. Titus did not put up a stubborn resistance; he did not look for excuses, as did Moses when God called him to go to Pharaoh. Rather, Titus was happy to accept the assignment.

This eagerness of Titus served to show Paul how successful Titus had been on his previous mission. If that mission had been a failure, or if Titus had met with exceptional difficulties and opposition from the Corinthians, he certainly would not now have been very eager to accept a second assignment, one that might, if the first one had been only a partial success, by its very nature offer more and greater difficulties than did the first. The fact that he was ready to go again assured Paul that the troubles and misunderstandings in Corinth had been completely overcome. Conditions again were normal, or at least a good way along on the road to normalcy.

(17) Paul says: ὅτι τὴν μὲν παράκλησιν ἐδέξατο, *because (my) urging, yes, he accepted (it).* But that is only part of the story. Paul continues: σπουδαιότερος δὲ ὑπάρχων αὐθαίρετος ἐξῆλθεν πρὸς ἡμᾶς, *but, being unusually eager, he is departing for you by his own choice.* The comparative σπουδαιότερος expresses the idea that the eagerness of Titus was greater than Paul had anticipated. Paul does not say ὤν, but ὑπάρχων, thereby indicating that Titus' eagerness was not superficial. It was genuine, deep-seated. The aorist, ἐξῆλθεν, is epistolary. Titus had not yet left for Corinth when Paul wrote his letter. Rather, Titus served as the carrier. Αὐθαίρετος, which Paul here applies to Titus, is the same word with which he describes the readiness of the Macedonians to participate in the collection (vs. 3). They did not wait to be prodded; rather, they themselves took the initiative. Titus was doing the same in this instance.

Titus had been with the Corinthians only a short while before, helping them to work out a most troublesome problem. The fact that he was ready so soon, yes, eager, to return in order to help them in what, under the circumstances, must have appeared as a most delicate matter, would certainly open their hearts toward him to receive him with full confidence and joy.

(18) During the disturbance caused by the false apostles in Corinth the collection had sagged seriously. Even now after the crisis had passed, and though the willingness of the Corinthians could not be questioned, the success of the collection still hung in the balance, if experienced help could not be provided. For this purpose Paul was sending Titus. But was one helper, even a man like Titus, sufficient? Paul did not think so. Therefore he was sending two companions together with Titus to assist him in the work.

In order that this step may not be misunderstood by the Corinthians, Paul explains his action in the present subsection of this part of his epistle. Twice, in vs. 18 and again in vs. 22, he begins with the verb συνεπέμψαμεν. This is the epistolary aorist, meaning, *we are sending together with him,* μετ' αὐτοῦ, i.e., Titus, and then αὐτοῖς (in vs. 22), i.e., Titus and his previously mentioned companion.

The first companion is described in these words: τὸν ἀδελφὸν οὗ ὁ ἔπαινος ἐν τῷ εὐαγγελίῳ διὰ πασῶν τῶν ἐκκλησιῶν, *the brother whose praise in the Gospel is (heard) throughout all the churches.* He is a man who is no novice in Gospel work. How far the expression πᾶσαι αἱ ἐκκλησίαι is to be stretched, Paul does not say, but, it includes, at least, all the churches among whom Paul was working at this time, all the churches in Macedonia. Among them and for them this man had done Gospel work. He had been faithful and efficient. The congregations were unanimous in their praise. The Corinthians would be pleased to receive such a helper in the company of Titus.

(19) But there is more to be said about him. Οὐ μόνον δὲ ἀλλὰ καὶ χειροτονηθεὶς ὑπὸ τῶν ἐκκλησιῶν συνέκδημος ἡμῶν, *But not only (that) but (who) has also been elected by the congregation as our fellow traveler.* His zeal and his ability had been previously recognized. Now it was further acknowledged by the churches of Macedonia in electing him as a traveling companion for Paul. Evidently this man was not one of Paul's regular assistants. The congregations of Macedonia had, in their own mission endeavors, recognized and employed

his special gifts. Just as some years previous the churches of Iconium, Lystra, and Derbe had noted the gifts of Timothy and had recommended him to Paul, so now the congregations of Macedonia had engaged the services of this brother, and on the basis of their observation had elected him as a traveling companion for Paul to deliver the collection in Jerusalem. We see from this that from the very beginning local congregations did not remain isolated. They joined hands with their neighbors to do Gospel work in common. They were sufficiently organized to carry out a joint election, as they now appointed this brother to be a traveling companion with Paul.

Who this man was, we cannot say. Most likely he was a Macedonian. The men who traveled with Paul to Jerusalem to deliver the collection are mentioned in Acts 20:4: "Sopater of Berea; and of the Thessalonians, Aristarchus and Secundus." Since Aristarchus was a regular assistant of Paul (cf. Acts 19:29), our present choice apparently is limited to Sopater and Secundus. But from Acts 20:5ff. we learn that also Luke, who seems to have remained in Philippi since Paul's second mission journey, accompanied Paul to Jerusalem. That raises the number of possibilities to three men.

We see how far the matter of the collection had progressed by this time. In the spring of the year it was not yet certain whether Paul himself would go up to Jerusalem when the collection was to be delivered (cf. I Cor. 16:4). That question had now been decided: Paul was going. And at least some of the congregations which took part in the collection had already elected their representatives who were to go with Paul. All this shows that special efforts were necessary if Corinth was not to fall too far behind.

Yet Paul never loses sight of the fact, and never allows his readers to forget, that the success of the collection is not a matter of human effort. It is a matter of God's grace. He describes it ἐν τῇ χάριτι ταύτῃ τῇ διακονουμένῃ ὑφ᾽ ἡμῶν, *in this grace which is being administered by us.*

Now he adds another thought. It is really not new but rather is given as a corollary to the former. If the collection represents the grace of God as a gift to us, then it must be gathered *in proportion to the honor of God and also to our willingness* in receiving His grace, or, as Paul had called it before, our ἁπλότης. Πρὸς τὴν αὐτοῦ τοῦ κυρίου δόξαν καὶ προθυμίαν ἡμῶν. The preposition πρός brings persons or things "face to face"; the specific import of this relation must be determined from the context. It may be direction, purpose, reference, and the like. In our case Lenski translates with "to show," to show the Lord's glory and our willingness. To me it seems advisable to leave the "face to face" relation a little more general, say, 'in proportion to.' The glory of the Lord is emphasized by the addition of αὐτοῦ, the glory of the Lord Himself, of the very Lord. The collection is to stand face to face with the Lord's glory, in proportion to it.

It is to stand in proportion also to our willingness. Who is referred to in the "our"? Not only Paul and Timothy, who are administering this grace of God, but also the Corinthians who are contributing, whose willingness Paul had praised in vss. 10ff. There was no doubt about their willingness, there could be no doubt, but because of adverse circumstances the size of their collection was far from being in proportion to their willingness. There was a sore discrepancy. Time was running out, and therefore the Corinthians would welcome any help that might assist them in raising their collection to the proportion of their willingness.

(20) Paul has another purpose in mind: στελλόμενοι τοῦτο, μή τις ἡμᾶς μωμήσηται ἐν τῇ ἁδρότητι ταύτῃ τῇ διακονουμένῃ ὑφ᾽ ἡμῶν, avoiding this that anyone may blame us in this abundance which is being administered by us. In making all arrangements for the collection, Paul is very careful to avoid any occasion for blame. The thought that perhaps somebody might suspect him of embezzlement is suggested nowhere in the entire discussion. What blame, then, did Paul wish to forestall? In vs. 4 we saw that one of the chief purposes of the collection was the strengthening of the κοινωνία of the Church, specifically the κοινωνία of the two branches, viz., the Jewish Christians and the Gentile Christians. This κοινωνία should stand out as clear as possible. Anything that might tend to overshadow it in the least must be avoided. There was danger that the Christians in Jerusalem might consider the collection more or less as a personal affair of Paul, and overlook the spirit of the congregations who so willingly cooperated with Paul in raising it. To avoid this impression, Paul had at first hesitated to be personally present when it was delivered. Since his presence had now been decided, he worked toward the end that the representation of the congregations both in raising and in delivering

the collection be as widespread as possible. Both in Jerusalem and among the Gentile congregations it should be clearly understood that the collection was a spontaneous expression of their spiritual fellowship.

(21) The thought which Paul thus had stated negatively he now renders positively: προνοοῦμεν γὰρ καλὰ οὐ μόνον ἐνώπιον κυρίου ἀλλὰ καὶ ἐνώπιον ἀνθρώπων, *for we are providing (all things to be) proper not only before the Lord but also before men.* Καλός speaks of the intrinsic quality of a thing. It may be translated with 'excellent,' or 'honorable,' or more generally with 'proper.' In making his preparations Paul takes chiefly this into consideration that every step be καλός. No matter how expedient any method may seem, if it lacks propriety in any measure, Paul will reject it. In the present case this means that every step must be in accord with the general purpose of the collection, namely, that of strengthening and sealing the unity of the Church.

Since that is the main test of propriety in this case, it is not sufficient that the propriety be evident before God; it must emphatically be evident to men's eyes.

(22) What Paul has said so far about sending Titus and the brother who had been chosen by the Macedonian group of congregations as Paul's traveling companion to Jerusalem, applies with equal force to his sending of a third man. We must note particularly what Paul says about this man by way of introducing him to the Corinthians.

Συνεπέμψαμεν δὲ αὐτοῖς τὸν ἀδελφὸν ἡμῶν, ὃν ἐδοκιμάσαμεν ἐν πολλοῖς πολλάκις σπουδαῖον ὄντα, *We are sending jointly with them our brother whom we have found often (and) in many tests to be earnest.* This man is evidently one of Paul's regular assistants. Paul has used him on many occasions for various kinds of assignments. He never disappointed Paul. Paul always found him faithfully applying himself to the tasks before him and successfully completing them. He never shirked, nor did he ever quit a task which was only half-finished.

But Paul has an additional reason for delegating him now with the other two to go to Corinth: νυνὶ δὲ πολὺ σπουδαιότερον πεποιθήσει πολλῇ τῇ εἰς ὑμᾶς, *but now being unusually eager with full confidence in you.* The comparative σπουδαιότερον does not compare this man with the other two delegates, but rather points out his present attitude as exceeding his ordinary eagerness. There is a reason for his unusual zeal: he has full confidence in the Corinthians. He feels sure of their general Christian attitude and specifically of the collection and their inner readiness for it. Assisting them in taking up the collection will not mean a battle. It will not even be uphill work; it will be the happy gathering in of a rich harvest. Such is the confidence of this third delegate whom Paul is sending to Corinth to help them complete the collection. He should receive a most hearty welcome.

This next brief subsection is in the nature of a concluding summary. So far Paul had presented in some detail the steps which he had taken to help the Corinthians finish the collection speedily and successfully, and had introduced to them the men whom he had dispatched for their assistance.

(23) What was the status, the "call," of these three men? How were they to be regarded by the Corinthians? Paul vouched for their competence, for their interest in the Corinthians, and for their faithfulness. Paul was not foisting them on the Corinthians as "bosses" who would give them orders, nor, on the other hand, were the Corinthians to regard them as their hirelings who should do their work for them. In what spirit, then, were they to receive them?

Local congregations have from the beginning experienced a twofold danger: on the one hand, isolationism, on the other, submersion in a larger body. First Corinthians shows that this congregation did not always appreciate the bonds of spiritual unity by which they were joined with all other Christians and Christian congregations in the spiritual body of Christ, the bonds of a common faith and of mutual love. They considered themselves as autonomous Christians who could manage their own affairs without regard for other churches. To counteract this unhealthy attitude, Paul frequently refers to the "other churches" and their customs (cf. I Cor. 4:17; 7:17; 11:16); he warns the Corinthians not to give offense to the "church of God" (10:32); he rebukes them sharply: "What? came the word of God out from you? or came it unto you only?" (14:36.) Although this spirit of self-sufficient isolationism had, under Paul's instruction, been recognized as sinful, and had to a great extent been subdued, yet careful vigilance was still in place in this respect.

But just as the spirit of isolationism violates true Christian liberty, so does the other extreme, that a local congregation simply waits for orders from superiors, from the leaders, e.g., of a larger church body.

Accordingly, Paul now gives brief instructions on the proper attitude of the Corinthians toward the three men whom he is sending to them.

He presents the theme in the form of a question with two parallel members, joined by εἴτε—εἴτε, 'whether—or.' The two members are parallel, but not quite on the same level. In the first one Paul uses the preposition ὑπέρ, in the second, the simple nominative: εἴτε ὑπὲρ Τίτου . . . εἴτε ἀδελφοὶ ἡμῶν, Now whether about Titus . . . or whether our brethren. Titus is singled out because he is serving, so to say, as chairman of the committee which Paul is sending. The first εἴτε thus mentions Titus alone, while the second refers to the committee as a whole.

What about Titus? He is κοινωνὸς ἐμὸς καὶ εἰς ὑμᾶς συνεργός, he is my partner and fellow helper concerning you. Titus represents Paul personally; he is Paul's associate in a special sense. The Corinthians must look upon Titus as though Paul himself had come to them. Wherever Paul goes, he goes in the spirit which he expressed in this epistle, 1:24: "Not that we have dominion over your faith, but are helpers of your joy." His was the spirit as he described it a little more fully a few months later in his Epistle to the Romans: "For I long to see you, that I may impart unto you some spiritual gift, to the end ye may be established; that is, that I may be comforted together with you by the mutual faith both of you and me. . . . I am a debtor both to the Greeks, and to the Barbarians; both to the wise, and to the unwise" (1:11-14). Titus is Paul's κοινωνός; he shares the same spirit. Now he is coming to the Corinthians as Paul's συνεργός, Paul's fellow laborer, εἰς ὑμᾶς, with respect to the special task which they have on their hands. He does not come as a master, to give orders, nor as a slave, to take orders, but as a brother to counsel and assist. As such he should be received by the Corinthians.

Εἴτε ἀδελφοὶ ἡμῶν, or whether our brethren. This does not refer to the two companions of Titus in contrast to Titus, but includes Titus; it refers to the whole committee. What about our brethren? In his answer Paul uses two terms, the one referring to their official position, the second to the general aim and purpose and the fruit of their labors, and their person.

The official position of all three men is ἀπόστολοι ἐκκλησιῶν, apostles of churches. Paul does not mean to say that some congregations sent these men as their delegates to Corinth. In the foregoing verses he had stated very clearly that he himself was the one who was sending these men. They were representing him in the assistance which they gave to the Corinthians in raising the collection. They were apostles apart from and before their present commission.

In New Testament times the title apostle acquired a new and very specific significance. The 12 men whom Jesus chose to proclaim His Gospel in all the world are commonly known as His Apostles. Jesus Himself gave them this title. St. Luke, in recording the calling of these men, describes the procedure as follows: "And when it was day, he called unto him his disciples: and of them he chose twelve, whom also he named apostles" (Luke 6:13). In the preceding verse Luke reported that Jesus prepared Himself for this solemn action by spending the night in prayer.

Jesus took the initiative. He summoned His disciples. This was not a call to faith. They had accepted Him as the promised Messiah at some time prior to this occasion. He did not ask for volunteers among His disciples. He Himself made the selection. Then He explained to them the work which they were expected to do, the special position which they were to hold in contradistinction to the other disciples by being called as apostles. The general function of an apostle was well known. This general relation should now mark their specific connection with their Savior.

On the day of His ascension Jesus, in correcting some gross misconceptions still held by His Apostles even then, told them that their specific task consisted in this that they were to be "witnesses" unto Him, and that they would be qualified for this task by a special gift of the Holy Ghost. Even on an earlier occasion Jesus had already told them: "And ye also shall bear witness, because ye have been with me from the beginning" (John 15:27). On the basis of this concept of the Christ-created apostleship, Peter, at the election of a successor to Judas, declared: "Wherefore of these men which have companied with us all the time that the Lord Jesus went in and out among us, beginning from the baptism of John, unto that same day that he was taken up from us, must one be ordained to be a witness with us of his resurrection" (Acts 1:21, 22).

On the method in which an apostle functions and on the scope of his work we get some light from a combination of terms as Paul uses them. In I Timothy 2:7 he says that he was appointed "a preacher

and an apostle" (κῆρυξ καὶ ἀπόστολος), and adds "a teacher of the
Gentiles" (διδάσκαλος). In II Timothy 1:11 he uses the same three
terms in the same order: "Whereunto I am appointed a preacher, and
an apostle, and a teacher of the Gentiles." Thus the function of an
apostle seems to lie somewhere between that of a κῆρυξ and that of
a teacher. A herald makes solemn announcements; an apostle does
more. A teacher trains his pupils by continued instruction in the
proper application of the truth. Thus an apostle does not seem to be
limited, as is a herald, to the bare announcement. He is to explain,
to amplify, to "put across" his message, while the teacher continues
this work by training the hearers on the basis of the apostle's exposition of the message.

The three men whom Paul is sending to Corinth are apostles of
congregations. Christian churches had employed them in some way to
carry the Gospel message abroad in their name. Now Paul is sending
these experienced men to Corinth.

They are also devoted men, who carry out their commission, not in
a mechanical way; but their heart is in their work. They themselves
are monuments to the glory of Christ, and they perform their work
with the sole purpose in mind of spreading the glory of Christ. They
are δόξα Χριστοῦ, *the glory of Christ.*

(24) How will the Corinthians respond to the mission of such
men? They themselves stand in need of help; three men are coming
to them who are not only experienced in Gospel work but are themselves models of devotion. What else can the Corinthians do but fall
in line with such leadership?

Paul connects his following statement to the foregoing with οὖν,
now then. The verb of the sentence appears in two different moods in
the various manuscripts. The simplest and most natural form is the
imperative, ἐνδείξασθε. The Nestle text has the more difficult form,
the present participle, ἐνδεικνύμενοι. In the latter case the imperative of
εἶναι would have to be supplied. The verb is accompanied by the
cognate object, ἔνδειξιν. The meaning of the combination would be to
give proof: τὴν οὖν ἔνδειξιν ἐνδεικνύμενοι.

To whom should the Corinthians give proof? Not to Paul, nor to the
three delegates. They do not need any proof. They understand the Corinthians and have full confidence in them. The Corinthians have an
obligation before all congregations of Christ. Their recent lapse has

grieved and offended many. Now they must undo the damage which they have caused, undo it as far as possible. Hence they must give proof εἰς πρόσωπον τῶν ἐκκλησιῶν, *in the sight of the churches.*

Of what must they give proof? First of all: τῆς ἀγάπης ὑμῶν, *of your love.* Love is a comprehensive term. It is the response to the χάρις of God, which Paul mentioned in the beginning of the chapter. It is an expression of the ἁπλότης, their singleness of purpose. It is the bond which cements the κοινωνία of believers.

In his plea Paul injects a personal element. They should give proof καὶ ἡμῶν καυχήσεως ὑπὲρ ὑμῶν εἰς αὐτούς, *and of our boasting concerning you before them.* Paul had great confidence in the Corinthians, and he had forcefully voiced his confidence before the delegates whom he is now sending. Now he asked the Corinthians to live up to his expectations. If they failed to do so, they would not only make him out to be an irresponsible braggart, if not a liar; they would shake his confidence, and would undo the blessings which had accrued to the churches from their successful struggle against the influence of the false apostles.

For the sake of the churches, give proof of Paul's truthfulness in praising you.

B. THE REAL PURPOSE OF THE COLLECTION

Chapter 9

1. 9:1-5

The first part of chapter 9 (vss. 1-5) concludes Paul's discussion of the steps which he took to aid the Corinthians in bringing their collection to a speedy and successful close. He begins by reminding them once more of their readiness to participate in the undertaking. If we bear this in mind, it will aid us greatly in understanding his argument.

He connects this section to the foregoing with γάρ. What statement in particular of the foregoing chapter is he going to explain? The word καυχῶμαι in vs. 2 provides the key. In vs. 24 of the previous chapter he had spoken about his and his associates' καύχησις concerning the Corinthians. He had pleaded that the Corinthians demonstrate the correctness of the boasts which Paul had made about them to the

Macedonians. In vs. 2 of the present chapter he again refers to his boasting, a boasting about the Corinthians' readiness.

(1) In concentrating on this thought, he first stresses, negatively, that he can omit a discussion of the collection as such. They understand the collection and are in full agreement with Paul's views. Περὶ μὲν γὰρ τῆς διακονίας τῆς εἰς τοὺς ἁγίους περισσόν μοί ἐστιν τὸ γράφειν ὑμῖν, *For concerning the ministration to the saints as such it is superfluous for me to write to you.*

What is the meaning of μέν? This particle is usually followed by δέ, German: *zwar—aber,* 'yes—but.' In the present case, however, no δέ occurs till we come to vs. 3; and the mutual relation of the two thoughts of vss. 1 and 2, on the one hand, and of vss. 3ff. on the other, does not seem to lend itself conveniently to a μέν—δέ association, an association in which μέν tends to throw the emphasis on the second member, the one introduced by δέ. In our case μέν, standing alone, simply serves to emphasize the subject of the clause which it introduces: the διακονία as such.

Paul mentioned the διακονία in vs. 4 of the previous chapter without discussing it. He mentioned a number of factors in connection with it, chiefly, that it is a part of God's χάρις; that it is an expression of the Christians' ἁπλότης; that it flows out of an appreciation of the Christians' spiritual κοινωνία and helps to cement it. He had mentioned also that a certain ἰσότης, equalization, is to take place in connection with it. He did not then discuss the διακονία itself, its nature, its meaning, its purpose, etc.

In our present verse he refers to the διακονία again, and declares a discussion to be superfluous. That the collection was εἰς τοὺς ἁγίους he had also mentioned before (8:4). He now declares any writing about this collection to the Corinthians to be περισσόν. In I Thessalonians 4:9 and 5:1 he expressed a similar thought with οὐ χρείαν ἔχετε: you have no need γράφειν ὑμῖν, or ὑμῖν γράφεσθαι. Paul might have used the same expression in the present case; yet περισσόν seems to express the superfluousness more strongly. We note, moreover, that Paul here prefixes the definite article τό to the infinitive γράφειν, *the* writing to you is superfluous for me. This places a certain stress on the writing. We keep this in mind when we read the following.

(2) Paul continues with an explanatory γάρ. Why would it be a waste of energy, perhaps even a violation of good taste, if he under-

took to compose an elaborate explanation of the collection as such? He answers: οἶδα γὰρ τὴν προθυμίαν ὑμῶν, *for I know your readiness, willingness, eagerness.* We note that Paul does not use a form of γιγνώσκω, but says οἶδα, thus emphasizing the objective certainty of the matter. The point is not whether he has any personal connection with their willingness. It is rather that he is sure of it on the basis of compelling evidence. Their zeal stood indisputably established. It was so evident that Paul did not hesitate in the least to boast about it: ἣν ὑπὲρ ὑμῶν καυχῶμαι Μακεδόσιν, *of which I am boasting for you to Macedonians.* Μακεδόσιν is anarthrous. Paul is not boasting to the Macedonians as a group; he is boasting to individuals, as the occasion may present itself.

He sums up the content of his boasting in the words: ὅτι Ἀχαία παρεσκεύασται ἀπὸ πέρυσι, *that Achaia stands ready since last year, since a year ago.* Paul does not limit his praise to the Corinthians; he includes all of Achaia. From Acts 17 we know that some people were won by the Gospel in Athens; and from Romans 16, that there was a church in Cenchrea, the eastern harbor of Corinth, on the Saronic Gulf. Acts 18:27f. informs us that Apollos carried on successful Gospel work in Achaia. The present epistle was addressed to the congregation in Corinth together with all the saints in all Achaia (1:1). About this entire group of Christian churches Paul is convinced that they stood ready for the collection since a year ago.

The verb παρεσκεύασται is the perfect tense, either of the middle or of the passive voice. Whether we read it as passive or middle does not alter the facts: Paul had prepared them, and they stood ready. With this verb Paul repeats the thought which in the previous verse he had summed up in the word προθυμία, their willingness, their zeal. It would be reading more into the word than the context warrants, when people assume that Paul meant to say that in Achaia the collection was practically finished a year before. What he means with προθυμία and παρεσκεύασται, he explained in the previous chapter by saying that they had then begun not only the doing but also the willing, οὐ μόνον τὸ ποιῆσαι ἀλλὰ καὶ τὸ θέλειν προενήρξασθε, but that the ἐπιτελέσαι had yet to be achieved (8:10, 11).

The dating of ἀπὸ πέρυσι we discussed briefly in connection with 8:10 (see p. 178). We now shall try to establish the sequence of events beginning with ἀπὸ πέρυσι. First Corinthians was written at Easter time in 57; Second Corinthians in late summer of the same year. First Corinthians presupposes the incest case and a previous letter of Paul concerning it (I Cor. 5:9); it presupposes the preparation for the collection (I Cor. 16:1); it presupposes also the invasion of the Corinthian congregation by the troublemakers; as least Paul had then already changed his travel plans (I Cor. 16:5). Hence Paul probably went to Corinth from Ephesus in the latter part of 56, to propose the matter of the collection. Soon thereafter the incest happened and Paul wrote a letter to Corinth (which we no longer possess). About this time also the troublemakers arrived. The Corinthians wrote a letter to Paul, submitting a number of questions (I Cor. 7:1), and sent a delegation of three men (I Cor. 16:17). Paul answered in First Corinthians. He stayed in Ephesus until the riot of Demetrius took place (the latter part of May), sending Timothy, and later Titus, to help the Corinthians in their troubles. After the riot of Demetrius he started for Corinth via Troas and Macedonia. It had been a year full of work and bitter troubles.

Yet Paul boasts of the Corinthians: Achaia stands ready since a year ago. He does so in all sincerity. Timothy, whom he had sent to Corinth when he considered his work in Ephesus as finished (Acts 19:22), before the riot of Demetrius, had returned and became the coauthor of Second Corinthians (1:1); and just recently also Titus had returned with a good report. Paul rejoiced over the success of the Gospel, and joyfully boasted about the readiness of the Corinthians for the collection. And many in Macedonia were encouraged thereby: καὶ τὸ ὑμῶν ζῆλος ἠρέθισεν τοὺς πλείονας, and your zeal encouraged and stimulated the majority (to greater and more cheerful efforts). In Macedonia, as in every congregation of Christians on earth, there were such as responded only feebly to God's grace when they were asked to give; but the majority — not a scant majority, rather, by far the greater majority — rejoiced in the zeal of the Corinthians and themselves gave more cheerfully.

The verb ἐρεθίζο occurs only twice in the New Testament. In Colossians 3:21 it is used in the bad sense of irritating, as fathers are addressed: Μὴ ἐρεθίζετε τὰ τέκνα ὑμῶν, while in our passage it is used in the good sense.

Under these conditions, did Paul have to write an exhaustive discourse on the proposed collection? Could he justify his action if he did?

We have heard: Paul has firm confidence in the zeal of the Corinthians for the collection, and he knows that they stand ready since a year ago, having been properly informed and motivated by Paul himself, and having wholeheartedly taken all necessary preparatory steps for doing their part. Therefore Paul finds it superfluous to explain the matter in writing. Why, then, is he now sending a committee of three prominent men to assist them? Does this step not tend to cast doubt on his words? Paul knows, and the Corinthians know, what a terrific spiritual struggle the congregation had just gone through, a struggle which threatened their very existence as a Christian church. Although the danger had been successfully averted, and the Christian character of the congregation, both in doctrine and practice, had been re-established, yet the aftereffects of the struggle were still in evidence, and it would take some time before all scars of the battle completely disappeared. Among other things, the collection had lagged woefully. Concerted efforts in this matter might serve to speed the healing process.

(3) For the present Paul concentrates his attention and his measures on the work of the collection in Corinth, and he uses the fact that Corinth was known throughout the Church as having been prepared since a year before in explaining the coming of the three helpers.

Ἔπεμψα δὲ τοὺς ἀδελφούς, ἵνα μὴ τὸ καύχημα ἡμῶν τὸ ὑπὲρ ὑμῶν κενωθῇ, *But I am sending the brethren lest our boasting on your behalf be emptied.* Note the change of number in the personal pronouns. Paul alone is doing the sending (I), while the praises of the Corinthians had been sounded also by his associates (our). Καύχημα is not the act of boasting (that would be καύχησις), but it is the content of the boasting. If the content is removed, then Paul's boasting would be reduced to empty words. And his boasting would appear empty and unfounded if the collection now produced only mediocre results. The completion should match the readiness. So Paul had said in the previous chapter (vs. 11). If it did not, then it would appear that either Paul's instructions or the Corinthians' response, or both, had been insufficient. Paul's praise of the Corinthians would be deflated.

SECOND CORINTHIANS

Paul and his associates had many words of praise for the Corinthians. They abounded, as he mentioned in 8:7, "in faith, and utterance, and knowledge, and in all diligence, and in your love to us." All of these virtues would become doubtful if now a failure, or even only a half-failure, would have to be registered in the execution of the collection. For that reason Paul adds the limiting remark: ἐν τῷ μέρει τούτῳ, *in this part* (namely, of our boasting). The collection will become a sort of test case: ἵνα καθὼς ἔλεγον παρεσκευασμένοι ἦτε, *that, as I was saying, you stood prepared.* This ἵνα clause serves to explain the meaning of τοῦτο τὸ μέρος. It is not final, but appositive (substantive). On the basis of Paul's praises the Macedonians anticipate a very sizable collection to be raised by the Corinthians. If the Corinthians measure up to these expectations, well and good; but if they do not, then both Paul and his associates will stand disgraced as irresponsible braggarts.

(4) Would such disgrace be very serious? In the following negative purpose clause Paul pictures a possible course of events which by all means should be forestalled. He says, μή πως ἐὰν ἔλθωσιν σὺν ἐμοὶ Μακεδόνες, καὶ εὕρωσιν ὑμᾶς ἀπαρασκευάστους, *lest, if (as is probable) there should come with me (some) Macedonians and should find you unprepared.* Such an eventuality must by all means be avoided. Paul will soon be coming to Corinth, perhaps at the end of the summer. Since he left Ephesus about June 1, and is writing this letter after his arrival in Philippi and some days after receiving the report of Titus, it may now be about the end of June. Since Paul plans to spend the winter in Corinth, there are still several months left in which to carry out the collection, sufficient to make it a success, provided no time is wasted.

Paul is coming, and there is great probability that some Macedonians will accompany him. The conditional clause with ἐάν and the subjunctive expresses "some prospect of fulfillment" (Chamberlain, p. 198, cf. Blass-Debrunner, #371,4). Paul does not know who or how many of the Macedonian Christians will come with him, but he is pretty sure that there will be some. The Philippians had from the very beginning shown an active interest in Gospel work. When Paul had been forced to leave Philippi and had taken up work in Thessalonica, they twice sent a contribution for his support during the few weeks of his stay in that city. Lydia, the first convert in Philippi, had insisted that Paul accept free lodging in her house. Together with the other churches in Macedonia, as we heard in the previous chapter, the Philippians had engaged a certain "brother" for joint Gospel work in their territory. Is it too far-fetched to assume that much of this can be traced to the faithful labors of Luke, "the beloved physician," who apparently remained in Philippi during the entire period of Paul's second and third mission journeys (Acts 16:11-20:5)? The Bereans had escorted Paul as far as Athens when the unbelieving Jews stirred up a persecution against him in their city and he was forced to leave. Would the Macedonians, who from the beginning showed such an active interest in Paul's mission work, now let him travel to Corinth alone? Paul does not think so; he expects that some of them will accompany him.

Since Paul had spoken in glowing terms about the staunch Christian character of the Corinthians, and since their example had served to stimulate and strengthen the zeal of the Macedonians, they would, of course, be greatly interested in the success of the collection in Achaia. They in their bottomless poverty had contributed much more than Paul in his fondest dreams had dared to hope. What would they find in prosperous Corinth? What would be their reaction if they should find (the same ἐάν with the subjunctive as above) the Corinthians unprepared? Ἀπαρασκεύαστος is the verbal adjective of the word which Paul used twice in the two preceding verses, plus the alpha privative prefixed. From the fact of a disappointing collection they would naturally draw the conclusion that also the preparation, both on the part of Paul and of the Corinthians, must have been deficient. The Corinthians were simply ἀπαρασκεύαστοι, from whatever angle you might look at them.

In that case, Paul says, we, who so confidently proclaimed their thorough preparation, must hang our heads in shame, μή πως . . . καταισχυνθῶμεν ἡμεῖς, lest . . . we, yes we, be put to shame, we with our unwarranted boasting on the basis of an unsatisfactory work of preparation. Would the Corinthians want such a thing to happen, they who, after some terrible aberration, have just found their way back to appreciation, love, and confidence toward the founder of their congregation? Paul is doing everything in his power to avert such a disgrace. He is dispatching three tried and faithful men to help the Corinthians expedite matters.

Would a failure in the collection bring disgrace only to Paul and to his associates? What about the Corinthians themselves? Paul adds, ἵνα μὴ λέγωμεν ὑμεῖς, *not to say you.* Paul does not feel guilty of any neglect. He had done his part in preparing the Corinthians for the collection so thoroughly that he finds it improper and superfluous to add anything now in his letter. If people will try to pin any blame on him, he will be suffering innocently. The fault will be all the Corinthians' for neglecting to act on the instructions which they had heard from Paul and his associates, and which they had understood and absorbed, but which they had carelessly failed to translate into action. The Macedonians, who knew Paul as a teacher from their own personal experience, would be quick to place the blame where it belongs. By a telling *praeteritio* Paul calls this fact to the attention of his readers.

Paul closes his purpose clause with the prepositional phrase ἐν τῇ ὑποστάσει ταύτῃ. We leave the phrase untranslated for the present, since the word ὑπόστασις calls for some investigation. According to its etymology it literally means 'something laid under,' 'a basis or foundation' (ὑπό and ἵστημι). Then by means of a metonymy it signifies something that rests on such a foundation. Practically, it then becomes a synonym to οὐσία. In this sense it occurs in Hebrews 1:3, where Christ is called the imprint of God's ὑπόστασις. This is erroneously translated with "person" in the King James Bible: "the express image of his person." The word received the meaning of person much later, during the Trinitarian controversies.

Usually, in this metonymical use the word was applied to some mental processes (metaphor) to indicate trust or confidence (and expressions of trust) as resting on safe grounds. Its opposite would be "imagination." (Compare the expression: φαντασίαν μὲν ἔχειν πλούτου, ὑπόστασιν δὲ μή.) In this sense the Epistle to the Hebrews uses it in the definition of faith as: the ὑπόστασις of things hopd for, i.e., the sure, well-founded conviction (Heb. 11:1). The same epistle encourages its readers to avoid the bitter root of unbelief (ἀπιστία) and to hold fast to the end their original Christian faith: ἀρχὴν τῆς ὑποστάσεως (Heb. 3:14). Thus Hebrews uses the word in two places for confidence. Paul uses the word only twice, both times for an expression of confidence. In our passage it means: *in this confident boasting.* In 11:17, where he is "bragging" in ἀφροσύνη, he speaks about ταύτῃ τῇ ὑποστάσει τῆς καυχήσεως, this 'venture' of boasting.

Might his confidence, after all, be without real ὑπόστασις? Might it have been misplaced? Neither Paul nor the Corinthians will want that to be the case.

(5) This verse concludes the present subpart and, at the same time, the whole section begun at 8:1. Paul states summarily his reason for sending a delegation to Corinth to help the congregation in completing the collection.

Ἀναγκαῖον οὖν ἡγησάμην, *Accordingly I considered it as necessary.* The connective οὖν shows that Paul deduced the necessity of his measure from a consideration of the various factors which he had pointed out in this section. Adding them up, he had arrived at the procedure of which he just has informed his readers. That is the meaning of ἀναγκαῖον, a word which he places at the head of the sentence. The course may have some unpleasant implications, but since no alternate plan presents itself that would hold out any prospect of success, he considers it imperative to adopt this one. He is willing to submit to this ἀνάγκη, the force of circumstances, and he expects his readers to do likewise. His resolve was, as we have seen, to send three men to aid the Corinthians in completing the collection.

The first step which Paul took in this direction was to win for his plan the three men whom he was sending. They, if they were to serve efficiently, had to be convinced that the plan was sound. If they were not, or if they were not wholeheartedly for it, if they would do their work only mechanically, then, perhaps, it would be better not to send them at all. Paul says: παρακαλέσαι τοὺς ἀδελφούς, *to urge the brethren.* He does not say how much urging he had to do. About Titus he had remarked before that he was eager of his own accord; he went αὐθαίρετος. About the second partner of Titus he said that he was eager to go because of his great confidence in all of the Corinthians. About the other brother he remarked that he had been chosen by the Macedonian congregations to be a traveling companion of Paul in delivering the collection to Jerusalem. Evidently, they all agreed with Paul that special help to the Corinthians was indicated by the circumstances. Evidently, Paul had no difficulty in persuading the brethren to accept their assignment ἵνα προέλθωσιν εἰς ὑμᾶς, *to go beforehand to you.*

The prefix πρό in προέλθωσιν is easy to understand. Paul is going to Corinth to take the collected funds and, together with some delegate of the congregation, deliver them in Jerusalem. The three brethren whom he is sending are to go to Corinth in advance, before him, to help in gathering the contributions. But this πρό is only the first one in a series of three: καὶ προκαταρτίσωσιν τὴν προεπηγγελμένην εὐλογίαν ὑμῶν, and complete in advance your blessing (which was) promised in advance. Καταρτίζω, from ἀρτίζω with perfective κατά, means 'to fit together completely.' The idea is the same as Paul had expressed in 8:11 with ἐπιτελέσαι. Now he prefixes πρό to it. The gathering of the collection was to be completed before Paul and his Macedonian companions arrived in Corinth. Already in his first epistle he had urged prompt action, "that there be no gathering when I come" (I Cor. 16:2). The original Greek sounds even more urgent: ἵνα μὴ ὅταν ἔλθω τότε λογίαι γίνωνται, "lest when I come then gatherings be made." If it was in place at that time (about Easter) to warn against easygoing complacency, it was much more so now, since during the disturbance much valuable time had been lost.

Paul prefixes a πρό also to ἐπηγγελμένεν. The Corinthians had enthusiastically agreed with Paul when he presented the matter of a collection to their congregation; they were for it heart and soul; there was a θέλειν, and they made promises to Paul. Paul is now not making new demands on them; he is just reminding them of promises which they themselves had made earlier, in fact, a year before. But although these promises were made so long before, they were still a far way from being redeemed. Hence the resolve of Paul to send able men to assist the Corinthians.

He calls the contribution of the Corinthians an εὐλογία, 'a blessing.' And he means just what he says. No doubt, the Corinthians agreed. They also intended their gift to be a blessing. But as things had been going, there was danger that this goal would not be reached. The three men are to help the Corinthians ταύτην ἑτοίμην εἶναι οὕτως ὡς εὐλογίαν καὶ μὴ ὡς πλεονεξίαν, that this be ready thus as a blessing, and not as (niggardly) stinginess. Thus Paul here again urges that the collection be ready when he comes. Then he adds not only ὡς, as a blessing, but reinforces this thought by inserting οὕτως, let it be ready thus as a blessing, so that at the first glance everyone can see that it is a blessing. The collection would fail of its main purpose, that of being an expression of the Christian κοινωνία, if it revealed a spirit of skimping. It would then, furthermore, demonstrate a lack of ἁπλότης, singleness of mind and purpose. It would arouse the suspicion that the Corinthian Christians were pretty far in arrears in the matter of banishing covetousness from their hearts.

The Corinthians have the correct understanding, but they are not fully alert to the situation. They need prodding, and should welcome assistance.

2. 9:6-15

Having explained the meaning of the delegation which he is sending to Corinth, Paul, beginning with vs. 6 and continuing to the end of the chapter, speaks about the grand purpose which he is aiming to achieve in connection with the collection. He uses the figure of sowing and reaping. Taking part in the collection may be compared to casting seed into a field, expecting it to reap a harvest in return.

(6) Paul calls special attention to what he is about to say with Τοῦτο δέ, *Now this.* The demonstrative pronoun τοῦτο here stands alone; grammatically it is not connected with the rest of the sentence. It is neither the subject nor the object of any verb. It exhibits somewhat the characteristics of an exclamation: Now this! Yet the meaning is very clear. What Paul wants to say is: Now this is what I have in mind, and what I would like to have you consider carefully.

Ὁ σπείρων φειδομένως, φειδομένως καὶ θερίσει, καὶ ὁ σπείρων ἐπ' εὐλογίαις, ἐπ' εὐλογίαις καὶ θερίσει, *He who sows sparingly, sparingly also shall he reap, and he who sows in a bountiful manner, in a bountiful manner also shall he reap.* The sentence stresses the relation of the harvest to the sowing, and the careful attention which a sower pays to this fact. Note how Paul places the adverbial modifiers, φειδομένως in the one case and ἐπ' εὐλογίαις in the second, next to each other. If the sowing is done φειδομένως, φειδομένως will also be the reaping. It is the same with ἐπ' εὐλογίαις.

This prepositional phrase is unusual. The new *Greek-English Lexicon of the New Testament** says that it is adverbial in nature and expresses manner. To illustrate, the Lexicon refers to an expression like κακοτρόπως καὶ ἐπὶ ῥαδιουργίας, "deceitfully and on trickery"; thus because the prepositional phrase is coordinated with a regular adverb.

---

*) Arndt-Gingrich, **Greek-English Lexicon of the New Testament** (University of Chicago Press, Chicago 57, Ill., 1957).

The said Lexicon lists our passage as the only case of its kind found in the New Testament. Not only the adverbial function but the meaning of the phrase as well is determined by its contrast to the adverb φειδομένως, ἐπ᾽ εὐλογίαις means: *in a bountiful manner.*

Since Paul calls special attention to this relation between reaping and sowing, we shall do well to take a little closer look at the expressions which he uses. He does not say, e.g., he who sows *a little,* but uses the adverb φειδομένως. We met the verb from the same stem in 1:23, φειδομένως ὑμῶν, "sparing you." There the participle does not stress the outward action of sparing, but calls attention to its motivation, namely, Paul's consideration for the Corinthians. Paul refrained from doing a certain thing because his love for the Corinthians prevented him. Also in our passage the φειδομένως does not merely suggest the small amount of seed that is used, but hints at a hesitancy of the sower about the act of sowing. The word εὐλογία, if anything, goes a little further in this direction, pointing not only to the amount of the seed, but to the willingness, the cheerfulness, with which it was sown.

In spite of the fact that Paul places the two adverbs φειδομένως, and the two phrases ἐπ᾽ εὐλογίαις, next to each other, they do not apply to the σπείρειν and to the θερίζειν in the same manner. As far as the sowing is concerned, it is entirely up to the sower whether he wants to sow sparingly or abundantly; but not so with the harvest. That depends entirely on the blessing of the Lord. So much is clear: from a niggardly sowing no rich harvest may be expected. But if the Lord does not grant His blessing, even the most bountiful sowing will not produce a rich harvest. Sowing demands a trust in God's providence on the part of the sower.

Thus, while it is true that a sower is guided in his sowing by a consideration of the size of the harvest which he wishes to reap, yet he must exercise confidence, a trust in God, when he sows much in the hope of reaping a rich harvest.

It is this cheerful, hopeful confidence which Paul is trying to stir up in his readers. As a sower does not consider the seed which he casts into the ground as wasted, neither should a participant in the present collection enter his gift in the loss column of his ledger. It is, rather, an investment from which rich profits may be expected. Paul uses the same figure of sowing and harvesting in his letter to the Galatians:

"For whatsoever a man soweth, that shall he also reap" (Gal. 6:7). This he says by way of encouragement, not to cultivate the lust of reward or the idea of merit. Remember how, in the very beginning, he placed the entire collection under the general heading of χάρις. The Corinthians had experienced the grace of God in a rich measure, not only when the Gospel message was brought to them, but recently in a special way, when they through a terrific spiritual struggle were led to a glorious victory.

(7) By comparing the collection with the seeding of a field, and by holding out the prospect of a rich harvest, Paul arouses the faith of the Corinthians in the grace of God to a cheerful response to the call for contributions. He does not say in what the harvest will consist, but will speak about that a little later. Yet if the collection serves as an expression of the spiritual κοινωνία, and will strengthen the bonds of this κοινωνία, that in itself would be a rich harvest.

At present, however, Paul is interested in setting forth another point. He reminds the Corinthians that any form of coercion or constraint is foreign to the matter. Ἕκαστος καθὼς προῄρηται τῇ καρδίᾳ, *Every one just as he has first made up his mind (or chosen in his heart).* Αἱρέομαι denotes a free choice, without any high-pressuring or coercion. This is to be exercised by the giver πρό, 'beforehand.' This privilege, this exercise of Christian faith and love, belongs to every member of the Church. His faith, the exercise and training of his faith, is a very individual, personal matter. Brethren may advise, they may admonish, they may urge and encourage, but in the last analysis even the size of a contribution is a question to be settled between the believer and his Lord.

After this general remark, Paul adds two specific dangers that are to be carefully avoided: μὴ ἐκ λύπης ἢ ἐξ ἀνάγκης, *not from grief or from compulsion.* Does a sower ever sow his seed from grief? Does he feel sorry that he has cast the seed into the ground? It is true, for him the seed is gone; he can make no further use of it. But does he feel sorry for that? He rejoices in the fact that he had seed to sow. He may even have gone so far that he borrowed the money to buy the seed to be cast away. Let a Christian giver look at his gift in the same light. If he gives with grief in his heart over the loss, his gift becomes tainted. Does he not appreciate the grace of God which enabled him to give? Is his ἁπλότης deficient? Does he cling to the treasures of this world? Does the κοινωνία mean little or nothing to him? Does he consider every mite that he spends on it, to express it and to strengthen it, as wasted?

Nor let a Christian give from compulsion, be it the compulsion of some quota system; be it the fear of the wrath of God; or be it the urge to "keep up with the Joneses." If any form of compulsion plays a role in determining the size of the gift, again the gift has become tainted.

Paul adds by way of explanation, ἱλαρὸν γὰρ δότην ἀγαπᾷ ὁ θεός, *for God loves a cheerful giver*—with the stress on *cheerful*. God is not interested in the gift as such. He is interested in the heart of the giver. If the heart is motivated by λύπη or ἀνάγκη, the gift loses its value. God does not need the gift. All the goods of the world are His. He created them. In the Psalm He says, "If I were hungry, I would not tell thee: for the world is mine, and the fullness thereof" (Ps. 50:12). If He needed a gift for His hungry children, He would not have to go begging. He can readily provide for them. If He asks others of His children to come to the assistance of their needy brethren, it is to give them an opportunity to exercise their new life, to show their love to their brethren and their thankfulness toward God. To invite them to contribute is, as Paul said from the very beginning, an act of God's grace. Let them respond cheerfully.

The words which Paul uses are adapted from Proverbs 22:8, which in the Septuagint translation reads, ἄνδρα ἱλαρὸν καὶ δότην εὐλογεῖ ὁ θεός, "God blesses a cheerful man and giver," while the Hebrew original says that "a kind-eyed one, he is blessed." For the specific term "to bless" Paul substitutes the more general idea "to love," ἀγαπᾶν, which does not mean merely 'to be pleased,' but to treat accordingly, thus including also the blessing. God actively loves a cheerful giver.

God Himself is a cheerful Giver. Not only can St. James say, "Every good gift and every perfect gift is from above, and cometh down from the Father of lights, with whom is no variableness, neither shadow of turning" (Jas. 1:17), but he also maintains that "God giveth to all men liberally (ἁπλῶς, i.e., 'simply giving') and up-braideth not" (vs. 5). His children, being born of Him and being created after His image, will manifest the same spirit.

A Christian giver realizes that what he is able to give he has first received as a gift from God. His gift will be a happy expression of thanks to God who enabled him to have the happy experience of giving. He will remember the word of Jesus which Paul quoted to the Ephesian elders: "It is more blessed to give than to receive" (Acts 20:35).

(8) God loves a cheerful giver. He promises to bless him. Can He? Yes, it is easy for Him. However, first He must perform a more difficult task; but He is able to do that also. The more difficult task is—since all men by nature are rather unwilling givers—that He transform the Corinthians into cheerful givers. He does so, not by command, not by promise of a reward to be earned by the giver, not by threats of dire punishment for anyone who does not comply. He does so by His life-giving, joy-creating grace.

The Corinthians had experienced the grace of God. They got their first taste of it when Paul brought them the Gospel of salvation for Christ's sake. They got another rich taste only a short while before, when the grace of God led them out of the trouble into which they had permitted themselves to be lured, had granted them a victory, and was leading them on the way of recovery. God had poured out His grace upon them richly. But that was only a beginning. He can do much more. Can He? Yes, He can.

Paul very emphatically places the verb δυνατεῖ at the head of the sentence; *He can,* there is not the least doubt about His ability. Let this truth sink in: God is able. What is it that God can do?

Δυνατεῖ δὲ ὁ θεὸς πᾶσαν περισσεῦσαι εἰς ὑμᾶς, *Able is God to increase (and make abound) every grace in you.* Every grace, every form of grace. They have experienced the manifold grace of God richly, but God can make it abound still more and more. Particularly, God can make them cheerful givers. We now note first what a bold picture Paul paints of a cheerful giver.

Ἵνα ἐν παντὶ πάντοτε πᾶσαν αὐτάρκειαν ἔχοντες, *that you (as people) who have in all things at all times all sufficiency.* . . . Note the repetition of the "all," πᾶν, in the description of the subject. The Corinthians have a complete sufficiency; they lack nothing. In his first letter Paul had written, "I thank my God always on your behalf, for the grace of God which is given you by Jesus Christ; that in everything ye are enriched by him, in all utterance, and in all knowledge; even as the testimony of Christ was confirmed in you: so that ye come behind in no gift" (I Cor. 1:4-7). In his second letter he had repeated, "Ye abound in everything, in faith, and utterance, and knowledge, and in all diligence, and in your love to us" (8:7). Well may he now say that they have complete sufficiency. And they have it in every respect, and at all times.

The limit has not yet been reached. God is able to increase every grace.

This particular grace of God has not yet had an opportunity to manifest itself in their participation in the present collection. To be sure, they were ready a year before for the doing with determination, but the spiritual struggle which they had undergone in the meantime had seriously interfered. But God is able to increase the operation of His grace also in this respect, ἵνα . . . περισσεύητε εἰς πᾶν ἔργον ἀγαθόν, *that you . . . increase in every good work.* Note another πᾶν, the fifth in a single sentence.

If anyone recognizes this ability of God, embraces it in a believing heart, and appreciates it: can he help but become a cheerful giver?— Now what about the harvest? Paul brings a quotation from the Old Testament.

(9) Καθὼς γέγραπται, *as it is written,* Paul says. Yes, there it stands before all men's eyes as a permanent record.

The quotation which Paul introduces with these words is taken from Psalm 112. This Psalm must be read against the background of Psalm 111. These two Psalms form a unit. They are not only alike in structure, but, as an old saying has it, where the one leaves off the other begins: *Ubi haec ode* (Ps. 111) *desinit, sequens incipit.* Both Psalms are acrostics, consisting of 22 lines beginning with the 22 letters of the Hebrew alphabet. In both Psalms two succeeding lines always form a pair, except that in each case the last six lines are grouped in two triplets. Concerning the thought presented in the two Psalms, Delitzsch quotes Hitzig as saying: "Whilst Ps. 111 celebrates the glory, might, and loving-kindness of Jahve in the circle of the upright (cf. vs. 1: in the assembly of the upright), Ps. 112 celebrates the glory flowing therefrom and the happiness of the upright themselves (cf. vs. 2: the generation of the upright shall be blessed), of those who fear Jahve. The two Psalms are twin in form as in contents."

St. Paul's quotation is from the second of this pair of Psalms, from the one which sings about the blessings of the God-fearing, and thus is very appropriate for the occasion. Moreover, while Paul had compared the Christians' contribution to the collection for the needy to a sowing, the Psalm also speaks about a "scattering" as of seed.

Ἐσκόρπισεν, ἔδωκεν τοῖς πένησιν, *He scattered, he gave to the poor* (*laborers*).

Ἐσκόρπισεν is the translation of a Hebrew Piel form, denoting an intensive act of scattering and spreading; while ἔδωκεν is the translation of a simple Qal form, telling us in what the scattering consisted. It was a giving to the poor. One is reminded of Proverbs 11:24: "There is that scattereth, and yet increaseth; and there is that withholdeth more than is meet, but it tendeth to poverty." (Luther: *Einer teilt aus, und hat immer mehr; ein anderer karget, da er nicht soll, und wird doch aermer.*)

In the Greek there is a difference between πένης and πτωχός. While πτωχός denotes a beggar, πένης applies to a poor man who lives from hand to mouth. (So Plutarch explains, according to the new Greek-English Lexicon.) Whether the translators of the Septuagint had this distinction in mind, may be difficult to determine; compare their translation of Psalm 40:17: "poor and *needy*" as πτωχὸς καὶ πένης; Luther: *arm und elend.* The distinction has little bearing on the point which the Psalmist is trying to put across, namely, that the fear of the Lord, which characterizes the "upright," expresses itself also in this way that he scatters and gives to the poor. He is not a pinchpenny; he is a cheerful giver. The blessing which he received from the Lord makes him such.

The point which Paul is trying to impress on the hearts of the Corinthians is that God loves and blesses a cheerful giver. So much for a description from the Psalm of what a cheerful giver is like. Now for the inducement it offers by holding out the promise of a bountiful harvest.

Ἡ δικαιοσύνη αὐτοῦ μένει εἰς τὸν αἰῶνα, *His righteousness endures unto the eon* (*for ever*).

What is δικαιοσύνη? In 3:9, Paul compared δικαιοσύνη with κατάκρισις. He contrasted the two terms and pointed out that the διακονία τῆς κατακρίσεως is the direct opposite of the διακονία τῆς δικαιοσύνης. Κατάκρισις is the act of a judge who after due investigation declares a defendant guilty. By way of contrast, δικαιοσύνη is a righteousness pronounced by a judicial verdict.

We take a little closer look at the use of this term in the Psalm from which Paul quotes. Psalm 111, which praises the works of the Lord, says in vs. 3: "His righteousness endureth for ever." Then, unfolding the doings of the Lord in His righteousness, the Psalmist says in vs. 9: "He sent *redemption* unto his people: he hath commanded *his covenant* for ever: holy and reverend is his name." That is the righteousness of the Lord which the Psalmist has in mind: not the legislative righteousness, in which He issues just commandments, not the retributive righteousness, according to which He without partiality and without respect of persons rewards the good and punishes the evil, but that righteousness of which Paul says in Romans 1:17, that it is revealed in the Gospel from faith to faith; and of which St. John writes: "If we confess our sins, he is faithful and *just* to forgive us our sins, and to cleanse us from all unrighteousness" (I John 1:9).

The Psalmist declares the fear of the Lord (*Gottesfurcht*) to be the beginning of wisdom, and concludes with the promise that if anyone acts accordingly ("do his commandments"), his praise will endure forever.

Here is where Psalm 112 takes over, singing about the blessedness of a man who shows this "wisdom" in his conduct, who "feareth the Lord" and "delighteth greatly in his commandments." Already in vs. 3 he declares: "His righteousness endureth for ever." The righteousness which he has received from the Lord in the forgiveness of his sins will ever guide him in his life and conduct. His whole behavior will demonstrate undeniably that he is a justified man. He will "show favor" (vs. 5) and "lend." He will scatter his gifts among the poor (vs. 9).

That is the δικαιοσύνη about which the Psalmist is singing, a righteousness effected by the righteous God, a righteousness proclaimed to the sinner in a sentence of justification, a righteousness which creates and motivates a life of righteousness. Of this righteousness the Psalmist sings that it endures forever. It will outlast this present life; it will outlast death and the grave; it will outlast the final judgment, and will follow him into heaven, as the Book of Revelation says: "Their works do follow them" (Rev. 14:13).

We are reminded of the description which Jesus gives us of the final judgment. He will use our fruits of righteousness to demonstrate before the world the correctness of His verdict, which He proclaimed by placing us on His right hand and by inviting us to inherit the kingdom prepared for us from the foundation of the world.

Neither the Psalmist nor Paul says that these works of righteousness are our own achievements, or that they merit us the favor of God. From the very beginning (8:1) Paul had placed the entire matter of the collection under the comprehensive heading of "the grace of God." He underscores this truth in the following short paragraph, using the thoughts of the Psalm passage as a starting point.

(10) When Paul introduced the comparison of the collection with the act of sowing, it was simply assumed that the man who was going to sow his field had the necessary seed on hand; that is was simply left up to his decision whether he would sow much or little. But where did his seed come from? The One who blesses the seed so that it produces a harvest is also the One who provided the seed in the first place. So it is with the collection. God will make it a blessing for the cheerful giver; but it was also God who provided the giver with the means to give.

'Ο δὲ ἐπιχορηγῶν σπέρμα τῷ σπείροντι καὶ ἄρτον εἰς βρῶσιν, *Now He who provides seed to the sower and bread for eating.* 'Ο ἐπιχορηγῶν, the substantivized present participle, is equivalent to our English verbal noun ending in -er, *the provider,* not one who just happens to provide, but one whose characteristic it is to do so. It is necessary to remind also Christians again and again of this truth. We too easily forget, and take things as they are for granted. There is a Provider of seed, and without His providing there would be no sowing.

The same God, however, who provides seed to the sower, by means of that act also provides bread for eating: to the scanty sower scantily, and to the sower ἐπ' εὐλογίαις, bountifully.

Apply this truth to the collection. The same Provider of natural seed and bread, He χορηγήσει καὶ πληθυνεῖ τὸν σπόρον ὑμῶν καὶ αὐξήσει τὰ γενήματα τῆς δικαιοσύνης ὑμῶν, *He will provide and multiply your (spiritual) seed and will increase your products of righteousness.*

It seems advisable to take the double verb χορηγήσει καὶ πληθυνεῖ as more than an ordinary hendiadys: He will provide richly. Rather, the first verb simply repeats the action named in the substantivized participle of the subject; then the second adds the thought: and He will do so richly, so that you will have no difficulty as cheerful givers to give ἐπ' εὐλογίαις.

The parallelism of the two statements: "The Provider of seed for the sower . . . will provide your σπόρος," indicates that it is advisable to take σπόρος in its literal sense used metaphorically, not as Lenski suggests, metonymically, for the crop which it produces. While σπέρμα always is concrete, the seed, the first meaning of the word σπόρος is the act of sowing.

The expression τὰ γενήματα τῆς δικαιοσύνης is found in the Septuagint translation of Hosea 10:12, which differs from the original in several points. In Keil's translation the passage reads: "Sow to yourselves for righteousness, reap according to love; plough for yourselves virgin soil: for it is time to seek Jehovah, *till He come and rain righteousness upon you.*" Instead of the last clause the Septuagint reads, ἕως τοῦ ἐλθεῖν γενήματα δικαιοσύνης ὑμῖν, *till there come products of righteousness to you.* Δικαιοσύνη, the same word which was used before, is the righteousness declared by God in His irrevocable verdict, and announced to sinners in the Gospel, the righteousness which manifests itself in the sinner by a new life of righteousness, over which God rejoices. The works of righteousness performed by the justified sinner are not his own achievements; they are γενήματα, products, of that imputed righteousness.

Paul holds out the promise that God αὐξήσει, "will increase" in number, in vigor, etc. For this idea the Prophet Hosea had used the figure: God will *rain* righteousness upon you.

(11) All glory to God!—The next verse, in a way, summarizes the thoughts which Paul developed beginning with vs. 6, and serves as a transition to the glorious conclusion of this second part of the epistle. Paul addresses the Corinthians as πλουτιζόμενοι, as *people who are being enriched.* The fact that Paul does not connect the participle in its case to the pronoun of the previous sentence, ὑμῶν, to which it refers, indicates that the new thought is not to be subjoined to the foregoing. It marks an independent statement, yet one closely related to the preceding one. He had spoken about God's providing various gifts, of multiplying and increasing them. By these gifts the Corinthians are being enriched. We bear in mind that Paul's general topic is the collection for the saints in Jerusalem, toward which the Corinthians had agreed to contribute. When we give toward any purpose, we sometimes have the feeling as though thereby we ourselves are being impoverished in proportion to the amount of our contribution. Paul

says to the Corinthians not only: No, but you are being enriched; he adds emphatically ἐν παντί, *in every respect*. There is a constant increase going on for the giver even in such things as, on the surface, might look like a setback.

The high point of this enrichment Paul mentions in the phrase εἰς πᾶσαν ἁπλότητα, *in complete singleness of purpose*. Paul mentioned the ἁπλότης before as evident among the Macedonians in connection with the collection; their Christian joy and their extreme poverty together resulted in a rich development of their ἁπλότης. Now, the Greek-English Lexicon* insists that in this case (8:2) ἁπλότης must be rendered with "liberality." Also our present passage (9:11) is listed as an example of this use of the word. There is, however, no compelling reason for the change. 'Απλότης expresses the attitude of the Christian heart which grasps the truth of Jesus' word to Martha: "One thing is needful," and that of Paul that God does "gather together in one all things in Christ" (Eph. 1:10).

There are many things in the world to distract a Christian's attention. To strengthen his ἁπλότης is indeed enriching him. The ἁπλότης sets its sights on the glory of God. With this thought Paul closes this transitional verse: ἥτις κατεργάζεται δι' ἡμῶν εὐχαριστίαν τῷ θεῷ, which (*by its nature*) *effects through us thanksgiving to God*.

῟Ητις, unlike the common relative pronoun, does more than to connect the new thought with the foregoing. It also implies that the antecedent such as it is, by its nature, produces the result stated in the clause.

The ἁπλότης as such, by its very nature, produces thanksgiving. How can it be otherwise? We are permeated with the recognition that by ourselves we are nothing; that by our own fault we are sinners; that we have justly merited God's wrath, temporal death, and eternal damnation; that by no means are we able to avert our doom; that we are unable to change our nature, but that, rather, by all our own efforts we sink only deeper into perdition. We are permeated with the knowledge that God spared not His own Son in order to save us; that He sent His Spirit to kindle faith in our rebellious hearts; that He by the power of His Word broke down our resistance to what seemed utter foolishness to us, and moved us to accept His gracious

---

*) Arndt-Gingrich, **A Greek-English Lexicon of the New Testament,** 1957.

offer as our only hope of salvation. In other words, we recognize that we who were beggarly poor by nature now have been made rich by God, and are continually being made rich over and over. Then, how can such concentrated realization do anything else than make us burst forth in thanksgiving? The more we recognize God as the sole source of all our blessings, the more will our ἁπλότης be strengthened, the more will it produce thanksgiving.

This applies also to the collection for the saints in Jerusalem. Deliberate participation in it will exercise and strengthen the ἁπλότης. What a wonderful hymn of praise it will help to produce, Paul will present in the last subpart of this second main part of his epistle, 9:12-15.

The subsection which we are to study now ends with a very brief expression of thanks to God. But the sentence preceding this doxology is rather lengthy and of a form which calls for some grammatical discussion. Since the Greek writers had at their disposal certain word endings indicating number, case, and gender which the English idiom lacks, they can at times express their thoughts with perfect clarity in a way which we simply cannot duplicate in our language.

The statement in our text is made in the form of an explanatory subordinate clause introduced by ὅτι, because. The first part, vs. 12, is quite regular, but the second, vs. 13, containing the participle δοξάζοντες, offers a construction which is foreign to our English grammar. The form of the participle is the masculine nominative plural; but there is no noun of that description, neither in the previous verse nor anywhere in the vicinity. Grammarians call it a nominative absolute. The subject of this participle must be taken from the ἁγίων mentioned in vs. 12. The purpose is to explain in some detail the εὐχαριστίαι mentioned in vs. 12. Thus the thought of vs. 13 is subordinate to vs. 12.

Verse 14 then contains another participle, this time in the genitive plural, ἐπιποθούντων, masculine, since it modifies αὐτῶν, which here refers to persons. The question is whether αὐτῶν . . . ἐπιποθούντων should be read as a genitive absolute, or whether the dative δεήσει should be coupled to the two datives of vs. 13 (τῇ ὑποταγῇ . . . καὶ ἁπλότητι) which depend on the preposition ἐπί. In that case the genitive αὐτῶν would be possessive, modifying δεήσει. This second alternative, although espoused by Bachmann in Zahn (Kommentar *zum Neuen Testament*), is not very likely. It would state that the recipients of the gift will glorify God for the Corinthians' ὑποταγή and ἁπλότης and for their own δέησις. It seems best to take the first alternative. Bachmann objects that in that case καί would have to be translated as *also*—"also they"—which, according to him, would presuppose a ὑμεῖς in the previous sentence, to justify the strong contrast which is implied in *also they*. Yet the καί does not necessarily have to be joined to αὐτῶν alone, but may refer to the thought of the entire genitive absolute. Not two groups of persons are being compared, but two actions of the same group.

To sum up, the skeleton of the sentence might be presented something like this: because the collection will result in much thanksgiving, as the recipients glorify God particularly for two products of His grace in the Corinthians, while they also long for their benefactors in their prayers.

Some minor points of grammar will be considered in the course of our study.

(12) In closing the previous section, where Paul compared the collection for the needy Christians in Jerusalem to a sowing for a harvest, he had mentioned as one of the important results the increase and strengthening of Christian ἁπλότης, their living in the truth that "One thing is needful," which is of such a nature that it effects and multiplies thanksgiving to God. This truth he now unfolds in the present section by pointing to the intended purpose of the collection.

What is it? The obvious purpose, as everyone could assume, was to bring relief to the brethren. There were many poor members in the Jerusalem congregation. It had been so from the beginning. Some of the better-situated members had at that time sold their possessions and placed the money at the disposal of the Apostles to procure food and clothing for the needy. This work soon became too burdensome for the Apostles; it interfered with the main task for which our Savior had called them. The Apostles pleaded with the congregation for a division of labor, and the congregation responded by electing seven almoners.

Poverty continued. When Paul and Barnabas, after their first mission journey, went to Jerusalem to discuss the question of circumcision and other Mosaic ceremonies, whether the Gentile Christians were obligated to observe them, the Jerusalem Apostles reminded the missionaries that they should not forget the poor and needy in the mother church. In this way things continued. When Paul in the year following the present epistle delivered the collection in Jerusalem, he found there four men who had a vow on them but were unable to pay for the required purification sacrifices. Paul took these expenses on himself.

Thus there were many poor people in Jerusalem, and the obvious purpose of the collection was relief. Yet that was really only a minor matter. Paul says, οὐ μόνον ἐστὶν προσαναπληροῦσα τὰ ὑστερήματα τῶν ἁγίων, *the collection is not only helping to replenish the things lacking the saints.* A few words and forms here demand our attention. The participle προσαναπληροῦσα is made up of three parts. There is the verb πληρόω. To it is joined the reinforcing particle ἀνά. This compound ἀναπληρόω is used for the fulfillment of prophecy (Matt. 13: 14), for fulfilling the law of Christ (Gal. 6:2), for the Jews' fulfilling of their sins at all times (I Thess. 2:16), for "occupying the room of the unlearned" (I Cor. 14:16), for supplying that which is lacking (I Cor. 16:17), etc. To this verb is prefixed a πρός. The collection which Paul's congregations are gathering will not completely supply the wants of the needy brethren, but it will materially work toward that goal; it will help to supply their needs.

That is one of the purposes, but it is by far not the chief one.

Before we take up a study of Paul's chief aim, it will help us to note under what category Paul includes the collection. In speaking of this ministry he calls it ἡ διακονία τῆς λειτουργίας ταύτης, *the administration of this service.* The word "service" which the King James uses for λειτουργία is really a little too weak to convey the meaning of the Greek word. The Greek-English Lexicon groups the various meanings of the word under two headings. First it is used of ritual and cultic services; then of other kinds of service to God. The word λειτουργία was originally used for a service which a citizen rendered to the community, and for which he bore the expenses; then in general for any public service. This meaning was then applied to religious services. The services which Zacharias, the priest, the father of John the Baptist, performed in the temple are called a λειτουργία (Luke 1:23). The Epistle to the Hebrews speaks of the tabernacle and its vessels of λειτουργία (9:21). Paul, in speaking about his own ministry of the Gospel, calls it θυσία καὶ λειτουργία (Phil. 2:17). Also the assistance which Epaphroditus was sent by the Philippians to render to Paul is called by this name (Phil. 2:30). By using this word λειτουργία in connection with the physical aid which the churches were sending to Jerusalem, Paul elevates the collection to the level of spiritual, religious service. Do we always realize that the contributions which we solicit for congregational or synodical work pertain even more directly to the kingdom of God than did the collection which Paul raised to help feed and clothe the needy saints in Jerusalem? We should do that work, and speak about that work, with reverential awe. It is λειτουργία.

Bearing this in mind, we shall sense more fully what Paul has to say about the deeper meaning and the higher purpose of his collection. Paul continues, ἀλλὰ καὶ περισσεύουσα διὰ πολλῶν εὐχαριστιῶν τῷ θεῷ, but (is) also extemely abundant (overflowing) through thanksgiving of many to God. We note that in this part of the statement, as well as in the first, we have a periphrastic present. Instead of the plain προσαναπληροῖ and περισσεύει we have the respective participles with the copula ἐστίν. This gives greater prominence to the action as such. Our attention is focused on the supplying in the first half and on the superabundance in the second. The administration of our sacred service achieves this double purpose.

Our whole life of sanctification can be summed up under the concept of thanksgiving. Taking part in the collection is in itself an expression of gratitude, but it is of such a nature that it causes also other Christians to increase their thanksgiving.

A question of minor importance is the understanding of πολλῶν. The King James takes it as an adjective modifier of εὐχαριστιῶν, many thanksgivings; so do also other translations, only they try to find some smoother expression, e.g., Moffat: "many a cry of thanks"; Goodspeed: "a wealth of thanksgiving." I prefer to follow Luther's lead, who translated: dass viele Gott danken. This shows that he took πολλῶν in the sense of masculine indefinite pronoun: the thanksgiving of many.

(13) In the previous verse Paul spoke about the collection as a διακονία, an administration, of a sacred service, a λειτουργία. In the present verse he still retains the concept of διακονία; but here he treats it as a test, successfully passed, with a resultant approval. In the matter of the collection the quality of the Corinthians' Chris-

tianity, their ἁπλότης, their εὐχαριστία, their κοινωνία, etc., are being put to a test, and they themselves are thereby given an opportunity to demonstrate that these qualities are genuine in them. That is the δοκιμὴ τῆς διακονίας.

With this aspect of the collection Paul begins the next part of his statement: διὰ τῆς δοκιμῆς τῆς διακονίας ταύτης δοξάζοντες τὸν θεόν, (*many will give thanks to God*) *as they are glorifying God* (*being moved*) *by the test of this service.* We discussed the construction of the participle δοξάζοντες above; we need not repeat. It is of utmost importance to consider what characteristics in particular of the Corinthians' faith the saints in Jerusalem will find established through this test which the collection afforded. Paul mentions two things, The first is ἐπὶ τῇ ὑποταγῇ τῆς ὁμολογίας ὑμῶν εἰς τὸ εὐαγγέλιον τοῦ Χριστοῦ, (*glorifying God*) *on the submission of your confession in* (*respect to*) *the Gospel of Christ.*

Τῇ ὑποταγῇ τῆς ὁμολογίας ὑμῶν. Here we have a noun with a genitive modifier plus a possessive pronoun. We find similar combinations quite frequently in Paul's letters. We take an illustration from Colossians 1:13: τὴν βασιλείαν τοῦ υἱοῦ τῆς ἀγάπης αὐτοῦ, which the King James translates, "the kingdom of his dear Son" (Luther: *das Reich seines lieben Sohnes*). Τῆς ἀγάπης is thus treated as a qualifying genitive modifying τοῦ υἱοῦ. And the possessive pronoun αὐτοῦ is taken, not as modifying the noun immediately preceding it (τῆς ἀγάπης), but the compound expression τοῦ υἱοῦ τῆς ἀγάπης: His dear Son (not: the Son of His love). Apply this observation to the expression now under investigation, and we get: your confessional submission in respect to the Gospel, i.e., your submission to the Gospel as it becomes manifest in your confession. The Greek-English Lexicon* paraphrases: "Your confessing the Gospel finds expression in obedient subjection to its requirements." This is a good statement except for the last word, "requirements," which may create the impression of rules and legalistic commandments (Bauer's German original is even worse: *Euer Bekenntnis zum Evangelium aeussert sich in gehorsamer Unterwerfung unter dessen* Forderungen).

Ὁμολογία points to a confession in words. Yet such confession alone is not sufficient in the case of the Gospel. The Gospel is a power

---

*) Arndt-Gingrich, **A Greek-English Lexicon of the New Testament,** 1957.

of God which creates a new spiritual life in its hearers. The birth of this new life is a revolutionary process. A few chapters back (5:17) Paul describes it in these words: "Old things are passed away, behold, all things are become new." What does a confession imply in a case of this nature? To laud the Gospel in words while continuing in the former life of sin would be rank hypocrisy: "having a form of godliness, but denying the power thereof" (II Tim. 3:5). Ὁμολογία in this case includes an expression of the new life within the heart by a new mode of living in the world. Participating wholeheartedly in the collection for the needy saints is a method of ὁμολογία. It shows that the Gospel is living and ruling in the hearts of the Corinthians, producing an active brotherly love.

A second reason for the increased thanksgiving of the saints Paul expresses in these words: καὶ (ἐπὶ τῇ) ἁπλότητι τῆς κοινωνίας εἰς αὐτοὺς καὶ εἰς πάντας, and (on the) singleness of (your) fellowship to them and to all. This phrase effectively disposes of the idea that by ἁπλότης Paul understands "liberality." The Corinthians took up a collection for the needy saints in Jerusalem, and they likely contributed liberally; but they did not take up a collection for all, which the addition of εἰς πάντας would imply if ἁπλότης is understood to mean "liberality." The meaning of "singleness of mind" or "singleheartedness" must be retained.

We note that Paul does not repeat the preposition and the definite article (ἐπὶ τῇ) with the second member of the phrase. Omitting these serves to unite the two datives most closely. The ὑποταγῇ τῆς ὁμολογίας and the ἁπλότητι τῆς κοινωνίας may not be separated. Just as Jesus Christ is the same yesterday and today and forever (Heb. 13:8), so is also His Gospel. And again, just as God is not the God of the Jews only, but also of the Gentiles (Rom. 3:29), so also the Gospel of Christ is a power of God unto salvation to everyone that believeth, to the Jew first and also to the Greek (Rom. 1:16). The Gospel does not create different kinds of believers, different types of Christians: e.g., Jewish and Gentile, but one Church in which there is neither Jew nor Greek, neither bond nor free, neither male nor female, but all are one in (the same) Christ Jesus (Gal. 3:28). This is the κοινωνία created by the Gospel. Thus submission to the Gospel and joining this fellowship are inseparably tied together. You cannot submit to the Gospel and at the same time deny the fellowship, just as you cannot join the fellowship while rejecting the Gospel. Paul combines the two concepts under one article.

The collection also in this respect evidences the singleheartedness of the Corinthians. There were many things that separated them from the saints in Jerusalem, not only distance and economical conditions, but also nationality, and historical and religious background. But while these differences continued outwardly, they could not affect the κοινωνία created by the Gospel. And the participation of the Corinthians in the collection gave expression to their singleheartedness also in this respect.

The collection which the Corinthians helped to raise for their needy fellow Christians in Jerusalem pointed out their κοινωνία with them. It did more. The Corinthians were not the only ones who contributed to the collection. Rather, in this collection they were joining hands with the Christians in Macedonia, and with those in Asia and in Galatia. It was a joint endeavor of the mission congregations, which Paul did not consider as mere coöperation in externals. He considered it as a truly spiritual undertaking: the collection as a conscious act of confessing proclaimed to the saints in Jerusalem the faith of the Corinthians in the Gospel of Jesus Christ and their wholehearted realization of the fellowship which this common faith entailed. This then would induce them to glorify God for His grace which He had granted to the Corinthians as well as to the Christians in Jerusalem. The solidarity of the Church would stand out in bold relief, and would be strengthened in the hearts of all concerned. It would be a rich spiritual harvest.

But that is only one side of the picture.

(14) In vs. 14 Paul adds another point. He does so, as we have analyzed the construction above, by means of a genitive absolute: καὶ αὐτῶν δεήσει ὑπὲρ ὑμῶν ἐπιποθούντων ὑμᾶς, *while they also with intercession for you give vent to their longing for you.*

Ἐπιποθέω denotes an anxious desire, a warmhearted longing or yearning. Such feelings will be the reaction on the part of the saints in Jerusalem to the interest which the Corinthians showed for their well-being in their collection. The collection will thus help to bring the hearts of both churches closer together. The interest of the Corinthians was purely spiritual, no external or temporal benefits accruing to them. Likewise the response on the part of the recipients, their longing for the Corinthians, would be purely spiritual, again without any outward advantages in sight.

Ἐπιποθεῖν is a process going on in the heart. As such it is not perceptible to human senses. It cannot be seen nor measured. Yet it is a powerful force, driving the Christians to fervent prayer and intercession. They will long for their benefactors δεήσει ὑπὲρ ὑμῶν, *with prayer for you.*

To be sure, the Christians in Jerusalem had offered up prayers for the Corinthians before this. They were constantly praying for the whole Church on earth. They were praying for the success of the Gospel. The Lord Himself had taught them to pray, "Thy kingdom come." And as early as at the election of almoners we are told that the Apostles would give themselves continually to prayer and to the ministry of the Word (Acts 6:4).

These general prayers for the Church certainly included also the Corinthians. Yet from now on there would be a change. The longing of the saints would not stop at such a general, all-inclusive supplication. It would urge them to single out the Corinthians and to mention them by name in their petitions.

What a rich blessing that would mean for the Corinthians! God promises to hear and answer prayer, and the effectual fervent prayer of a righteous man availeth much (Jas. 5:16). What then if the members of a whole congregation unite to bring their requests before the throne of God for another of His congregations? Jesus is in the midst of two or three who are gathered together in His name, and promises that what the two or three may agree to ask shall be done for them by His Father in heaven (Matt. 18:19, 20).

A rich harvest! Who will receive the credit for it? Will the Corinthians for their willingness? Will the saints in Jerusalem for their ready response? Who made the Corinthians willing? And who prompted the Jerusalem Christians to respond? All honor belongs to God. Paul states this in a διά phrase: διὰ τὴν ὑπερβάλλουσαν χάριν τοῦ θεοῦ ἐφ᾽ ὑμῖν, *on account of the superabundant grace of God to you.* Ἐφ᾽ ὑμῖν expresses the dative idea in an intensified degree: 'to you, on you, upon you.' The Corinthians must realize that their participation in the collection was nothing but an act of God's grace. If it had not been for the grace of God, they never would have thought of joining in the collection. If they had heard about the collection at all, it would have seemed undiluted foolishness to them. It was grace that brought them the Gospel in the first place. It was grace that led them to accept the Gospel. Again it was grace that had led them out of their recent self-incurred difficuties: grace, pure grace, without any merit or worthiness on their part. It was rich grace, "superabundant" grace Paul calls it, a grace that overcame the strongest resistance and did not rest till it had gained its point.

The saints in Jerusalem thank God and glorify His name because He granted His grace to the Corinthians; and they pray to Him to continue and to increase His grace in them.

(15) Paul concludes the entire part on the collection with the brief but powerful shout of thanksgiving: Χάρις τῷ θεῷ ἐπὶ τῇ ἀνεκδιηγήτῳ αὐτοῦ δωρεᾷ, *Thanks to God for His indescribable gift.*

A gift from beginning to end, a free gift! Indescribable, unfounded, unlimited: nothing on earth to compare with it, not even a mother's self-sacrificing devotion. She may forget, but God will never. For as the heavens are higher than the earth, so are His ways higher than our ways. God can and will do exceeding abundantly above all that we ask or think.

Yes, thanks be to God for His indescribable gift of grace.

III. THE INTRUDERS

Chapters 10-13

Chapters 10 to 13 form the third and last part of Second Corinthians. The Epistle clearly falls into three main parts, each one dealing with a specific subject. The break between the second and third parts is especially marked, so sharp indeed that many critics consider the following chapters as a separate letter, or at least as a part of another letter. They call this part the "Four-Chapter Epistle." Yet, although the language and the tone of these chapters is very much different from that of the two preceding parts, they clearly belong to our present Second Corinthians, as a part of which they appear in all old codices. "No abbreviated text has ever been discovered to raise even the faintest question on this score, and no text with an omission or with omissions has ever been found" (Lenski).

Parts One and Two, though they treat their respective subjects with great clarity, still raise a number of questions which they leave unanswered. To mention a few: Why does Paul so elaborately explain that a change in his travel plans does not affect the unchanging truth of the Gospel message which he proclaims? Why does he maintain that his purpose in deferring his visit to Corinth to a later date was to spare the Corinthians? Why does he enlarge on the superiority of the New Testament over the Old, charging the Jews that they read their Old Testament with a veil over their heart? The collection for the needy Christians in Jerusalem, which a year earlier the Corinthians had endorsed enthusiastically, had lagged seriously. Why? And why is Paul so extremely careful in explaining his sending of helpers to organize and speed up the gathering of funds?

Such and similar questions call for an answer, which is not given in Parts One and Two. The Corinthians, no doubt, knew the reason, but they needed instruction and guidance in dealing practically with the unhealthy situation. This instruction and guidance Paul now gives in the form of a personal defense. His person is involved, and for the sake of the Gospel he must vindicate himself. He does not relish the task, yet in the interest of the spiritual well-being of the Corinthian church he considers it necessary. It is well to bear this in mind throughout the study of this section. According to the principle Paul had expressed in 5:12: "For we commend not ourselves again to you, but give you occasion to glory on our behalf, that ye may have somewhat to answer them which glory in appearance, and not in heart"— according to this principle Paul is now defending himself against the accusations and insinuations which the troublemakers peddled in Corinth, and which the Corinthians failed, or were not able, to meet effectively—and by which their faith was greatly endangered.

For a brief listing of the events during the year just prior to the writing of Second Corinthians see page 193.

A. PAUL'S STANDARD
Chapter 10

1. 10:1-6

(1) With a bold αὐτὸς δὲ ἐγώ Paul announces that he is now taking up a personal matter. What he had written so far was on the whole a joint message from him and Timothy, with an occasional personal remark (cf. e.g., 1:23ff.). The section which now follows has to do directly with Paul only. An occasional "we" indicates that the derogatory remarks of the troublemakers had not spared his assistants; they had also been "smeared" (cf. vs. 2).

Paul begins with a plea, παρακαλῶ. Παρακαλεῖν always denotes an appeal, with a wide range of form in which it may be issued, from mild to severe, from a gentle request to the sternest rebuke. In the present case he bases his appeal on *the meekness and gentleness of Christ*, διὰ τῆς πραΰτητος καὶ ἐπιεικείας τοῦ Χριστοῦ. The single article before the two nouns combines them into a compound unit. Meekness is the inner attitude of the heart, which manifests itself in gentleness when dealing with men. The word ἐπιεικής is never used of Jesus, except by Paul in the present passage, while πραΰς is predicated of

Him twice in the Gospel of St. Matthew. Jesus invited us to learn from Him ὅτι πραΰς εἰμι καὶ ταπεινὸς τῇ καρδίᾳ (Matt. 11:29). And regarding His entry into Jerusalem, Matthew cited the prophecy of Zechariah to the effect that Zion's King is coming πραΰς. Jesus' dealings with poor sinners were always prompted by a heart filled with ἐπιείκεια and in a manner guided by πραΰτης. But let no one get the idea that His ἐπιείκεια and πραΰτης was a spineless nonchalance. Think of the stern woes which He uttered against all hypocrites; think of His purging of the Temple.

He manifests His ἐπιείκεια and πραΰτης by laying down His life for the world; and it is by His ἐπιείκεια and πραΰτης alone that we live. The precious ἐπιείκεια and πραΰτης of our Lord, which the Corinthians experienced in a rich measure when the Gospel was first proclaimed to them, and which they only recently experienced again in a special way when by its power they overcame their difficulties, should move them to guard this treasure most jealously. Paul leads them to consider that the real attack of the Judaizing troublemakers was directed against the ἐπιείκεια and πραΰτης of the Lord, to rob the Corinthians of this treasured possession. Their life, flowing from and resting in the ἐπιείκεια and πραΰτης of the Lord, is at stake. Hence Paul bases his appeal on this grace of Christ. The very ἐπιείκεια and πραΰτης of the Lord is put out of commission for them by the errors of the false apostles. To the Galatians Paul expressed this truth with the words: "Christ is become of no effect unto you, whosoever of you are justified by the law; ye are fallen from grace" (Gal. 5:4).

In form the attack of the troublemakers was directed against the person of Paul. Paul adds it in a relative clause, ὃς κατὰ πρόσωπον μὲν ταπεινὸς ἐν ὑμῖν, ἀπὼν δὲ θαρρῶ εἰς ὑμᾶς, who in my personal presence (am) humble indeed among you, but from a (safe) distance I dare to act boldly toward you. The sentence apparently is not Paul's own; it reads like a quotation. If the words are not the identical ones which Paul's slanderers used, they at least reproduce very correctly the derogatory opinion which the troublemakers held concerning him, and which they foisted on the gullible members of the Corinthian congregation.

Paul was indeed ταπεινός. On the Damascus road the Lord's πραΰτης and ἐπιείκεια had overpowered him. He had learned this attitude from his Master. Although he labored more than the other Apostles, he considered himself as the least among them, not worthy to be called an apostle. In his Gospel work he practiced true sympathy. When dealing with the weak, he became as weak; to those under the Law, as under the Law; to those without the Law, as without the Law. He was gentle with the newly won Christians "even as a nurse cherisheth her children" (I Thess. 2:7). It may not always have been easy for Paul to practice this type of ταπεινοφροσύνη, since by nature he was quick, energetic, active. He gave sad evidence of his natural boldness during the time before his conversion by the way in which he carried on the persecution against the Christians. When he became a Christian, the natural traits of his character were not removed; they were sanctified and placed into the service of the Gospel. It was not cunning calculation when Paul in his Gospel work employed ταπεινοφροσύνη; he did it for the Gospel's sake. It was for him a way of growing in sanctification that he might be a partaker of the Gospel jointly with his hearers (cf. I Cor. 9:23).

This method of Paul in his work, which he had applied also in Corinth, his detractors deliberately misconstrued as personal cowardice. They knew better. Paul had met the fierce attacks of the Judaizers in Antioch after his return from his first mission journey. He had courageously defended the Law-free Gospel at the council in Jerusalem. Whether they had been present personally at these encounters or not, it was their group which had gone down in defeat before the undaunted Paul. Yet they did not blush to insinuate that Paul dared to put on a bold front only at a safe distance, but when he was personally present among them was an easy "pushover."

What steps is Paul going to take to clear himself of these insinuations? He does not outline in detail the course which he will follow, but merely asserts that his opponents will get a taste of his boldness, which they foolishly question; and he pleads with the Corinthians not to become personally involved. They should clearly dissociate themselves from the troublemakers.

(2) Δέομαι δὲ τὸ μὴ παρὼν θαρρῆσαι, I pray, however, that I may not (have to) be bold in my presence. As the personal object of δέομαι we readily supply ὑμᾶς from the first sentence, where it is the object of the verb παρακαλῶ, and accordingly as the object of θαρρῆσαι we supply εἰς ὑμᾶς. It seems that the troublemakers were still present in Corinth, and Paul was planning some drastic action against them. He is now pleading with the Corinthians that it may not become necessary

for him to use boldness against them also. This would happen, when he uses boldness against the troublemakers, to such as have not dissociated themselves from them.

He is determined to spare no one, and trusting in the power of the Gospel, he is confident that no one will be able to withstand his attacks. He is going to proceed τῇ πεποιθήσει ᾗ λογίζομαι τολμῆσαι ἐπί τινας, *with that confidence with which I calculate to act boldly against certain ones.* Πεποίθησις is a verbal noun denoting the action. Paul is persuaded, he has the sure confidence. This is not human boldness. It is not a reliance on his superior knowledge or ability. It is the confidence of faith, born out of the Gospel, which had overpowered his own fiercely resisting heart, and had been graciously confirmed to him by the many triumphs of the Gospel which had been privileged to witness. In spite of opposition and persecution his mission work had been one glorious triumphal procession (cf. 2:14).

In this confidence he now calculates to challenge the troublemakers. Τολμῆσαι he says. This is an aorist infinitive, thus stressing the action as such. No idea of duration, iteration, completion, or success is added. Paul realizes that there is no other way, he simply must attack the gainsayers; and attack them he will. His attack will result in the defeat of the opponents; he is confident of that. His only concern is that none of the Corinthians should become involved in his attack. If they cannot themselves shake off the intruders, they must at least avoid them. Else *mitgegangen* would result in *mitgefangen* and *mitgehangen.*

It is interesting to note how Paul describes the troublemakers. He does not mention them directly, he refers to them as τινας, certain ones, τοὺς λογιζομένους ἡμᾶς ὡς κατὰ σάρκα περιπατοῦντας, *who consider us as (people) walking according to (the) flesh.* We have here in λογιζομένους a present participle of the verb λογίζομαι, which Paul used in the first part of this verse with a slightly different shade of meaning. There Paul was considering and determining a course of action which he was to take; here the enemies of Paul are considering him and his associates, evaluating his principles and mode of procedure. They look at Paul and his associates as περιπατοῦντας, as walking about, as conducting themselves, as managing their affairs. In doing this they have no idea of the πραΰτης and ἐπιείκεια of Christ, which Paul learned from his Master. They have no understanding of this spiritual principle. They imagine that Paul is guided and determined in his actions by considerations of expediency, of human shrewdness—and by human weakness. It is κατὰ σάρκα ever to bear in mind that "discretion is the better part of valor." Paul's detractors will soon find out that his ταπεινοφροσύνη is not something dictated by human considerations.

(3) Yes, Paul is still living ἐν σαρκί, and his flesh hampers him very much in doing his work. He had to change his travel plans, to mention one example, because in his human limitations he could not foresee the inroads which the Judaizers would attempt in Corinth. He is, to use another figure, carrying the rich treasure of the Gospel in a weak earthen vessel. This is according to God's plans, "that the excellency of the power may be of God, and not of us" (4:7).

Although thus περιπατοῦντες ἐν σαρκί, yet οὐ κατὰ σάρκα στρατευόμεθα, *we are not campaigning according to the flesh.* For a military campaign considerable planning must be done; proper implements must be provided; enthusiasm must be instilled in the army. Apply this to the mission campaign of Paul. Human strength, human ingenuity, human enthusiasm had nothing to do with it. This mission campaign, both in its broad outlines and in its minutest details, lay completely in the hands of God. If this mission campaign were to be conducted κατὰ σάρκα, it would be doomed to failure. Just as no man can by his own reason or strength believe in Jesus Christ or come to Him, so likewise, no human reason or strength can lead another man to faith or bring him to Jesus. No force of argument, no human inducement will avail. God alone can provide efficient implements.

(4) Paul singles out the implements of operation: τὰ γὰρ ὅπλα τῆς στρατείας ἡμῶν οὐ σαρκικὰ ἀλλὰ δυνατὰ τῷ θεῷ, *for the weapons of our campaign are not fleshly, but mighty for God.* The whole equipment which Paul and his associates need for their campaign is from God; above all, the weapons both for attack and for defense. In one word, their sole equipment is the Gospel of Jesus Christ. Nor is the skill in using this equipment produced by human training, but rather, according to the promise of Jesus, it is provided by the Holy Spirit: When they hail you before their courts, "take no thought how or what ye shall speak: for it shall be given you in that hour what ye shall speak" (Matt. 10:19).

Since Paul here opposes δυνατός to σαρκικός, it is evident that by thus speaking of the flesh he has chiefly its weakness in mind. Although he is living in weakness, he is not doing his work in weakness.

His work is in the nature of a warfare, requiring powerful weapons, which no human flesh can provide. But the weapons which God supplies are powerful for God to achieve God's purpose.—The dative τῷ θεῷ sounds a little strange. Many take it as qualifying the adjective δυνατά: divinely powerful. It expresses more. The weapons are to be used in God's campaign, and they are qualified for just that purpose; they are mighty for God to achieve the victory for Him.

They are powerful πρὸς καθαίρεσιν ὀχυρωμάτων, *for the razing of fortresses.* A kingdom erects fortresses to protect its boundaries and to prevent hostile inroads. The enemies of God and of His Gospel also constitute a well-organized kingdom with many mighty strongholds to ward off the Gospel. If the Gospel is to bring salvation to the world, it cannot bypass these fortifications; it must be able to wreck them. To mention some of these strongholds, we take a list from John's First Epistle, where he describes the world as holding its own with "the lust of the flesh, and the lust of the eyes, and the pride of life" (I John 2:15-17). We know e.g., what a massive stronghold in Paul was the pride of life. It was not only the natural inborn idea of work-righteousness, it was that idea religiously fortified by a misunderstanding of God's Law. Paul himself describes this zeal in Romans 10:2f.: "They (sc. of Israel) have a zeal of God, but not according to knowledge. For they being ignorant of God's righteousness, and going about to establish their own righteousness, have not submitted themselves unto the righteousness of God." Yet the Gospel was strong enough to break down this apparently impregnable fortress and to make Paul a prisoner of war for itself.

Again, a formidable stronghold in some people is the lust of the flesh in its coarser forms. What an insurmountable barrier it seems to offer to the Gospel! Think of the pride of the Greeks in their achievements in philosophy, in poetry, in the arts of sculpture and architecture. Yet also these fortresses fell before the onsets of the Gospel. The weapons of Paul's warfare are indeed mighty for the wrecking of strongholds.

In order to impress the Corinthians still more with the divine power of the Gospel which he proclaims, Paul, still continuing the metaphor of warfare, partly translates the figurative language into direct statements. In an easy way he connects his new thought to the foregoing with a present participle. Case, number, and gender of this participle show that it refers to the subject of the main clause. We, the Apostles, are λογισμοὺς καθαιροῦντες, *wrecking thoughts and designs and calcula- tions,* etc. He retains the idea of wrecking, but he specifies the strong- holds as thoughts and designs. He is therewith, of course, not referring to human plans in the fields of politics, or economics, etc., but to such as are in the religious field, such as the ideas underlying all the com- mon forms of idol worship. Although coarse idolatry had at this time lost much of its appeal (cf. *Haruspex, cum haruspicem videt, ridet),* yet the basic ideas of work-righteousness and of buying the favor of the gods with sacrifices had been developed scientifically by the various schools of philosophy. Thus the inborn *opinio legis* had been tremen- dously reinforced by the λογισμοί of the philosophers.

The word λογισμός refers both to the content and to the activity of our thinking. In the other passage of the New Testament in which the word occurs, Romans 2:15, the λογισμοί are represented as accusing and excusing. Note the English words which the New Greek-English Lexicon lists: "calculation, reasoning, reflection, thought"—also "de- signs." For our passage the Lexicon suggests: "sophistries."

Paul had successfully stormed these fortresses of human λογισμοί. Think of his encounter with the leaders of the Stoics and Epicureans on the Areopagus. They ridiculed him when he spoke of the resur- rection; still "certain men clave unto him, and believed: among the which was Dionysius the Areopagite, and a woman named Damaris, and others with them" (Acts 17:34). The Gospel had succeeded in breaking down their philosophic fortification.

(5) In the following verse Paul unfolds the picture in several directions. While so far he has mentioned strongholds in general, he now singles out the most formidable ones: καὶ πᾶν ὕψωμα ἐπαιρόμενον, *and every height that is being raised up.* The most impregnable fortifications are erected on inaccessible heights of land, the more in- accessible the better. The natural difficulties of approach are elaborately developed and supplemented artificially. Satan fortifies his kingdom by developing the natural tendencies of the world (enumerated by John as the lust of the flesh, the lust of the eyes, and the pride of life) to their highest potential, by undergirding them with sophistry, making them appear as reasonable, as beneficial, as desirable, and their op- posites as foolish. Yet Paul says that he in his Gospel work is battering

down every height, without exception, no matter how elaborately it had been erected.

The participle ἐπαιρόμενον not merely points to the ingenuity and the labor that goes into the building of these fortresses, it also points to the purpose which they are to serve. The phrase, ἐπαιρόμενον κατὰ τῆς γνώσεως τοῦ θεοῦ, erected against the knowledge of God. What the knowledge of God is we may learn from Jeremiah 31:34: "They shall all know me . . . for I will forgive their iniquity, and I will remember their sin no more." The same truth is expressed by Zacharias in his Benedictus: "To give knowledge of salvation unto his people by the remission of their sins" (Luke 1:77). This is the knowledge of God in which, according to Jesus' word, eternal life consists: "This is life eternal, that they might know thee the only true God, and Jesus Christ whom thou hast sent" (John 17:3).

This knowledge of God is not a mere intellectual acknowledgment that there is a God, Creator, and supreme Ruler of the universe; it is not a mere admission that God is Triune, Father, Son, and Holy Ghost. It is a personal meeting of God and contact with Him through the forgiveness of sins which He imparts to the heart, and the serene peace of conscience which accompanies that forgiveness as its fruit. All of this God announces to us through the Word of His Gospel and seals to us by means of His Sacraments. It is a personal contact which God establishes by kindling faith in our hearts through His aforementioned means, a faith which appropriates the proclaimed forgiveness. All of these different factors taken together constitute a unit blessing, which the Scriptures call the "knowledge of God." Wherever this knowledge of God is established, there Satan has suffered a defeat; a stronghold, a high fortress has been wrecked, and his kingdom begins to crumble. Paul's Gospel warfare accomplished just that since the day that God commissioned him as His standard-bearer in this campaign.

The second part of vs. 5 introduces another term taken from the language of warfare: αἰχμαλωτίζοντες. The form is the present participle, plural masculine, nominative, agreeing with "we," the subject since vs. 3. The meaning of the word is: to take prisoners of war. In speaking about the destruction of Jerusalem, Jesus used the word: "And they shall fall by the edge of the sword, and αἰχμαλωτισθήσονται into all nations: and Jerusalem shall be trodden down of the Gentiles"

(Luke 21:24). Prisoners of war were sold as slaves. In Romans 7:23, Paul uses the verb metaphorically: "I see another law in my members, warring against the law of my mind, and αἰχμαλωτίζοντα me to the law of sin . . ." The sense is the same, making me a slave, forcing me into service. The verb occurs once more in a metaphorical sense, II Timothy 3:6: "For this sort are they which creep into houses αἰχμαλωτίζοντες silly women laden with sins, led away with divers lusts, ever learning, and never able to come to the knowledge of the truth." The simple noun αἰχμάλωτος occurs in a quotation from the Old Testament in Luke 4:18, meaning a prisoner, a captive. Paul uses the compound συναιχμάλωτος twice (Rom. 16:7; Col. 4:10) to designate someone as a fellow laborer in the Gospel, being a fellow captive of Jesus.

This verb, αἰχμαλωτίζειν, Paul now introduces to describe the success of the Gospel campaign, καὶ αἰχμαλωτίζοντες πᾶν νόημα εἰς ὑπακοὴν τοῦ Χριστοῦ, *and taking captive every thought for the obedience of Christ.* With the word νόημα Paul takes up the idea which in the previous verse he had expressed with λογισμός. He is referring to men whose thoughts and designs were formerly used as ramparts against the progress of the Gospel, but which are now taken captive by the Gospel and are forced to serve the Gospel. Paul never calls himself directly an αἰχμάλωτος of the Lord (only by implication, calling others his συναιχμάλωτοι), yet his Christian career most impressively illustrates the meaning of αἰχμαλωτίζειν. Paul's was a keen mind, a strong will, a firm character. All of these characteristics he originally developed and employed against the Gospel. But in his conversion Christ took over the control of these same characteristics and made them work in the interest of the Gospel. Now, what happened in Paul's case in a very spectacular way, happened, and happens, in every conversion to a greater or lesser degree.

This (as just outlined) is the power and method of Paul, as any one may readily see who follows his career as a missionary, from Cyprus through Galatia and Macedonia and Achaia to Ephesus. Let not the Corinthians be deceived by derogatory remarks of his opponents. Paul will employ the same method with the same force on his announced arrival in Corinth.

(6) With another present participle masculine plural nominative he continues: καὶ ἐν ἑτοίμῳ ἔχοντες, *and keeping (ourselves) in readi-*

ness. Our translation is a little too heavy, as is also Lenski's, who says: "and continuing in readiness." Ἔχειν with an adverb really does not say more than εἶναι with an adjective; thus: *being ready.* That is all that Paul says. He is not making any special preparations to meet his opponents in Corinth; rather, in the same way in which he has always handled the Gospel, he will also now apply it to the intruders in Corinth. He cannot add anything to the power of the Gospel, nor does it require any supplementing. Having the old Gospel, he is ready.

Ready for what? ἐκδικῆσαι πᾶσαν παρακοήν, *to right every disobedience.* Ἐκδικεῖν may have either a good or a bad connotation; it may mean either to 'avenge' or to 'correct.' When the widow pleaded with the unjust judge, she said, ἐκδίκησόν με: "Protect me in my rights" (Luke 18:3). In his instructions to the Romans Paul warns: μὴ ἑαυτοὺς ἐκδικοῦντες, "not avenging yourselves" (Rom. 12:19). In 7:11 of our present epistle we found the verbal noun ἐκδίκησις, as the climax in a process of recovery in Corinth, a thorough righting of their sad state of affairs. In the present case Paul aims at repentance—or else a "delivering unto Satan" of the disobedient. The details of this procedure will be mentioned in 13:1ff.

In the meantime, so he hopes, the Corinthians will develop and strengthen their own ὑπακοή: ὅταν πληρωθῇ ὑμῶν ἡ ὑπακοή, *when your own obedience shall have been fulfilled.* Ὅταν anticipates that the action mentioned in the clause will come about. It is not as loose as "whenever" nor as rigid as "as soon as." The action is called πληρωθῇ. This verb stresses both the amount and the degree. When speaking of a filling—filling in, filling out, filling up—the specific meaning must be gathered from the existing situation. What is it that stands in need of filling? We know the conditions in Corinth. False apostles had invaded the church, had shaken the faith of the believers and infected them with error. A remedy for the disease was called for to begin a checking process. Under those conditions the sense of Paul's sentence is: when your obedience shall have been fully restored to its former normal health. This will not only mean that Paul then does not have to spend much labor on the Corinthians to bring them back to a sound faith, but that he can devote his attention entirely to the opponents. But this will mean much more, namely, that the Corinthians themselves, having fully recovered from the error of their way, will rally to his support in dealing with the troublemakers.

This is Paul's program. For this he is trying to prepare the Corinthians in the following section of his epistle; and for this he has laid the groundwork in the previous two sections: a thorough freeing of the hearts from the poison injected into them by the false apostles, and a strengthening of their spiritual life.

2. 10:7-11

Paul had received the assurance from his associate Titus that the crisis in Corinth had passed, that the danger which threatened the life of the congregation from the false apostles had been checked, that the congregation was on the way to recovery. However, the Christians in Corinth still needed much tender care. The false apostles, apparently, had not left the city; at least, they still had some following in the congregation. This fact presented a constant menace to the progress of recovery, if not an actual danger of relapse for some members.

Paul announced, in the introductory section to this third main part of his epistle, that he was ready to come soon and to deal decisively with the troublemakers. His concern was that some of the faithful yet weak members of the church might become implicated with the troublemakers, and would then have to be dealt with together with them. He therefore earnestly, yet tenderly, tried to help them extricate themselves completely from any entanglements, and to build them up in their faith. The beginning of this effort we have in the section now up for consideration.

(7) The words of the first sentence admit of three different constructions. They read: Τὰ κατὰ πρόσωπον βλέπετε. These words speak about *looking at things right before one's eyes*. The question is: Are they to be read as a statement of fact? or as a command? or as a question? All three constructions are possible: You are (in the habit of) looking at things right under your eyes. Or: Keep looking, etc. Or: Are you in the habit of looking, etc.? Since the context alone can determine the sense, we shall defer a consideration of the problem till we have taken a look at the continuation.

Paul makes the evident fact that every member of the Corinthian congregation considered himself to be a true Christian the starting point of his appeal: εἴ τις πέποιθεν ἑαυτῷ Χριστοῦ εἶναι, *if anyone is convinced for himself to be Christ's.* Πέποιθεν is a perfect tense of πείθω.

This verb offers the translator considerable difficulties. The great number of expressions suggested in the lexicons merely shows their helplessness in finding a good one. The English word "persuade" comes close, but it includes the idea of success. The Greek verb expresses "suasion," but not necessarily "persuasion." To say "try to persuade" might lead one to assume that the verb form is conative. As for the perfect tense, it is difficult to accustom ourselves to the fact that in this verb form the action itself (past and completed) is practically forgotten; only its lasting result is stressed. Thus in our present case Paul is not interested in the type of suasion which a man applied to himself. He stresses the fact that the man has reached a certain conviction, which remains in him and by which he is motivated in his decisions and actions.

That conviction in this case is: that he is Christ's, a redeemed of Christ, a believer in Christ, a follower of Christ, a servant of Christ. Once a lost and condemned sinner by nature, he is now saved, justified, sanctified by Christ. Once without hope in the world, he is now a hopeful heir of eternal life, assured by Christ's all-sufficient sacrifice.

Since this conviction is the controlling factor in the addressed person's life, Paul directs him to draw an evident, yes, inescapable inference: τοῦτο λογιζέσθω πάλιν ἐφ' ἑαυτοῦ: *let him consider (infer) this in turn concerning himself.* Τοῦτο has the emphasis of position; in the following ὅτι clause Paul will explain to what he is referring. Λογιζέσθω is the present imperative, thus not only indicating the action to be taken, but adding the idea that this should not be a passing thought held for a moment, but should be considered again and again. Ἐφ' ἑαυτοῦ, for himself, based on himself, on his condition as one who is a member of Christ's.

Now the content of the important consideration: ὅτι καθὼς αὐτὸς Χριστοῦ, οὕτως καὶ ἡμεῖς: *that just as he (is) Christ's, just so (are) also we.*—How does this follow? By using the present imperative, λογιζέσθω, Paul had pointed to a thorough process of consideration. Whomever Paul's admonition may concern, he should ask himself: You are a Christian. How did you become one? You were not born in a Christian community, your parents served idols, and so did you. You did not go out into the world, seeking for Christ. Strange missionaries came to town and proclaimed His Gospel. Many rejected it as foolish. You accepted it. You came to faith. The Gospel of Christ answered all your vexing questions for you, and in it you found peace for your sin-troubled conscience. How did you come to faith? It was the Gospel of Christ itself that worked its way into your heart and won your confidence.

Now consider that, if it had not been for those strange missionaries and their strange Gospel, you never would have become Christ's member. You are Christ's now because they were Christ's first. If they had not been Christ's, they never would have brought you the Gospel of Christ, and you never would have been joined to Christ.

The false apostles maintained that Paul was not a true apostle, that they themselves were far superior to him. Yet they never brought the Gospel to Corinth. They never brought the Gospel anywhere. They waited until the Church had been planted in a certain place; then they broke into the field, lured the people away from their missionaries, and exploited them.

If the Corinthians are Christ's, a little reflection will show them that Paul and his associates are also Christ's—or they never would have brought them the Gospel, which united them with Christ.

After studying this major part of vs. 7, we can return to the first part, and answer the question about its proper construction. Paul is in the second part of the verse directing the Corinthians what to do. It is most natural to understand the first part in the same way: *Just look at the things before your eyes.* A statement, "You are looking at things right before your eyes," does not prepare for the directive to do some considering. To take the sentence as a question, "Do you look at things plainly on the surface?" would require us to supply: Well, then look at this one. (The KJ Version translates as a question; so does Luther.)

(8) So far Paul merely said, We are Christ's. Is that all that he can say? He can say more, but he will not do so for the present. His detractors, as he had quoted them in vs. 1, said that he was bold when he knew himself to be at a safe distance. If now he said more than just this that he is Christ's, then they might distort his words and try to use them against him in support of their insinuations. However, Paul indicates that he will have more to say some time than just this that he and his associates are Christ's as well as anyone in Corinth.

He says, ἐάν τε γὰρ περισσότερόν τι καυχήσωμαι: *for if in addition I shall boast somewhat more.* The postpositive τε connects the whole statement to the foregoing as adding a new thought, not only the conditional clause in which it is found. The conditional clause with ἐάν and subjunctive aorist expresses something to be anticipated: if I shall boast, as I expect to do. The boasting will pertain to something περισσότερον, something considerably more than merely that he is Christ's.

What this is he states in the words περὶ τῆς ἐξουσίας ἡμῶν: *concerning our authority.* The Judaizers and all troublemakers constantly questioned Paul's authority as an Apostle. They did so in Galatia, and so they did in Corinth. Paul had not been with our Savior during His earthly career, as had Peter and the other Apostles: How then can his Gospel be considered as authoritative? Over against the Galatians Paul emphatically declared that he was an Apostle "not of men, neither by man, but by Jesus Christ" (Gal. 1:1). In our verse he speaks about his authority, and in 12:12 he will point to the "signs and miracles, and mighty deeds" done by him as his credentials which establish his apostleship.

What is his authority? First of all, it was a gift from God: ἧς ἔδωκεν ὁ κύριος, *which the Lord has given.* The aorist ἔδωκεν emphasizes the reality of the past act, while κύριος identifies the Giver as the Savior Himself. It was Jesus Christ who Himself had commissioned Paul. But the main thing is: what powers did this authorization from the Lord confer on Paul? He says, εἰς οἰκοδομὴν καὶ οὐκ εἰς καθαίρεσιν ὑμῶν: *for your building up, and not for your tearing down.* Ὑμῶν is naturally the objective genitive. Paul, who has received the authority, uses it on the Corinthians as the object. Tearing down what Paul had built, tearing down the faith of the Corinthians, that was what the false apostles were actually doing. The authority which Paul had received was also a wrecking machine, but for the strongholds and fortresses of Satan. It was no wrecking machine against the Corinthians. As far as the Corinthians were concerned, it was given to Paul for the sole purpose, and was used by Paul for the sole purpose, of building them up, of creating, nourishing, preserving faith in their hearts.

What will happen if Paul, as he intends to do later, shall boast somewhat about this authority? Many a man has made himself ridiculous by his boasting. *Hic Rhodus, hic salta,* has brought many a braggart to fall. Paul does not fear this fate. He continues: οὐκ αἰσχυνθήσομαι: *I shall not be put to shame.* The facts will bear him out.

This last remark is of great importance. He had used his God-given authority on the Corinthians. What was their experience? They had been down in the depths of sin, some in debauchery and vice, some in careless abandon, some in self-pride, some in despair. Paul with authority had built them up. By his preaching they had become new creatures. If Paul here should repeat his λογιζέσθω from vs. 7, everyone would have to testify that Paul had never broken him down spiritually, but had always strengthened and built up his faith. He had done so in a highly effective, yet very gentle and sympathetic way.

If the Corinthians remembered what blessed fruits the authority of Paul produced in them, will a reference to his authority then frighten them? The word "authority" may have a somewhat terrifying sound, but the Corinthians, when they think of their experience, must rather rejoice. Where would they be if it had not been for the authority of Paul?

(9) If we keep this in mind, then the following ἵνα clause will not be so difficult, nor seem so unconnected with the foregoing: ἵνα μὴ δόξω ὡς ἂν ἐκφοβεῖν ὑμᾶς: *that I may not appear as frightening you.*

That was not his purpose, neither in his personal work nor in his letters. It was not true that he was meek in his personal presence, but bold and boastful in his letters. He adds: διὰ τῶν ἐπιστολῶν. This was the third epistle which he sent to the Corinthians. The first one we no longer possess; it is referred to in I Corinthians 5:9. The second was the one which is called First Corinthians in our Bibles. In it Paul used some strong language, so that he himself feared for a time that he might have been too severe (cf. 7:8 in our present epistle).— All the letters which we possess from Paul's pen are forceful and clear. In them he was always very tender while dealing with the difficulties that troubled the weak brethren; but he was also very outspoken and sharp in denouncing the errors of false teachers (e.g., Phil. 3:2, where he does not hesitate to call them dogs). Now compare with his letters the oral addresses of Paul which Luke has preserved for us in Acts, whether delivered in a synagogue, before philosophers, before governors and kings, or before a mob. These addresses are just as clear and just as forceful, suited to the occasion.

(10) Yet the opponents of Paul pounced on his letters, and criticised them for their severity. They evidently made an impression on some of the believers in Corinth. In the following verse Paul quotes one person. Whether it was one of the troublemakers or a member duped by them is not clear, and it really makes no difference. The quotation illustrates the underhanded attacks that were made on Paul: ὅτι αἱ ἐπιστολαὶ μέν, φησίν, βαρεῖαι καὶ ἰσχυραί: *for the letters, indeed, he says, are weighty and strong.* Some manuscripts have changed the singular φησίν to the plural φασίν; but since the next verse continues with the singular, both in the subject and in the verb, referring to the speaker of the present verse, the form φησίν is preferable. Although μέν and δέ balance the two parts of the sentence, the μέν is here more emphatic than in most cases. The speaker grants, and grants with some emphasis, that the letters of Paul are far from trivial both as to content and as to form. But he stresses this fact only for the purpose of belittling all the more, by way of contrast, the personal presence of Paul.

The sentence continues: ἡ δὲ παρουσία τοῦ σώματος ἀσθενὴς καὶ ὁ λόγος ἐξουθενημένος: *but his bodily presence is weak and his speech contemptible.* Τοῦ σώματος is a qualifying genitive. It does not mean the presence of his body only, while the soul is absent, but simply denotes his bodily presence. When Paul is present in person, this man says, he does not make any impression on the people. Ἐξουθενημένος is passive perfect participle of ἐξουθενέω, 'to despise,' 'to disdain.' Jerome translates *contemptibilis.* This sentence sounds bad as it is, but when read on the background of the μέν member, the disdain which it expresses stands out still more in bold relief.

(11) But let no one be misled by such remarks. Paul continues: τοῦτο λογιζέσθω ὁ τοιοῦτος: *let the (fellow) of that type consider this.* Τοιοῦτος equals 'such a one,' which is here preceded by the definite article: 'the man of this kind,' or, to bring out a little more of the scorn expressed by the word here: 'the fellow of this type.' — Λογιζέσθω is the same present imperative as in vs. 7. Again τοῦτο is placed in the emphatic position at the head of the clause.

What is it that the deluded fellow should well consider? Ὅτι οἷοί ἐσμεν τῷ λόγῳ δι' ἐπιστολῶν ἀπόντες, τοιοῦτοι καὶ παρόντες τῷ ἔργῳ: *that just as we are by (our) word through letters in our absence, just such also in our presence with (our) work.* The detractors of Paul

imagined that they could see a great difference between a preaching
Paul and a letter-writing Paul, a present Paul and an absent Paul.
But Paul calls attention to the fact that he is always the same, as his
whole past career bears out. This is something for his detractors to
think about. Let them trace his career as a missionary. Let them evaluate
the opposition which he encountered in every city. Let them imagine,
if they can, the persecutions which he suffered. And in every place
where he preached he planted a church. If they honestly considered
this, would they still insist that his bodily presence is weak, and his
speech contemptible? Let them consider how he met and routed the
Judaizers in Antioch and Jerusalem. If Paul's word then was contemptible, what about the presence and speech of his opponents, the
Judaizers? Let them consider this and repent before it is too late. And
let the Corinthians beware lest they become entangled with these false
apostles.

3.   10:12-18

(12) In the opening remarks of the third short subpart Paul launches
an attack on the false apostles with stinging sarcasm: Οὐ γὰρ τολμῶμεν
ἐγκρῖναι ἢ συγκρῖναι ἑαυτούς: *For we do not dare to classify or compare
ourselves.* Paul couples this part to the foregoing with γάρ, explaining
and motivating his previous statement, although the words at first
sight give the impression that Paul was afraid that he had made too
bold a statement, and was now ready to tone down his claim somewhat.
He says, οὐ τολμῶμεν, *we do not dare, we have not the courage, we
consider it foolhardy.* What they are not bold enough to do he states
in two infinitives ἐγκρῖναι and συγκρῖναι: 'to count ourselves among'
and 'to compare ourselves with.' To judge ourselves and certain other
people, and on the basis of such judgment to declare ourselves to belong to the same class, is the first act that Paul will not risk to do.
The second is that he will not dare to examine himself and certain
others, and then on the basis of such investigation to claim a certain
similarity of himself to the others.

Who are these others for whom Paul seems to have such high
regard? He describes them thus: τισιν τῶν ἑαυτοὺς συνιστανόντων: *with
some of those who commend themselves.* With these words he refers
to the troublemakers in Corinth. They never tired of praising themselves, their ability and their achievements. If you heard them, you

might get the impression that Jesus could congratulate Himself on having such superfine apostles. Paul does not dare to count himself as belonging to their class, or even to have his work mentioned side by side with theirs.

What did they have to boast about? Paul describes their method in the following: αὐτοὶ ἐν ἑαυτοῖς ἑαυτοὺς μετροῦντες καὶ συγκρίνοντες ἑαυτοὺς ἑαυτοῖς: *measuring themselves by themselves, and comparing themselves with themselves.* Paul places the ἑαυτοῖς in the emphatic position both times, once at the head, then at the close of the phrase. By thus producing a chiasm he strengthens the emphasis on this word. The standard by which they gauge themselves, and the model with which they compare themselves is always themselves. No wonder that they always achieve a rating of 100 per cent.

It is surprising that the Corinthians were deceived by such tactics. Now that Paul had tactfully opened their eyes, they must have felt ashamed of themselves, and, no doubt, they were greatly strengthened in their faith in the Gospel which Paul had proclaimed to them. They realized how ridiculous was the intruders' self-recommendation even before they read Paul's judgment in the two words, which form a litotes, οὐ συνιᾶσιν: *they have no understanding, they lack common sense, they are making fools of themselves.*

No wonder Paul is afraid to classify himself, or even compare himself, with that type of people.

(13) What does Paul consider a sensible way of gauging an apostle's work, and by what standard does he want his own work to be evaluated?

First he answers the question negatively: ἡμεῖς δὲ οὐκ εἰς τὰ ἄμετρα καυχησόμεθα: *but we shall not boast on the basis of unmeasurable (factors).* Ἄμετρος simply means something without measure. When the false apostles measure themselves by themselves, they are really not doing any measuring at all. Paul will not be caught doing that kind of boasting. That is what he says in these words. And that is really pronouncing a most devastating verdict on the tactics of the troublemakers. It is reading something into the text, and at the same time considerably weakening Paul's statement, when some translators render the clause: We will not boast beyond limits. What Paul says is that he will not, like some, be such a fool as to apply himself as a standard when rating himself.

He then continues positively: ἀλλὰ κατὰ τὸ μέτρον τοῦ κανόνος οὗ ἐμέρισεν ἡμῖν ὁ θεὸς μέτρου: *but according to the measure of the standard which God imparted to us as a measure.* In measuring himself, Paul will apply a certain fixed rule or standard, a κανών. By doing this the result will not be an ἄμετρον. Where does he get his standard? If he provided it himself, the result of his measurement would still be an ἄμετρον. It is God Himself who established the rule and who handed it to Paul. The word μερίζω originally means to divide. The genitive of the relative pronoun, οὗ, is by attraction to the genitive of the antecedent τοῦ κανόνος; it then draws the predicative noun into the same case, μέτρου.

What is this standard with which God Himself has provided Paul for gauging his own work? ἐφικέσθαι ἄχρι καὶ ὑμῶν: *to come also as far as unto you.* When Jesus called Paul to be His Apostle, He did not appoint him to serve as pastor or teacher in some established congregation. He appointed him to do pioneer work, to carry the Gospel into places where it was not yet known. When Paul had planted the Church in any place, then God would in some way (usually by persecution) give him a signal that it was time to move. If we follow Paul in his mission work, we can readily see how strictly he adhered to this rule. By applying this standard, he could correctly gauge his own work; and according to this rule he could boast before the Corinthians over against the false apostles. It was he who brought the Gospel to Corinth. The false apostles were intruders who broke into his congregation. Why did they not carry the Gospel to virgin fields? The world was wide enough.

(14) In the following verse Paul unfolds his rule a little, and shows its application to the present case: οὐ γὰρ ὡς μὴ ἐφικνούμενοι εἰς ὑμᾶς ὑπερεκτείνομεν ἑαυτούς: *for not like noncomers to you are we overreaching ourselves.* The present participle, ἐφικνούμενοι, is here used to indicate a characteristic: 'noncomers.' If we wish to stay closer to the participial form in our translation, we would have to change the tense to the perfect: people who have not come to you. In obeying the call from God, Paul came also to Corinth to do pioneer work in the Gospel. He is not overreaching himself in making that claim. What about the troublemakers?

Paul not only came to Corinth with the Gospel, he was the first to do so: ἄχρι γὰρ καὶ ὑμῶν ἐφθάσαμεν ἐν τῷ εὐαγγελίῳ τοῦ Χριστοῦ: *for even as far as to you we came first with the Gospel of Christ.* Our KJV misses the force of ἐφθάσαμεν; φθάνω means more than ἐφικνέομαι. It means, according to the new Greek-English Lexicon, *to come before, to precede.* (Note the archaic "prevent," e.g., in I Thess. 4:15.) Yes, Paul can say: We were the first to come all the way to you in proclaiming the Gospel of Christ.

This is the rigid standard by which Paul gauges his own work, and by which he requests the Corinthians to gauge it. It is a fair standard, no one will contest that. But what if it were to be applied to the activities of the false apostles? Once the attention of the Corinthians has been called to the very questionable methods of the troublemakers, when this standard is applied to their work, they will be strengthened in their determination to shed the contamination of the false Gospel and to return wholeheartedly to the genuine Gospel of Christ, as it was brought to them by Paul.

(15) Grammatically, the verses 15 and 16 are a continuation of the sentence beginning in vs. 14; but as to content, they are speaking of a new application of Paul's standard: οὐκ εἰς τὰ ἄμετρα καυχώμενοι ἐν ἀλλοτρίοις κόποις: (*we are) not boasting in unmeasurable things in connection with (on the basis of) other men's labor.* This part merely repeats in a brief summary the thought which Paul had presented and developed in the foregoing. It is here used in a concessive way: while we are not doing this. Although this is the unalterable rule of Paul's conduct, yet it will not prevent him from working under it in a way not mentioned so far. The attention of the reader is aroused by this manner of approach. What are Paul's plans which, though still strictly within the limits of his rule, yet indicate a modification of its application?

He continues: ἐλπίδα δὲ ἔχοντες αὐξανομένης τῆς πίστεως ὑμῶν ἐν ὑμῖν μεγαλυνθῆναι: *but entertaining (the) hope, as your faith continues to increase, to be made greater among (by) you.* Here Paul uses two verbs, both of which contain the idea of increase: the passive of αὐξάνω and of μεγαλύνω. Jerome translates the former with *crescere,* the latter with *magnificari,* thereby indicating that the former has practically acquired the force of an intransitive verb, while in the latter the passivity of the subject is still felt. Of the faith of the Corinthians Paul says that it *grows,* while about himself that he will *be made greater.*

The growth of the faith of the Corinthians is mentioned in a genitive absolute. The participle is present, thus denoting continued action: while the faith of the Corinthians keeps on growing. The function of this genitive absolute is not purely temporal, it is causal. The growth of faith is presupposed; the hope which Paul entertains is conditioned on it. Should that growth of faith cease, then Paul's hope would fail.

His hope is that he will become greater. He has already reached a certain measure according to his standard; he hopes to attain a greater measure. But in this he hopes to be helped by the Corinthians, as their faith increases. He mentions the people whose help he solicits with ἐν ὑμῖν. This ἐν is very wide in its application. It does not specify any particular form of support; it leaves room for that in many ways. We shall have to come back to this point after we have heard what plans Paul has in mind.

He first repeats that his plans lie strictly within the scope of the rule which God has given him: κατὰ τὸν κανόνα ἡμῶν: *according to our rule.* But he adds emphatically that he is looking for a great increase, εἰς περισσείαν: *for abundance.* The phrase, placed at the end for emphasis, modifies the infinitive μεγαλυνθῆναι: *to be increased abundantly.*

(16) What he means by this increase he now states in an infinitive phrase: εἰς τὰ ὑπερέκεινα ὑμῶν εὐαγγελίσασθαι: *to carry the Gospel to the regions beyond you.* What does Paul mean with "beyond"? He began his work in Antioch of Syria. While ministering there, he was commissioned for Gospel work in the Gentile world, and he went west to Cyprus and Galatia. On his second journey he went still farther west to Macedonia and Achaia, reaching Corinth. On his third journey he made Ephesus in Asia his headquarters, covering the territory which by divine order he had bypassed on his second journey. But he then already had his sights set on Spain. Beyond Corinth, perhaps way beyond Corinth, refers to the countries west of Greece, as far as the Atlantic.

Paul plans to stop over in Rome. Rome lay within the field that had been assigned to him; but since there was a church in Rome already, which could take care of the mission opportunities in Italy, he did not plan to do any mission work there. He would confine himself to a strengthening of the brethren. All this was to be done according to the rule which God had given him.

There were also the countries between Corinth and Rome, which Paul might have in mind with his ὑπερέκεινα ὑμῶν. But in his letter to the Romans, written from Corinth just a few months after Second Corinthians, he mentions that "from Jerusalem and round about unto Illyricum" he had fully preached the Gospel of Christ, and that he has "no more place in these parts" (Rom. 15:19, 23), so that we may safely assume that with the countries beyond Corinth he has Spain in mind.

To go to Spain, that would indeed greatly increase his credit. And it would be strictly according to the rule which God gave to Paul. In his Epistle to the Romans he expresses this in 15:18: "For I will not dare to speak of any of those things which Christ hath not wrought by me, to make the Gentiles obedient." And again in vs. 20: "Yea, so have I strived to preach the Gospel, not where Christ was named, lest I should build upon another man's foundation." In our text he continues: οὐκ ἐν ἀλλοτρίῳ κανόνι εἰς τὰ ἕτοιμα καυχήσασθαι: *not to boast in another (man's) rule on things (already) prepared.* To boast about things which have already been prepared by someone else, where the Gospel has already been preached and a church founded, that is not Paul's rule; that is not according to the rule which God Himself devised. That is a strange rule devised by the false apostles and applied by them in measuring themselves for self-praise. Paul will carefully avoid that.

Now we may take up the question in what sense the Corinthians can help Paul to increase his credit. He said ἐν ὑμῖν, which leaves the specification of the method open.

Paul's hope presupposed that there would be a steady and full recovery of faith in the Corinthians. As long as their faith was still endangered by the false apostles, it would not have been safe for Paul to proceed beyond Corinth. He would leave a ruined congregation behind, which would, moreover, serve the false apostles as a base of operations. If Paul established the Gospel in any city to the west, then they would sally forth from Corinth, where they were entrenched, to wreck the new congregations which Paul had founded. His work would have been in vain. First the situation in Corinth had to be cleared up. Only then could Paul proceed to carry the Gospel to other parts. Thus, in a somewhat negative way, they would assist Paul in increasing his credit.

Another way is suggested by a comparison with vs. 6. There Paul expressed the thought that his dealings with the false apostles would not only be simplified, but would also be greatly assisted, when the faith of the Corinthians was fully restored. So also now Corinth could serve as a basis for Paul's future mission operations, once it had been cleared of the wreckage which the false apostles had caused. Instead of being a basis for the enemy, it could be one for him. If in no other way, then, at least, fervent prayers would rise to God from the Corinthian Christians for the success of Paul's Gospel work.

Here we may remember that, in 2:11, Paul referred to the "devices" of Satan in connection with the incest case, without, however, stating specifically how he understood Satan's designs. Now we can see what he had in mind. Satan was not primarily interested in destroying the spiritual life of the sinner and of the persons whom he had wronged. Nor was he primarily interested in laying waste the one church in Corinth: his design was, by wrecking Corinth, to block the way of progress for the Gospel in general and for Paul's further mission work in particular.

(17) The chief point still remains to be stated. The false apostles claimed credit where none was due them. Paul pointed out where, according to the proper standard, credit must go. But now he goes to the root of the whole matter. Where, ultimately, does all credit belong?

'Ο δὲ καυχώμενος ἐν κυρίῳ καυχάσθω: *Now he who boasts, let him boast in the Lord.* This statement says more than: Let him boast according to the Lord's standard. Paul worked according to God's standard; but how had he been enabled to do so? Was it his own achievement? Over against the false apostles he could maintain that his credit was earned honestly, while they stole theirs. But in spite of this fact Paul confesses that he really deserves no credit. Originally he destroyed the Gospel, which he now preached. God, at His own time, had taken hold of him and had given him a new heart, or as he described this in vs. 5 above, Jesus had made of him a prisoner of war, so that now he used his natural endowments in the service of Christ. But what about his natural endowments? Where had they originally come from? They were a gift from God, which he, however, in the beginning had used against God. Paul could not boast of them as though he had produced them himself.

Moreover, who was it that sustained Paul in his work, in all his troubles, afflictions, persecutions to which he was subjected in his ministry? Again, it was the Lord of the Church Himself, who is seated at the right hand of the Father and rules even in the midst of His enemies.

Paul remembered all this and said, "Now he who boasts, let him boast in the Lord," even as he himself had done, "I labored more abundantly than they all: yet not I, but the grace of God which was with me" (I Cor. 15:10). This was something which the false apostles forgot entirely. They claimed credit for themselves where none was due them even according to human standards.

(18) With the next verse Paul concludes the present point, and leads over to the following one, where he will begin some real boasting.

The verse reads: οὐ γὰρ ὁ ἑαυτὸν συνιστάνων, ἐκεῖνός ἐστιν δόκιμος, ἀλλὰ ὃν ὁ κύριος συνίστησιν: For not the one commending himself, he is approved, but (he) whom the Lord commends.

Even according to popular sentiment, self-praise has a bad odor. To Christians it is a sign of a very low spiritual life and insight to indulge in self-glorification. One who honestly confesses that he could not by his own reason or strength come to Jesus or believe in Him, cannot claim credit for anything that the Lord may do through him in His kingdom. He will always be conscious of his own inability, and will attribute his work and his success to the grace of the Lord alone. That is the reason why Paul is so reluctant to list any of his credits over against the troublemakers. He yields (under pressure) to the needs of the Corinthians.

B. THE DANGEROUS WEAKNESS OF THE CORINTHIANS IN YIELDING TO THE INTRUDERS
Chapter 11:1-21a

1.   11:1-6

St. Paul concluded the tenth chapter with the remark that self-recommendation does not mean anything. To be valid, a recommendation must come from the Lord, to whom all glory belongs. Paul observed this rule, we might say automatically, during his whole career.

Think, for example, of the physical ailment he suffered on his first mission journey, of his persecution in every city, of his stoning in Lystra, and of his strenuous efforts to preach the Gospel under such adverse circumstances. And then listen to his report on his return to Antioch, Acts 14:27, "They rehearsed all that God had done with them." (Cf. also Acts 15:4; 21:19.) In these reports Paul kept his own person completely in the background; he gave all glory to God.

If we bear this in mind, we can begin to feel how unpalatable, how repulsive, it was for Paul to speak about himself, his efforts, his sacrifices, his achievements. He would much prefer to speak about his own weaknesses, so that the glory of God might shine forth in greater brilliance. Yet in order to deflate the shameless boasting of the troublemakers in Corinth, and to break the spell which they held over some of the Corinthian Christians, there was no better way than to let the Corinthians see the sham work of the false apostles against the background of the real Gospel work as Paul was performing it. Distasteful though it was to him, he is ready to yield to the necessity. When we hear him call it folly, or foolishness, let us remember that he means just that. But from the very outset his Corinthian readers must have gotten the feeling that, if it is folly for Paul to engage in boasting, then what about the bragging of the false apostles?

(1) When Paul now begins by pleading for a little forbearance on the part of his readers, he again means just that. Self-praise never has a very pleasant odor. Paul really hates to impose on his Corinthian converts, but for the sake of the cause it simply is necessary.

Ὄφελον ἀνείχεσθέ μου μικρόν τι ἀφροσύνης, *Would that you would bear with me with regard to a little (excursion) of folly.* The origin of ὄφελον, as generally assumed, is a corruption of the second aorist of ὀφείλω (for ὤφελον). The meaning then would be: 'I owed,' or, 'I was obligated.' But it is difficult to see how that expression could develop into the use of a particle introducing an unattainable wish: 'Oh, that,' or 'Would that.' Hence others take the word to have been a participle with ἐστιν to be supplied (Blass-Debrunner, #67,2). It is used also to introduce attainable wishes. So in our case. The tense of the verb is then regularly the imperfect, to denote the present time.

Paul's request is that the Corinthians grant him a little ἀνέχειν, 'a little enduring,' 'bearing with,' 'putting up with.' The person for whom one practices this consideration is expressed in the genitive, in our case μου, and the unpleasant thing which one tolerates for a while is stated in the accusative, in our case μικρόν τι, a little something. A little something of what? ἀφροσύνης. Paul is now in his letter going to digress for a little while and to a short distance from his sane and sober presentation of the Gospel, and from his direct invitations and exhortations to accept it and abide by it, and from his serious warnings against error. He is going to indulge in a little folly—and thus meet his opponents on their own ground.

He had never played this role before in his dealings with the Corinthians. For that reason he pleads for their patience, that they put up with this for a little while.

The interpretation of the added clause, ἀλλὰ καὶ ἀνέχεσθέ μου, hinges on the answer to two questions. The first is: to what does ἀλλά introduce a contrast? And the second: what is the mood of the verb ἀνέχεσθε? The two problems are closely connected. The answer to the first question is really decided by the understanding of ἀνέχεσθε. This may be either the indicative, *You are bearing with me,* or the imperative, *Do bear with me!* If we read it as an indicative, then the translation would be: But that is precisely what you are doing already. If we read it as an imperative, the sense would be: I do not only entertain the wish, but expressly plead with you to bear with me (Blass-Debrunner, #448, Note 6). The following sentence, introduced with a motivating γάρ, seems to support the second alternative. Paul earnestly requests a little unusual consideration. Why?

(2) Ζηλῶ γὰρ ὑμᾶς θεοῦ ζήλῳ, *For I am deeply concerned about you with God's concern,* or, *I am zealously striving for you with God's zeal.* Ζηλόω expresses an earnest striving to obtain and to hold. The genitive θεοῦ is best taken as a real genitive of possession. Some understand it as a qualifying genitive, a divine zeal. But Paul's zeal in this case is not merely godly in quality; it is the very zeal of God Himself. God's zeal is stated in John 3:16; I Timothy 2:4; II Peter 3:9; Ezekiel 33:11. This zeal had won Paul, and this same zeal now filled his heart. His plunge into a little foolishness is not prompted by levity; it is motivated by, and is an expression of, the deepest concern for the spiritual welfare of the Corinthians.

To illustrate the situation and to impress upon the Corinthians the delicacy and seriousness of the matter, Paul compares his work of winning their souls for Christ to that of a man winning a bride for his friend: ἡρμοσάμην γὰρ ὑμᾶς ἑνὶ ἀνδρὶ παρθένον ἁγνὴν παραστῆσαι τῷ Χριστῷ, *For I betrothed you to one as (your) husband to present (you) as a pure virgin to Christ.* The verb, an aorist middle, contains the root from which we derived our English word 'to harmonize'; very significant for the use which Paul here makes of the word.

Paul is not the first one to use the comparison. John the Baptist did the same. In his case the application was different. If he was trying to win followers for Jesus, should he feel jealous when he saw the multitudes turning to the person to whom he himself directed them? Just as little as the friend of the bridegroom when he sees the success of his negotiations. Paul here makes a different application. He brought the people of Corinth to Christ. He is as deeply concerned about their undivided loyalty to Christ as is the friend of the bridegroom concerning the fidelity of the bride whom he secured for his friend.

According to his own testimony, Paul on his arrival in Corinth had determined "not to know anything . . . save Jesus Christ and him crucified" (I Cor. 2:2). He proclaimed Jesus Christ to the Corinthians as the Savior whom God sent into the world, as the God-Man who humbled Himself and assumed the form of a slave, becoming obedient unto death, the death of the cross; and who thereby redeemed them that were under the curse of the Law, and won for them the adoption of sons. By this proclamation Paul kindled faith in the hearts of his hearers. He filled their hearts with the truth that, though their sins had been scarlet, they had been washed away completely by the blood of Jesus Christ. Through his preaching a new spirit had been created in the hearts of the people, a spirit which recognized its own inability to do or think anything of any spiritual value, but rejoiced in the forgiveness and freedom secured by Jesus. That is the relation which Paul had established between the Corinthians and Christ, their Savior.

Now he is concerned that no foreign thoughts or desires enter into their hearts. It would spoil the union between Christ and the Corinthians if they began to trust in their own merits, if they tried to add, for example, their circumcision or their observance of the Jewish food and festival laws in order to supplement Christ's redemption or to make it more secure. It would also spoil their relation to Christ if they began to despise the suitor whom He had sent to them in the person of Paul. More of similar things might be mentioned. Paul's is a delicate position, and he is as deeply concerned about the sincerity of the congregation which he had led to Christ as is a suitor about the bride whom he has led to one man to be her husband.—Take ἑνί as the indirect object of ἡρμοσάμην, and add ἀνδρί to it as predicative.

(3) So far Paul spoke about his deep concern for the purity of the Corinthians' faith. Now he adds a suspicion which had turned his concern into anxiety: φοβοῦμαι δὲ μή πως, ὡς ὁ ὄφις ἐξηπάτησεν Εὔαν ἐν τῇ πανουργίᾳ αὐτοῦ, But I fear that in some way, as the serpent utterly deceived Eve with his trickery, etc. (The Greek negative μή after words of fear correspond to the English positive that. In the English a substantive clause follows verbs of fear, while the Greek, in a clause of purpose, express their desire—which, of course is the opposite of what they fear.) From the beginning there existed the correct relation between Eve and her God. It was a union of pure faith and love. She stood in wonderment and admiration before the world —which God had created for her service, to provide her with food and comfort. She was perfectly happy in receiving these blessings from the hand of the Lord. Warm gratitude filled her heart, till the serpent came and with great cunning and trickery suggested that greater happiness was to be found if she broke away from God. Then her pristine purity was gone.

Paul is for the present interested merely in the fact that this happened. He does not, at this point, make anything of the fact that the real instigator operating through the serpent was the devil, nor does he mention the dire consequences of Eve's aberration. But the fact stands out in bold relief that Eve lost her purity.

Things that have happened may happen again. The devil is still going about like a roaring lion seeking whom he may devour. Hence Paul fears—he fears for the purity of the Corinthians: φθαρῇ τὰ νοήματα ὑμῶν ἀπὸ τῆς ἁπλότητος καὶ τῆς ἁγνότητος τῆς εἰς Χριστόν, (that) your thoughts be corrupted (away) from the single-mindedness and the purity respecting Christ. Here the word ἁπλότης occurs again, which Paul had used with telling force in connection with the collection for the needy Christians in Jerusalem. There it was that the collection should be a manifestation of the Christians' single-mindedness. Here it is the single-mindedness itself which is at stake, that their devotion to Jesus in faith and love might be disturbed by foreign influences and interests.

In passing we note that here the meaning of "liberality," which some try to foist on ἁπλότης in the chapters about the collection, would completely wreck the force of Paul's comparison. A groom is very much interested in the singleness of thought and devotion of his bride, and he would deeply resent too great a "liberality" on her part. A bride is married to one man as her husband.

Paul is afraid that such single-mindedness and purity of heart toward Christ may have suffered already in Corinth. He uses the strong word φθείρω, 'to ruin,' 'to destroy.' For if a Christian permits only a slight foreign interest to creep into his relation to Christ, then that relation is not only contaminated; it has been ruined. Whoever is not entirely for Christ is against Him.

(4) This fear of Paul implies a serious indictment against the Corinthian Christians. How can Paul entertain such fears without violating the Eighth Commandment, not to mention brotherly love, which unites him with all Christians? Paul might be assailed by misgivings of that nature, but he would never permit them to lodge in his heart without compelling reasons. He has such, and he hastens to mention them.

Εἰ μὲν γὰρ ὁ ἐρχόμενος ἄλλον Ἰησοῦν κηρύσσει ὃν οὐκ ἐκηρύξαμεν, For if the one coming (to you) palpably heralds another Jesus, whom we did not herald, etc. The conditional clause is one of reality. It assumes that someone did come and did preach. The μέν, standing alone, without a following δέ, serves the purpose of emphasis. It is difficult to reproduce in English. We might use "indeed." I used the word "palpably." The matter is so evident that no one can question it. Paul does not have to adduce any further evidence. The recent disturbances are sufficient evidence of the nefarious work done by the recently arrived false apostles, and of the impact they made on the Corinthian believers. Μέν emphasizes that his presupposition, on which his suspicion rests, is a definite, incontrovertible fact.

Ἄλλος does not necessarily mean a different or a second person. The false apostles did not question the identity of Jesus of Nazareth. They spoke about the same person as Paul had done, and as did all the Apostles. Yet the Jesus whom they proclaimed was an ἄλλος. Dr. Jekyll and Mr. Hyde were one and the same person physically, yet each one was an ἄλλος, the one a respectable citizen, the other a vicious criminal. So the Jesus whom the false apostles preached was an ἄλλος, different from the real Jesus. The real Jesus proclaimed the unconditional promise that He would give rest to everyone coming to Him with his burdens; that He would give His flesh and lay down His life as a ransom for the world; that anyone who believes in Him should not perish but have everlasting life. It is an entirely ἄλλος Jesus if anyone pictures Him as a wise teacher who informed us how we might work out our salvation, or as a model man who left us an example to follow. A Jesus who teaches us what *we* should do and how *we* should live, who in His life provides a pattern for us to copy as best we can, or who epitomizes His message in the Golden Rule—he is not the Jesus in whom we believe by invitation of the Gospel. He is an ἄλλος.

The substantivised participle in the singular does not necessarily mean that only one false apostle came to trouble the Corinthians. The participle is descriptive, and the definite article generic. In the very next verse, vs. 5, Paul speaks about the false apostles in the plural.

In our present verse he adds two more of the effects of their nefarious work, which make him uneasy concerning the spiritual purity of the Corinthians. He continues: ἢ πνεῦμα ἕτερον λαμβάνετε ὃ οὐκ ἐλάβετε, or if you receive a different spirit which you did not receive. We notice at first sight that Paul uses a new word for "other," ἕτερος. While ἄλλος may refer to the same person, only presenting it under a different aspect, ἕτερος presupposes an essentially different individual, one not only different in quality.

The purpose of Christ is to bestow a new spirit on the world, to give men a new heart. So it was foretold in the Old Testament, for example, in Ezekiel 11:19, "And I will give them one heart, and I will put a new spirit within you; and I will take the stony heart out of their flesh, and will give them an heart of flesh." This new spirit is born of the Holy Ghost of God, whom the Father sends into our hearts, crying, and teaching us to cry, "Abba, Father." It is a spirit which delights in the Word of God, which relishes the grace of God, and produces fruits of a new obedience. This was the spirit which the Corinthians received when Paul brought them the message of Jesus Christ.

Now they have received, and are still receiving and nourishing a different spirit, not a modification of the Christ-given spirit, but one completely crowding out and replacing their former spirit. It is not a spirit of adoption by grace. It is a spirit which reckons with its own works. What then about the Corinthians' purity as the bride of Christ?

Paul adds a third symptom: ἢ εὐαγγέλιον ἕτερον ὃ οὐκ ἐδέξασθε, *or another Gospel which you did not accept.* Paul repeats the word ἕτερος. There is only one Gospel. If anyone tries to modify this Gospel by additions, by omissions, by alterations of any kind, he simply destroys the Gospel, and substitutes a counterfeit. The Judaizers brought a ἕτερον εὐαγγέλιον to the Galatians, but Paul told them that this was not an ἄλλο Gospel, neither superior nor inferior to the one which they had received. It simply was no Gospel at all; and Paul pronounces a solemn curse on anyone who presumes to preach such a "gospel" (Gal. 1:6-9).

Now the Corinthians received another Gospel which was *toto coelo* different from the one they had learned from Paul. And they accepted it. Paul uses a new verb, ἐδέξασθε. The verb λαμβάνειν usually makes the recipient somewhat passive: something is being given to him; whereas δέχεσθαι points to the readiness of the recipient, he accepts. Thus when Paul brought the genuine Gospel to the Corinthians, they not merely received it, they absorbed it and made it their own. They were imbued with the Gospel truths.

We take notice of the fact that Paul so far did not stress his own person. Only once did he mention himself and his associates, and then only in the pronominal ending of the verb, ὃν ἐκηρύξαμεν—without an additional ἡμεῖς. In speaking of their reception of the Gospel and of the spirit, he does not even mention himself as the carrier. The contrast here is not between Paul and the false apostles. It is between the different work which they did and the results which they produced for the Corinthians, the different effect on their hearts. The Jesus as He was portrayed before their eyes, the spirit which He instilled into their hearts through the Gospel as it had been proclaimed to them should have prepared them so that they would—instinctively—reject any falsification. Had they?

With a sad heart Paul continues: καλῶς ἀνέχεσθε, *you bear with it (or him) well.*—Ἀνέχεσθαι, that is what Paul had requested for himself (vs. 1), and that is what they are according to the intruders and to their harmful activity. And they are doing it καλῶς, in a very accommodating way, they are receiving them *with open arms.*— Whether we read ἀνέχεσθε, the present tense, or ἀνείχεσθε, the imperfect, makes no material difference. The former, the Nestle reading, states that that is what they are doing as a matter of habit, while the latter would say that, whenever an intruder came to them, they would welcome him.

It is evident that Paul is here speaking about actual conditions in Corinth. He is not speaking about possibilities, nor is he offering suggestions. Both the King James and the Luther Bible do not do justice to the text. Both seem to take the conditional clause as expressing a possibility (or an irreality), and then translate the apodosis as containing a piece of advice: "ye might well bear with him"— *so vertrueget ihr's billig.* Both also make the adverbial modifier καλῶς the main predicate of the statement, in the sense of: If anyone brought you an advancement in the Gospel, you would do well if you bore with him. But Paul is not speaking of possibilities, he states it as a fact that the Corinthians are bearing with the apostles of error, and are doing it καλῶς, in grand style.

(5) On the basis of the facts as just outlined Paul is justified in his fears about the spiritual purity of the Corinthian congregation. What is he going to do about it? He attacks the intruders at their most vulnerable spot. They boasted of their superiority as Christ's apostles. Paul thoroughly demolishes their claim. But in doing so he must of necessity now draw in his own person, and show up the imaginary greatness of the intruders against the background of his own achievements, as established by a strict application of God's standard described in the previous section.

Paul begins with an understatement: λογίζομαι γὰρ μηδὲν ὑστερηκέναι τῶν ὑπερλίαν ἀποστόλων, *For I reckon to be lower (to have come behind) in nothing than the superfine apostles.* In comparing himself with the intruders, Paul is not thinking of his personal qualifications, but rather of the work which he did, its quality, and of the blessings which he brought to the Corinthians and the manner in which he brought them. He says, λογίζομαι; he is calculating, taking inventory, comparing both the credit and the debit side of his ledger. He compares the result with the much vaunted excellence of his opponents. He states in the word μηδὲν ὑστερηκέναι, he did not fall short in anything, and hence does not hold an inferior position. Ὑστερηκέναι is a perfect infinitive, which denotes the continuing result of a past complete action. In nothing does he find an inferiority in his work, no, not in the least. The meaning of this litotes is that his work is, rather, far superior to that of the intruders.

He calls them ὑπερλίαν ἀπόστολοι. Ὑπερλίαν is really an adverb, meaning 'exceedingly,' here by position functioning as an adjective modifier: the superfine apostles, as they consider themselves. The King James translates: "the very chiefest apostles" and seems to be thinking of the original Twelve. But Paul is not referring to them, he is dealing with the troublemakers in Corinth, who claimed great superiority for themselves over against Paul. He is not inferior to them, though they consider themselves superapostles in comparison with him.

Some of the early copyists (e.g., the Vatican Codex) were troubled by the connective γάρ; they substituted the adversative δέ. Yet γάρ is in place. Paul connects the thought of vs. 5 not only to the directly preceding one, but to the entire complex situation which he discussed in the whole paragraph. He charged the Corinthians that, by admitting the false apostles, they had jeopardized their purity of heart in which he had presented them to Christ as their spiritual groom. He would not dare to have voiced the suspicion if his work were really inferior to that of his opponents. This he does not admit. Why? The reason is stated in vs. 6, and thus the γάρ is in place.

(6) In this connection we may recall a word found in 5:12. There Paul called attention to the tendency of some people to boast about superficial advantages, and not to go down to the heart of the matter (ἐν προσώπῳ and not ἐν καρδίᾳ). When his opponents belittled his work, they used external things only as their criteria. For the sake of argument Paul is ready to grant that in a certain sense they may be right; he is not going to contest the point. That point has no bearing on the main question at issue. He introduces it: εἰ δὲ καὶ ἰδιώτης τῷ λόγῳ, *But granted that I am only a layman (a nonprofessional) in my speech.* The opponents evidently boasted that they were masters of rhetoric, professionals in oratory.

We possess a number of letters from the pen of Paul, and are thus in a position to judge his style. It is not the most elegant; Luke and the author of Hebrews were superior to Paul in this respect. Yet Paul's style is always very lucid and forceful. He knows how to get his thoughts across to his readers. His opponents were ready to admit as much with respect to his letters: "For his letters, say they, are weighty and powerful" (10:10). But they denied this as far as his oral delivery was concerned: "but his bodily presence is weak, and his speech contemptible." How does this charge comport with the unbroken chain of successes which Paul registered in his mission work? Paul referred to this in 10:4,5. But we do not merely have to infer from Paul's successes that his speeches must have been as powerful as were his letters. We can study the style of his speeches directly from the samples which Luke preserved for us in Acts. To mention some: the address in the synagogue at Antioch of Pisidia, his off-the-cuff remarks in Lystra, his address on Areopagus, his unprepared speech before the lynch mob in Jerusalem, his farewell address to the elders of Ephesus, his defense before the governor Felix, his defense before King Agrippa and Governor Festus— sufficient material to evaluate the style of Paul as a public speaker, and sufficient to show that Paul's addresses were very forceful.

Why did his opponents question his ability in this respect? Whom would they on their part consider as a master of oratory? Fortunately, Luke preserved a speech for us that was prepared by a professional according to the rules of rhetoric. It is the speech in which Tertullus presented the charges against Paul before Felix, the Roman governor. Tertullus was an "orator," being an attorney; and since the Jewish leaders engaged him, we may well assume that he had a good reputation as an orator. We need not study his whole speech, it will suffice for our purposes to look at the introduction. Acts 24:2,3 (according to Moffat's translation): "Your excellency, as it is owing to you that we enjoy unbroken peace, and as it is owing to your wise care that the state of this nation has been improved in every way and everywhere, we acknowledge all this with profound gratitude."* What has all this to do with the charges against Paul? It is flattery, and rather hollow at that. Look at the three points which he mentions. The first is "unbroken peace." Josephus reports: "The affairs of the

---

*) The NEB has: "Your Excellency, we owe it to you that we enjoy unbroken peace. It is due to your provident care that, in all kinds of ways and in all sorts of places, improvements are being made for the good of this province. We welcome this, sir, most gratefully."

Jews grew worse and worse continually, for the country was again filled with robbers and imposters who deluded the multitude." Felix put to death some of the robbers, but had ordered the high priest Jonathan to be murdered by the *sicarii*, and in general "did the violence of the seditions prevail over all right and justice." Then, when Nero deposed Felix and replaced him with Festus, the leaders of the Jews went to Rome to prefer formal accusations against Felix. Yet here Tertullus suggests that he really deserves the much-coveted epithet of *pacator provinciae*. Secondly, Tertullus refers to "improvements" and reforms, of which there is otherwise no record. Lastly, he mentions "wise care." The Greek word πρόνοια is the equivalent of a Latin word found on many coins in connection with the name Caesar: *providentia Caesaris*. Tertullus suggests that Felix had the qualifications for becoming the next Emperor. Almost nauseating flattery—with no bearing whatsoever on the case in hand.

This is a sample of the rhetoric in vogue at the time, of the rhetoric with reference to which the false apostles claimed that Paul was a layman, a rhetoric which most likely they employed in luring people away from the pure Gospel. Paul alluded to this type of rhetoric when in chapter 2 he spoke of καπηλεύειν and in chapter 4 of δολοῦν τὸν λόγον. Paul was happy to admit that he was nonprofessional in this art.

Paul concentrated on the truth which he was to proclaim. He tried to penetrate ever deeper into an understanding of the truth and to become ever more "expert" in presenting it forcefully. In chapter 2 he said that he spoke as from sincerity, as from God, in the presence of God; and in chapter 4, that he spoke, by the publishing of the truth appealing, and thus commending himself, to every man's conscience. Now he says, "Granted that I am a nonprofessional with respect to λόγος, what of it?" Ἀλλ᾿ οὐ τῇ γνώσει, *but (I am) not (a layman) with reference to (the) knowledge.*

How skillfully Paul could present facts in a convincing and winning way, we may learn from his reply to the charges of Tertullus. When Felix gave him the nod, he said (again according to Moffat's translation): "As I know you have administered justice in this nation for a number of years, I feel encouraged to make my defense" (Acts 24:10). Since Felix had served as a judge among the Jews for many

years, he had the opportunity to familiarize himself with their customs and manners. Paul does not have to make lengthy explanations
to be understood. All he has to do is to present the pertinent facts,
and Felix will be in a position to evaluate them properly. Hence
Paul is not afraid to make his defense. He will get a fair hearing,
and expects a fair verdict. Very complimentary, but far from Tertullus' hollow flattery. Moreover, every word has a bearing on the case.
That is a sample of Paul's rhetoric, which he calls being an expert
in knowledge.

The Corinthians knew this, not from hearsay but from personal
experience. Paul concludes this little paragraph: ἀλλ' ἐν παντὶ φανερώσαντες ἐν πᾶσιν εἰς ὑμᾶς, *but in every way having in all things demonstrated (it, the truth) to (among) you.* Paul's work was to bring
the truth to light among people where it was unknown. He performed
this task among the Corinthians. And he did so both ἐν παντί and
ἐν πᾶσιν, in every way and in all things. In his farewell address to the
Ephesian elders he stated twice, "I kept back nothing that was profitable unto you, but have showed you" (Acts 20:20). And again,
"I have not shunned to declare unto you all the counsel of God"
(vs. 27). The same he had done in Corinth, so that he can truthfully
say ἐν πᾶσιν. In Acts 20:20 he adds, "and have taught you publicly,
and from house to house." In I Thessalonians 2:11 he wrote: "Ye
know how we *exhorted* and *comforted* and *charged* every one of you."
Yes, ἐν παντί, in every way, in every respect he brought the Gospel
to light. The Corinthians knew. They had the evidence before their
eyes. In 10:7 he had directed them: Τὰ κατὰ πρόσωπον βλέπετε. In our
present verse he refers to it with φανερώσαντες εἰς ὑμᾶς.

If in spite of the wonderful change which they had witnessed in
the lives and conduct of a goodly number of their fellow citizens, and
the wonderful new life that had been created in their own hearts,
all as a result of Paul's preaching, they permit themselves to be
"taken in" by the intruders with their hollow rhetoric. Is it any wonder
that Paul is worried about them? Can anyone charge that he is unduly suspicious, or that in violation of the Eighth Commandment
he is judging their hearts, and is thinking evil of them?

It is God's zeal with which he is jealous of them. Their virgin
purity and singleness of purpose toward Christ is under a cloud.

2. 11:7-11

When Paul at the close of the previous subsection declared emphatically that in every way in all things he had given evidence to the Corinthians that in γνῶσις he was anything but an ἰδιώτης, he paved the way for the introduction of a possible objection. He takes it up in vs. 7, introducing it with ἤ, 'or.' If this objection could be upheld, it would prove a serious deficiency in Paul's handling of the Gospel. But, on the other hand, if it can be shown to be baseless, it will shed new light on Paul's thorough work.

(7) The objection is Ἢ ἁμαρτίαν ἐποίησα ἐμαυτὸν ταπεινῶν ἵνα ὑμεῖς ὑψωθῆτε, *Or did I commit a sin humbling myself in order that you might be exalted?* What Paul means by "humbling" himself, he goes on to explain in a ὅτι clause: ὅτι δωρεὰν τὸ τοῦ θεοῦ εὐαγγέλιον εὐηγγελισάμην ὑμῖν, *in that I proclaimed the Gospel of God to you without charge.*

When the Corinthians listened to the false apostles, they may not have thought of Paul's work in their midst as resulting in their exaltation. Yet only a moment's reflection must have impressed upon them how fittingly the word which Paul chose described both the nature and the result of his labors. Before Paul came to them, they had been lost in the depths of sin and despair. They may not have fully realized it at the time; they may even have resented his approach. But now, after their eyes had been opened through his message, they were aware of their former lost condition.

Nor could they have failed to recognize the glory of their estate to which Paul had elevated them. They had the forgiveness of their sins; they were united to God as His dear children; they had the hope of eternal life in heaven. Although for a time some of them had questioned the coming resurrection, yet Paul had given them the blessed assurance that death has been completely swallowed up in victory. Yes, through Paul's work they had been exalted.

But had he adopted the proper mode of procedure? In his efforts to bring about their exaltation he had humbled himself, so much so that his opponents ridiculed his personal presence as weak and his speech as contemptible. Ought he not, in order to underscore the exalting nature of his message, have shown in his bearing a consciousness of his high position, and evinced a dignity and commanded a respect conformable to his high calling? Did he not by his humility degrade the message which he was carrying?—In asking this question Paul does not use the simple verb, "Did I sin?" He says, "Did I perpetrate a sin?"

In speaking about his self-humiliation, Paul hastens to limit the expression. He did not conduct himself unseemly in a general way. The Corinthians well knew that his conduct always was above reproach. His self-humiliation consisted in this that he demanded no compensation for his work. He places the word δωρεάν, 'free,' 'gratis,' 'without charge,' into the emphatic position at the head of the clause: that is the idea which he wishes to draw to the attention of the Corinthians.

About his message he speaks in glowing terms. He not only calls it the Gospel; he calls it God's Gospel, which God Himself prepared, which God is sending forth into all the world as His final word to mankind, which God backs up with all His majesty. He repeats the idea of Gospel in the verb, literally: "I gospeled the Gospel of God to you." The Corinthians must recall how pure and unadulterated was his proclamation of God's forgiving grace in Christ, with no terms or conditions attached, no ifs or buts. It was Gospel from beginning to end.

The Corinthians will also remember how stern was his rebuke when the Jews contradicted and blasphemed. "He shook his raiment, and said unto them, Your blood be upon your own heads; I am clean: from henceforth I will go unto the Gentiles" (Acts 18:6). Paul preached the Gospel and permitted no tampering with it. In adding that it was God's Gospel, he indicates that he is well aware of the fact that he is God's messenger, that he has to represent God's majesty and that on the other hand, God's majesty was fully backing him up. But he did his work absolutely δωρεάν, just as God justifies the sinner δωρεάν (Rom. 3:24).

It should not have escaped the notice of the Corinthians, and we also do well to pay attention to the fact that, in describing his method, Paul uses terms which he otherwise employs in speaking about the two states of Christ (cf. Phil 2:8,9). Only with reference to the exaltation of Christ he uses a compound verb ὑπερύψωσεν, while in speaking about the Corinthians he uses the simple verb ὑψωθῆτε. From the Philippians passage we may gather that this was Paul's customary way of speaking about the two states of Christ. As Christ had humbled Himself that we might be exalted, so also did His messenger.

(8) In the following verse Paul describes how it was possible for him to preach the Gospel to the Corinthians free of charge. He does not mention that he worked with his own hands day and night to support himself and his colaborers. The Corinthians remembered that he had found employment in the shop of Aquila, the tentmaker. He does not have to mention that now, but he does say that other Christians with their gifts had enabled him to go to Corinth and begin his Gospel work there: ἄλλας ἐκκλησίας ἐσύλησα λαβὼν ὀψώνιον πρὸς τὴν ὑμῶν διακονίαν, *Other churches I robbed, receiving support (from them) for the ministry to you.* 'Οψώνιον, originally the pay of mercenary soldiers, came to be used in a general way for pay, sustenance, support, etc. John the Baptist told the soldiers who came to hear him that they as a fruit of their repentance must be content with their ὀψώνια. In First Corinthians Paul, speaking about the salary due to ministers of the Gospel, says that no one ever goes to war on his own ὀψώνιον (9:7). Death is the ὀψώνια of sin (Rom. 6:23).

From whom did Paul receive his support in the present case? He may be thinking of the Berean Christians. When the Jews of Thessalonica started a persecution against Paul in Berea, the brethren "sent him away" to the sea and then "conducted him unto Athens" (Acts 17:14,15). Who paid the fare? Is it too much to assume that they who conducted him did so?

Yet, here Paul is most likely thinking of other Christians, the Philippians. In his letter to this church he mentions with warm approval that they had held "fellowship in the gospel from the first day unto now" (Phil. 1:5). This general, all-inclusive term he, in a later part of the same epistle, describes as meaning also that they manifested a keen interest in Gospel work and cooperated actively in its spread (Phil. 4). From his prison cell (most likely in Rome) he thanked them for having remembered him with a gift to support him in his work. In this connection he mentions that they had tried to come to his aid much sooner, but had "lacked opportunity" (vs. 10). He remembers with thanks that, when he was working in Thessalonica after leaving Philippi, they had twice sent a contribution for his support (vs. 16).

We remember two things—and this demonstration by the Philippians of their interest in the spreading of the Gospel will impress them on us with still greater force. The first is that Paul was permitted to stay in Thessalonica for "three sabbath days" only (Acts 17:2). In so short a time the Philippians twice sent him a gift. The second point to remember is that the Philippians were not a wealthy congregation. In our present Epistle to the Corinthians Paul refers to their "deep poverty" (8:2), in spite of which they contributed "to their power," yes, "beyond their power," to the collection which he was taking up for the needy saints in Jerusalem (vs. 3).

The fellowship of the Philippians in the Gospel manifested itself in so great a measure that Paul, in speaking about it, borrows some terms from bookkeeping (receipts and disbursements): "Now ye Philippians know also, that in the beginning of the gospel, when I departed from Macedonia, no church communicated with me as concerning *giving* and *receiving,* but ye only" (Phil. 4:15).

When Paul left Macedonia he went to Athens, and then to Corinth. The contributions which he had received from the Philippians helped to tide him over during the beginning of his stay in Achaia, and supplemented his income after he found employment in the shop of Aquila.

It may be assumed that the Corinthians were familiar, at least to some extent, with the conditions as just outlined. They must have sensed the peculiar flavor of one word which Paul here used: "I *robbed.*" Accepting support from so poor a congregation made Paul feel guilty, as though it bordered on robbery.

(9) That was not all. Not only did the Philippians help him get a start in Corinth; even later, during his 18 months' stay in that city they came to his assistance: καὶ παρὼν πρὸς ὑμᾶς καὶ ὑστερηθεὶς οὐ κατενάρκησα οὐθενός, *and while present with you and having come behind, I did not burden anyone.* Paul was not always able to make ends meet. Though working day and night (I Thess. 2:9), so that, pointing to his calloused hands, he later could say to the Ephesian elders: "Ye yourselves know, that these hands have ministered unto my necessities, and to them that were with me" (Acts 20:34), yet it would happen that his funds became exhausted. Did he then appeal to the Corinthians for help? He had a perfect right to do so. "If we have sown unto you spiritual things, is it a great thing if we shall reap your carnal things?" (I Cor. 9:11). Paul did not avail himself of this right. He did not burden anyone. The verb which he here uses he repeats also in 12:13, 14, where vs. 13 contains the same form which we have in our present

verse, while in vs. 14 the future tense appears. The meaning is the same in all three instances, yet Jerome uses three different expressions in his translation. In our verse he has *onerosum esse;* in 12:13, *gravare;* and in 12:14, *gravem esse.* He treats the verb as intransitive, while there are indications that in classical Greek it was used as transitive in the sense of "stupefy" or "disable." The new Greek-English Lexicon of the N.T. offers two English words: "burden" and "be a burden." The German words are more expressive: *zur Last fallen, beschwerlich werden.*

By the choice of this word Paul indicates how careful he was to preach the Gospel without charge to the Corinthians, and how much importance he attached to that fact.

So far his statement was purely negative: he became a burden to no one. Yet his admission that there were times when he failed to meet his financial obligations from his own earnings raises a question which demands an answer. Paul continues with a positive statement: τὸ γὰρ ὑστέρημά μου προσανεπλήρωσαν οἱ ἀδελφοὶ ἐλθόντες ἀπὸ Μακεδονίας, *for my shortage the brethren coming from Macedonia helped to fill up.*

In referring to a visit by Macedonian brethren, Paul is telling the Corinthians nothing new. They remembered. Paul says *"the* brethren" with the definite article of previous reference. Incidentally, this gives us a glimpse of the close contact which the early congregations maintained among themselves. Already in 9:4 Paul had stated that he expected some Macedonians to accompany him on his visit to Corinth. Here we learn that during his 18 months' stay in that city they had visited him and the young congregation which he had founded.

It happened that just at the time of their visit he was in arrears with his payments. Then they προσανεπλήρωσαν his shortage. This is the same verb which he had applied to the collection which he gathered for the needy saints in Jerusalem: It was helping to fill up their want. So now the brethren from Macedonia helped to fill up Paul's want.

Paul repeats emphatically, καὶ ἐν παντὶ ἀβαρῆ ἐμαυτὸν ὑμῖν ἐτήρησα καὶ τηρήσω, *and in every way unburdensome I did keep myself, and shall keep myself to you.* The stress is on the idea "in every way unburdensome." The new thought is that Paul intends to continue his method in the future as in the past, stressing that this is a set policy with him.

(10) This raises the question: Why? What may be Paul's reason? Paul gives the answer in the words: ἔστιν ἀλήθεια Χριστοῦ ἐν ἐμοί, *There is Christ's truth in me.*

This statement is understood by many as an asseveration, a solemn declaration, a mild form of oath. Jerome's translation is noncommittal: *Est veritas Christi in me,* followed by a *quoniam* clause. But the King James says, *"As the truth of Christ is in me."* So also the RSV. Luther: *So gewiss die Wahrheit Christi in mir ist.* Phillips in his "Letters to Young Churches" uses even a stronger form: "By the truth of Christ within me." We grant that Paul might have chosen a plain statement like the present to express a solemn affirmation— as in the very next verse he says, "God knows," and as in I Thessalonians 2:5, he says, "God is witness." Yet more frequently he indicates it by his phraseology when he wants his words to be understood as an emphatic affirmation of the truth. Compare in this same chapter verse 31: "The God and Father of our Lord Jesus Christ which is blessed for evermore, knoweth that I lie not." Compare also 1:23: "Moreover, I call God for a record upon my soul." Yet though the form does not decide anything either one way or the other, and since it does not rule out the assumption of a mild oath, the question remains: Which of Paul's statements, either because of its importance or because it was questioned by someone, calls for such a solemn reinforcement? The translations which treat the statement as a solemn affirmation apply it to the immediately following ὅτι clause. Here is the whole verse in Phillips' translation: "By the truth of Christ within me, no one shall stop my being proud of this independence through all Achaia." In the original the clause reads: ἡ καύχησις αὕτη οὐ φραγήσεται εἰς ἐμὲ ἐν τοῖς κλίμασιν τῆς Ἀχαΐας, *this boasting shall not be blocked for me in the regions of Achaia.*

Paul connects this clause to the foregoing with the conjunction ὅτι. Jerome translated this with *quoniam*: 'because,' 'since,' 'seeing that.' Lenski takes ὅτι here to be consecutive: 'so that.' It is not necessary to ascribe to ὅτι any such specific meaning. This conjunction had a wide range of uses, and frequently is impossible of translation. (Compare e.g., the so-called ὅτι *recitativum* before direct quotations.) We may in this connection think of the peculiar use of ὅτι in I Timothy 6:7, "For we brought nothing into this world, ὅτι we can carry nothing out." Moffat, Goodspeed, and the RSV substitute a simple "and" for ὅτι in this Timothy passage. A similar connection seems indicated in our Corinthians passage.

Καύχησις is the act of boasting, not, as Phillips translates, "being proud." The fact that Paul adds the demonstrative αὕτη forces us to look for this act of boasting somewhere in the near vicinity of the present verse. Does he mean what Phillips calls "independence"? Was it a spirit of "independence" that prompted Paul to preach the Gospel to the Corinthians free of charge? To refuse taking remuneration? Paul feels that someone might even consider it as a sin, and he himself called it a self-humiliation. In the following he even indicates that by some his method was interpreted as evincing a lack of love.

The boasting which Paul had done was contained in vs. 7, namely, that he had "gospeled the Gospel of God," and that he had done this in full γνῶσις, and had given unmistakable evidence of his γνῶσις of the Gospel before the Corinthians in all things and in every way (vs. 6). This boasting is based on fact. It stands on a firm rock, and no efforts of the false apostles will be able to shake it. Paul could repeat without fear of contradiction: There is Christ's truth in me. The intruders may try, but they will never succeed in blocking Paul's boasting. Rather, by attacking him they will merely show that their own "gospel" is false.

This is Paul's boasting, which shall not be blocked for him in Achaia. Would Paul appeal to the truth of Christ within him to corroborate his statement? Does that seem quite appropriate? By the truth of Christ within me, no one will effectively cut off my act of boasting? If he had said, I call upon God, or, God is my witness, that this boasting shall not be blocked, that would be understandable; but an appeal to the truth of Christ within him seems odd. It seems indicated that we should look for some other understanding of the words, "Christ's truth is in me."

We have above already briefly indicated how we understand them. They are a summary statement of his claim that he is a true preacher of the true Gospel. We take a little closer look at the statement. We note that ἔστιν is in the emphatic position. Paul stresses the fact that what he says in this clause is really so, unmistakably so. Christ's truth actually is in him. That fact stands out in bold relief. No matter what the false apostles may proclaim as Christ's truth, no matter what they may say against Paul's message, no matter whether Paul is a professional or a layman in rhetoric, no matter how often Paul may have to change his travel plans: all this in no way affects Christ's truth which he proclaims. This is something which the Corinthians should remember: The truth *is* in Paul.

We note further that Paul states the fact in an arresting manner: Christ's truth *is in me*. He had summarized Christ's truth in 5:19 and 21: "God was in Christ, reconciling the world unto himself, not imputing their trespasses unto them. . . . For he hath made him to be sin for us, who knew no sin; that we might be made the righteousness of God in him." This truth of God's unmerited, boundless saving grace is in Paul, not only in the message which he proclaims, but also in the method by which he does so. He not only announces the truth, but in his announcement lives the truth, so that his very life becomes an illustration of the way in which God deals with lost sinners: granting them free pardon. We may go a step farther. Paul is so anxious to proclaim God's grace in all its splendor because he himself is an outstanding example of its free saving power. When stressing in I Timothy 1:15 that "Christ Jesus came into the world to save sinners," he adds significantly, "of whom I am chief." When in I Corinthians 15 he mentions the fact that the risen Christ was seen also by him, he describes himself as "one born out of due time" (i.e., an abortion). He is an example of Christ's truth; now he proclaims Christ's truth, he illustrates Christ's truth by proclaiming it δωρεάν.

We may add a little more. Not only is Paul's message the Gospel of free justification and salvation by grace alone; not only does Paul by his method of proclaiming the Gospel without charge illustrate its nature: Paul in his very person is an outstanding example. In his youth he had persecuted the Gospel. He was not an ordinary opponent. He forged ahead of the other members of his group: "above many my equals (in age) in mine own nation" (Gal. 1:14). He was "exceedingly mad against them (the believers), [and] persecuted them even unto strange cities." He did this from conviction: "I verily thought with myself, that I ought to do many things against the name of Jesus of Nazareth" (Acts 26:11 and 9).

What happened to this Paul? In his first letter to Timothy he calls himself the chief of sinners, and then adds: "Howbeit, for this cause I obtained mercy, that in me first Jesus Christ might show forth all long-suffering, for a pattern" (I Tim. 1:16). He came to faith as "one born out of due time" (I Cor. 15:8). How did this happen? The answer is: "It pleased God" (Gal. 1:15). Without merit or worthiness. out of pure grace, without charge, δωρεάν. Thus Paul in his very person is a classical case in point; he is an outstanding example of the Gospel which he proclaims.

Yes, the truth of Christ is in him. He assures the Corinthians that this boasting shall not be blocked for him in the regions of Achaia.

The last remark has a peculiar ring. Why does he use that expression in referring to Corinth? Is he *"sore"?* Is he scolding the Corinthians? Is he angry at them? It is true, false apostles had tried to "smear" Paul. They had tried to undermine his reputation. And the Corinthians had not met their slanderous remarks properly. They had, in part at least, accepted them. Their hearts had turned away from Paul, had to some extent turned against him. It would have been only human if he had been somewhat embittered.

(11) Paul himself now asks the question διὰ τί, why? Why does he speak in this way? Why will he not permit his boasting to be blocked in the regions of Achaia? He assumes that someone might interpret his words and his actions as evincing a lack of love, a certain bitterness: ὅτι οὐκ ἀγαπῶ ὑμᾶς, (*Is it*) *that I do not love you?*—A person cannot read this epistle to the Corinthians without being impressed by its spirit of warm love and affection, which it breathes on every page. A deep interest in their affairs, a tender concern for their well-being: all this goes to show that Paul loved the Corinthians as fervently as ever. But if he were called upon to prove that he loved the Corinthians, that in spite of his sharp rebuke he loved them, yes, that even his stern words were prompted by his love—it would have been impossible to do so. The false apostles, who boasted of outward things only and never went to the heart of a matter, would have been quick to suggest that his words and actions were incontrovertible evidence of resentment. Realizing this, Paul appeals to God as witness: ὁ θεὸς οἶδεν, *God knows.* Here we have a strong affirmation in the nature of an oath.

This should have been sufficient. It would have been if Paul were interested only in clearing his good name. But he is interested in strengthening the faith of the Corinthians. They were impressed by the slanders against him, spread by the false apostles. Their faith had

become shaky. Paul seeks to brace it, and to lead them back to a
more healthy condition.

In the last few remarks we have already indicated that Paul's question, "Why this?" is not to be limited to the last point, namely, his
preaching the Gospel to the Corinthians without charge. That point
was only a part of a wider complex of arguments, the center of which
was Paul's doubts about the Corinthians' sincerity and fidelity to
Christ. Without mincing words he pointed to their questionable attitude toward the carriers of a false Gospel, and with unusual stress
he pointed to the truth of Christ which he by word and example had
brought to them. Why this uncomplimentary reminder and this sharp
rebuke? Paul appeals to God's omniscience that it was nothing but
fervent love which motivated him.

3.   11:12-15

In the conclusion of the previous subsection Paul appealed to the
omniscience of God in support of his claim that the motive for his
somewhat harsh treatment of the Corinthians was nothing but loving
concern for their spiritual well-being. He now points out a special
purpose which he is trying to achieve by calling attention to the
special manner in which he proclaimed the Gospel.

(12) He takes up the thought by saying, Ὅ δὲ ποιῶ, καὶ ποιήσω:
The thing that I am doing and will continue to do. This is the way
Luther translates the relative clause: *Was ich aber tue and tun will;*
while the KJ treats the καὶ ποιήσω as a main clause: "But what I do
that I will do." Thus the KJ drops the καὶ altogether. If the καὶ ποιήσω
is to be elevated to the rank of a main clause, then the translation
will have to be: That I *also* will do. That would mean a stressing of
Paul's plan to continue his mode of procedure. Such stress does not
seem in place now. Already in vs. 9 Paul had emphatically declared:
"In all things have I kept myself from being burdensome unto you,
and so will I keep myself." Now he is referring to that announcement.
That makes it seem advisable to follow Luther's example and to take
the second verb into the relative clause. This construction, however,
makes it necessary to supply a thought; as also Luther does: *das tue
ich darum.* In reading the Greek text it is not necessary to insert these
words; a pause after the relative clause will achieve the purpose.

We note that Paul is not speaking about his conduct in general. He refers specifically to his method of preaching the Gospel without charge to the Corinthians. He indicates this by using the singular of the relative pronoun. If he were speaking about his general conduct, the plural would have been required. In the Greek it is clear at once that he is referring to some specific thing. This is not so clear in either the German or the English translation.

What particular purpose is Paul trying to achieve by his method of preaching the Gospel free of charge? His general purpose he stated above, but what is his specific purpose in the present situation? His purpose over against the boastful false apostles? We remember that he stressed emphatically: "Christ's truth is in me," and that also his method of preaching the Gospel without remuneration served the purpose of underscoring the unmerited and unrepayable nature of God's grace and of our redemption. Teachers of philosophy in those days were wont to collect fees from their pupils. If Paul had done the same, he thereby might have created the impression that his Gospel was on a level with the various systems of philosophy, so that people would imagine themselves to have a choice between Stoicism and Epicureanism or the Gospel. In order to impress on all minds the uniqueness of the Gospel he, as a matter of principle, refrained from taking remuneration.

Now with respect to this particular thing which he had done and plans to continue to do, he says that it will serve a special purpose in his clash with the false apostles. We may paraphrase the relative clause somewhat like this: Now as to the thing which I am doing, and shall continue to do, the specific purpose is this: ἵνα ἐκκόψω τὴν ἀφορμὴν τῶν θελόντων ἀφορμήν, *in order that I may cut off the occasion of those who (just) want (or, are looking for) an occasion.* Ἀφορμή is literally a starting point, a springboard; then a base of operation; a pretext; an occasion, an inducement; also food for argument, material or subject for discussion; in a very special sense: the capital of a banker. In our case no special coloring seems to attach to the term, and we take it in its general metaphorical sense of 'occasion.' Paul wants to cut off, once and for all, the occasion for those who are eagerly looking for just some occasion. Note that ἐκκόψω is the aorist, thus stressing merely the action as such, without any suggestion of duration or lasting result.

It is clear that with the expression: "those who want an occasion," he is referring to the false apostles. Although they preached a Christ who was totally different from the historical Christ; although their message conveyed a spirit which was the very opposite of the spirit which Paul's message carried; although thus their Gospel was a counterfeit: yet they pretended to be, and demanded to be acknowledged as, true apostles of Christ. They claimed to be more efficient apostles, and to bring the Corinthians a better grade of Gospel.

Yet they were eagerly looking for an occasion to create the appearance as though in a way they were like Paul. Therefore Paul has deliberately pursued a certain course, and will continue to pursue that course, for the purpose of cutting off the desired occasion, namely, ἵνα ἐν ᾧ καυχῶνται εὑρεθῶσιν καθὼς καὶ ὑμεῖς: *in order that in the thing in which they boast they may be found just as also we (are).* If they are really penitent believers in Christ, if they are grateful disciples, if they are solicitous apostles, eager to win souls for Christ, then let them show it in self-sacrificing service, as Paul did. But what about it? They are interested in remuneration more than in the welfare of souls. To preach the Gospel without charge is beyond them. Here, then, is the point where they may be tested, here is where their true nature appears. The Gospel does not mean enough for them to forego their pay. They use their Gospel work as a convenient source of income.

(13) They looked for an occasion to be found just like the true Apostles. Paul effectively cuts off that occasion for them. They now stand exposed as what they are. Paul does not mince words: οἱ γὰρ τοιοῦτοι ψευδαπόστολοι, *for men of that type (are) pseudo apostles.*

The Greek text does not contain the copula; it must be supplied somewhere. Luther places it before the participle a little farther on in the sentence, and uses pseudo apostles (together with "evil workers") as the subject of the resulting periphrastic verb form: they "are transforming—or disguising—themselves." It seems preferable, however, to follow the lead of the KJV, which supplies the copula before "pseudo apostles." Paul has spoken about "superfine apostles," who had come to Corinth proclaiming a different Jesus and conveying another spirit, and, in short, representing a Gospel which had nothing in common with the true Gospel except the name. He had said that they were seeking an occasion to appear like Paul and his associates.

Now he brands them as pseudo apostles. They pretend to be messengers of Christ, but the content of their message, its effect, and the manner in which they conduct themselves while posing as Christ's apostles, shows clearly that they are not messengers of the Gospel of Christ. Christ did not send them. They have no divine commission to do what they are doing. They are like the false prophets whom God described to Jeremiah: "The prophets prophesy lies in my name: I sent them not, neither have I commanded them, neither spake unto them: they prophesy unto you a false vision and divination, and a thing of naught, and the deceit of their heart" (Jer. 14:14). For the same reason Paul's opponents are pseudo apostles.

Fictitious as is their commission, so is also the work which they do, and the results which they produce. They are ἐργάται δόλιοι, *fraudulent workers*. The effect of their dishonest work was evident among the Corinthians: a Jesus in an unrecognizable guise, a spirit of an altogether different stripe, a counterfeit Gospel. They do this μετασχηματιζόμενοι εἰς ἀποστόλους Χριστοῦ, *changing their appearance into (that like) apostles of Christ*. Paul, of course, is not referring to the physical appearance of the false apostles, but to their pious talk, to their pious admonitions, to their insinuating manners, to their glorious promises. But pity the Christians who let themselves be deceived by this mask! Only the true Gospel of Christ is a power of God unto salvation. An adulterated Gospel, which is no Gospel at all, leads to destruction, no matter how cunningly it may be camouflaged to resemble the original.

(14) Where do the false apostles learn their tricks?

Paul continues, καὶ οὐ θαῦμα αὐτὸς γὰρ ὁ σατανᾶς μετασχηματίζεται εἰς ἄγγελον φωτός: *And no wonder: for Satan himself transforms (disguises) himself into an angel of light*. In vs. 3 Paul compared the recent happenings in Corinth to the tragedy in the Garden of Eden. In Eden it was a serpent (manipulated by Satan) who deceived Eve with its trickery. Now similar things were going on in Corinth with similar results. In vs. 3 only the similarity of the two events themselves was pointed out; no causal connection between them was predicated. Now Paul indicates that everything is clear if we realize that the false apostles, just like the serpent in Eden, are in the employ of Satan. As in Eden Satan exploited a serpent, so he is now engaging the false apostles in his murderous work. And just as in Eden he did not show his hoofs and horns, but appeared as a harbinger of a more abundant life, so now he deceived the Corinthians by pretending to be an apostle of Christ. Note the present tense of the verb: such trickery is his regular mode of procedure. "Deep guile and great might are his dread arms in fight."

(15) Satan, the father of lies, resorts to disguise for success. It is to be expected that he will teach his agents the same mode of procedure. Above Paul had used the word "no marvel." Now he expresses the same idea in a somewhat milder term. He says, οὐ μέγα οὖν. *It is, then, not a great thing*—rather it is to be expected. What? εἰ καὶ οἱ διάκονοι αὐτοῦ μετασχηματίζονται ὡς διάκονοι δικαιοσύνης: *if also his servants transform (disguise) themselves as ministers of righteousness.* Paul uses the word διάκονος, not δοῦλος. The latter would be in place if the point were to stress the fact that these men take their orders from Satan. That certainly is true, but it is not the point which Paul here wants us to note. These men are agents of Satan, engaged in carrying out Satan's designs. They are his administrators, promoting his affairs. He is the one who sinned from the beginning. He introduced sin into the world by tempting man to disobey God. His business is to perpetuate sin in the world by leading men into temptation and causing them to fall, so that they must die. Since Christ came into the world and as the Lamb of God took away sin by His vicarious suffering and death, the specific design of Satan is to prevent people from accepting Christ and His righteousness in simple faith.

And yet, while engaged in perpetuating sin he teaches his agents to pose as administrators of righteousness, i.e., of the righteousness which Christ won for us by being made sin for us, and which He administers by proclaiming free justification to men, and sending His Holy Spirit to create faith in their hearts. He gave to us the message of reconciliation and established among us the blessed ministry of reconciliation. It is not a great or unusual thing that Satan, the liar from the beginning and the father of lies, in order to deceive the people so much the more easily, teaches his agents to assume the pose of ministers of righteousness, and to use this guise for spreading unrighteousness all the more effectively.

As a warning Paul concludes this part with the announcement: ὧν τὸ τέλος ἔσται κατὰ τὰ ἔργα αὐτῶν: *whose (i.e., but their) end will be according to their works.* The relative pronoun serves merely to connect this clause to the foregoing. Such mode of connection is extremely rare in English. We substitute a demonstrative, usually together with some coordinating conjunction. In our case, the relation being slightly adversative, we use "but." The false apostles do make a great show, but their work is sham. The bubble will burst. Their works will be made manifest in their true nature. They will not stand up in the judgment of the Lord. Being exposed as works of unrighteousness, they will bring down damnation on the heads of Satan's agents. And all who permitted themselves to be misled by them will share their fate.

With this warning Paul concludes the part begun in vs. 2, where he remarked that he is zealous about the Corinthians with the very zeal of God. He is going to indulge in a little foolishness, but not in trifling flippancy; it is extremely serious business for him. Life and death is at stake, righteousness and unrighteousness, eternal salvation or damnation.

4. 11:16-21a

(16) In vs. 1 of this chapter Paul had asked for the indulgence of his readers if he engaged in some foolishness. Having now demonstrated what a serious matter his request concerns, he repeats the original appeal in a modified form in vs. 16. He asks, πάλιν λέγω, μή τίς με δόξῃ ἄφρονα εἶναι: *Again I say, let not anyone think that I (really) am a fool.* With πάλιν referring back to the wish expressed in vs. 1, Paul now pleads that no one misunderstand his method. His talk will sound like a fool's, but it will not be done in the spirit of a fool. Fools boast for self-glorification. They will speak about themselves, their qualifications, their efforts, their achievements. When they are present, no one else will have a chance to get a word in edgewise. They will conveniently forget about their own shortcomings. Oh, yes, they may condescendingly say, "We all make mistakes. That's why we have erasers on our pencils." But that is not to be taken too seriously. In their boasting they will also exaggerate.

In a boastful way Paul is now going to speak about his own work and that of the intruders. Of course, he will abstain from untruthful exaggeration; but his words might be misconstrued in that sense by unfriendly critics. For that reason he pleads with his readers not to assume that he is actually a fool.

But if his boasting should sound too realistic, if his readers cannot quite come up to his request, then, he pleads, they should at least listen to him: εἰ δὲ μήγε: *but if not, i.e., if you do not grant my request.* Paul adds the emphatic particle γε for a stress which is difficult to reproduce in English. Words like *even, indeed, at least,* etc., are a little too heavy. The Greek-English Lexicon of the N.T. suggests for our passage: *otherwise at least.* The KJ has simply "if otherwise," while Luther renders it: *wo aber nicht.* If the Corinthians find it utterly impossible to grant his request, then what? Paul continues, κἂν ὡς ἄφρονα δέξασθέ με: *even if as a fool, receive me.* With δέξασθε Paul not only asks his readers to listen to him carefully, but also to consider well what he has to say. In form his words may be like a fool's talk, but the content will be of the utmost importance. Hence, δέξασθε: listen and absorb, ἵνα κἀγὼ μικρόν τι καυχήσωμαι: *that also I may do a little bit of boasting.* Thus Paul repeats his request of vs. 1, that the Corinthians should bear with him in a little folly.

(17) Before he begins his boasting, Paul inserts another explanation—we might call it an excuse—for this manner of procedure in proclaiming the Gospel and instructing believers. He says, ὃ λαλῶ, οὐ κατὰ κύριον λαλῶ ἀλλ᾽ ὡς ἐν ἀφροσύνῃ: *What (i.e., the thing that) I am saying, not in the Lord's manner am I saying (it), but as in folly.* We must not overlook the fact that Paul uses the singular of the relative pronoun. He is not referring to his manner of teaching in general. He is speaking specifically of the request which he is making, that the Corinthians permit him to do a little boasting. In boasting like a fool he is palpably deviating from the manner in which the Lord proclaimed His Gospel and instructed His hearers. There was no occasion, and there could not arise a situation during our Lord's earthly career, that would call for a manner of procedure such as Paul now plans to follow. Someone might object that since the Lord never employed this method, it was a clear indication that the method itself was improper, and that Paul really stood self-condemned by stooping to employ it. Ordinarily Paul would not think of using it, and he shows considerable uneasiness now that he decided to try it. He appears quite uncomfortable in the role he is about to play.

This is evident also from the explanatory remark which he adds, ἐν ταύτῃ τῇ ὑποστάσει τῆς καυχήσεως: *in this venture of the (my) boasting.* He calls his boasting a ὑπόστασις. This word literally means 'a basis,' 'a foundation,' and, used metonymically, it may designate the building erected on a foundation. Metaphorically, it denotes the basis on which some assumption rests, and then, metonymically, that assumption itself. Thus in Hebrews 11:1, our faith is called the ὑπόστασις of things hoped for; and in the same verse in the synonymous parallel member the word ἔλεγχος, conviction, is used to express the same idea.

In our present case Paul is undertaking something new, something which makes him feel rather uncomfortable, yet something which he is convinced is proper and will be effective. To express these ideas I used the English word "venture." (Moffat and Phillips simply say "business," while Goodspeed has "reckless way.") By the way, when Paul in this verse says that he is not speaking κατὰ κύριον, he is not referring to inspiration. He does not mean to say that the Lord has nothing to do with the matter and is not giving him the very words by His Spirit, as the RSV, Moffat, and Phillips seem to imply. RSV: "I say not with the Lord's authority." Moffat: "What I am now going to say is not inspired by the Lord." Phillips: "I am not now speaking as the Lord commands me." Paul is simply referring to his method of speaking in the given situation.

This still leaves the question unanswered: Why did Paul choose this method of boasting? The next verse mentions the occasion, but only hints in a very veiled way at the real reason.

(18) Ἐπεὶ πολλοὶ καυχῶνται κατὰ τὴν σάρκα, κἀγὼ καυχήσομαι: *Since many are boasting according to the flesh, also I shall boast.* The desire to boast is very common and is in agreement with the flesh. "Flesh" is here, of course, not to be taken in the sense of sinful nature. Paul would never deliberately boast in a sinful manner. It merely refers to a certain weakness of all human nature. It is human to feel the urge for boasting, and, on the other hand, just as human to resent having to listen to someone else's boasting. To this common trait of human nature Paul refers when he says that many indulge in boasting. It is a very common practice. "Everybody's doing it."

While making this general observation, Paul naturally keeps the situation in Corinth in mind. The Corinthians have recently been exposed to very much boasting. They should really be "fed up." But that does not seem to be the case. Hence Paul will fall in line; he also will engage in boasting. The Corinthians should not resent it, rather, on the basis of their past behavior toward the false apostles, they might be expected to enjoy it. At least, it seems to Paul to be an avenue of approach to the Corinthians' heart that is worth trying.— The irony of the next verse is designed to blast the last roadblock.

(19) Ἡδέως γὰρ ἀνέχεσθε τῶν ἀφρόνων: *For with joy you endure the fools.* Note the contradiction in terms between the verb and its adverb modifier: ἀνέχεσθαι means 'to endure,' 'to put up with.' As a rule persons will endure something with dull resignation or with silent patience. But never will such endurance be the source of joy and happiness. In the case of the Corinthians things were different. They had to put up with fools, but they were happy doing it. They enjoyed it, and never did they seem more elated than in the company of those fools

Paul will have more details to add to this statement later on, in vs. 20. For the present he describes the motive for the peculiar conduct of the Corinthians in a participial phrase: φρόνιμοι ὄντες: (*you do this*) *being intelligent people.* Do intelligent people enjoy the prating and bragging of fools? By being pleased and delighted with the treatment which they received from the intruders, the Corinthians clearly show that they are anything but intelligent people.

Is Paul justified in speaking to the Corinthians with such bitter, biting irony? In support of his charge he points out to them what their acceptance of the intruders really means. He may be speaking as a fool, but the matter is serious, and he is in dead earnest about it. He continues with an explanatory γάρ, and presents the meaning of the Corinthians' reaction to the false apostles from five different angles.

(20) The first is: ἀνέχεσθε εἴ τις ὑμᾶς καταδουλοῖ: *You endure it if someone reduces you to slavery.* Paul had brought them the truth of the Gospel, the truth which, according to Christ's promise, made them free. The intruders brought them another Christ, a counterfeit Gospel, and a heterogeneous spirit, whereby they resubjected them to the yoke of bondage. By accepting additions of Law elements to the Gospel, the Corinthians had lost Christ and had fallen from grace. They had become entangled again in the bondage of the weak and beggarly elements of this world. This is what the intruders had done to the Corinthians. And they took it with a smile. They enjoyed it.

Looked at from a different angle, what the intruders had done to the Corinthians can be described as: εἴ τις κατεσθίει: *if someone devours you*. The intruders not only robbed the Corinthians of their spiritual liberty and made slaves of them; they also charged heavy fees and collected exorbitant payment. Again the Corinthians did not resent it. They complied most willingly.

In a way that is similar to the first statement, yet going slightly beyond it, the third εἰ clause says: εἴ τις λαμβάνει: *if anyone takes you* (*i.e., takes possession of you, captures you*). Paul does not say, takes *from* you, or robs you, but, takes you personally, so that you become his slaves and he your master. Paul had emphatically declined such a position for himself. "Not for that we have dominion over your faith, but are helpers of your joy" (1:24). That is in full agreement with the attitude which Peter enjoined on all bishops: "Neither as being lords over God's heritage, but being ensamples to the flock" (I Pet. 5:3). Peter had learned this from the Lord Himself: "Neither be ye called masters: for one is your Master, even Christ" (Matt. 23:10). And Paul had warned the Corinthians: "Ye are bought with a price: therefore glorify God in your body, and in your spirit, which are God's." And again: "Ye are bought with a price; be not ye the servants of men" (I Cor. 6:20; 7:23). Yet the Corinthians permitted themselves to be taken captive by men. They let men lord it over them—and seemed to enjoy it.

A fourth way of expressing it is closely related to the third: εἴ τις ἐπαίρεται: *if anyone is presumptuous* (Luther: *so jemand euch trotzet*). This attitude of the intruders stands in sharp contrast to Paul's "meekness and gentleness," which he had learned from Christ, and at which the intruders sneered, saying that his personal presence was weak and his speech contemptible. Yes, Paul had even "abased" himself that they might be exalted. Then the intruders came, putting on airs, acting presumptuously, and even becoming abusive. And the Corinthians took it meekly; they even gloried in it.

Lastly Paul says that they bear it εἴ τις εἰς πρόσωπον ὑμᾶς δέρει: *if someone slaps you in the face*. The Corinthians had learned from Paul to rejoice in the Gospel of the free forgiveness of their sins, of their adoption into God's family. Now they were told by the intruders that they had been duped by Paul, and that the Gospel which they had accepted was a very inferior brand. That was like a slap in the face. Yet the Corinthians meekly and joyfully submitted. They felt honored.

Such was the treatment which the Corinthians had received, as it appears when viewed in the light of the facts. How was it possible that they had submitted?

(21a) Paul answers: κατὰ ἀτιμίαν λέγω: *I am speaking according to disgrace*. The picture which Paul sketched in a few bold lines certainly is a disgraceful one; and Paul is actually ashamed to present it. On whom does the disgrace fall? On the intruders for doing such shameful things? On the Corinthians for submitting to such treatment? Shameful for themselves and for their Savior, who is thereby crowded out of His rightful place? Paul feels that the shame falls on himself and his colaborers: ὡς ὅτι ἡμεῖς ἠσθενήκαμεν: *namely, that we (now) stand there as weaklings.*

The combination ὡς ὅτι occurs three times in Paul's letters: in II Thessalonians 2:2; and in our present Epistle in 5:19, besides the verse under consideration. We discussed it briefly in connection with 5:19. Some grammars do not explain it at all; some, like *Blass-Debrunner*, simply equate it with plain ὅτι. Jerome has two different translations. In our passage and in II Thessalonians 2:2 he says *quasi, as though;* Ὡς, the relative adverb of manner, is best changed to a demonstrative according to the English idiom, and the ὅτι clause explains what is meant. Paul is speaking by way of disgrace, namely, because "we now stand there as weaklings."

Paul had brought the Gospel to Corinth. He had instructed the Corinthians in the faith. Through his service they had learned to know their Savior and had received the Spirit. Then when the false apostles came, the Corinthians received them with open arms, and readily accepted their false gospel in the manner which Paul has just outlined in a concise summary: They took it with a smile when they were made slaves, etc.

Paul now says, That reflects on our work. When the Galatians permitted themselves to be taken in by the Judaizers, Paul wrote, I am surprised, I cannot understand "that ye are so soon removed from him that called you" (Gal. 1:6). Here he says, We must be weaklings, we must have done a very poor job, seeing that "fools" can so easily shake you and win you over to their error, and treat you as the intruders did—and you even feel happy and proud about it.

The Corinthians well remembered how thorough Paul had been in his work. All the more they must now feel ashamed of themselves, having permitted themselves to be duped so easily.

Now Paul is ready to begin his own boasting.

C. BOASTING IN WEAKNESS

Chapter 11:21b to Chapter 12:18

The ground now has been well prepared. Paul has warned the Corinthians that he believes he has reason to suspect them of a lack of singleness of purpose and purity of heart in their relation to Christ. The warm reception which they accorded the false apostles shows their instability. In spite of the fact that the false apostles brought them a different Jesus, another spirit, and another gospel, they readily accepted the counterfeit. Paul, though not in excellency of speech and in rhetorical eloquence, yet with rich understanding and in sincere modesty, had raised them out of the depths of darkness and despair and exalted them to peace and joy in the Lord. Yet apparently with no difficulty at all the false apostles by their boasting had destroyed the work of Paul. The Corinthians even seemed to relish the boasting and the boasters, although it meant spiritual enslavement for them. Now Paul says, that points a possible way of approach for him to their hearts. It may not be the Christlike way, it may be loathsome to Paul personally, yet he is willing to try it. He also will resort to boasting. He will not exaggerate. He will present facts, and let the facts speak for themselves.

1. 11:21b-29

(21b) The false apostles had indulged in some "tall" boasting. Paul will match them point for point: ἐν ᾧ δ' ἄν τις τολμᾷ, *but in whatsoever anyone is daring.* The δέ is slightly adversative. In the previous part of the verse Paul had spoken about his own "disgrace." Since his work in Corinth had been so quickly overthrown by the intruders, does that fact not reflect unfavorably on the nature of his work? Does it not show that he had done a very "poor job"? If he had been more efficient, ought not the Corinthians to have stood more firm? Ought they not to have resisted the false apostles? Yet, though this may be the first impression which an observer gets, Paul will not concede the point, rather, in whatsoever anyone dares to claim something, Paul is ready to call the bluff. Note the very wide scope of the relative pronoun. Paul asks for no exceptions. He leaves it to the opponent to bring in any challenge he chooses.

Before writing the apodosis, Paul once more expresses his aversion to this type of procedure. He remarks parenthetically, ἐν ἀφροσύνῃ λέγω, *I am speaking in folly*. The false apostles were in earnest when they boasted about themselves. They were very much concerned about their own honor and their pocketbooks. If Paul now starts to boast, the Corinthians might get the impression that he is similarly concerned— something which would defeat the very purpose of Paul, who is concerned about one thing only: viz., that "Christ be formed" in them (cf. Gal. 4:19).

If the Corinthians keep Paul's aversion to boasting in mind, then he will now take up the gauntlet which the opponents had thrown at his feet: τολμῶ κἀγώ, *daring am I also*— with no fear of being bested.

Paul said that he would meet the boasting intruders on their own ground. Whatever claim they may advance, he will take it up and match it. They boasted in outward things, without going to the heart of the matter. This fact we must bear in mind when Paul now mentions some of their claims.

(22) He takes up three of their vaunted excellences, which he maintains he can easily duplicate, but which for him had a different meaning than for the false apostles. Ἐβραῖοί εἰσιν; *They are Hebrews?*— Ἰσραηλῖταί εἰσιν; *They are Israelites?*—σπέρμα Ἀβραάμ εἰσιν; *They are Abraham's seed?*—In each case he can say, κἀγώ, *So am I.* For the intruders these three terms meant merely outward membership in God's chosen nation. In that sense already Paul could say, I too. As far as nationality is concerned, he could say more. He was not only an ordinary Hebrew, but, as he says in Philippians 3:5, he was "an Hebrew of the Hebrews," a purebred Hebrew in descent, in customs, in language, without any foreign admixture.

Israel was the name given by God to Jacob on his return from Mesopotamia, when Jacob in faith and prayer wrestled with God for the promised blessing: "For as a prince hast thou power with God and with men, and hast prevailed" (Gen. 32:28). The opponents of Paul were Israelites only outwardly; Paul was one in the true sense of the word. "They are not all Israel, which are of Israel" (Rom. 9:6).

The same applies to the name "seed of Abraham." Abraham is the father of believers: "They which are of faith, the same are the children of Abraham" (Gal. 3:7). Paul does not stress this important distinction here; he is meeting his opponents on their own ground of externalism.

(23) The same applies to the next point, διάκονοι Χριστοῦ εἰσιν; *Are they ministers of Christ?*—Paul calls himself a δοῦλος Χριστοῦ, one who takes all his orders from Christ, one who has no interests of his own but is completely absorbed in the business of his Master (e.g., Rom. 1:1; Phil 1:1). He does not use that word here. He also calls himself a ὑπερέτης of Christ (I Cor. 4:1), an underling, a "performer of any strong and hard labor," an "inferior minister to perform certain defined functions" (Trench). He does not use that word here. Here he speaks of διάκονοι.

This word, according to Trench, "represents the servant in his activity for the work"—or in the words of Cremer: *die Ruecksicht auf die einem andern zu gute kommende Arbeit.*

When comparing his work done for the Gospel and his service rendered to the Lord with that of the false apostles, Paul can say, ὑπὲρ ἐγώ. In this respect he is "'way above" them. But he inserts, παραφρονῶν λαλῶ, *I am talking as one beside himself.* His words may sound silly, but he is really ministering to Christ in a manner which the false apostles never even approach. When he works for the Lord, he actually toils and labors strenuously: ἐν κόποις περισσοτέρως, *in labors excessively.* The Corinthians knew how Paul labored in his ministry among them, proclaiming the Gospel publicly in the house of one Titus Justus, and instructing, admonishing, warning, rebuking individuals privately. At the same time he labored with his hands in the shop of Aquila, in order to support himself and his associates. How much did the false apostles labor, who came into the established congregation and posed as lords? Περισσοτέρως is not meant to compare the unusually great amount of Paul's labors with a comparatively small amount of work done by his opponents, but is to be taken in the absolute sense: great by comparison with an ordinary or regular amount of work, by comparison with what might reasonably be expected.

The last paraphrase naturally does not apply to the next expression: ἐν φυλακαῖς περισσοτέρως, *in prisons excessively.* A law-abiding citizen does not expect to be cast into prison; but in the administration of the Gospel, which is "unto the Jews a stumbling block and unto the Greeks foolishness," such treatment may await the faithful minister. Whether Paul was ever cast into prison while in Corinth, is not recorded in Acts. He came pretty close to it when the Jews dragged him before the tribunal of Gallio; and he had been in prison in Philippi shortly before he came to Corinth. Were the false apostles ever arrested for their ministry of the Gospel? Or threatened with imprisonment?

These two points would be sufficient to support Paul's ὑπέρ, but they are mild in comparison with what he can say in addition: ἐν πληγαῖς ὑπερβαλλόντως, in beatings superabundantly. These were not beatings by some excited, rioting mob; they were beatings ordered and administered by some Jewish or Roman court. Paul will speak about them more specifically in the following verse. There is very little difference, if any, between περισσοτέρως and ὑπερβαλλόντως. Both express the idea of excess, of more than enough.

Ἐν θανάτοις πολλάκις, in deaths often. His work in the Gospel ministry often brought Paul to death's door: in his dangerous travels by land and by sea, from unruly mobs, from unreasonable court orders.

This is what it meant for Paul to be a minister of Christ. How many badges of this type could the false apostles produce? Could they say like Paul, "I bear in my body the marks of the Lord Jesus"? (Gal. 6:17.) He was ὑπέρ them with regard to labors excessively, with regard to imprisonments excessively, with regard to stripes superabundantly, yes, he had faced death, not only once or twice, but often.

(24, 25) In these two verses Paul explains in some detail what he means by facing death: ὑπὸ Ἰουδαίων πεντάκις τεσσεράκοντα παρὰ μίαν ἔλαβον: From Jews I five times received forty less one. In the case when a criminal was sentenced to a beating the Jewish judge was limited by law to 40 stripes (Deut. 25:3). In order to guard against the error of a miscount, the Jews stopped every beating at 39. This was not done out of any consideration of pity for the convict, but purely out of a mechanical interpretation and treatment of the law. The criminal was beaten unmercifully, and far less than 39 stripes might cause death or permanent deformity. Paul received the limit five times, and every time faced the possibility of death. When and where these beatings by the Jews took place is not recorded.

These were not the only beatings; τρὶς ἐρραβδίσθην, *three times was I beaten with rods*, i.e., by the Roman lictors. Luke records one of these beatings in Acts 16:22,23. In this case the procedure was illegal, as the judges learned to their consternation and humiliation on the next day, since Paul was a Roman citizen. But in the confusion caused by the mob they had failed to hear Paul's protest, or had ignored it, taking for granted that Paul stood outside the protection of the pertinent statutes. When the other two scourgings before Roman courts occurred is not recorded. They were severe. Even Pilate was moved to exclaim, "Behold the man," when he saw Jesus after His scourging.

Paul came even closer to death by other means than by these scourgings. He names four other occasions. One was a stoning: ἅπαξ ἐλιθάσθην. This happened in Lystra (Acts 14:19). It must be considered as a special miracle of God that Paul survived this ordeal.

Three shipwrecks brought Paul face to face with death, one case being especially grueling. He was forced to spend 24 hours, a night and a day, in the deep, clinging to some wreckage of the ship most likely; τρὶς ἐναυάγησα, νυχθήμερον ἐν τῷ βυθῷ πεποίηκα: *three times I was shipwrecked; I spent a night and a day in the deep.* The last verb is a perfect tense, thus not historical, merely recording the fact, but indicating that this shipwreck left its marks either on the body or in the mind of Paul. He is a man who once was adrift on the sea for a night and a day. On his mission journeys Paul crossed parts of the Mediterranean and of the Aegean Sea on several occasions. Just when the shipwrecks occurred, is not recorded by Luke.

(26) All of these near-deaths threatened Paul because he was a minister of Christ. They happened on his journeys in the interest of the Gospel. Was he deterred? No, he was a minister of Christ, called to cover a certain territory; so he must travel, no matter what the dangers. He was *on journeys often,* ὁδοιπορίαις πολλάκις, facing eight different kinds of danger. Paul is here still demonstrating in what respect he as a minister of Christ is 'way ὑπέρ the false apostles. It is by his mission travels. That explains the first dative, ὁδοιπορίαις. The following datives denote the manner in which these mission travels were carried out, namely, κινδύνοις ποταμῶν, κινδύνοις λῃστῶν, κινδύνοις ἐκ γένους, κινδύνοις ἐξ ἐθνῶν, κινδύνοις ἐν πόλει, κινδύοοις ἐο ερημίᾳ κινδύνοις ἐν θαλάσσῃ, κινδύνοις ἐν ψευδαδέλφοις, *with perils of rivers,*

with perils of robbers—with perils from (my) race, with perils from Gentiles—with perils in a city, with perils in a solitude, with perils on sea—with perils among false brethren. The first pair uses the subjective genitive, rivers and robbers causing the perils which theatened Paul. The second pair has the preposition ἐκ, thus indicating the source from which the perils arose, both from Paul's own kin and from Gentiles. The next group (three members) points to the places where Paul met the dangers: with the preposition ἐν. The last phrase has a single word: false brethren, who pretend to be brethren, but in reality are traitors. 'Ἐν means *in their midst*.

No further comment is required. Traveling was dangerous in those days. Though the Romans had done much to improve the highways and to clear the land of robbers and the sea of pirates, they succeeded only in part. The story of the Good Samaritan, which happened not far from Jerusalem, was taken from life. In the interest of the Gospel Paul never hesitated to undertake any voyage by land or by sea in spite of the concomitant dangers.

(27) From his extensive journeys in the interest of the Gospel, all connected with trying perils of various kinds, Paul now turns to his labor for the Lord. He began the previous paragraph with a dative of reference. He was 'way ὑπέρ the false apostles ὁδοιπορίαις, with his perilous travels. Similarly he now says that he is 'way ὑπέρ them κόπῳ καὶ μόχθῳ, *with toil and exertion*. Κόπος (from κόπτω, to strike, to smite) indicates difficulty, troublesome and exhausting labor. Μόχθος (from μοχθέω, to be weary, to be sore distressed) is a synonym, meaning hardship or distress. Paul's work as a minister of Christ was a daily grind, a never-ending ordeal. With four ἐν phrases he mentions some of the grueling circumstances.

The first is ἐν ἀγρυπνίαις πολλάκις, *in sleeplessness often*. Time and again it would happen that Paul could not refresh his tired body and his weary mind with a little sleep. He kept many, not self-chosen, but inflicted vigils, imposed by the labor he was performing as a minister of Christ.

The second ἐν phrase mentions two distressing experiences, which form a pair: ἐν λιμῷ καὶ δίψει, *in hunger and thirst*. Many a time he had to skip a meal because his service of Christ demanded his attention; often he may not have been in a financial position to pay for a meal. And since he would not be burdensome to anyone, he went without food and drink. In this manner he did his difficult work for Christ on may occasions: ἐν νηστείαις πολλάκις, *in involuntary fastings often*. The Pharisee in the Temple boasted of fasting twice in a week. Paul was ὑπέρ in point of number; only he did not count his fastings as meritorious works, for which he would demand a reward, but as necessary adjuncts incidental to the ministry for Christ.

Lastly he mentions ἐν ψύχει καὶ γυμνότητι, *in cold and nakedness*. On his many travels for the Gospel Paul may frequently have been caught unprepared for a sudden drop in the temperature from day to night. His ministry for Christ, in itself taxing a man's ability to the breaking point, was made unusually difficult by these grueling accompaniments. Yet Paul considered them as comparatively insignificant, when compared to the real burden of his work.

(28) He calls them little "extras": χωρὶς τῶν παρεκτός, *apart from these secondary matters*. To us the list of dangers and privations incidental to Paul's ministry of the Gospel may seem very impressive. Paul rates these things as minor matters. The really weighty part of the ministry he calls ἡ ἐπίστασίς μοι ἡ καθ᾽ ἡμέραν, *the daily pressure on me*. The word ἐπίστασις occurs, besides in our passage, only in Acts 24:12. There Paul in his defense before Felix points out that during the scant 12 days which he had spent in Jerusalem nobody had found him in the Temple arguing with anyone, nor causing an ἐπίστασις of the crowd (a *concursus*, Jerome translates), nor in the synagogues, nor anywhere in the city. In this reference there is a hint of violence in ἐπίστασις. In our present passage, where the ἐπίστασις is directed at Paul, a certain pressure seems to be indicated, which the crowd daily exerted on him. Physical violence is not indicated.

To this he adds ἡ μέριμνα πασῶν τῶν ἐκκλησιῶν, *the anxious concern for all the congregations*. The genitive ἐκκλησιῶν is objective. Besides the pressure of the problems of the local group among whom Paul is working to establish a church there are the problems of the congregations already in existence elsewhere. We learn that they wrote letters and sent delegations to Paul, e.g., the Corinthian congregation, also the churches in Galatia and in Colosse. Paul revisited his churches to "see how they do," e.g., the churches in Galatia. He sent some of his assistants and wrote letters. In all of these letters we see how deeply he was concerned about the welfare of these churches. There was heart-taxing μέριμνα. That was the heavy burden of his ministry, in comparison with which all the before-mentioned perils and hardships pale into insignificance. What do the false apostles in their ways ever get to feel of such ἐπίστασις and μέριμνα?

(29) All this adds up to immense weakness and pain for Paul. He poses two questions to drive home this point: τίς ἀσθενεῖ, καὶ οὐκ ἀσθενῶ; *Who is weak, and I am not weak?* Paul does not use the personal pronoun ἐγώ. There is no special emphasis on his person. He is not comparing himself with others in respect to weakness. He is comparing weakness with weakness. Does anyone think he is overburdened? Just let him look at my load, if he wants to see a real burden. All this because Paul is carrying the combined load of weakness of all churches.

The second question contains the pronoun ἐγώ. Thus Paul is here comparing himself with others: τίς σκανδαλίζεται, καὶ οὐκ ἐγὼ πυροῦμαι; *Who is caught in a death trap, and I (on my part) am not being burned?* This is figurative language. If anyone has to suffer trials and temptations that threaten his very faith, his spiritual life, let him look at me, who am assailed from without and within with most devastating attacks. "O wretched man that I am! who shall deliver me from the body of this death?" (Rom. 7:24.)

That is what the ministry of Christ meant for Paul, a load under which he would break down were he to bear it in his own strength. That it would be just so had been announced to him when he received his call. Jesus instructed Ananias to "show him how great things he must suffer for my name's sake" (Acts 9:16). And such was one of the first experiences which he had in his newly received ministry, as he will tell us in the following short section.

2. 11:30-33

In the previous section Paul started out with boastful defiance. He challenged his opponents to mention any of their excellences or merits, and he would match them. He wound up by speaking of his own weakness and painful, deathly "burning."

Paul is not inconsistent; he is not veering; he is not losing sight of his aim. He is still pointing out that regarding the ministry of Christ he is far ὑπέρ his boasting opponents. The ministry of Christ entails labor and perils. The opponents may think that the ministry

of Christ means an easy life of honor and quasi luxury. They do not
realize that with ideas of that type they are actually disqualifying
themselves for any part of Christ's ministry.—He continued to point
out that the excessive labor under perils and sufferings required of
Christ's ministers is not carried out with their own strength. Paul
feels the pain, he realizes his own weakness. He of himself is not
equal to the task. If the opponents do not realize their own insuf-
ficiency, that is no sign of superiority. They merely reveal thereby
again that they are actually not qualified for the service of Christ.
They are pretenders and deceivers.

Although Paul here introduces this fact over against the boasting
of the opponents, it is not the first time that he has mentioned it.
After speaking about the glory of the New Testament ministry in
chapter 3 he continued in chapter 4: "But we have this treasure in
earthen vessels" (vs. 7), and supported this statement with a reference to various aspects of the apostles' weakness (vss. 8-12). This is
so, not by accident. The purpose is that the power of God may shine
forth in all its glory (vs. 7). Consciousness of one's personal weakness
and unworthiness is a necessary prerequisite in the make-up of every
minister of Christ.

This is the reason why Paul in his venture of boasting led over to
his "weakness" and "burning."

(30) He adds the summary statement that, if any boasting at all
has to be done, he will forget everything else and will concentrate on
his weakness. Boasting was necessary for Paul in this case. It was pro-
voked by the baseless boasting of his opponents. His words are:
εἰ καυχᾶσθαι δεῖ, *if to boast is necessary,* as it is in this case, then
τὰ τῆς ἀσθενείας μου καυχήσομαι, *then I will boast (boastfully mention)
the things of my weakness.*

The kingdom of Christ is the very opposite of the kingdoms of
this world. In the kingdoms of this world it is power that counts. Not
so in Christ's kingdom. The disciples of Jesus argued on several occasions who of them should be the greatest in His kingdom. Two even
requested the distinction of being seated one on the right hand and
the other on the left of Jesus in His kingdom, while the other ten
resented that these two had thus tried to "steal a march" on them.

On each of these occasions Jesus rebuked His disciples sharply.
"It shall not be so among you: but whosoever will be great among you,

let him be your minister; and whosoever will be chief among you, let him be your servant: even as the Son of man came not to be ministered unto, but to minister, and to give his life a ransom for many" (Matt. 20:26-28).

Paul had been initiated into this nature of Christ's kingdom from the very beginning of his apostleship. Ananias had announced to him that he must suffer many things for the name of Jesus. And Paul did not have to wait long before he got a taste of persecution.

Yet to boast of one's weakness seems such an unusual, abnormal procedure that Paul sees fit to add a special assurance to his plain statement of vs. 30. He wants those words to be taken at full face value. He does not want them to be toned down as though he were jesting or exaggerating. God knows that he is stating plain facts in plain language.

(31) The point of this verse is, ὅτι οὐ ψεύδομαι, that I am not lying. The point which Paul is trying to get across to his readers is of utmost importance, and yet very difficult to realize even for believers. Paul appeals to God's infallible knowledge. He says, ὁ θεὸς . . . οἶδεν, God knows.—He is, however, speaking of God not, e.g., as the wise Creator or Ruler of the universe. He calls Him πατὴρ τοῦ κυρίου Ἰησοῦ, the Father of the Lord Jesus.—In the work of Jesus, God demonstrated the truth: per aspera ad astra, the way to the crown leads through the cross. In encouraging the Corinthians to participate cheerfully and according to ability in the collection for the needy saints in Jerusalem, Paul referred to the poverty of our Savior that, being rich, He became poor for our sakes, in this way to make us rich. In his letter to the Philippians a few years later he spoke specifically about the two states of Christ. The author of the Epistle to the Hebrews formulates it thus: "Jesus . . . for the joy that was set before him endured the cross, despising the shame" (Heb. 12:2).

Paul adds, ὁ ὢν εὐλογητὸς εἰς τοὺς αἰῶνας, He who is blessed forever. We must join in the praises of our God, first of all, by accepting for our salvation wholeheartedly His principle which is so offensive to our flesh; and we must learn to live and to regulate our life by that principle. "Not unto us, O Lord, not unto us, but unto thy name give glory, for thy mercy and for thy truth's sake" (Ps. 115:1).

(32) Ἐν Δαμασκῷ ὁ ἐθνάρχης Ἀρέτα τοῦ βασιλέως ἐφρούρει τὴν πόλιν Δαμασκηνῶν πιάσαι με: *In Damascus the ethnarch of King Aretas was guarding the city of the Damascenes to arrest me.*

This statement of Paul raises a number of questions which cannot be answered definitely. Was Damascus under Arabian rule at this time? In connection with this: Was the ethnarch of King Aretas governing the city itself, or was he perhaps some Arabian sheik near the city? Why does Paul call it the city of the Damascenes? Does he mean to hint some form of home rule? Was the control by Aretas only nominal, even nonexistent, though claimed by him?

Josephus speaks about King Aretas quite extensively. This king seems to have ruled approximately from 9 B.C. to 40 A.D. He was the father of the first wife of Herod Antipas, who divorced her in order to marry Herodias, his niece, the wife of his brother Philip. When the daughter of Aretas learned of her husband's plans, before he knew that she had been informed, she escaped to her father via the fortress Machaerus. In the war which Aretas then waged against Herod to avenge the honor of his daughter (and about some border disputes), Herod's army was utterly routed. The Jews interpreted this as a judgment of God on Herod for the murder of John the Baptist.

Herod appealed to Rome; and Vitellius, at this time proconsul of Syria, was sent to make war on Aretas and to deliver him to the emperor dead or alive. While Vitellius was on the march, the report reached him of the death of the Emperor Tiberius (March 16, 37 A.D.). The expedition was discontinued. The next emperor, Caligula, was rather favorably disposed toward Aretas, and the Arabian affairs were settled peaceably in 39. Whether he turned Damascus over to Aretas is not stated. Perhaps Aretas, during the time of confusion, arrogated some authority to himself.

While Paul says that the ethnarch of King Aretas guarded the city to arrest him, St. Luke records that the Jews instigated this persecution. They evidently were the prime movers, and the ethnarch was a tool in their hands.

(33) Paul's escape was not a heroic, glorious affair. Διὰ θυρίδος ἐν σαργάνῃ ἐχαλάσθην διὰ τοῦ τείχους, *Through a door in a basket was I lowered through the wall.* The door was a small opening in the wall. It must have been very inconspicuous, so that, while they were carefully guarding the gates, nobody seems to have thought of this door. It was

a round, plaited basket (σπυρίς, Acts 9:25) in which Paul was lowered to the ground.—Καὶ ἐξέφυγον τὰς χεῖρας αὐτοῦ, *and (thus) I made my escape from his hands.* Thus began the career of the Apostle who brought to Corinth the Gospel of Christ, filled with "the power of God unto salvation."

3. 12:1-5

In the previous chapter Paul had dared the false apostles to present their claims and had announced that he would match them point for point. He did so, but soon came to a pass where he could declare that as far as the real ministry of Christ is concerned he is 'way beyond them. Then in vs. 30 he had touched on the question if it is really necessary to engage in boasting. The only boasting that will serve to provide a proper background for setting off the superabundant saving power of the Gospel is a boasting about one's own weakness. This procedure, of course, is something utterly foreign to the false apostles' way of thinking. They may misinterpret this turn in the argument in their favor, namely, that Paul, because he is aware of his weakness, knowing that he has no personal excellences, now tries to make the most of a bad case by turning a deficiency into a virtue. Paul is ready to meet them.

(1) Καυχᾶσθαι δεῖ, *It is necessary to boast (to keep on boasting) about oneself.* There are many variant readings of this verse, showing what difficulty the copyists had in grasping Paul's meaning. It seems that the reading adopted by Nestle is the best, except for the punctuation. The brief sentence listed above should be followed by a period. It is as though Paul meant to say: Boasting (about oneself—middle voice) is necessary, but so far we have barely scratched the surface. Let us proceed to mention some truly outstanding matters. He prefaces his statement with a clause marked as concessive by the particle μέν: οὐ συμφέρον μέν, *It may not be an aid* (to your faith). Yet: ἐλεύσομαι δὲ εἰς ὀπτασίας καὶ ἀποκαλύψεις κυρίου, *I will proceed to visions and revelations of the Lord.*

Paul calls his supernatural experiences "visions and revelations." By using the plural he indicates that he had several experiences of this nature. He will, however, mention only one. These experiences were granted to Paul for a strengthening of his personal faith. In his ministry of the Gospel he had many most grueling experiences, which severely taxed his powers of resistance. In order that he might not lose courage and that his faith might not break down under the strain, God granted him also exceptional experiences of glory. They were meant to serve Paul personally. And Paul realized that to mention them to others, to such as had not been exposed to similar excruciating afflictions as had struck him, might create a wrong impression. They were no aid to the Corinthians' faith, and Paul now reluctantly decides to mention them only because he is forced to it by the necessity of boasting.

(2) Οἶδα ἄνθρωπον ἐν Χριστῷ, *I know a man in Christ.* Paul is speaking about himself, naturally. The progression of the argument and the use of the middle voice of the verb for boasting demand this assumption; and the content of his statements corroborate it. Yet Paul avoids the use of the personal pronoun, first person singular; he speaks about himself in the third person. He maintains only that he has incontestable knowledge of the case.

He calls himself merely a man, a human being. Ἐν Χριστῷ seems to belong to ἄνθρωπον. It can hardly be explained as modifying the verb. Paul is not qualifying the nature of his knowledge of the man as being mediated by Christ. It was the man who was united with Christ. Prepositional phrases used as adjectival modifiers are ordinarily limited to abstract nouns of verbal derivation. Here we have a concrete noun, a man, which would really require the definite article before the prepositional modifier. However, since ἄνθρωπος is anarthrous, the modifier must be left without the article also.

The vision happened more than 14 years before, πρὸ ἐτῶν δεκατεσσάρων. Since Paul wrote Second Corinthians in 57, these 14 years will carry us back to 43, or perhaps 42. That was several years after his inglorious escape from Damascus. It must have been during his stay in Tarsus after his visit in Jerusalem (Gal. 1:21), perhaps shortly before Barnabas called him to Antioch (Acts 11:25, 26).

Before relating the vision itself, Paul cuts off several curious questions that might be raised by someone, a discussion of which would detract from the main point. He does not know whether he was bodily carried to heaven or without his body; on both points he says οὐκ οἶδα. It is enough that God knows these details.

The experience itself Paul relates in the words: ἁρπαγέντα τὸν τοιοῦτον ἕως τρίτου οὐρανοῦ, (he knows) *the man just described as having been snatched up to the third heaven.* With τοιοῦτον Paul calls special attention to the character and position of the man (scil., himself). The man had no merits to show; the vision was pure grace. It consisted in this that he was "snatched up"—suddenly, rapidly. Unexpectedly he found himself in the "third heaven." As Paul indicates in the parallel repetition of the statement, he understands the third heaven to be the heaven of the blessed. He calls it "paradise." It may be assumed that he counted the clouds and the starry skies as first and second heavens; or, perhaps, he did not count at all, and used the numeral merely to denote eminence.

(3) Paul repeats that he is sure about the experience. He says, καὶ οἶδα τὸν τοιοῦτον ἄνθρωπον, *and I know the man, the such-a-one.* By repeating that he does not know anything about the manner, but leaves this entirely to God, he sets forth with great emphasis that there cannot be the least doubt about the reality of the main fact.

(4) For the participle of verse 2 Paul now substitutes a ὅτι clause, without affecting the meaning, and for the "third heaven" he substitutes "paradise": ὅτι ἡρπάγη εἰς τὸν παράδεισον.

Then he relates the experience which he had during the vision: καὶ ἤκουσεν ἄρρητα ῥήματα, *and he heard unutterable utterances.* With the peculiar combination ἄρρητα ῥήματα Paul indicates, on the one hand, that he heard real, meaningful words, but, on the other, that it is impossible for him to reproduce them. He does not say anything about the contents, but evidently the words were such as fit the glory of heaven, the opposite of the "wailing and gnashing of teeth" in the outer darkness. They were strengthening and cheering. Paul had a real foretaste of eternal life.

He might like to pass the joy on to others, but that is not possible. He adds, ἃ οὐκ ἐξὸν ἀνθρώπῳ λαλῆσαι, *which is impossible for a man to voice.* The verb ἔξεστι usually means that something is proper or permitted; but both the German Bauer and the New Greek-English Lexicon list also the meaning: *it is possible.* Since ἄρρητος suggests impossibility rather than impropriety, it seems best to understand ἐξόν here as: it is impossible. The human organs of speech are not constituted to reproduce even the sounds of the words which Paul heard in heaven, let alone that any human being should be able to express the heavenly ideas.

It was a glorious, strengthening experience for Paul.

(5) Ὑπὲρ τοῦ τοιούτου καυχήσομαι, *about such a one I will boast.*
This boasting of Paul is the same as singing praises to God. The
man was just a man, a creature of God, a sinner. He was in Christ. By
the grace of God, on the basis of the redemption of Christ, without any
merit or worthiness of his own he had become a child of God, living
in communion with his heavenly Father. This grand vision was nothing
but pure grace. Thus boasting in it means glorifying God.

By the way of contrast Paul continues: ὑπὲρ δὲ ἐμαυτοῦ οὐ καυχήσομαι
εἰ μὴ ταῖς ἀσθενείαις, *but concerning myself I shall not boast except
in (my) weakness.*

4. 12:6-10

Although all glory belonged to God in these wonderful experiences,
and although all boasting would naturally proclaim His praises, yet,
due to the presence of the Old Adam, there was the danger that Paul
might develop a feeling of pride for having been granted such exceptional revelations. But Paul received an antidote, a painful reminder,
to keep him humble.

He envisions the possibility that on some occasion he might consider personal boasting to be indicated. He actually did so in the
previous chapter. He presented a number of points in which he was
the equal of the false apostles, he mentioned others in which he was
ahead of them. Yes, even earlier (11:6) he had protested his superior
γνῶσις. Was this boasting wrong?

(6) Paul says, ἐὰν γὰρ θελήσω καυχήσασθαι, *for if (as is possible)
I shall (at some time) decide to boast.*—Ἐάν with the aorist subjunctive
implies a certain expectancy. This thought is introduced by way of
explanation, γάρ. He said in vs. 5 that in boasting of himself he will
always take into due consideration his weaknesses, and will boast
of them. If he did otherwise, his boasting would not be true, and he
would become a fool. The weaknesses are a fact, and any boasting
which would overlook or ignore them would be untrue. Hence Paul
now says that whenever he might want to boast: οὐκ ἔσομαι ἄφρων,
ἀλήθειαν γὰρ ἐρῶ, *I will not be a fool, for I shall speak (the) truth.*
Yet he says, φείδομαι δέ, *but I refrain,* even from truthful boasting,
boasting which gives due attention to the weaknesses. Why? It might
create a wrong impression. The danger he wants to avoid, is: μή τις εἰς

ἐμὲ λογίσηται ὑπὲρ ὃ βλέπει με ἢ ἀκούει ἐξ ἐμοῦ, *lest anyone consider about me above what he sees (in) me or hears from me.*

(7) Paul refrains from boasting because it might be misunderstood. There is also a personal danger lurking for him in boasting about the visions. He might become proud because of this preferential treatment.

There are two peculiarities in this verse which it would seem best to dispose of first. One is the position of the dative noun τῇ ὑπερβολῇ. For the purpose of emphasis it has been placed forward, even ahead of the conjunction introducing the clause. The second difficulty arises from the use of διό. What thought connection does it express? The manuscript evidence for and against this inferential conjunction is of about equal authority. Being derived from διὰ ὅ, διό literally means *wherefore.* Yet it does not always indicate a very strong causal connection. In our case both Goodspeed and Moffat render the connective with a simple "so." Διὸ ἵνα μὴ ὑπεραίρωμαι, *so in order that I may not be unduly elated (with pride),* τῇ ὑπερβολῇ τῶν ἀποκαλύψεων, *by the grandeur of the revelations.* Since the verb is in the middle voice the dative is not strictly instrumental. The grandeur of the revelations, rather, would serve as the occasion for unwarranted pride. Paul was human, by nature somewhat inclined to pride (compare his ambition to exceed his pals at school, Gal. 1:14).

In this case God Himself provided a powerful antitoxin, to counteract and neutralize any inclination Paul might have to be tempted to undue pride: ἐδόθη μοι σκόλοψ τῇ σαρκί, *there was given to me a thorn for the flesh.* This is, of course, metaphorical language, pointing to some very painful physical condition. Paul considered it as a "gift" from God. It did not come to him by accident. It was not a natural result of his labors and of his enforced mode of living. It was directly imposed by God. Just when this happened to Paul, cannot be determined. The revelation which he described had occurred 14 years before. It is hardly probable that the "thorn" came simultaneously with it, not even that it came very soon thereafter.—It was one revelation that he was granted 14 years ago; in our verse he speaks of revelations in the plural. It is possible, but not necessarily so, that other revelations had preceded this particular one, and that this one formed a certain climax. It is just as possible that this particular revelation marked the beginning, to be followed by others from time to time. Since Paul did not deem it necessary to indicate the time elapsed since he had been troubled with that "thorn" in his flesh, it would be idle for us to speculate. The purpose of the "thorn" is the important thing.

Paul stated it in the ordinary way in this part of vs. 7, placing the emphasis on the grandeur of the revelations, which might occasion an undue elation on his part. He calls special attention to it at the end of the verse by repeating: ἵνα μὴ ὑπεραίρωμαι.

Paul explains the nature of his suffering by saying that it was an ἄγγελος σατανᾶ, *a messenger of Satan,* who was sent ἵνα με κολαφίζῃ, *in order to maul me.* This is again a figurative description. It is not to be assumed that the messenger of Satan appeared in visible form and struck Paul with his fists physically. The verb κολαφίζω is used in the literal sense in Matthew 26:67, where the members of the Sanhedrin, after declaring Jesus to be guilty of death, spit in His face and ἐκολάφισαν αὐτόν. Peter uses the verb for the punishment of slaves (I Pet. 2:20). In our present passage, however, Paul is evidently speaking figuratively.

In what the affliction consisted, cannot be determined. (We may safely disregard the half column which the New Greek-English Lexicon devotes to a listing of seven guesses on the nature of Paul's sufferings.) The use of the expression "thorn" and of the present subjunctive κολαφίζῃ suggest a continuing sharp and nagging pain, which greatly hampered Paul in his work.

The special visions and revelations, which were granted to Paul for strengthening his faith in the exceptional tribulations which marked his ministry of Christ, might become the occasion of pride for the Old Adam in Paul. God provided an antidote: a messenger of Satan was sent to plague him.

As Paul was willing to bear his tribulations, labors, wants, persecutions, imprisonments, perils of death, so he also took this special "thorn in the flesh" without complaint. Yet, because it seemed to hamper him in his work of proclaiming the Gospel, he prayed the Lord to relieve him.

(8) Paul reports: ὑπὲρ τούτου τρὶς τὸν κύριον παρεκάλεσα: *Concerning this (matter) I three times (urgently) entreated the Lord.* What is the antecedent of τούτου? We might be inclined to refer the demonstrative to ἄγγελος σατανᾶ. But since the messenger of Satan

is mentioned merely as the instrument for inflicting the special ailment on Paul, it is more likely that τούτου refers to the entire matter, the ailment itself and the manner in which it was inflicted. In other words, we take τούτου to be neuter, not masculine. It was so understood by Jerome, who translated: *Propter* quod *ter Dominum rogavi.*

Paul does not tell us when this ailment began and just how it affected him. Yet the expressions he uses seem to point to a continuing sharp and nagging pain, rather than to intermittent attacks, with alternating periods of comparative relief. If that is correct, then the three specific prayers which Paul mentions cannot be understood as referring to three specific attacks, probably the first three. It seems, rather, that while the malady continued, Paul on three different occasions in his regular prayers made special mention of his concern. Also the following verb, ἀποστῇ (Jerome: *decederet*), seems to presuppose a continuing ailment.

Paul describes his prayer as παρεκάλεσα. This verb denotes an earnest appeal, the nature of which must be determined from the context. (Jerome uses eight different Latin verbs: *rogare, orare, consolare, deprecari, obsecrare, hortari, adhortari, exhortari.*)

The Apostle's urgent request was: ἵνα ἀποστῇ ἀπ᾽ ἐμοῦ, *that it might go away from me.*—While we use a substantive clause after verbs of petition to denote the content of our request, the Greek states the content as the purpose to be achieved by our request. In the Koine, however, ἵνα lost much of its final meaning. Cessation of the ailment is what Paul desired.

(9) καὶ εἴρηκέν μοι, *and (the Lord) said to me.* We have no smooth expression in English to bring out the full force of the perfect tense in εἴρηκεν. The manner in which the Lord's answer came to Paul whether in a dream, in a vision, in a revelation, in an oral address, is immaterial. The important point is that it was definite and final. The Lord's words are still ringing in Paul's ears and glowing in his heart. It was an answer which cleared his mind, tempered his feelings, steeled his will.

This answer stood ever before him in bold relief. It was: ἀρκεῖ σοι ἡ χάρις μου, *sufficient for thee is my grace.* The verb ἀρκεῖ as an answer to Paul's request reveals to us the ideas that had motivated him in his petition. He was called to preach the Gospel, to preach it under the most grueling difficulties. Such work required strength. The ailment weakened him, hampered him in his efforts, obstructed his work. In the interest of the Gospel, he thought, it should be removed. The verb ἀρκεῖ overrules all of Paul's scruples. The grace of God is spreading the Gospel. Just as the grace of God alone achieved our redemption, without the necessity of any supplementary efforts on our part, so the grace of God alone is spreading the Good News, and the grace of God alone is making the Gospel effective, creating faith thereby in the hearts of sinners *ubi et quando visum est Deo;* and our physical strength or mental ability cannot add one ounce of effectiveness to its power.

The grace of God, however, is not meant to be an easy pillow of indolence for any God-appointed messenger of the Gospel. No one may say, If it is the grace of God that does the work and achieves the results, then I can take it easy. The Lord's answer said σοί, sufficient *for thee.* The grace of God had chosen Paul as a tool for its operation. It did not operate outside of Paul, but through Paul. It activated him. It took possession of his physical vigor and permeated his mental faculties. The grace of God reached distant countries through Paul's physical travels, and touched hearts through Paul's clear, vigorous, warm appeals. But it was, after all, only the grace of God which produced the results.

Grace is sufficient for Paul. To be rid of his serious ailment is not necessary for his work. Yes, there is even a great advantage in it. The Lord added a statement to explain this seeming paradox, introducing it with γάρ. He says, ἡ γὰρ δύναμις ἐν ἀσθενείᾳ τελεῖται. Before we translate this sentence, we must get clear on a few terms. The Lord is speaking about δύναμις, 'power.' Since He uses the definite article, He is speaking, not of force in general, but of some very definite power. What power? Some manuscripts add μου, My power. In the last analysis it is the Lord's power, as Paul indicates in the last part of this verse, ἡ δύναμις τοῦ Χριστοῦ. Yet the reading without the μου seems to be the better attested. Then the close connection with the statement about the sufficiency of grace for Paul's work would suggest that it is the power of grace to which God refers: *its* power.

The verb in the sentence, τελεῖται, means *to bring to the end, to finish, to complete.* Our KJV: "is made perfect," presupposes the reading τελειοῦται. What the Lord meant to say, is that the power of grace is fully unfolded and comes to full view when it works through means that are hampered in their operation by some palpable weakness. The N.T. *Woerterbuch* of Schierlitz more than 50 years ago suggested the translation for our passage: *sie zeigt sich am kraeftigsten, wirksamsten.* Paul unfolded the truth which he here learned from the Lord in answer to his prayer already in chapter 4 of this epistle: "that the excellency of the power may be of God, and not of us" (vs. 7). Yes, the power (of grace) is most fully unfolded in (the) weakness (of the instrument with which it operates).

Once before, in 11:30, and again in 12:5, Paul had stated it as his rule to boast in his own weakness. It seemed a rather odd way of boasting, especially over against the claims of superiority raised by the false apostles. But it is a procedure in line with the principles laid down by the Lord Himself; and the false apostles are marked by their very boasting as men who subvert the ways of the Lord and of His Gospel.

We now readily grasp Paul's resolution: ἥδιστα οὖν μᾶλλον καυχήσομαι ἐν ταῖς ἀσθενείαις, *Most gladly, then, will I rather boast in my weaknesses.* The future καυχήσομαι is volitive, rather than temporal: I will do my boasting, I will continue to boast. The function of μᾶλλον is not quite clear. Jerome left it untranslated. The translation "rather" could put the continued boasting of Paul in contrast to his former praying for relief. It would also make good sense if we combine it as a modifier with καυχήσομαι, all the more will I boast.

Ἵνα ἐπισκηνώσῃ ἐπ' ἐμὲ ἡ δύναμις τοῦ Χριστοῦ, *in order that the power of Christ may spread its tent over me* (so Lenski). Jerome's translation is impossible: *ut inhabitet in me virtus Christi.* The preposition ἐπί does not allow the idea of *in*dwelling.

The purpose, expressed in this clause, is not one to be realized at some time in the future. Rather, the overshadowing of Paul by the power of Christ is the primary factor which produced also this correct evaluation of his own strength in the work of the Lord. This overshadowing by the power of Christ would be greatly disturbed if he engaged in boasting about his own achievements and failed to give all glory to Christ. This is something which Paul will avoid by all means. Once and for all the power of Christ must spread its tent over him. Hence the aorist ἐπισκηνώσῃ. Paul will glory in his own infirmities, so that this relation to the power of Christ may not be upset.

(10) With a διό clause Paul sums up the thoughts developed in this section, and makes a practical application. Διὸ εὐδοκῶ, *accordingly I rejoice*. Διό, from δι᾽ ὅ, 'because of which,' states a causal relation but not always in a strict and sharp sense. It corresponds somewhat to our English 'accordingly.' Εὐδοκέω, literally 'to consider as good' or 'to consent to,' may also mean 'to be well pleased with' or 'to take delight in.' Under the conditions as outlined above Paul agrees to, yes, takes delight in and rejoices—in what? ἐν ἀσθενείαις (weaknesses), ἐν ὕβρεσιν (insults), ἐν ἀνάγκαις (necessities), ἐν διωγμοῖς (persecutions), ἐν στενοχωρίαις (difficulties; German *Klemme*), provided they are ὑπὲρ Χριστοῦ, for Christ's sake.

5.　12:11-13

(11) With jubilant tones Paul concluded the previous section. Upon further reflection he continues: γέγονα ἄφρων, *I have become a fool*. The perfect tense in γέγονα is very vivid: I am a fool, here I stand as a fool. Why did I permit myself to slip into this awkward position? Ὑμεῖς με ἠναγκάσατε, *You (were the ones that) forced me (into it)*.

The Corinthians compelled Paul to boast, not by any form of violence, but by their unappreciative attitude toward his Gospel, and by their fawning servility before boastful and showy deceivers. Their faith and salvation were in danger. Paul could not stand idly by. He had to do something to avert disaster, and, disagreeable though it was to him, he had to resort to boasting, since that method of procedure held out some promise of success.

It was a comparatively simple thing to diagnose the danger which threatened the Corinthians. If they had stood firm in the Gospel which Paul had brought to them, what would have been their reaction to the inroads of the false apostles? It would have been, as Paul tersely states it in the second part of our present verse: ἐγὼ γὰρ ὤφειλον ὑφ᾽ ὑμῶν συνίστασθαι, *for I ought to be commended by you*. By using the personal pronoun ἐγώ, Paul stresses his own importance in relation to the false apostles, not because of his personal qualifications, but because he was the representative of the true, saving Gospel, which the false apostles adulterated. Ὤφειλον, imperfect tense: it was your solemn obligation. Your faith, if it was genuine, should have, and would have, spoken up in defense of the Gospel which I had brought to you. Sad to say, you failed, and you compelled me to become a fool.

Οὐδὲν γὰρ ὑστέρησα τῶν ὑπερλίαν ἀποστόλων, *for in nothing was I inferior to those superfine apostles.* I was 'not inferior' is a litotes. Paul was in every respect superior, far ahead of the intruders: in his understanding (γνῶσις), his labors, his sufferings, his visions and revelations. He admits: εἰ καὶ οὐδέν εἰμι, *even though I am nothing.* Where does that leave the false apostles? Paul nothing, and they far below him!

(12) Paul personally was nothing, but the grace of God was with him in full power, and his apostleship was irrefutably confirmed in the presence of the Corinthians. Paul reminds them: τὰ μὲν σημεῖα τοῦ ἀποστόλου κατειργάσθη ἐν ὑμῖν, *the signs of an Apostle were performed among you.* The ability to perform supernatural acts was promised to the Apostles of Jesus to serve as their credentials and to corroborate the message which they were proclaiming. Such wonderworks were performed by Paul also in Corinth. The definite article before ἀποστόλου is generic. The word is here not applied to some individual who served as an Apostle, but to the class as such. This use of the definite article is rather limited in the English language, where usually the indefinite article is preferred. The verb κατειργάσθη has the perfective κατά. The works were real; they could not be denied, nor explained away, nor brushed aside. All the more reprehensible was it in the Corinthians not to have heeded this testimony of the Lord. The difference between Paul and the false apostles was too obvious.

The signs which Paul performed in Corinth were not monotonously uniform. There was variation. Paul mentions three groups: σημείοις τε καὶ τέρασιν καὶ δυνάμεσιν, *both in signs and wonders and power-works.* Σημεῖον indicates that the miracles were not mere "stunts," they were meaningful, significant deeds; τέρας denotes that they were awe-inspiring; δύναμις, that they gave evidence of supernatural power.

Such miracles did not happen only on rare occasions, few and far between. Paul says, ἐν πάσῃ ὑπομονῇ, *in all endurance,* or *perseverance.* St. Luke does not record any of these miracles from Paul's stay in Corinth, but he does say something about Paul's activity along these lines in Ephesus (cf. Acts 19:11, 12). On the basis of Paul's present remark we may safely assume that similar things happened in Corinth.

Before going on to the next verse we take notice of a solitary μέν in this verse: τὰ μὲν σημεῖα, no δέ following. This particle serves the purpose of reinforcing the statement; it is approximately the equivalent of our English "indeed." It indicates the importance which Paul attached to the fact that he could refer to his miracles as his credentials, as incontestable evidence of his apostleship.

(13) The γάρ with which Paul introduces this verse does not indicate a motivation of the foregoing statements, nor is it explanatory; it is mildly inferential: "well, then," or "now, then," or, simply "then."

Τί γάρ ἐστιν, *What, then, is it?* ὃ ἡσσώθητε ὑπὲρ τὰς λοιπὰς ἐκκλησίας, *in which you were slighted beyond the other churches?* Ὅ is the adverbial accusative. The verb ἡσσώθητε (from ἑσσόομαι, a secondary form for ἡττάομαι) contains a comparative idea, ἥσσων, inferior, weaker. The question thus is: In what respect were you accorded an inferior treatment? Ὑπέρ then is the ὑπέρ of comparison, in place of ἤ or the genitive (cf. Luke 16:8; Heb. 4:12). Jerome in our verse translates with *prae.* The Corinthians have no reason to assume that they were slighted in anything.

In one respect, Paul admits, they did receive differential treatment, εἰ μὴ ὅτι αὐτὸς ἐγὼ οὐ κατενάρκησα ὑμῶν, *except that I, on my part, did not burden you.* Paul discussed this matter more fully in 11:7ff. and there stated his reasons. He now asks them to forgive him this "injustice," χαρίσασθέ μοι τὴν ἀδικίαν ταύτην.

6. 12:14-18

(14) With ἰδού Paul calls attention to a change in his discussion. The general topic will remain the same: he is still concerned with the havoc the intruders caused in Corinth, but he will discontinue his "foolish" boasting.

Ἰδοὺ τρίτον τοῦτο ἑτοίμως ἔχω ἐλθεῖν πρὸς ὑμᾶς, *Behold, I am ready to come to you this third time.* Paul is speaking about his announced but delayed visit, his travel plans having been changed even before First Corinthians was written. The route was changed, the visit was delayed but not canceled. Paul is on his way and at the present moment is ready to set sail for Corinth soon. He calls it his third visit. Luke in Acts so far recorded only one visit of Paul to Corinth. That was when he founded the congregation and spent 18 months in the city. We discussed his second visit in connection with the collection which was to be taken up for the needy saints in Jerusalem. It took place about a year before Second Corinthians was written.

On his coming third visit Paul will not change his conduct as far as remuneration or sustenance is concerned: καὶ οὐ καταναρκήσω, *and I will not be a burden (to any one of you)*. He states the reason in the words: οὐ γὰρ ζητῶ τὰ ὑμῶν ἀλλὰ ὑμᾶς, *for I am not seeking your possessions but you*. One might ask the question if these two things really are mutually exclusive. Does the accepting of financial support prevent, or at least hamper, the winning of souls? Paul accepted support from the church at Philippi with no harm to their spiritual wellbeing. But Corinth was different. It was a commercial city, in which financial matters played a great role. The principle which Paul urged on the new mission fields in Crete certainly applied also to Corinth, but here had to be handled in a special way, owing to the special conditions just mentioned. When Paul urged Titus to "bring Zenas...and Apollos on their journey diligently, that nothing be wanting unto them," he added the instruction, "And let ours also learn to maintain good works for necessary uses, that they be not unfruitful" (Titus 3: 13, 14). In Corinth Paul applied this part of Christian training by instructing them about their obligation toward the needy Christians in Jerusalem. But if he had taken personal support, that might easily have been misunderstood and misconstrued. By his example he impressed upon the Corinthians the proper attitude toward earthly possessions.

Paul is the spiritual father of the Corinthians, and as such he is ever concerned about enriching his children spiritually. In a most fatherly, friendly way he adds, οὐ γὰρ ὀφείλει τὰ τέκνα τοῖς γονεῦσιν θησαυρίζειν, ἀλλὰ οἱ γονεῖς τοῖς τέκνοις, *for the children ought not store up treasures for their parents, rather the parents for the children*. Paul had told the Corinthians in his First Epistle, "For though ye have ten thousand instructors in Christ, yet have ye not many fathers: for in Christ Jesus I have begotten you through the gospel" (4:15). The statement that Paul as spiritual father of the Corinthians is following the general custom that parents lay up treasures for their children, not vice versa, must be understood in the connection in which Paul made it, and must not be stretched beyond his own application. Any attempt to draw from it general rules regulating the financial relations between parents and children is mere quibbling; thus, e.g., when some miser uses the words as a pretext to cover the hoarding of his goods.

(15) Paul's is a genuine care for his spiritual children: ἐγὼ δὲ ἥδιστα δαπανήσω καὶ ἐκδαπανηθήσομαι ὑπὲρ τῶν ψυχῶν ὑμῶν, *but I on my part will most gladly spend, yes, be completely spent for your souls.* The welfare of their souls is at stake. And in the interest of their souls Paul on his part will spend with the greatest of pleasure. He names no object; none is necessary. He will not shrink from spending all that he has, his health, his strength, his convenience, his love. He will risk and spend all, and will do it gladly. More than this. He is ready to be himself completely spent—ἐκ is prefixed for stress— as he also stated his willingness in Philippians 2:17: "Yes, and if I be offered upon the sacrifice and service of your faith, I joy, and rejoice with you all." First a life of service and self-sacrifice. Then to be made a bloody sacrifice on the altar of martyrdom will be a joy to him. So it was in the case of the Philippians; so in the case of the Corinthians.

So great is his devotion to his calling as an Apostle, and so is his love toward his "children." How do they respond to it? εἰ περισσο- τέρως ὑμᾶς ἀγαπῶ, ἧσσον ἀγαπῶμαι; *If I love you more fervently, am I being loved the less?* Paul is not pleading for personal appreciation from the Corinthians, nor for their personal affection; nor is he complaining about its lack. He is pleading for their spiritual understanding and appreciation of the Gospel which he had brought to them and of the Savior whom he had proclaimed. The greater this spiritual appreciation, the greater will also be the esteem in which the Apostle of this Gospel is held. The lack of reverence for the messenger reflects unfavorably on the Corinthians' love and appreciation of the Gospel and of the Savior. It is a searching question for the Corinthians: "Am I being loved the less?"

But may not Paul's apparently selfless devotion have been mere sham? May it not have been a ruse to cover up insidious greed and foul play? It seems that the intruders had put some such construction on his conduct.

(16) Paul begins this verse with a concession, ἔστω δέ, *but granted.* The question, however, remains: Who is making what concession? It might be that Paul is referring to his question in vs. 15 about his being loved less, the more he practices love. It might be that he wants to say, "Now let that be as it may. Let us drop that matter." Yet, in that case the connection with the following statement would not be

clear. Some connective would be required. As it stands, the sentence, ἐγὼ οὐ κατεβάρησα ὑμᾶς, *I on my part did not burden you*—stands in close relation to ἔστω δέ, expressing the conceded point. It seems that Paul, though not quoting directly, is referring to some derogatory statement of his opponents in which they granted that he personally did not burden the Corinthians, but insisted that that proved nothing concerning his alleged unselfishness.

They put an altogether different construction on his action: ἀλλὰ ὑπάρχων πανοῦργος δόλῳ ὑμᾶς ἔλαβον, *but being a (dyed-in-the-wool) trickster I took you by guile.* Πανοῦργος (literally, "ready to do anything," German: *zu allem faehig*—together with the abstract noun πανουργία) is, although neutral in itself, like its German equivalent commonly used with a bad connotation. Ὑπάρχων is similar in meaning to ὤν, but stronger. It is Paul's habitual method, they say, to employ crooked means in order to attain his evil ends, unsuspected and undetected. So also his simulated modesty is only a dirty trick.

(17) Paul answers the charge with a question about the Corinthians' past experience: μέ τινα ὧν ἀπέσταλκα πρὸς ὑμᾶς, δι' αὐτοῦ ἐπλεονέκτησα ὑμᾶς; *did any one of those whom I sent to you—did I through him take advantage of you?* The accusative τινά, placed forward for emphasis, has nothing on which it depends, neither verb nor preposition. (Compare the German folksong: *Den liebsten Buhlen, den i han, der liegt beim Wirt im Keller.*) It is taken up again with δι' αὐτοῦ. Paul challenges the Corinthians to scrutinize the records of anyone and everyone who came to them as his representative. (That is the force of the perfect ἀπέσταλκα.) Did Paul defraud them through any one of his assistants? Could they find any trace even of only doubtful dealings?

(18) Together with this letter Paul is sending two men to Corinth to assist the congregation in gathering the gifts for Jerusalem. Titus is coming at Paul's request, and with him he is sending a brother as he had mentioned previously in the letter: παρεκάλεσα Τίτον καὶ συναπέστειλα τὸν ἀδελφόν.

Titus is well known in Corinth. He had been there just a few weeks before to help them find the way out of the sad situation which the false apostles had caused. Μήτι ἐπλεονέκτησεν ὑμᾶς Τίτος; *you do not mean to say that Titus took advantage of you, do you?* Since Titus heads the present delegation, it is sufficient to inquire about him and his record. The other brother, being an associate with Titus, will naturally conform to his guiding. Moreover, it seems that he had never been in Corinth before. The record of Titus was clear.

A double question concludes this section. What does a comparison of Paul's record and that of Titus' show? Was Paul a rogue who, while he himself posed as a very modest, unselfish, yes, self-sacrificing man, fleeced his victims through his accomplices whom he sent to them? Οὐ τῷ αὐτῷ πνεύματι περιεπατήσαμεν; οὐ τοῖς αὐτοῖς ἴχνεσιν; *Did we not walk in the same spirit? yes, in the very same tracks?* The perfect agreement between Paul and his representatives, the fact that no member of the Corinthian congregation could point to a single instance where either Paul or one of his messengers had solicited a penny for personal use, was conclusive evidence of the established policy of Paul—and of the malicious nature of the opponents' slanderous remarks.

The rest of the chapter and chapter 13, still dealing with the intruders, are devoted to his impending visit, which he has been planning for some time, and which he had briefly mentioned in verse 14.

D. PAUL'S APPROACHING VISIT
Chapter 12:19 to Chapter 13:10

1.   12:19-21

Titus had spent some time in Corinth as Paul's assistant, helping the congregation to recover from the attack by the false apostles and to undo the damage which they had done. God had blessed his efforts with success. The congregation as a whole had seen the error of its ways. The members in general had recognized the true nature of the intruders and had learned to avoid them. When Titus returned to Paul he brought a glowing report of improvement achieved in Corinth. He never tired of repeating his report and of adding new incidents to complete the picture. And when the lagging collection for the needy saints in Jerusalem made special assistance advisable, Titus was more than willing to return to render the extra help. He had full confidence in the sincerity of the Corinthians.

This does not mean that conditions were perfect; that everything was running smoothly; that there were no old sores to smart occasionally; that there were no more dangers lurking here and there. Basically the congregation had recovered, but there were still many details that had to be adjusted.

We must remember that even before the false apostles came to Corinth there were divisions and cliques in the congregation, such as marred also the celebration of the Lord's Supper. Paul's first letter did much to allay these difficulties, but we dare not assume that the restored harmony was perfect in every respect. It had been gained in principle, but traces of the old divisions were bound to show up from time to time and needed constant watching and care. The inroads of the false apostles at this juncture did not help matters in this respect. Rather, it may be assumed that the old dissensions were stirred up anew by them, and, in part at least, explain the easy success of their efforts.

So far we have spoken of the congregation as a whole. We must remember, however, that every congregation is made up of members no two of whom are completely alike. Some are strong, some are weak; some are quick, some are slow; some have a deep understanding, some are superficial; and so on. Thus the reaction of the individual members to the work of Titus and to the epistles of Paul will not have been equally favorable.

If we keep this picture of the situation in mind, it will help us to understand the present and the following sections of Paul's discussion of his coming visit.

(19) The sentence with which Paul opens this section does not have the form of a question, but in its sense it approaches a question very closely. He states what he assumes might be expected as the Corinthians' reaction to his explanation and vindication of his apostleship in answer to the spurious claims and the disparaging remarks of the false apostles. Πάλαι δοκεῖτε ὅτι ὑμῖν ἀπολογούμεθα: *All this while you are assuming that we are defending ourselves before you.* Πάλαι (cf. παλαιός, old) refers to the past, usually to the remote past. Here it points back to the beginning of the section in which Paul spoke about his apostleship. All the while that the Corinthians were reading it, listening to it, considering it, they were under a certain impression, perhaps increasingly so, which Paul expresses in the clause ὅτι ὑμῖν ἀπολογούηεθα. Both the verb and the dative object have a certain stress and belong closely together. This circumstance, in a way, modifies

also the sense of the verb. It is true, Paul was vindicating his apostleship, but his act is not to be understood as an attempt at clearing himself in the manner of a defense in court. It was not an ἀπολογία in that sense, least of all ὑμῖν, as though the Corinthians were the legitimate judges when Paul's apostleship was on trial.

Was not Paul violating brotherly love by assuming this arrogant attitude on the part of the Corinthians? Paul knew the Corinthians and their weaknesses. Had they not been sitting in judgment on his apostleship long ago, when one said, I am a Paul man, another, I am an Apollos man, and a third, I am a Cephas man? Paul had rebuked them then: "With me it is a very small thing that I should be judged of you, or of man's judgment: . . . judge nothing before the time, until the Lord come" (I Cor. 4:3,5). And had they not recently listened to the judgment of the false apostles and to a certain extent joined them in it and made it their own, that Paul was a rather inferior apostle? Well might he tell them to their face that he could not escape the assumption that they might be posing even now as judges who were considering his vindication of his apostleship as an attempt to clear himself in their court.

His "defense" has an altogether different meaning, and a different purpose. His speech belongs to an altogether different category. Paul continues, κατέναντι θεοῦ ἐν Χριστῷ λαλοῦμεν: *Before God in Christ we are speaking.* This clause has a familiar ring. With precisely the same words and in the same order it occurs in 2:17. There Paul is glorying in the fact that God always granted him a triumph while proclaiming the Gospel: "For we are unto God a sweet savor of Christ, in them that are saved, and in them that perish. To the one we are the savor of death unto death; and to the other the savor of life unto life" (vs. 15,16). Then in answer to the question whence this ability ("Who is sufficient for these things?"), he emphasizes that it is from the Word of God, without additions or adulterations, which he by the grace of God is proclaiming, κατέναντι θεοῦ ἐν Χριστῷ λαλοῦμεν.

The phrase in our present verse must be viewed with 2:14-17 as a background, and in the light of that passage. Even when describing and vindicating his apostleship in the form of foolish boasting, Paul is carrying out his assignment of proclaiming the Gospel of Christ.

And the purpose? τὰ δὲ πάντα, ἀγαπητοί, ὑπὲρ τῆς ὑμῶν οἰκοδομῆς, *and all this, friends, for your edification.* There is no contrast between the thoughts which Paul expresses. There is a contrast between the way the Corinthians view Paul's action and its real meaning. To express this relation, "but" (or any other conjunction denoting antithesis) would be a little too heavy; "and" is sufficient. Δέ here merely connects this part of the sentence to the foregoing. Addressing his readers here with ἀγαπητοί adds a plea to the thought, the plea that the Corinthians, getting to feel Paul's warm concern, should take notice and give due consideration. Also this part of Paul's work concerns their "edification," their spiritual advancement, their strengthening in faith and in sanctification. If they remember their earlier and their most recent fumblings, remember how rather shamefully they acted towards Paul, they will realize how much they stand in need of edification, and will appreciate the fact that the much maligned Paul takes such a warm interest in aiding their edification.

An important part of edification is the battle against, and the victory over, pet lusts. But this involves a painful procedure, especially if the Apostles, in order to achieve it in their hearers, will have to apply warning, rebuking, castigating, and the like. It is less painful, yes, it will afford a certain spiritual "thrill," if the Christians can achieve their own edification before the Apostle applies the "rod" (cf. I Cor. 4:21). Let the Corinthians make good use also of Paul's foolish boasting for this purpose. It will be more pleasant for everyone concerned.

(20) Paul knows the conditions in Corinth. In spite of the fact that the damage which the false apostles had caused had been overcome in principle, there was still much awry, and some members evidently were not concerned as zealously about correcting their error as they should have been. Paul begins this verse with φοβοῦμαι γάρ, *for I fear.* This verb is here followed by three clauses beginning with μή, stating what Paul fears. Twice the clause is modified with an enclitic πως, *perhaps.*

The first is: μή πως ἐλθὼν οὐχ οἵους θέλω εὕρω ὑμᾶς, κἀγὼ εὑρεθῶ ὑμῖν οἷον οὐ θέλετε, *lest perhaps on my arrival I find you not as such as I wish, and I on my part will be found of you as you do not want (me).* This terse statement calls for no further explanation. It strikes home with telling force. There are two matters to which attention may be called. The first is the dative ὑμῖν. In the Latin the dative is used with the passive to denote the agent only in connection with the gerundive; in the Greek this use is found also in connection with other passive verb forms. In the sentence under discussion the agent in the first parallel member is ἐγώ (in the verb ending). Over against this, the second parallel member dare not remain without naming the agent in some way. This consideration suggests that the dative ὑμῖν should not be considered as the *dativus commodi,* but as the dative of agent. Hence not: I should be found *for* you, but *by* you. The second is the different position of the negative: I may find you not exactly as I would like to see you; but you will find me as you definitely do not want me.

The second clause reads: μή πως ἔρις, ζῆλος, θυμοί, ἐριθεῖαι, καταλαλιαί, ψιθυρισμοί, φυσιώσεις, ἀκαταστασίαι, *lest there perhaps be strife, jealousy, (acts of) anger, (of) rivalry, (of) backbiting, (of) whispering, (of) self-conceit, (of) disorder.* The first two nouns in this list are in the singular, the rest in the plural. The plural of these abstract nouns denotes manifestations of the moral deformities they mention. We translate "acts of."

One of the words, the fourth in the list, calls for a little investigation; ἐριθεία, though often treated as being derived from ἔρις, does not seem to be etymologically connected with this word. It goes back to ἔριθος (both masculine and feminine) meaning a 'wage earner.' Ἐριθεία is derived from this noun, as the accent indicates, not directly, but via the verb ἐριθεύειν. Aristotle uses the word for the "self-seeking pursuit of political office by unfair means." It occurs in several passages of the New Testament. The clearest light on the meaning is probably found in James 3:14, 16, where it is used as synonymous with πικρὸν ζῆλος. It denotes *Lohnsucht,* and the dubious and unfair practices that go with it, such as "chiseling," rivalry, and the like.

We readily realize that all the sins which Paul enumerates are concomitants of the factionalism which plagued the Corinthian congregation earlier, and had been fanned into more violent outbursts by the recent doings of the intruders. This, then, is the point where the edification of the Corinthians must begin: true repentance over these sins and an earnest effort to curb them. If they neglect this phase, then all other apparent progress will be but sham.

(21) Paul devotes an entire verse to his third fear, nor does he soften the clause with a modifying πως. He states this fear with two verbs, the one being more general, the second specific, explaining the general term.

We take the general expression first. Μὴ πάλιν ἐλθόντος μου ταπεινώσῃ με ὁ θεός μου πρὸς ὑμᾶς, (I fear) lest, when I come again, my God humble me in your presence. The πάλιν will ordinarily be connected with the participle immediately following, but the commentators who assume that Paul's second visit to Corinth took place between First and Second Corinthians and that Paul on this occasion suffered some very humiliating treatment from the congregation, so that he left in a huff, ignore this natural connection and maintain that the adverb modifies the main verb of the clause. While Paul is speaking about his announced new visit, they try to make him speak about a repeated humiliation. We have discussed the chronology on a previous occasion.

Paul calls it a humiliation for himself if things in Corinth are not as they should be. But would not this humiliation rather fall first of all on the Corinthian Christians themselves? It would. But Paul is aware of his responsibility for his congregations so keenly that he feels their shame as his own. What makes the matter more painful for him is that this humiliation will take place in their presence, before their very eyes. In an earlier section Paul had expressed the hope that his next visit would be marked with joy all around (chap. 2:1ff.). Will it? Paul now expresses grave misgivings, he fears that God will humiliate him.

He pinpoints his fears: καὶ πενθήσω πολλοὺς τῶν προημαρτηκότων καὶ μὴ μετανοησάντων, and I (must) mourn for many of those laden with the guilt of former sins, and not having repented. Paul, who was hoping for joy on his coming visit to Corinth, fears that he will experience grief, humiliating grief, instead. There are people in the Corinthian congregation who committed sins some time ago (προ-) and are still burdened with the guilt—the perfect tense stresses the lasting result of the completed action—since no repentance took place (note the aorist) to remove the stain. These are not isolated cases. Paul fears that there are many.

These unrepented sins reach back farther than to the recent disturbances. Paul lists: ἐπὶ τῇ ἀκαθαρσίᾳ καὶ πορνείᾳ καὶ ἀσελγείᾳ ᾗ ἔπραξαν, for the uncleanness and fornication and licentiousness which they have committed.

From First Corinthians we learn that the attitude of the congregation toward sex sins was rather lax. When the incest case happened, the members were not shocked. Paul writes, "Ye are puffed up, and have not rather mourned" (5:2). That case had been settled. The "punishment (censure) which was inflicted of many" on the sinner had led him to acknowledge his wrong and to grieve over it even to such a degree that he stood in danger of being "swallowed up with overmuch sorrow" (II Cor. 2:6,7).

This was not the only case. There was great carelessness, if not laxity, of the members with respect to idol festivities (cf. I Cor. 8 and 9). Note furthermore the list of excesses which Paul assembled in I Cor. 6:9,10, adding in vs. 11: "and such were some of you." Also to sex sins they applied the axiom: "All things are lawful," and placed the gratification of the sex drive on a par with eating and drinking. Paul had to set them straight: Yes, "all things are lawful unto me, but all things are not expedient. . . . Meats for the belly, and the belly for meats: but God shall destroy both it and them." So far the axiom is valid. Now Paul continues: "Now the body is not for fornication, but for the Lord; and the Lord for the body. . . . Know ye not that your bodies are the members of Christ? shall I then take the members of Christ, and make them the members of an harlot?" (I Cor. 6:12ff.)

The fleshly mind of the Corinthians expressed itself in other ways. It did so even in connection with the Lord's Supper, where the agape was degraded to a gourmand's feast (I Cor. 11:21).

By stating expressly, μὴ μετανοησάντων, Paul indicates that those people refused to repent and kept on defending their actions. They ceased to be weak brethren who had lapsed into sin. They persisted. It was clear that all admonitions were to no further avail.

2.   13:1, 2

In these two verses Paul outlines the course of procedure which he plans to follow. They thus, in a way, form the conclusion of the previous section, 12:19-21. In the main, however, they serve as an introduction to the next section, which speaks of the power of Christ in weakness. We examine it briefly.

(1) Paul repeats with some emphasis that he is coming to Corinth. The carrying out of his promise that he would visit Corinth was important. In I Corinthians 4:18ff. he complained that some questioned his sincerity in this respect: "Now some are puffed up, as though I would not come to you. But I will come to you shortly, if the Lord will, and will know, not the speech of them which are puffed

up, but the power. . . . What will ye? shall I come unto you with a rod, or in love, and in the spirit of meekness?"

In Second Corinthians he commented on a change in his travel plans. It did not mean that he had abandoned them, forgetting his promise and canceling his visit. Much less did it mean that his Gospel message was unreliable. It meant simply that he intended thus to spare the Corinthians some very unpleasant embarrassment (1:15ff.).

It seems that some diehards refused to be convinced. Hence Paul here emphatically repeats, τρίτον τοῦτο ἔρχομαι πρὸς ὑμᾶς, *Now for this third time I am on my way to you.* He says ἔρχομαι. He may have touched Troas recently; he may have stopped off for some time in Philippi and Thessalonica: but those places do not mark the end of his present journey, they are merely stopping stations. His real aim of this journey is Corinth. That is the destination for which he set out. He is on his way. This circuitous route was chosen in order to give the Corinthians time to remove the offenses and scandals themselves, before Paul would arrive. His third visit is not forgotten. He is coming. They may expect him soon. And he will attend to business.

He says, ἐπὶ στόματος δύο μαρτύρων καὶ τριῶν σταθήσεται πᾶν ῥῆμα, *On the mouth of two witnesses and three shall every case be established.* This contains a reference to Deuteronomy 19:15: "One witness shall not rise up against a man for any iniquity, or for any sin, in any sin that he sinneth: at the mouth of two witnesses, or at the mouth of three witnesses, shall the matter be established." Compare also Deuteronomy 17:6; Numbers 35:30. To convict a man of a crime with which he was charged, the testimony of at least two unimpeachable witnesses was required. Their testimony had to cover the same case, and had to agree. On the other hand, if there was the agreeing testimony of two unimpeachable witnesses, it had to be accepted. Even the death penalty could be pronounced and executed on the strength of it.

It might be asked, however, why Paul should appeal to that Old Testament regulation. Was not the sin of the respective members in Corinth manifest before the eyes of all? And was not also their refusal to repent public knowledge? That may have been true in a number of cases, and then a formal investigation would seem superfluous. To conduct one nevertheless might make the whole procedure look ridiculous and would blunt the divinely intended effect.

In vs. 20 of the previous chapter, however, Paul had referred to backbitings and whisperings. Some brethren may have been maligned innocently. That also must be stopped. No one will be dealt with on mere rumor. If anyone voices a charge against a brother, he must be able to produce the evidence, or he himself will become guilty of what God denounced in the Mosaic law. "If a false witness rise up against any man to testify against him" (Deut. 19:16), then the court shall carefully investigate, and if they find that his testimony was false, "then shall ye do unto him, as he had thought to have done unto his brother" (vs. 19). "So shalt thou put the evil away from among you."

In passing we mention a curious toying with the words by some of the commentators, who try to identify the three visits of Paul with the three witnesses required by the Law. Even Bachmann in Zahn's *Kommentar zum Neuen Testament* says: *Darum nehmen wir an, Paulus habe sich, indem er sein* τρίτον τοῦτο *schrieb, in innerer Bewegung vergegenwaertigt, wie damit in eigentuemlicher Weise ein alttestamentlicher Rechtssatz sich erfuelle. Er kommt sich, indem er jetzt zum zweiten, bzw. zum dritten Male nach Korinth geht, vor, wie wenn er 2 bis 3 Zeugen den Korinthern gegenueberstelle, die ihr Zeugnis ueber und in diesem Falle wider sie ablegen.* *

(2) This second verse contains a phrase which greatly puzzles the commentators: ὡς παρὼν τὸ δεύτερον καὶ ἀπὼν νῦν. The question is: To what do παρών and ἀπών refer? The present absence seems clear, but to what does the second presence refer, to what time and what event? Paul uses a similar expression in I Corinthians 5:3: "as absent in body, but present in spirit." In that case it is clear that presence and absence coincide; they denote the same time and condition, viewed from two different angles. The case is similar in Colossians 2:5: "For though I be absent in the flesh, yet am I with you in the spirit." The case is different in vs. 10 of our present chapter: "I write these things being absent, lest being present I should use sharpness." Here

---

*) Therefore we assume that, when Paul wrote his τρίτον τοῦτο, he had, in his inner agitation, imagined that hereby an Old Testament legal ordinance was being fulfilled in a unique way. In now going to Corinth for the second, resp. the third time, he thought of himself as placing before the Christians two to three witnesses, who give their testimony about them, and in this case ,against them.

two different times and conditions are being contrasted as one following the other. A contrast is evident also in Philippians 1:27:
"Whether I come and see you, or else being absent, I may hear of
your affairs."

It seems that in our present verse νῦν modifies not merely the ἀπών,
but rather the entire phrase. Paul is now both present and absent.
Then τὸ δεύτερον would also refer to both conditions. It is now hap-
pening for the second time that Paul is both present and absent as
far as the Corinthian congregation is concerned. It happened for the
first time when the incest case had to be handled, and it happens now
again when there are many unrepentant members to be dealt with.

Paul says προείρηκα καὶ προλέγω. Considering the tenses we may
transcribe Paul's thought: *I have warned you in advance, and that
warning stands; and I repeat (it).* When Paul was both absent and
present for the first time, he wrote: "I will come to you shortly. . . .
What will ye? shall I come unto you with a rod, or in love, and
in the spirit of meekness?" (I Cor. 4:19, 21). That was his advance
warning, which he gave them then, and which still stands. Now being
both absent and present for the second time he merely repeats—
still in advance. He did so in vs. 1.

Whom does his advance warning concern? He says, τοῖς προημαρτη-
κόσιν καὶ τοῖς λοιποῖς πᾶσιν, *to those who still have their former sins
on their conscience, and to all the rest.* With the word: they "which
heretofore have sinned," he refers to those whom he described in 12:21
as unrepentant. His words to them were a call to repentance—in the
First Epistle, and they are so now again. If they take the warning to
heart, no one will be happier than Paul. He will speak about this a
little farther down.

Paul's warnings are addressed also to all the rest. The sins of any
member concern and affect the whole group. The Church is the
spiritual body of Christ. "Whether one member suffer, all members
suffer with it" (I Cor. 12:26). One little toothache can upset the
whole system. Hence, when one church member falls into sin or becomes entangled in error, the whole church must get into action in an
attempt to rescue the infected member, in order to disentangle him and
bring him to repentance. Jesus outlined the mode of procedure in
Matthew 18. If the affected member persists in his sin, he must be
excommunicated as a publican and heathen man; if he persists in his

error, he must be excluded. How his spiritual life is affected by his error, will depend on the nature of his error. An unrepentant sinner cannot be tolerated in the church without endangering the spiritual life, the faith and sanctification, of every member. And if a persistent errorist is tolerated and permitted to make propaganda for his false views, then purity of doctrine cannot be maintained.

When Paul urges action against the unrepentant sinners, he is not advocating undue haste. The congregation must take a firm stand, and must act with a firm hand. But firmness is not the same as haste. There are people who confuse the two—to the great harm of the Church. True firmness must be coupled with love, and can afford to be patient. For proper dealing with sinners and men caught in error Paul always insisted on patience. But when unrepentance of sin and persistence in error become manifest, then love demanded decisive action.

In Corinth the dealings with the incest case had been carried out, but dealings with other still unrepentant sinners seem to have lagged. Hence Paul's advance warning to all the rest. He hopes that they will be aroused to take the proper steps.

If they do, and even if their manner is weak and perhaps clumsy, Paul will be happy. But if not, his warning is, ὅτι ἐὰν ἔλθω εἰς τὸ πάλιν οὐ φείσομαι, If (and when) I come again, I will not spare. Paul, of course, will not employ any kind of force outside that of the Spirit, but he will not put on "kid gloves"; he will not mince words. He will not deal gently with their shortcomings, but will expose them unsparingly. He will pronounce God's judgment on their delinquency in straightforward and unequivocal terms.

This brings to a close the matter of dealing with unrepentant sinners; at the same time it opens the way for a brief discussion of Christ's and His Apostle's power in weakness.

3. 13:3-6

In verses 1 and 2 of this chapter Paul announced that on his coming visit, the third one which he would make to the Corinthian congregation, he would take care of the pending cases of discipline, whether they called for excommunication of impenitent sinners or "for "avoiding" of manifest makers of divisions and offenses. In unmistakable terms he added that he would not "spare."

(3) In the opening words of our present section he adduces a rather startling reason: ἐπεὶ δοκιμὴν ζητεῖτε τοῦ ἐν ἐμοὶ λαλοῦντος Χριστοῦ, *since you are seeking (or demanding) a proof of the Christ speaking in me.*

We might ask, what is the connection between the disciplinary action of the congregation and their demand for a proof of Christ's presence in Paul's work? Do not the cases of discipline stand on their own merits? Does not the congregation in those cases have to base its action on the factors which it observes? If the sinner manifests impenitence by refusing to listen to the admonitions of the congregation, is not excommunication then called for? If anyone is observed to be causing offenses and divisions contrary to the doctrine of the Church, is he then not simply to be avoided? In that case must not all formal connections be severed and all exercise of church fellowship be suspended? What has the demand for a proof of Christ as speaking in Paul to do with the manner of handling those cases?

Yet Paul introduces the present clause with ἐπεί, *because, since.* His preannounced action will be influenced by their (expressed or implied) demand. We see that Paul regards cases of discipline not as isolated matters, where we simply follow a certain mode of procedure according to the nature of the case as we observe it. No, it is not as simple as that. Discipline is an integral part of the Church's activity.

No member of the Church is perfect in this life. Everyone must continue to grow; everyone is subject to the danger of falling away; everyone is exposed to attacks from the enemy. As a result, the life of a congregation becomes very complex. It embraces mutual encouragement, mutual strengthening, mutual warning, mutual admonition. This activity, especially the last-named phase, assumes special forms when a brother becomes entangled in a sin, or is seduced by some error. Then admonition and rebuke become very prominent, which, if rejected by the brother, will lead to excommunication or to severance of fellowship, as the case may be.

Since discipline is an integral part of the life of a church body, many factors come into consideration in carrying out the individual cases—as Paul here indicates by referring to a demand of the Corinthian congregation. Christian discipline presupposes not only a thorough familiarity with the "rules" that Christ gave us; it taxes above all our spiritual judgment. There is nothing mechanical or simple about it. The demand of the Corinthian congregation for a certain proof on the part of Paul—unreasonable though it was —had to be considered by him in planning his dealing with the cases in Corinth. In the present instance, for example, this demand made it impossible for Paul to "spare."

All along Paul had taken various factors into consideration. Before the troubles arose in Corinth, he had planned an earlier return to the congregation. But then he changed his travel plans. He considered it to be better for the congregation if he advised them through one of his assistants, and gave them the opportunity to straighten out the matter by themselves before his arrival. He took the risk that his change of plans might be misunderstood and misconstrued to his disadvantage, as actually did happen. We heard his correction of this misunderstanding in chapter 1. He used his judgment in staying away from Corinth for the time being. He himself calls it a judgment (ἔκρινα), and even emphasizes the word by placing it at the head of the sentence (2:1). He reported a part of his deliberations in that chapter.

But the "sparing" which Paul considered as proper then was now no longer in place. That peculiar "demand" of the Corinthians made a sterner step necessary.

For the "demand" Paul uses the word ζητεῖτε, *you seek*. Most likely it was not expressed in the form of a demand. It may have taken the form of a complaint about the absence of "proof," or the form of a question: what proof could he present for his claims? The intruders maintained—and apparently many of the Corinthians accepted their word—that Paul's letters were weighty and strong indeed, but that his speech was contemptible; that in his absence he used big words, but, when present, would not live up to his claims. All this implied the demand for a demonstration. If it is really Christ who is speaking through Paul, then Paul should not disgrace Christ by his humble conduct. He must assert his authority and demand recognition. Since Paul did not even take remuneration for his service, how could they recognize him as an Apostle of the glorified Savior who is at the right hand of God, all power having been given to Him in heaven and on earth and under the earth, and angels and principalities having been made subject to Him? In all this there was implied the demand for a proof, a demonstration.

Paul says that they will get a proof in the "unsparing" way in which he will handle their cases of discipline. Perhaps the people who complained the loudest about Paul's weakness will get this proof with the sharpest reproof for their own slovenly, inadequate way, their own inaction in the serious matter at hand.

The demand is really out of place, and shows a deplorable lack of understanding. Paul says of Christ, ὃς εἰς ὑμᾶς οὐκ ἀσθενεῖ ἀλλὰ δυνατεῖ ἐν ὑμῖν, *who is not weak (in His sway) over you, but is powerful among you.* They want proof of the power of Christ. They have it right before their eyes, and do not see it. Let Paul be as weak as he may, yes, the weaker the better. The weaker Paul is, the clearer can the power of Christ be seen.

How is it that there is a Christian congregation in Corinth? Who brought about the radical change in the hearts of its members? Natural man does not receive the things of the Spirit; they are foolishness unto him: how was it that the Corinthians accepted the foolish preaching by the weak preacher Paul? It was Christ who was not ineffective on them, but was and is present with them in all His might and glory. Recently men had come to them with enticing, seductive words, and caused great havoc in the Church. How did it come about that the congregation survived and now is on the way to recovery? It was Christ's work. What better proof of Christ's power do they want? Or do these things mean nothing to them? Is their spiritual mind so obtuse?

(4) Why are they disturbed by Paul's meekness, the absence of any show of power? Why do they let Paul's meekness lead them to overlook the mighty work which Christ's power performed on them when He made new creatures of them by the word of reconciliation which Paul preached to them? They evidently do not understand the real nature of Christ's power and its operation.

Paul begins both parts of vs. 4 with καὶ γάρ. This combination of conjunctions always introduces an explanatory remark. The explanation may be mild in nature, something like one introduced by our English "namely." Sometimes it may be pretty sharp, implying even a rebuke for the ignorance of the reader: he ought to know better, and he would have known better, had he only considered the following explanation. That is the case here in vs. 4. The Corinthians should have known better about the power of Christ than to be misled by Paul's meekness and, as a result, to demand proof.

The truth of which the Corinthians had lost sight is ἐσταυρώθη ἐξ ἀσθενείας, ἀλλὰ ζῇ ἐκ δυνάμεως θεοῦ, (*Christ*) *was crucified out of weakness, but He is living out of God's power.* In order to perform His stupendous task of redeeming the sin-lost world, Christ entered into the state of exinanition. Though He was in the form of God, He did not deem this something to be displayed continually by living on an equal level with God. But He voluntarily emptied Himself of the heavenly mode of living and took on the form of a servant, becoming obedient unto death, even the death of the cross. He was crucified from voluntarily assumed weakness. Was He weak? Did He lose?

By His work in extreme lowliness He achieved the tremendous, glorious result that the sin-laden world now stands reconciled before God. He who knew no sin was made sin for us, that we might be made the righteousness of God in Him.

And now He lives to dispense this treasure to the world. The pleasure of the Lord prospers in His hand. He is at the right hand of God, directing the affairs in heaven, on earth, and under the earth. God gave Him the name which is above every name, that at His name all knees must bow of the dwellers in heaven, the dwellers on earth, and those under the earth. He lives by the power of God.

If this is the method which Christ applied effectively in procuring the salvation of the world, is there any reason for questioning the presence of Christ's power when His ministers come to us in meekness? Does not the demand for proof actually reveal an abysmal, unpardonable ignorance? With an emphatic καὶ γάρ Paul continues: ἡμεῖς ἀσθενοῦμεν ἐν αὐτῷ, ἀλλὰ ζήσομεν σὺν αὐτῷ ἐκ δυνάμεως θεοῦ εἰς ἡμᾶς, *we are weak in Him, but we shall live jointly with Him by God's power (made felt) upon you.* As Christ performed His work in weakness, so we on our part, who are in connection with Him, are also weak with Him.

In regard to the apodosis, we take notice of a few special points. Paul uses the future, ζήσομεν. This is not to be taken in the temporal sense: at some time in the future we shall live with Him. Then the εἰς ὑμᾶς would not make good sense, no matter whether we combine it with δύναμις or with ζήσομεν. The εἰς ὑμᾶς takes the Corinthians as they are now living under the Gospel of Christ. Ζήσομεν refers to the present conditions. Hence it is logical rather than temporal. If Christ after His labors in weakness now is living vigorously by the power of God, then it is to be expected that He will lead His Apostles over the same road: outwardly weak, but effectively proclaiming the Gospel of salvation.

Paul stresses that we are joined to Christ. We are not only in the company of Christ—μετά would express that idea—we are σὺν αὐτῷ, united with Him, specifically in that we are doing His work. "Lo, I am with you," He said. Our work is His work.

With εἰς ὑμᾶς Paul indicates that the Corinthians are the recipients and beneficiaries of this work. With this thought he leads over to the following verse.

(5) In vs. 3 Paul mentioned the fact that the Corinthians are demanding a "proof," δοκιμή. He now takes up this term and applies it in different ways, not only in the last remarks of the present section but also in the beginning of the next one. Δοκιμή may be applied in different ways to different situations, and will then show different shades of meaning.

The Corinthians were demanding a δοκιμή from Paul. By calling attention to the fact that his work had been done on them, εἰς ὑμᾶς, Paul charges that their request is misdirected. A tree is known by its fruit, and a man's ability is gauged and determined by the work which he produces. If the Corinthians are seeking a test and a proof of the Christ speaking in Paul, then they ought to examine themselves; for Paul's work was done among them and his words were directed to them. Ἑαυτοὺς πειράζετε, *examine yourselves*. The ἑαυτούς has the emphatic position in the sentence.

In what respect are they to examine themselves? Paul came to Corinth preaching the Gospel of salvation through Christ. His aim was to lead his hearers to faith in Christ as their Savior. And that is the point at which they must apply the test: εἰ ἐστὲ ἐν τῇ πίστει, *if you are in the faith*. Paul is here repeating an argument which he had used in 10:7. There he had said: Look at the things right before you. If anyone considers himself to be a believer in Christ, where did he get such faith? Did not we bring Christ to you? Realize, then, that we also are in Christ. Here he repeats, If you are in the faith, living by the faith, hoping for eternal salvation as the goal of your faith, why then ask for a proof of Christ's speaking in us? You have it in your very faith! It was Christ's power, and His power alone, that could kindle a spark of faith in your dead hearts. It did, and the mere fact that faith is now present in you is sufficient proof, incontrovertible proof, of Christ's power in my work.

But the fact that the Corinthians were demanding a proof from Paul was a sign of danger, a symptom of some spiritual ailment. It indicated that they were working with standards foreign to the Gospel. Their faith seemed to have absorbed some earthly elements. Hence Paul, who is concerned about building up their faith, about strengthening and purifying it, repeats emphatically, ἑαυτοὺς δοκιμάζετε, *prove yourselves.* Yes, you yourselves are the ones who need attention, you yourselves need testing, watching, guarding, and improving.

Paul now expresses the same thought in another form. He begins with ἤ, *or,* i.e., to put it another way. Οὐκ ἐπιγινώσκετε ἑαυτοὺς, *do you really not know your own selves?* Namely, ὅτι Ἰησοῦς Χριστὸς ἐν ὑμῖν, *that Jesus Christ is in you?*

The meaning of this expression, "Jesus Christ in you," is best set forth by Paul in his letter to the Galatians. Speaking of himself and Christ's living in him, he says: "I am crucified with Christ: nevertheless I live; yet not I, but Christ liveth in me: and the life which I now live in the flesh I live by the faith of the Son of God, who loved me, and gave himself for me" (Gal. 2:20). Do the Corinthians not realize that Christ crucified is the dominating power of their life? Their life may be hampered by the flesh, as was Paul's, but they resist the temptations of their flesh, and follow the lead of Christ's Spirit, as is invariably the case when Christ occupies a heart, and only then when He does.

If that is not the case with the Corinthians, if Christ does not rule in their hearts, what then? Εἰ μήτι ἀδόκιμοί ἐστε, *unless you simply are failures.* Εἰ μήτι, according to the Greek-English Lexicon of the N.T. (Arndt-Gingrich), means "unless perhaps" or "unless indeed." The idea of δοκιμή here turns up in the negative ἀδόκιμος, meaning that they did not pass the test which was applied to them; that they failed.

These are the two alternatives: either Jesus Christ is in them as indicated above, or else they are failures. Hence, instead of demanding a proof from Paul, they should keep watch over themselves. Paul still hopes that a check will bring to light the first alternative.

(6) In this sense we understand vs. 6: ἐλπίζω δὲ ὅτι γνώσεσθε ὅτι ἡμεῖς οὐκ ἐσμὲν ἀδόκιμοι, *But I hope that you will recognize that we (on our part) are not failures.* This is the result of the Corinthians' self-examination which Paul hopes for. He hopes that they will find themselves standing in the faith of Jesus Christ. He expresses the thought as though he were concerned about his own credit, but that is only a polite and startling way of saying it. If the Corinthians proved to be failures, such a result would be considered and recognized as casting a shadow on Paul, namely, that his work was not adequate. If Paul's work was successful, the result will show in the faith of the Corinthians. Thus for the Corinthians' sake Paul hopes that their test will demonstrate that he was not a failure. That just this was on his mind, comes out clearly in the following section.

4.   13:7-10

(7) This verse is devoted entirely to an elucidation of the last expression used in vs. 6. Εὐχόμεθα δὲ πρὸς τὸν θεὸν μὴ ποιῆσαι ὑμᾶς κακὸν μηδέν, *Now we are praying to God that you may not do anything bad.* A Christian's hope is always accompanied by prayer. Thus Paul here simply substitutes prayer for the word 'hope' which he had used in the previous verse. Paul's (and his associates') prayer is that God may keep the Corinthians from doing anything wrong, without pointing out any wrong specifically. He indicates by implication that all good things come from God, that it is also God alone who can and will preserve us in our Christian faith and protect us from taking a false step or making a wrong move. Thus, when Paul said that he hoped to come out of the Corinthians' self-examination as fully approved, he did not mean that any credit was due him. No, all honor belongs to God. With these suggestions he paves the way for the following protest.

Οὐχ ἵνα ἡμεῖς δόκιμοι φανῶμεν, *not in the sense that we might appear approved.* We take notice of a new verb. In the previous verse the reading was simply ἐσμέν (οὐκ ἐσμὲν ἀδόκιμοι). Here Paul substitutes φανῶμεν, that we may appear, i.e., that people may see and acclaim us as the great men of God, as the powerful preachers of the Gospel. That is not Paul's purpose in his prayers for the Corinthians, *rather* (ἀλλ') ἵνα ὑμεῖς τὸ καλὸν ποιῆτε, *that you yourselves be doing the proper thing.* That is the one concern of Paul: that the Corinthians stay on the right track, that they do so, under God, on their own initiative, without constraint, or coaxing and steering from Paul. He was their teacher, but now he would like to see them able to stand on their own feet. (We are reminded of a humorous definition of the aim of a good teacher. It is: to make himself superfluous. Paul's aim was just that.) But what will that outcome do to Paul? And particularly to the proof demanded of him by the Corinthians?

Paul adds: ἡμεῖς δὲ ὡς ἀδόκιμοι ὦμεν, *but (that) we be, so to say, unproved.* Paul used the word ἀδόκιμος twice before in the sense of "failure." Here he uses it in the purely negative sense: *without a test,* and hence without proof. Since the faith of the Corinthians is the only proof which Paul has for the efficiency of his work, then if the Corinthians learn to stand on their own feet and to follow the proper course on their own initiative, then his only proof is taken away. He will have nothing to show for his efforts. He is ά-δόκιμος. But, Paul says, such an outcome does not worry him. He will be glad to stand there without proof, if only the Corinthians keep on doing the proper thing. That is his one concern.

(8) The situation gives Paul an opportunity to repeat his warning against the false apostles, and to point out the nefarious nature of their work. When they came to Corinth, they found a flourishing congregation. They could not claim credit for founding it. But they did aim to acquire the credit of being superior apostles. What did they do? They began to criticize Paul and to belittle his work. They criticized his Gospel as being insufficient and inferior. Though he had preached the Gospel of Jesus Christ, they found fault with it. They began to wreck the work which Paul with great labor and patience had performed. They showed their superiority in tearing down.

Such methods are simply out of the question for Paul. Οὐ γὰρ δυνάμεθά τι κατὰ τῆς ἀληθείας, *For we are unable (to do) anything against the truth.* To uproot the truth, that is the work of the Old Serpent and his trickery; it is the work of Satan, who is a liar from the beginning, and the father of lying. That type of work, says Paul, we on our part are utterly unable to do. We can work only in the interest of the truth. Paul had mentioned before (11:23ff.) what it meant for him to be a minister of Christ and thus to work for the truth which no man by nature wants to hear. Now he simply says, ἀλλ' ὑπὲρ τῆς ἀληθείας.

(9) He does not, however, regret that he cannot demonstrate his strength by wrecking the truth. He has been taken completely captive by the truth. He has embraced the truth, and the truth of Christ is the very element by which he lives. Whenever and wherever he meets the truth, he rejoices, no matter whether it means strength and honor for him or weakness and disgrace (cf. 6:8): χαίρομεν γὰρ ὅταν ἡμεῖς ἀσθενῶμεν, ὑμεῖς δὲ δυνατοὶ ἦτε, *For we rejoice whenever we on our part are weak but you on your part are strong*; whenever we see you do the proper things by yourselves without our assistance or prodding, we are happy. In an earlier part of the letter he stated the motivation for this peculiar joy as follows: For we are not proclaiming ourselves as the Savior, but Jesus Christ, and ourselves as your slaves for Jesus' sake (cf. 4:5).

All the thoughts thus carried out by Paul are in line with the great truth referred to in vs. 4, viz., that Christ performed His work of redemption, not in the full luster of His heavenly glory, but in a state of deep humiliation; and that in a similar way also His ministers proclaim His salvation in weakness and humility.

When Paul ends this verse with the remark, τοῦτο καὶ εὐχόμεθα, τὴν ὑμῶν κατάρτισιν, he is not adding a new item. The καί is not copulative. It might be considered as explicative or even ascensive. He had mentioned his prayer before. In vs. 7 he said that he prayed to God to keep the Corinthians from doing evil, and to help them do the proper thing. Here again he speaks of his prayer, connecting his statement to the rest of the sentence with καί, thus indicating that he is repeating his thought in a somewhat specialized form. We may paraphrase: *and this is the very thing which we are praying for, your complete restoration*. Καταρτίζω means to put in order properly; figuratively, it means to put into proper condition. Κατάρτισις is a verbal noun denoting this process. The restoration of Christians is never completed in this life. It is never an accomplished fact, an attained state or condition. It is a continuing process. The prayer of Paul is that this process may keep on going in the Corinthian congregation in spite of obstructions and interruptions.

(10) The same is also the purpose of the present letter: Διὰ τοῦτο, *because of this* his earnest desire before God, ταῦτα ἀπὼν γράφω,

I am writing these things while yet absent. When he comes, he would like to find them strong, doing the proper thing, in full progress of restoration. Otherwise he might experience λύπη and cause λύπη, as he said in chapter 2. Here he expresses the unpleasant experience which he would like to avoid, and for the avoiding of which he is writing this letter, in these words: ἵνα παρὼν μὴ ἀποτόμως χρήσωμαι. We must supply ὑμῖν as the object of the verb: *in order that when present I may not have to treat you sharply.* The time for gentle and sparing treatment is past. They have had time and opportunity enough for making some headway in their "house cleaning." If they have allowed the time to slip by, and if they failed to make proper use of the assistance which Paul sent them in the person of Titus and his companions, then Paul will now have to take matters firmly into his own hands, and that may mean that he will have to be curt and treat them sharply. This letter, written very shortly before his planned arrival, is his last warning.

Yet if he does treat them curtly, it will not be to harm them or to tear down their congregation. It will be κατὰ τὴν ἐξουσίαν ἣν ὁ κύριος ἔδωκέν μοι εἰς οἰκοδομὴν καὶ οὐκ εἰς καθαίρεσιν, *according to the authority which the Lord has given to me for building up, and not for tearing down.* The power of the Gospel which Paul wields is indeed a strong power for wrecking the strongholds of the enemy (cf. chapter 10), but Paul does not consider the Corinthians as enemies of Christ. They are being troubled by the enemies, and they may have allowed themselves to become unduly entangled with the enemies. Therefore, although they are not to be considered as enemies themselves, yet sharp measures will be necessary to sever such alliances, and that course will hurt. Some members may even have been infected with the ideas of the enemy and may not be willing to give them up. Paul (in 12:21) referred to some people who thus far have refused to repent. Excommunication or severance may be called for (as the Latin poet phrased it: *Ense recidendum est, ne pars sincera trahatur*). That will be extremely painful. Such painful operation may be necessary to achieve the building up of the congregation.

If such painful disciplinary action can be avoided at Paul's visit, if the Corinthians take care of these matters themselves, they will spare both Paul and themselves some embarrassing moments.

CONCLUSION

Chapter 13:11-13

(11) *Finally, brethren, farewell.* We note that he calls them brethren, and considers them as such in spite of all the bad things he had to say to them and about them. Χαίρετε, literally, 'rejoice,' is best rendered with *farewell* at the close of a letter.

There follow two passive imperatives: καταρτίζεσθε, παρακαλεῖσθε, *be restored, be admonished.* Paul tried to restore them to the proper condition: they should let his efforts take effect. He admonished them: now they should willingly accept the admonition.—Two active imperatives follow, which are closely connected in meaning, τὸ αὐτὸ φρονεῖτε, εἰρηνεύετε, *be united in your (Christian) mind, have peace among yourselves.* By doing these things they will show that Christ is still in them. And the promise still applies to them, καὶ ὁ θεὸς τῆς ἀγάπης καὶ εἰρήνης ἔσται μεθ᾽ ὑμῶν, *and the God of the (true) love and peace will be with you*—with His help and with His blessing.

(12) There is church fellowship among the Christians in Corinth, and with the whole Christian Church on earth. Consider this fellowship most highly and seal it in a solemn formal way, ἀσπάσασθε ἀλλήλους ἐν ἁγίῳ φιλήματι, *greet one another with a holy kiss.* Note the aorist of simple action in ἀσπάσασθε, indicating that that is the proper thing to do. We may well imagine that some members on account of the recent disturbances felt doubtful if it was still proper to continue the custom. Paul says it is. On the kiss of peace compare also I Corinthians 16:20; Romans 16:16.

(13) The fellowship extends farther than the boundaries of the Corinthian congregation: ἀσπάζονται ὑμᾶς οἱ ἅγιοι πάντες, *all the saints salute you.* Note the present tense. They are sending their (fraternal) greetings. By their greetings they show their sympathy. They are with the Corinthians in spirit, supporting them before the throne of God with their prayers. In spirit they are standing shoulder to shoulder with them in their struggles against the forces of evil.

(14) Paul concludes his epistle with what has become known as the apostolic blessing: ἡ χάρις τοῦ κυρίου Ἰησοῦ Χριστου καὶ ἡ ἀγάπη τοῦ θεοῦ καὶ ἡ κοινωνία τοῦ ἁγίου πνεύματος μετὰ πάντων ὑμῶν.

We refrain from commenting. Let the blessing stand in its simple pristine beauty.

EPILOGUE

The question may be asked: What did Paul achieve with his letter?

Luke records that after Paul had gone through Macedonia and "had given them much exhortation, he came into Greece, and there abode three months" (Acts 20:1,2). After the winter, yet some time before the Passover (cf. vs. 6), he left Corinth to deliver the collection in Jerusalem.

Some time during his three months' stay in Corinth Paul wrote his Epistle to the Romans, in which he said: "From Jerusalem, and round about unto Illyricum, I have fully preached the Gospel of Christ." And again: "Now having no more place in these parts" (Rom. 15: 19 and 23).

The Word of God in Paul's letter did not return void.